THE RUSSIAN DAGGER
Cold War in the Days of the Czars

BOOKS BY VIRGINIA COWLES

LOOKING FOR TROUBLE

NO CAUSE FOR ALARM

WINSTON CHURCHILL
The Era and the Man

GAY MONARCH
The Life and Pleasures of Edward VII

THE PHANTOM MAJOR
The Story of David Stirling and His Desert Command

THE GREAT SWINDLE
The Story of the South Sea Bubble

THE KAISER

1913
An End and a Beginning

THE RUSSIAN DAGGER
Cold War in the Days of the Czars

VIRGINIA COWLES

THE RUSSIAN DAGGER

Cold War in the Days of the Czars

1817

HARPER & ROW, PUBLISHERS

NEW YORK AND EVANSTON

LIBRARY OF CONGRESS CATALOG CARD NUMBER: 69-15303

For my sister and brother-in-law
Mary and Carl Holtz

Contents

Illustrations

Preface

===

THIS IS THE STORY of Russia's attempts to expand in Europe in the sixty years before the First World War, against a background of dynastic relationships which made the rivalries personal and acute. A love of conspiracy has always been part of the Russian character; and the author has tried to show how the rise of the revolutionary movement affected Russian techniques of expansion. In 1881 Count Leo Tolstoy was horrified by the assassination of Alexander II. He felt that the terrorists, descendants of Nihilists and Nechaevsti who preached the destruction of moral ethics, were spreading a poison that threatened the whole fabric of Russian society. He asked the new Czar to pardon the regicides as an act of Christian mercy, which might have the effect of jerking the country to its senses. Alexander III not only refused, but allowed his officials to employ the same methods of violence and treachery in extending Russian influence in Europe. The two movements, subversion at home and subversion abroad, not only stimulated but fed one another. Although their aims were very different, one to overthrow the Czar, the other to increase the Czar's power, both were revolutionary.

They flourished side by side, and did not cease with the Bolshevik seizure of power in 1917. Nechaev's belief, postulated nearly half a century earlier, that the end justifies the means, became part of Russian Communist policy, and the imperialism of the white Czars was copied and improved by the red Czars.

The similarity between the two Russias, past and present, is startling and depressing. Russia has produced many great writers and musicians, but very few great rulers. It is impossible to separate government and governed for ever. Why is there always a new tyrant to take the place of the old? Does it spring from the Asiatic streak in the Russian character? Or, as Tolstoy prophesied, is it a natural consequence of the rejection of Christianity? This book does not attempt an answer, but tries to show what happened.

VIRGINIA COWLES

April, 1969   *19 Chester Square, London, S.W.1*

I

Philosophers at Court

IT WAS NO SECRET, in the winter of 1839, that the romantic, twenty-year-old Grand Duke Alexander, eldest son of Nicholas I of Russia was touring the German kingdoms in search of a wife. The tyrannical Czar doted on his heir and had given him permission to make his own choice, provided the lady was not a commoner and not a Roman Catholic. The Empress Alexandra, on the other hand, favoured one of the Baden girls, and anxiously awaited news from the poet Zhukovsky, her son's tutor and travelling companion. When the letter arrived, however, it was plain that the Karlsruhe visit had been a failure. The poet scarcely mentioned the Baden princesses, observing tactfully that he had "nothing to tell about the Grand Duke's heart. It keeps its own secret."

Darmstadt was not on the Grand Duke's itinerary except as a place to change horses *en route* to Mainz, and to pay a brief courtesy call on the Grand Duke Louis II of Hesse-Darmstadt. But the Russian entourage arrived in the small, out of the way capital some hours behind schedule and the Grand Duke's aide persuaded his master not to proceed farther until the morning. Louis was delighted to entertain such distinguished company. He took his guests to the opera and arranged a late supper at the palace. He presented to Alexander his three sons, the youngest of whom was the sixteen-year-old Prince Alexander of Hesse, and his only daughter, the fifteen-year-old Princess Marie. Marie had huge eyes and a delicate, oval face. Not only was she beautiful but "alarmingly intelligent."

The Grand Duke Alexander could not take his eyes from her. The next morning he sought out the faithful Zhukovsky and told him that he had fallen hopelessly in love. "Just where we least

13

expected it to happen it has happened," Zhukovsky wrote exultingly to the Empress Alexandra. "To call him happy would be hardly enough . . . I am convinced that it is God's intention for him . . . The aim of all our travels is at last achieved . . . Now he will be waiting for your Majesty's blessing and consent . . ."[1]

The Princess had fallen just as deeply in love, for the tall, blue-eyed Alexander not only was gentle and thoughtful but the handsomest prince in Europe. He cancelled his tour and the lovers spent idyllic days together until a special courier arrived from St. Petersburg with a shattering letter from the Czar. He forbade the engagement and demanded Alexander's instant return to Russia, reminding him that he was due to visit the Court of St. James in two months' time. No explanation was given. White-lipped, Alexander saw the Grand Duke Louis and told him that despite the Czar's attitude he considered himself betrothed to Marie and would never marry anyone else. His father was fond of him, he said, and he was certain that in the end he would overcome his objections.

Not until he reached the Russian capital did he learn the reason for the Czar's attitude. It sprang from stories concerning the unconventional behaviour of Princess Marie's mother, the Grand Duchess, who had died some years earlier. Apparently this well-connected lady, whose four sisters had shared the thrones of Russia, Sweden, Brunswick and Bavaria, resented her husband's many infidelities, and after bearing him three sons, decided to strike out on her own. She took as her lover the Court Chamberlain, the Baron Augustus von Senarclens Grancy. Fourteen years after the birth of her last child she became pregnant again; first came Alexander, then Marie. Tongues wagged furiously but the Grand Duke remained impervious, and his unruffled acceptance of paternity forced the Grand Duchess's detractors to keep their indignation under control.

The Czarevitch was unmoved by this disclosure; if he had to choose between Marie and the throne, he said, he would prefer to relinquish the throne. Nicholas sympathised, for he had fallen deeply in love with Alexandra when, as the beautiful Princess Charlotte of Prussia, she had become engaged to him; and he continued to love her all his life. Within a few days he was defending the choice his son had made. "When the Emperor paid me the honour of discussing the probability of the marriage of his son to the Princess of Darmstadt," the Austrian Ambassador wrote to Prince Metternich that April, "he told me he knew all that was said about the irregularity of her birth but as the Grand Duke took no notice of it, he found nothing to object to on that account."

The Empress Alexandra was not so easy to win over. "I know that secretly this choice pains the Empress. She is very vexed by the doubts over the Princess's birth, or at least by the rumours of it in Germany."[2] The Empress had other objections, for Marie's mother had died of consumption and Marie herself was known to suffer from "a delicate chest." The final decision was that Alexander must put aside all thought of an engagement for at least a year; at the end of the period his parents would reconsider the proposal. Then they packed him off to England.

The Grand Duke's upbringing had been so thorough that he managed to conceal his agitation from the twenty-year-old Queen Victoria and to be a model of charm and attentiveness. He accompanied her to concerts and theatres, and partnered her in lively mazurkas and German country dances which were quite new to her. "I never enjoyed myself more," she wrote in her Journal. ". . . I got to bed by ¼ to 3 but could not sleep till 5. I really am quite in love with the Grand Duke; he is a dear, delightful young man."[3] However, the sharp-eyed French nobleman, the Marquis de Custine, who met the Grand Duke at Ems on the return journey from England, noticed an "inward suffering." Although he remarked on Alexander's Grecian profile and described him as "one of the finest models of a prince I have ever met with" he observed "that he is under the influence of some cause of grief; his eyelids are cast down with a sadness that betrays the cares of a riper age."[4]

Alexander's confidence in his father was not mistaken, and the wedding took place in St. Petersburg in the spring of 1841. Marie's brother, the eighteen-year-old Alexander of Hesse, agreed to settle permanently in Russia in order to be near his sister. He was commissioned as a colonel in the *Chevalier Gardes* and given the Order of St. Andrew as a souvenir of the marriage. "Nobody has ever earned an Order more easily," he wrote in his diary, "unless it can be looked upon as a merit to have participated at a wonderful wedding breakfast where the horseshoe table was loaded with gold plate and the ladies all sat on the left in Russian costume and the men in their gala clothes on the right."[5]

The wedding breakfast was only an opening salvo, for the festivities lasted two weeks. The most elaborate party was the fancy-dress ball at the Winter Palace attended by 42,000 people. What delighted Prince Alexander even more, however, was the Czar's military review in which 40,000 cavalrymen of the Guards regiments took part. The climax came when the squadrons massed together and rode at full gallop toward the Imperial stand. The Czar stood motionless until the thundering cavalcade was nearly on top of the marquee, then raised his hand and brought it to a dead stop. According to the young Prince, "not a single horse projected beyond another by so much as a head."

If Marie had captured the most elegant prince in Europe, she had also acquired the most alarming father-in-law. Nicholas had an air of such freezing *hauteur* that people did not dare look him in the face. Long after his death one of his generals entered a room and turned the sovereign's portrait to the wall. "I had . . . such fear of the original," he explained, "that even a copy with those terrible eyes fixed on me, frightens and embarrasses me."[6] What made the gaze so awesome, apparently, was that the left eye was slightly asymmetrical "like a nail at white heat," disconcerting even Queen Victoria, who welcomed Nicholas to England in 1841. "He is certainly a *very striking* man," she wrote, "still very handsome, his profile is *beautiful*, and his manners most dignified and graceful . . . but the expression of the *eyes* is formidable and unlike anything I ever saw before . . ." The Queen was disappointed to find that he could talk of nothing but politics and military matters, felt that his education had been "neglected" and came to the conclusion that he was "not very clever." "His mind," she wrote, "is an uncivilised one."[7]

The truth was that Nicholas thought of himself as a soldier not a statesman. "I am," he once confided to the Austrian Ambassador, "a sentry at outpost to see all and observe all. I must stay here until

I am relieved."[8] Although God may have recognised Nicholas as a humble sentry, the Russian people saw him as a merciless drill sergeant. "I cannot permit that one single person should dare defy my wishes the moment he has become exactly aware of them," he had written soon after his accession. He looked upon the fifty million people of Russia as troops to be drilled and bludgeoned for, as he once explained to the poet Pushkin, "Russia . . . does not yet stand as a whole: the elements composing her are not yet harmonised . . . Take away the limitless all-powerful will of the monarch and at the least shock she would crumble."[9] Unlike other autocrats, such as the King of Prussia and the Emperor of Austria, Nicholas did not have to share his power with the aristocracy for riches and ancient names counted for nothing in the state hierarchy. Russia was divided roughly into two classes, forty million serfs on one side, ten million bureaucrats on the other; and the bureaucrats—church, military and civil service alike—were forced into the *tschinn* system, a ladder containing fourteen rungs each one of which had a prescribed rank and salary. As promotions were dependent on the Czar's pleasure the bureaucracy grovelled and Nicholas ruled. He was aided, of course, by his secret police, the dreaded Third Section, an institution established at the outset of his reign, which not only crawled with informers but contained an alarming number of blackmailers.

The "mighty potentate," as Victoria called him, only relaxed in the bosom of his family. Although Marie and Alexander lived in the vast Anitchkov Palace and had their own court, they were summoned only too frequently to dine at the Winter Palace which stretched for a quarter of a mile along the Neva. Nicholas's most human quality was his affection for his sons and daughters, and his passionate love for his wife, the still-beautiful, bird-like Alexandra. He called her "Mouffy" and she called him "Nicks." If he was separated from her for more than a few days at a time he grew as homesick as a small boy. "Oh, I have thought of you and cried for you," he wrote from Moscow, soon after the wedding of Marie and Alexander. "Tears are always coming into my eyes. Then we go to your room . . . I kissed your son there when he was born, and then we went together to pray in the chapel; there I could weep at my ease, for I could bear it no longer."[10] Nicholas heaped so many precious stones on Alexandra that her room looked like a jewellery shop; yet he himself lived the spartan existence of a soldier. He ate very little, occupied a small room decorated with army maps and icons, and always slept on a straw mattress on a camp bed. Indeed when he visited Queen Victoria he startled the English courtiers by sending his servants to the stables to get straw for the canvas mattress he always carried with him.

Although Nicholas liked to spend the evening playing the cornet or listening to readings from Sir Walter Scott, the morning always found him as imperial and glacial as ever. He had come to believe in his own omnipotence and there was no department in which he did not feel qualified to interfere. He countermanded military plans and upset financial policy. If the St. Petersburg fire bells rang, he ran out and told the firemen what to do. He banished Prince Yussupov to the Caucasus because he was having a love affair of which his mother did not approve; and when the daughter of a courtier was treated badly by her husband he had the marriage annulled and wrote majestically: "This young person shall be considered a virgin." In the morning he worked at his desk; in the afternoon visited the parade ground or rode through the capital in a carriage drawn by a magnificent Orlov trotter, pulling up unexpectedly at schools, barracks or hospitals as the fancy took him. If he noticed the slightest infraction of the rules the culprit would be given thirty days' imprisonment or dismissed from his job. And there were plenty of rules to observe. No one was allowed to smoke, not even on the streets, as Nicholas did not like the smell of tobacco; only Guards officers were allowed to wear moustaches, but the moustaches had to be black, dyed if necessary, because that was what Nicholas preferred. Once he dismissed the head of a school because pupils in the sick-bay stared at him out of the window with un-shaven faces. Occasionally he committed an act of kindness. When he saw a poor unattended hearse making its desolate way through the streets he walked behind it until he had collected a crowd of 8,000 people. And when he entered a building and found the porter asleep at his desk over a half-written letter—"I am in despair. Who will pay my debts?"—he leaned over and wrote: "I, Nicholas I."

One of the worst features of the Emperor's character was his tendency to declare people insane if he did not agree with them. When Peter Chaadaev, the darling of the Moscow intellectuals, produced a *Philosophical Letter*, published in the *Telescope* in 1836, arguing that Russia floated in space, belonging neither to West nor East, he gave instructions that the writer must be kept under medical supervision as he was "mentally unbalanced." Later he grew even more stringent. He dispatched a young student, the grandson of a Minister, to a lunatic asylum for organising opposition inside the University and sent a Professor of French, M. Rigaud, to the same institution for remaining seated during Divine Service in the Orthodox Church.

Nicholas laboured under the belief that ruling Russia was simply a matter of example and discipline. Yet foreigners who visited the country during this period were horrified by the poverty and backwardness, the corruption and deceit, that permeated every corner of life. The French nobleman, Custine, was disconcerted to find the hotels swarming with vermin, and to learn that not even the Winter Palace was free from the scourge; and the German doctor, Mandt, found it curious that cows were kept at the top of the Palace near the rooms of the Maids of Honour in order to provide the kitchen with milk. English travellers remarked on the appalling roads and the fact that there were only twenty miles of railway line in the country; this particular track had been constructed to connect the royal palaces at Tsarsko Selo with St. Petersburg. The Russian middle class, they noted, was practically non-existent. The merchants, architects, engineers, were German, French, English or Levantine. There was scarcely a Russian doctor, and not a single Russian apothecary, in the whole Empire; even the professors were foreigners. The peasants lived in the utmost wretchedness and were so primitive that some of them believed that the Czar went to Heaven once a week to hold a consultation with God.

But what dismayed tourists most of all was the venality and ineffectiveness of the supposedly educated bureaucracy. It was impossible to get a passport or a travel permit without days and sometimes weeks of delay. The grandest officials were not above accepting a bribe, while the lesser officials, impressive in velvet collars and gold buttons bearing the imperial crest, were so poor that their feet were wrapped in rags. The veneer of western civilisation that displayed itself in French furniture, elaborate entertainments, over-polite conversations, only served to worsen the impression. An English traveller was astonished to see his cosmopolitan host reprimand his servant in the middle of dinner for passing the wrong dish by felling him to the ground; while the Marquis de Custine discovered sadly that ladies frequently wore Paris dresses over unwashed bodies and that beds were often merely status symbols; even rich nobles frequently rolled up for the night in carpets on the floor to save the bother of removing their clothes.* But these were trifles compared to the deficiencies of character. "They have a dexterity in lying, a natural proneness to deceit which is revolting," wrote the Marquis de Custine. "In Russia fear replaces, that is paralyses, thought. This sentiment when it reigns alone can never produce more than the semblance of civilisation . . . it is not order but the veil of chaos."[11]

The Frenchman's censure was sharpened by the pretentiousness of Nicholas's court. The vermin and the squalor might have been forgiven were it not for the outrageous splendour of the Emperor's hospitality which Custine regarded as the trappings of a civilisation that did not exist. Nicholas, however, was a shrewd showman. He wished to be feared and respected, and judged correctly that magnificence was the surest means of conveying might. Furthermore, like Louis XIV, he felt safe when he saw his nobles dissipating their energies. "Let people amuse themselves," he said. "It keeps them out of mischief."

The Emperor liked dramatic effects and thought nothing of employing thousands of workmen to transform gardens into oriental palaces hung with silk and glowing with candles, or ballrooms into gardens banked with flowers from the Crimea, complete with rockeries and fountains. At every large ball the ladies were required to wear court dress; white silk gowns with red velvet bodices trimmed with gold lace, red velvet head-dresses encrusted

---

* When Count Leo Tolstoy brought his bride to Yasnaya Polyana in 1862 she was horrified to find that her husband never slept between sheets but rolled up in a blanket like the Moujiks.

with jewels, and wonderful embroidered trains. This provided a spectacular setting for the gentlemen in uniforms of peacock splendour slashed with ribbons and orders. The sovereign's body-guard lined the staircase leading to the ballroom; the supper-tables groaned with caviare from the Caspian, quail from the Caucasus, wines from France. Mirrors reflected the flicker of candles, the flash of fabulous jewels. "It was magnificent," wrote the French artist, Horace Vernet. "One could literally trample on diamonds . . . one walked on pearls and rubies; it has to be seen to be believed."

During "the season" the Emperor gave a ball every Monday night in the White Salon of the Anitchkov Palace, quite apart from the fêtes and galas at the Winter Palace. The Empress was mad about dancing and performed the mazurka more gracefully than any Polish woman; and as it was Nicholas's greatest pleasure to see "Mouffy" enjoying herself the parties never ended before dawn. Although the Emperor always opened the ball with a stiff bow which set the quadrille in motion, he spent most of the evening wandering through the vast supper rooms talking to guests who were usually too frightened to do anything but nod agreement.

It was not surprising that these gargantuan entertainments, designed to impress, turned the heads of many courtiers who began to feel that Russia's future was limited only by the confines of the globe; indeed, the Empress Alexandra's favourite poet, Tyutchev, dashed off a startling verse entitled "Russian Geography" which no one thought in the least extravagant.

> Seven inland seas and seven mighty rivers
> From the Nile to the Neva
> From the Elbe to China
> From the Volga to the Euphrates
> From the Ganges to the Danube
> Such is our Empire to be.

Although most Russians did not go as far as Tyutchev they dilated glowingly on the inevitability of Russian expansion as though it were some sort of cosmic explosion which no one could control. Their talk of Constantinople as Russia's rightful capital stemmed back to the fifteenth century when, nineteen years after the infidel

Turk had destroyed Byzantium, Ivan III had married the niece of the last emperor. Very fancifully the Grand Prince of Muscovy proclaimed himself the heir to the Byzantine Empire, incorporating the double-headed eagle on his escutcheon and assuming the name of Caesar or Czar. As missionaries from Constantinople's great church, Santa Sophia, the fount of the Greek Orthodox religion, had converted Russia to Christianity, the desire to possess Constantinople assumed the character of a Holy Crusade and became known as Russia's "historic mission."

By the nineteenth century, however, the longing for Constantinople, gateway to the Mediterranean, and the covetous glances towards South-Eastern Europe, were unmistakably political. The sanctimonious arguments employed to disguise ambition rarely failed to annoy foreigners; that such a vast, backward, barbarous country should take upon itself the role of saviour seemed an outrageous impertinence. "In order to cleanse herself from the impious sacrifice of every liberty, public and personal, the prostrated slave dreams about conquering the world," wrote the Marquis de Custine. Western Europe she saw as "a prey which will sooner or later be handed over to her by our dissensions." " 'Europe,' they say at Petersburg, '. . . is enervating herself by a vain liberalism, whilst we continue powerful precisely because we are not free; let us be patient under the yoke; others shall some day pay for our shame'."[12]

It was not easy for the seventeen-year-old bride of the Heir Apparent to understand this vast, schizophrenic country, so different from the postage-stamp kingdom she had left behind. Although Marie made an effort to win the affection of her husband's large family she disliked the glitter and pomp of court occasions and escaped from St. Petersburg whenever she could. She looked upon the Alexander Palace at Tsarsko Selo as her real home, for life was quieter here and she had time to think. Within twelve months she had mastered the Russian language and was able to share fully her husband's life. Alexander could not bear to be parted from her and read State papers sitting on her bed, underlining controversial passages and asking for her comments. "Those were the years of untroubled family happiness for the Grand Duke," wrote the historian, Tatischev. "There were almost daily gatherings at the young court . . . Nothing was formal or forced . . . There would be reading aloud, music, cards . . . The host and hostess charmed everybody by their manner."[13]

The person Marie admired most in St. Petersburg was Alexander's aunt, the remarkable Elena Pavlovna, wife of Nicholas's brother the Grand Duke Michael. Despite the disparity in age the two Grand Duchesses had much in common. Both were German princesses and both had been educated far above the customary standard for royal ladies. The Emperor referred to the tall, fair Elena with the finely chiselled face as "the scholar of our family." "She never chatters: she talks," wrote Count Kisselev. "Everybody who has met her marvels at the extent of her knowledge . . . Her court is magnificent, and her dinners and evening parties exquisite and quite unique of their kind. She does not choose her guests from the upper social layer . . . but by a recognition of people's personal quality, promise and achievement, and she is inevitably censured by many who place rank first . . . Her liberal gestures often produce little storms in society."[14]

The two Grand Duchesses showed considerable finesse in helping to turn the stifling forties into a decade of intellectual challenge without antagonising the Czar. They not only patronised music and the arts but filled their salons with novelists, poets, politicians and philosophers. As the secret police were not allowed to file reports on royal gatherings guests were encouraged to speak their minds freely. Indeed, the Grand Duchess Elena helped to stimulate the new school of literature that blossomed in the forties. For the first time writers portrayed a world of venality and poverty and produced such masterpieces as Lermontov's *A Hero In Our Times*, Gogol's *Dead Souls*, Dostoevsky's *Poor People*, Turgenev's *Sportsman's Sketches*.

The revolution began with Gogol's *Government Inspector*, a biting satire on the corruption of the bureaucracy. The censors refused to pass it until Elena's friend, the poet Zhukovsky (who had conducted Alexander on his tour) sent a copy of the play to the Emperor and obtained the sovereign's approval. Nicholas could not see what all the fuss was about as he regarded the work as nothing more than an uproarious comedy. The actors, however, did not know what to make of the script. For years the Russian theatre had confined itself to highly stylised foreign melodramas which required no effort apart from giving the characters Russian names. "When Gogol read *The Government Inspector* to the actors at Sosnitsky's most of them, brought up on comedies of the old-time authors, far removed from real life, were perplexed. 'What is it?' they whispered to each other at the end of a reading. 'Can it be a comedy? He reads well but what language! The servant talks like a servant, and the locksmith's wife is no more than a common peasant-woman, right out of the market place . . .' Actors as well as many writers did not dare remove their powdered wigs, or take French cloaks from their shoulders in order to put on real Russian clothes, like Abdulin's coat or Osip's worn, soiled, frock-coat."[15] The opening night was packed and the audience laughed until the tears ran down their cheeks, but Gogol was depressed. He had tried to make a serious contribution to society by pointing out the misuses of bureaucratic power but the public had seen only a vulgar farce.

This was far from the truth, as Gogol's masterpiece not only opened the floodgates to a literature that explored every facet of Russian life but started people thinking and talking about the necessity of reform. The most crying evil was the plight of the peasants. The Heir Apparent and the two Grand Duchesses believed that serfdom must be abolished. So, oddly enough, did the merciless Nicholas. Despite the fact that most members of his family told him it was impossible to alter the system, he felt a deep and paternal obligation to the defenceless people who formed the bulk of his population. "They know they have no other protector but me," he once told a friend. From the outset of his reign he searched for a solution to the terrible dilemma. Two years after his accession he appointed General Kisselev Minister of National Lands. "You know this custom of serfdom cannot remain in its present state," he said. "My Ministers do not understand my feelings; in my own family my brothers are against my plans . . . I ask your help. I know I can count on you . . . God will inspire and guide us."[16]

Although Kisselev set up directorates, redistributed land, re-apportioned taxes, introduced a police code, and made many other reforms, the basic problem seemed insoluble. Four-fifths of Russia's population consisted of peasants. How could any fundamental changes be made without destroying the whole economic system? Half the serfs, twenty million, were in the service of the Crown, the other half were the property of private landowners. Freedom, bestowed by the stroke of a pen, would create forty million paupers overnight, for where could the money be found to make each peasant family self-supporting? Nicholas appealed repeatedly for the co-operation of the landowners in seeking a solution, but they dug in their toes and sabotaged his efforts. "All these plans of emancipation," one of his ministers, Count Nesselrode, wrote in 1843, "... can only lead to peasant riots and the ruin of the nobility." "The peasants," Nicholas countered, "cannot be considered as property and still less as a thing. The nobility must help me to change gradually the state of the serf so as to forestall a radical upheaval." But the landowners increased their opposition, other problems intervened, and toward the close of his reign Nicholas said resignedly: "Three times I attacked serfdom; three times I had to stop; it was the hand of Providence."[17] Clearly Providence intended the problem to wait for Alexander.

Russian literature and peasant reform were absorbing; but of all the fierce controversies of the forties the Grand Duchess Marie was most fascinated by the battle between "Westerners" and "Slavophiles" that split the philosophical world in two. The impetus came from the *Philosophical Letter* of Peter Chaadaev, the man whom Nicholas had declared insane and placed under medical and police supervision for a whole year. Chaadaev not only depicted Russia as floating aimlessly between East and West but flatly asserted that Russia's contribution to civilisation was nil.

"Alone of all the peoples in the world we have not given anything to the world, and we have not learned anything from the world. We have not added a single idea to the pool of human ideas. We have contributed nothing to the progress of the human spirit, we have disfigured it ... We have only borrowed deceptive appearances and useless luxuries from the devices of others. A strange fact! Even in the all-inclusive scientific world our history is not connected

with anything, does not explain anything, does not prove anything . . .''[18]

It is not surprising that Chaadaev set the philosophers on a course
of furious reappraisal. Alexander Herzen welcomed the *Letter* as
"a shot that rang out in a dark night; it forced all to awaken."
Herzen, a revolutionary thinker who in 1847 quit Moscow for
London, where he produced a radical paper *The Bell*, led the
Westerners. Herzen argued that backward Russia must reject its
Asiatic heritage and pass as quickly as possible through all the stages
of development already experienced by Western Europe; for the
West alone could lead the way to Hegel's universal culture. "Only
the mighty thought of the West . . . is able to fertilise the seeds
slumbering in the patriarchal mode of life of the Slavs."[19]

The Slavophiles on the other hand were fascinated by Chaadaev's
theme of Russian remoteness. Although they deplored his "blank
sheet" theory, they were flattered by the notion of Russian singular-
ity. "We have never walked hand in hand with other nations. We
do not belong to any of the great families of mankind, either to the
West or to the East, we do not have the traditions of either. We
exist as if beyond the limits of time and as if we were never troubled
by the universal education of humanity."[20]

The Slavophiles were a handful of Moscow intellectuals led by
Youri Samarin and the two Aksakov brothers, Constantine and
Ivan. Russia must not ape the West, they said, but develop its own
culture by finding a way of life that was wholly Russian, a compromise between Europe and Asia. Western civilisation, they argued,
was based on the classical heritage of Rome, refined by German
philosophical thought; but this civilisation had taken so many wrong
turns that it was certain to tear itself to pieces over such irreconcilable beliefs as individualism, authoritarianism, rationalism,
scepticism, socialism, materialism, secularism and hosts of other
"isms." "We Russians do not belong to this doomed school and we
can say so while yet paying due respect to all that is great in the
European achievements in art, science and history."[21]

The Slavophiles referred to themselves as the Greco-Slav school.
Their roots must remain in religion and the land; and they must
cling to a patriarchal system free from tyranny. Culture must develop

through the village commune and true Christian brotherhood. To emphasise this last point some of the Slavophiles began to wear the *murmolka*, an outmoded peasant cap, and costumes so national that village people frequently mistook them for visiting Persians. "The mistake of the Slavophiles lies in their imagining that Russia once had an individual culture . . ." jeered Alexander Herzen. He attacked their right to call themselves intellectuals. "Slavism, or Russianism," he wrote, "not as a theory, not as a doctrine, but as a wounded national feeling, as an obscure tradition and a true instinct, an antagonism to an exclusively foreign influence, has existed ever since Peter the Great cut off the first beard." Although he poked fun at them he thought their movement dangerous for he saw in it "fresh oil for anointing the Czar, new chains laid upon thought, new subordination of conscience to the slavish Byzantine Church."[22]

The Grand Duchess Marie was not averse to "anointing the Czar" and embraced the Slavophile cause with fervour. Anything that could make her more Russian and bring her closer to Alexander was bound to appeal to her. She preached Orthodoxy with the fanaticism of the convert, and frequently attended mass twice a day. The poet Tyutchev, also a passionate Slavophile, dedicated verses to her and became her Chamberlain. He drew his friend, Ivan Aksakov, into the Court circle. Even her ladies-in-waiting were chosen for their devotion to the Church and their belief in the Slav future. Alexander smiled at her enthusiasm, but remained detached; philosophic arguments had little bearing on the practical decisions of everyday life.

Academic discussion was halted by the tremendous events of 1848. The revolutionary tidal wave which rolled across Europe threatened to bring an end to the monarchical principle. Louis Philippe was swept off the throne of France by what was known as "the revolution of contempt." The Emperor of Austria had to flee twice from his capital, while his chief minister, Metternich, who for twenty-four years had served as the policeman of Europe, was unseated. Italy, united in a league of princes, revolted against Habsburg rule under the leadership of a liberal pope, while Hungary broke away from Austria and declared itself independent.

In Prussia things were almost as bad. The Empress Alexandra's brother, King Frederick William IV, abandoned his capital in the face of a mounting insurrection which spread to many of the smaller German states. "You have heard about Berlin," wrote Zhukovsky, the Grand Duke's tutor, from Baden. "Poor, poor King of Prussia . . . To think that the Prussian monarchy should have been bested by such brigands . . . One's only hope lies in Russia. Let her turn away from the West and stand firmly behind her stout high walls . . . Here, all authority and power are in the hands of a tattered mob . . . They call it 'the will of the people' . . . Baden is a volcano, Frankfurt a seething cauldron . . . The entire stage is occupied by brigands in tatters, drunkards, escaped prisoners, and Jews, and the rightful rulers of Germany dare not make their voices heard . . ."[23]

Only the thrones of Russia and England remained steady. Nicholas I closed the frontier "to stop the deadly virus" and intervened effectively to bolster the tottering thrones of his neighbours. He warned the German revolutionaries that if they declared a republic he would send troops to restore the old Prussia. And when a federation of German states was formed at Frankfurt and offered the throne to the King of Prussia he warned his brother-in-law against dealing with an "illegal authority." Consequently Frederick William IV declined the gift, explaining haughtily that he did not wish "to pick up a crown from the gutter." But it was to the Habsburgs that Nicholas rendered the greatest service. As the Austrian Emperor was powerless to bring Hungary back into the fold, Nicholas sent a Russian army under Paskewitch to surround the Hungarian insurrectionists at Vilagos and forced them to surrender.

Meanwhile the Emperor Nicholas was taking no chances in Russia. Those who looked upon the early forties as oppressive found the late forties suffocating. Universities were placed under police supervision and chairs of metaphysics and moral philosophy were withdrawn. Foreign travel was prohibited; public meetings banned; and the works of Gogol, Turgenev and even Pushkin placed upon the Index. The censorship became rigorous to the point of comedy. A commission was appointed to examine music for conspiratorial cyphers; even the rows of dots in arithmetic books were scrutinised with magnifying glasses.

All "Westerners" were suspected of entertaining socialist theories and pursued doggedly by the Third Section. In 1849 a sensation was created by the arrest of Michael Petrashevsky, a junior member of the Foreign Office, and twenty youthful friends who were in the habit of holding Friday evening discussion groups. Among those picked up were two writers, M. E. Saltykov and Feodor Dostoevsky. None of the accused had done anything but talk, except for a young man named Durov who had bought a second-hand printing press which stood in his house, still in its pristine wrappings. But the talk was subversive. It ranged from criticism of serfdom and the censorship to arguments in favour of abolishing church, state and private property. Dostoevsky had committed the crime of reading aloud Belinsky's famous letter to Gogol which, of course, was prohibited.

After languishing for some time in the Fortress of St. Peter and St. Paul the group was subjected to a mass trial. All twenty were sentenced to death. The execution was scheduled to take place in the Semenovsky Parade Ground. Not until the young men were waiting to go before the firing squad was "a gracious reprieve" read out, commuting the sentences to imprisonment. This little drama had been planned by Nicholas I as part of the punishment. Years later Dostoevsky immortalised the terrible scene in *The Idiot*. The first group of three was ordered to don the traditional death garments, and hoods were placed over their heads. "My friend was eighth on the list," wrote Dostoevsky through the lips of Prince Myshkin," and he would therefore be in the third group to be marched to the posts. The priest went to each of them with the cross. It seemed to him that he had only five minutes to live. He told me that those five minutes were like an eternity to him, riches beyond the dreams of avarice . . ." Suddenly a retreat sounded, the men were led back from the posts and the pardon read out. All were condemned to Siberia. Petrashevsky received life imprisonment, Dostoevsky four years' hard labour followed by four years in the army as a private.

Not only "Westerners" but also "Slavophiles" were looked upon as potential traitors. Nicholas I suspected the Slavophiles of trying to draw into their orbit the Slavs of other lands; and this was a crime against the monarchical principle. Foreign Slavs owed allegiance to foreign kings. No matter how tiresome those kings might be, Russians who inflamed subjects to rebel against their royal rulers were traitors. Indeed, Nicholas had experienced too much trouble with the Poles to encourage any form of insurrection.

Consequently, in 1849, the year of the Petrashevsky trial, he ordered the arrest of the Grand Duchess's friends, the two Slavophile leaders, Youri Samarin and Ivan Aksakov. They were asked to define for the benefit of His Imperial Majesty the meaning of Slavophilism. "Men who are devoted to Russia with all their might and all the power of their soul . . ." replied Aksakov. And the relation of Slavophilism to Panslavism? (This question was of paramount importance, for three years earlier the Third Section had tracked down a Ukrainian "Brotherhood" which was preaching that "each Slavic people should have its independence" and advocating a federation. This had prompted Count Uvarov, the Minister of Public Education, to send a directive to Moscow pointing out that the Slav cause had two sides to it; ". . . one which malicious men could use to incite minds and spread dangerous propaganda, criminal and provocative . . . Russian Slavophilism in its purity should express unconditional loyalty to Orthodoxy and Autocracy.") Aksakov gave the right answer. "We do not believe in Panslavism," he explained, "because the greater part of the Slav people are already infected by the influence of barren Western Liberalism which is contrary to the spirit of the Russian people and which can never be grafted on to it."[24]

Although Nicholas I released the prisoners he was not altogether satisfied. With surprising perspicacity he saw that Panslavism was a natural, almost inevitable progression from Slavophilism. "Under the guise of compassion for the supposed oppression of the Slav people," he wrote on the depositions of the two men, "there is concealed the idea of rebellion against the legitimate authority of neighbouring and, in part, alien states, as well as the idea of a general unification which they expect to gain not through God's will but through disorder which would be ruinous for Russia."

In the end the pieces were glued together. Russia remained steady; and out of the European chaos Nicholas managed to re-establish the old order. The King of Prussia gradually regained control and the "democratic federation" broke up; the eighteen-year-old Franz Joseph imposed his authority on the Austro-Hungarian Empire; and Louis Napoleon finally proclaimed himself Emperor of the French. Nicholas had defeated the first flow of Western Liberalism and stood supreme.

Although the Grand Duke Alexander himself had liberal sympathies, he loved his father and accepted his reactionary measures without a protest. He was so tactful that he managed to keep in the good graces of his aunt but he cautioned Marie to forget her Slavophile leanings and busy herself with her household. During the first twelve years of marriage the Grand Duchess had given birth to six children. The eldest, a charming little girl, Alexandra, had died of consumption at the age of seven, and the second, Nicholas, was a constant anxiety because of recurrent fevers; but the others, Alexander, Vladimir, Alexis and Marie were all strong and healthy. Although the Grand Duchess engaged English nannies to look after them—which scarcely accorded with Slavophile views—she devoted much time to the nursery.

In 1851, however, the children were far less of a worry to Marie then her gay, feckless brother, Alexander of Hesse. This romantic character, who looked like an Assyrian God, seemed far removed in spirit from his serious, devout sister; yet the two blossomed in each other's company and loved one another with a tender devotion all their lives.

For ten years Prince Alexander of Hesse had revelled in the life of a Russian cavalry officer; short days of work and long nights of cards, women and parties. He did not endear himself to the Emperor for the simple reason that he flirted outrageously with Nicholas's daughter, the beautiful Grand Duchess Olga. He persuaded hostesses to seat him next to her at dinner, followed her to the ice-rink and even walked romantically outside her window. Nicholas I seethed with rage at the behaviour of the insolent puppy and no doubt would have banished him to Siberia if it had not been for Marie. Instead he seized the opportunity of making his displeasure felt at a military review. As the Prince passed the Emperor's stand, at the head of his cavalry regiment, his horse began to wheel and side-step and he found himself bringing his sword to the salute with his back to his sovereign. This was humiliating enough, but the climax was worse. The review ended with the great massed gallop towards the royal marquee. Although Alexander had equipped himself with a fresh horse the curb broke and the animal bolted straight for the imperial family. It only stopped after a violent collision with an officer in the Emperor's suite. The Prince rejoined his comrades, smarting with shame, but Nicholas was determined to humiliate him further. As his troop was leaving the grounds Nicholas rode up to him and called out angrily: "See to it that you get a horse that will carry you properly. Understand? You are no ornament to your regiment. You throw it in confusion."[25]

Although this public rebuke did not deter Alexander of Hesse, Olga was an obedient girl who long ago had resigned herself to a dynastic marriage. Prompted by her father, she asked the Prince if he was considering taking part in the new military campaign in the Caucasus. This slap in the face could not be overlooked; Alexander felt he had no alternative but to volunteer. He arrived at the Commander-in-Chief's headquarters in Tiflis with a suite of twenty-seven people consisting of a doctor, a valet, a scullion, two non-commissioned officers, twelve Cossack orderlies and ten privates. He also brought thirty-seven horses.

He was away for nearly a year. The warrior Shamyl was far too skilful for the Russian forces and almost scuppered the lot. The Prince arrived back at Sebastopol to find Nicholas holding a grand review of the Black Sea fleet and army manœuvres in which 22,000 horses and 189 squadrons of cavalry took part. Although the onlookers were deeply impressed by the might of Russia, the harrowing ineptitude of the Caucasian campaign was still fresh in Alexander's mind and he wrote to his sister: "I hardly dared hope that I should see you again, my dear Marie." Meanwhile the Prince learned that the engagement had been announced of the Grand Duchess Olga to the Prince of Württemberg, a nephew of the Grand Duchess Elena.

Marie hoped, quite naturally, that her impoverished brother would marry an heiress and settle down in Russia. Unfortunately in 1851 Alexander fell madly in love with Marie's lady-in-waiting, the Countess Julia Hauke. This was nothing short of disaster, for the pretty Countess was not considered grand enough to marry a prince of Hesse-Darmstadt. Her grandfather was a German soldier who had moved to Warsaw before the French Revolution. Her father, Maurice Hauke, fought with the Polish Army against Napoleon. After the establishment of a Polish Kingdom under Russian suzerainty, Hauke was raised to the Russian hereditary nobility with the rank of general and count, and given the post of Minister of War. When the Polish revolt took place in 1830 he did his best to protect the Governor-General, the Grand Duke Constantine, by confronting the insurrectionists and pleading for their loyalty. He was shot down in cold blood; but his bravery was rewarded by the appointment of his daughter, the Countess Julia, as lady-in-waiting to the Grand Duchess Marie.

When the Hessian prince told his sister he had decided to marry Julia, Marie and Alexander were horrified. It was impossible for the brother of a future Empress to marry a lady-in-waiting of humble origin. As Julia could only become a morganatic wife, the Czar was certain to banish Alexander from the Russian Court. And as neither Julia nor the Prince had a penny between them, life would be hazardous. They begged the twenty-eight-year-old Alexander to think carefully before he took such a rash step, for his whole career was at stake.

The Prince, however, refused to change his mind and events took place as Marie had prophesied. The Czar not only banished Alexander but struck him off the army list. After ten glorious years, his life in Russia was over. In October, 1852, he left St. Petersburg for Darmstadt; Julia followed and they were married the same month. As a morganatic wife she was not allowed to call herself Hesse. Later her children were permitted to take the name Battenberg.

For eighteen months Prince Alexander floundered about looking for employment. When Marie and Alexander paid a visit to Darmstadt in 1852 the Czarevitch asked the Grand Duke Louis of Hesse if he could not appoint his brother the Commander of the Hessian Forces, but Louis replied that the morganatic marriage was even more embarrassing in a small kingdom like Hesse-Darmstadt than in Russia. Marie then decided that Alexander must try for a job in the Austrian Army. She prodded her husband into asking the Emperor Franz Joseph if he could not give him a commission as a Major-General. The Austrian Emperor replied that it would not be possible unless the Czar reinstated Alexander on the Russian Army List; otherwise malicious tongues would say that the Austrian Army was accepting a "reject." Under pressure from the Heir Apparent Nicholas finally agreed to give him the right to wear a Russian uniform again; and in July, 1853, the Austrian Emperor sent word that Alexander could enter the Austrian Army as a brigadier.

Never had the prestige of a Czar stood higher than that of Nicholas I in the summer of 1853. The storm of 1848 had proved the Russian autocracy unbreakable, the word of the Czar decisive in all the capitals of Europe. The French Minister, M. de Castelbajac, referred to the sovereign as "this great spoilt child" and was fearful that he might become too ambitious. He was not far wrong, for now nothing seemed impossible. Inflated by success, emboldened by flattery, corrupted by power, Nicholas I decided that the time had come to bring new lustre to the Russian Crown. All the great Czars had added territory to the Russian Empire and Nicholas certainly considered himself a great Czar. Although his armies were moving forward steadily in the Caucasus he regarded Asian success as nothing more than the maintenance of order in his back-yard.

True glory meant an extension of power in Europe by further inroads on the crumbling Ottoman Empire. Russia had already fought seven wars against Turkey, one of which had been instigated by Nicholas himself in 1828. It was not difficult to pick a new quarrel. Nicholas sent an envoy to Constantinople demanding Orthodox rights in the Holy Places, and recognition of Russia as the protectress of all the Sultan's Christian Slavs. At the same time he summoned Sir Hamilton Seymour, the British Minister in St. Petersburg, and blandly suggested partitioning Turkey's European possessions between England and Russia. The reason he gave was that the Sick Man might suddenly die "and be on our hands."* Russia would retain her rights over Moldavia and Wallachia (which later became Romania); Serbia and Bulgaria would enjoy Russian protection as independent states; and England could have Egypt and Crete "if that island suits you . . ." A few weeks later Nicholas produced a new plan generously assigning the Adriatic to Austria and promising that Constantinople would become a free city with a Russian garrison on the Bosphorus and an Austrian garrison on the Dardanelles.

It is scarcely surprising that England doubted the sincerity of Nicholas's religious fervour. The British Ambassador in Constantinople advised the Sultan to grant the Czar Orthodox rights in the Holy Places but flatly to reject his demand for a protectorate over Turkey's Christian subjects, as this was seen as the thin end of the wedge.

Some people thought that Nicholas had gone mad. What was he after? Constantinople and its shipping lanes or the whole of South-East Europe? He thrashed about, toying with one idea after another, railing against this person and that. He spoke of "those Turkish dogs," that "cad" Palmerston, that "adventurer" Napoleon III. He wrote a private letter to Queen Victoria extolling his own Christian virtuosity and received the cutting reply that "the personal qualifications of a sovereign are not enough in international transactions."[26] The truth was that Nicholas had been over-confident of doing a deal and was furious at being balked. He tried to frighten the Powers by predicting excitedly that the Greeks and the Bulgars and the Serbs would rise to the last man when the Russian Army of "liberation" began its march. And he talked excitedly about his duty to God and Christianity.

Nicholas had gone too far to draw back. Although it was clear that England and France would side with Turkey he was not unduly worried, for he was confident of Austrian support. After all, he had shed Russian blood in 1848 to prevent the break-up of the Habsburg Empire. For forty years the two countries had worked in harmony and now young Franz Joseph was bound to show his

* He had suggested the same partition for the same reason when he visited London in 1844. "Russia," commented Lord Palmerston, "is just a great big humbug."

gratitude. In July 1853, the month when Prince Alexander of Hesse was commissioned in the Austrian Army, the Czar sent troops into Moldavia and Wallachia which were tributary to Turkey but under the protection of Russia. Turkey demanded Russia's evacuation and when the latter refused, declared war on her; a month later the Russian Navy retaliated by sinking the Turkish fleet off Sinope.

Now came Austria's treachery. She joined England and France in presenting Nicholas with an ultimatum asking for an immediate Russian withdrawal. The Emperor could scarcely believe his eyes. "Do you want England and France ruling in Constantinople?" he wrote to the Emperor Franz Joseph on 14th November. "No, a thousand times no. It would be better for us two to remain united, so as to counteract such an infamous combination." And on 4th January, "Are you really intending to make common cause with the Turks? Does your conscience permit you, the Apostolic Emperor, to do so? If this proves to be the case, Russia must march alone . . . under the sacred symbol of the Cross . . ." And on 17th February, "The possibility of hostilities between us appears to me a *monstrous absurdity* when I think that you might come to attack Russia, which only a few years ago came of its own accord to sacrifice its blood in order to reduce your rebellious subjects to order."[27]

The truth was that the Emperor Franz Joseph did not trust Russia any more than did the English, or for that matter the other Great Powers. If Russia gained control of South-Eastern Europe where would Austria be? And if Nicholas could appeal to the Christian Slavs over the head of the Sultan, was it impossible that some future Czar might appeal to the Austrian Slavs over the head of their Emperor? Franz Joseph's suspicions were not unfounded for Michael Pogodin, a History Professor at Moscow University and an ardent Panslavist, was already expressing such opinions. Pogodin had managed to keep in the good graces of the Imperial Court by passionately affirming his loyalty to Autocracy, Orthodoxy, Nationalism. Furthermore, he had the good sense not to make his views public but to send private memoranda to his friend, the Countess Antoinette Bludova, the Grand Duchess Marie's lady-in-waiting. Sometimes she passed his notes to the Emperor. "Where are we to look for allies?" he asked in a letter written at the end of

1853. ". . . our most helpful and powerful allies in Europe are the Slavs, our kinsmen by blood, tongue, heart, history and faith, and there are ten million in Turkey, twenty million in Austria . . ."28 Pogodin proposed that the liberated Slavs should form a federation headed by the Czar with its capital in Constantinople. The union was to include not only the Slavic people but Greece, Hungary, Moldavia, Wallachia and Transylvania.

Although Nicholas considered that these views were "not entirely well founded and do not lend themselves to practical fulfilment," he was no longer outraged at their treasonable implications. The stresses of the moment were too great for anger and he was grateful for Pogodin's devotion. Nevertheless, his dislike of Panslavism had not diminished. It was one thing to raise the banner of the Slav against the Mussulman; another to encourage the Slav against a Christian King. Nicholas played politics within the established rules. He was willing to appeal to the Orthodox Christians of Turkey to rise in defence of their religion—but not in defence of Slavdom.

England and France declared war on Russia in March 1854. Although Franz Joseph did not join in the declaration he promised the allies diplomatic support. This temporisation was not enough to win the friendship of the Western powers, yet more than sufficient to incur Russia's deep and lasting hatred. Prince Alexander of Hesse found the situation particularly intolerable. He wrote freely to his sister Marie, while she and her husband replied with remarkable candour in view of the censorship. "The unfortunate turns of an incomprehensible policy may place me in a camp hostile to Russia, but they will never succeed in altering my sacred feelings of loyalty . . ." declared Prince Alexander. "It grieves me deeply," replied Marie, "to think that you are in the service of an ungrateful and perfidious country like Austria. But what can one do? One must just make the best of things . . ." "Your remarks about Austria's infamous policy," wrote the Czarevitch, "seemed to me so right that I submitted them to the Czar . . ."29

It was not difficult for the Grand Duke Alexander to consult his father as, despite the war, the entire Imperial Family—Emperor and Empress, sons and daughters and grandchildren—were summering together at Peterhof in the Gulf of Finland. Nicholas I was one of the few sovereigns who declined to lead his troops into battle. He had taken charge of the army in 1828 at the battle of Schoulma. But everything disgusted him; the blood and disease and the untidy appearance of the soldiers who did not have time to polish their boots and buttons. So he had simply packed up and returned to St. Petersburg, declaring many years later, "It is not God's will that I should distinguish myself at the head of my army."

He saw no reason to reverse this decision in 1854 and, as it took weeks to receive news from the Crimea, where the main action would be fought, life at Peterhof was remarkably untouched. In June, however, the monotony was broken by the silhouette of the English fleet, not for any purpose, it transpired, but merely as a reminder that Britain ruled the seas. "The enemy fleet has appeared at Kronstadt: first 18, then 20 ships," wrote Mlle Tyutcheva, one of the ladies of the Court, in her Journal. "At six o'clock in the evening, the Grand Duchess Marie summoned us to the farm: we were going to drive in carriages to see the enemy. The Czarevitch and his wife and four children seated themselves in an English charabanc. Even little Alexis, scarcely four-years-old, was there, very excited to be waiting for the English. About half a dozen of us were invited . . . We stopped at Oranienbaum and had tea with the Grand Duchess Elena. Quite a battery of telescopes had been installed on the balcony with which to see the enemy, but owing to the fog we could not see very much . . ."[30]

Meanwhile Slavophiles and Westerners once again were at each others' throats. "What is beginning," exulted Tyutchev, "is not a war, not a policy: it is the birth in pain of a new world . . . it is the decisive battle of the West and Russia." Alexander Herzen, on the other hand, inveighed from Italy against Russian officialdom, "a dumb unit without a flag and without a name, the cord of slavery around its neck . . . with the insolent pretensions of the Byzantine Empire . . ."[30]

Nicholas I was too preoccupied to hear what anyone was saying for the war had taken a dangerous turn. In September, 1854, the allies landed at Eupatoria to the north of Sebastopol. The attacking troops routed the Russians on the banks of the Alma and probably could have entered Sebastopol if they had pressed on. Their hesitation gave the Russian Army time to strengthen its defences, and the siege lasted eleven months.

The war revealed cruelly the cracks in the Czar's glossy Empire. Despite the fact that corruption and inefficiency existed on both sides, the Russian shortcomings were appalling. Although Russia now boasted 600 miles of railway, supplies took longer to reach the front line from Moscow than by ship all the way from England. There were no railways in the Crimea; and the roads were deep with mud and strewn with the carcasses of horses who had fallen from thirst and hunger and whose rotting bodies spread a wave of epidemic. Medical supplies were almost non-existent, there was mould in the biscuits, weevil in the salted meat; the water was tainted; the soldiers' boots falling to pieces. Yet everyone whispered of the great profits made by the Army Commissariat whose duty it was to victual the army. War correspondent, Count Leo Tolstoy, sent home dispatches praising the dogged courage of the Russian soldiers in face of these frightful conditions. Yet everyone felt that things could never be the same again. The omnipotent bureaucracy had been shown to have feet of clay, and the mystique of Russian power exposed as a fraud.

Nicholas knew that his system had failed. In February, 1855, he caught cold on parade in St. Petersburg and neglected to take ordinary precautions. Pneumonia developed and his German doctor, Martin Mandt, began to fear the worst. The Czar lay on his iron camp bed covered by two blankets and a military greatcoat. The only light in the room was a flickering candle. The wind howled in the chimney and snow-flakes fluttered against the window-panes. The Czar's breathing was laboured. "Tell me, Mandt," he said, "am I going to die?" Mandt took the Czar's left hand, pressed it, and answered with brutal frankness, "Yes, your Majesty." "What is wrong?" "The lung is beginning to collapse, your Majesty."[31]

Mandt explains in his memoirs that many years earlier the Czar had made him promise to let him know when the end was near. He also says that if the last sacraments had not been administered in time the Russian doctors would have held him responsible. Nevertheless it is not surprising to learn that Nicholas did not linger long after this depressing conversation. A courier arrived with despatches but the Czar waved them aside. "This has nothing more to do with me. Henceforth I belong wholly to God."

Sebastopol fell in August; and in February, eleven months after the death of Nicholas, peace was signed in Paris. The terms were not as severe as the new Czar had feared, although he was indignant at having to cede part of Bessarabia to Turkey, and enraged to learn that the Black Sea could no longer be used as a base for Russian warships. But Prince Gortchakov, the Emperor's plenipotentiary, thought that Russia had not fared badly. "Sir," he said consolingly, "it is good the treaty is signed. We could not afford to go on . . ."

II
The New Reign

THE CORONATION of Alexander II in 1856 threw a glittering
cloak over the humiliation of the Crimean defeat. Byzantine Moscow with its hundreds of domes and cupolas was gilded and painted
until it blazed in the August sun. Not only were the great palaces
redecorated but dozens of ornate pavilions were especially built by
rich provincial landowners to house their families for the occasion.
For weeks the roads leading into Moscow were crowded with
coaches and carts as over a million people from all over Russia
poured in. The gentry brought their own food and bedding as
though preparing for a siege, for the resources of the city were known
to be inadequate. Thieving became widespread. "We were advised
to have all our provisions packed into coaches and not carts," wrote
a Russian lady, Vera Liarsky, to a friend. ". . . On the way here all
the carriages had to wait a considerable time in Tverskoy Boulevard
on account of heavy traffic . . . It must have been during the delay
that the last of the three coaches had its doors opened and all its
contents taken out by thieves . . . It must have been done very
cunningly because neither the coachman nor the footman on the
box noticed anything . . . Among other things, that coach contained
several sacks of flour and ten hams. They say that not a bag of flour
is to be bought anywhere . . . Luckily, there are several sacks of
rusks in another coach . . . Poor Nathalie Kourakina has fared much
worse; *her* larders and still-rooms were raided one night . . . and that
in spite of several bolts and locks."[1]

The coronation procession entered the Kremlin through the Gate
of the Redeemer and stretched for over a mile, a ribbon of high-
stepping horses, glittering breast-plates, marching feet. All the

important dignitaries of the Empire rode past; then came the Imperial servants in a riot of fancy-dress; Masters of Ceremony carrying silver wands with double-headed eagles; major-domos, valets and runners; huntsmen from Gatchina; boatmen from Peterhof; choristers from Tsarkoe Selo; even eight "Court Arabs" who were, in fact, huge Negroes from Abyssinia. Finally came the thirty golden coaches of the Romanov family, the occupants dressed in velvets and blazing with jewels. Even the steps of the carriages and the harnesses of the horses were studded with precious stones. The Dowager Empress Alexandra passed first in a carriage lined in garnet velvet, her coachmen and *piqueurs* in livery to match, and her horses sporting plumes of white ostrich feathers. The Czarina rode in a more modest carriage of silver and blue, preceded by four Cossacks of the Household, and followed by a hundred nobles wearing ancient Boyar dress.

And then came Alexander II in a wonderful glass and silver coach drawn by eight greys. He sat alone, his head bare. As he neared the Cathedral 8,000 bells from Moscow's 1,600 churches began to peal. Crowds of onlookers fell to their knees, not only as an act of homage, but in a sudden impulse of thanksgiving, for there was no doubt that a new era had begun. The Coronation Manifesto had set the tone; pardons were granted to the Decembrist mutineers of 1825, and to the Petrashevsky "conspirators" of whom Dostoevsky was one. Altogether thirty clauses of amnesties were read out and remissions of fines and taxes granted on a sweeping scale.

Although the coronation ceremony lasted five hours, the spectators were not bored for it was so ill-rehearsed they had plenty to gossip about. The singing was glorious but Count Bludov and Prince Shakovsky allowed the cushion bearing the Order of St. Andrew to fall just as they were about to hand it to the Emperor; and when the four court ladies tried to fix the crown on the Empress's head it nearly clattered to the ground, only saved by the folds of her cloak. That night the Emperor gave an outdoor banquet for 300,000 of the populace. The sky was illuminated by fireworks; the fountains flowed with wine; and three regiments of infantry served the food. Scarves and coronation medals were distributed by the thousand.

While the people were singing and dancing in the streets, Queen Victoria's Special Envoy, Lord Granville, was taking a sceptical view. Although the Emperor's manner was "singularly gentle and pleasing" the Ambassador did not think he had much strength of intellect or character. "His Imperial Majesty," he reported to Windsor, "is not supposed to have that power of will which will enable him to deal with the mass of corruption which pervades every class in this country. The Empress is a woman of sense and ability and is believed to have great influence with her husband when he is with her, but he is generally guided by the person who speaks last to him before he acts . . ."[2]

Although Marie possessed her husband's confidence and played a decisive part during the first years of the reign, Alexander was not as weak as Granville supposed. His veneration for his father had kept him scrupulously loyal during the years of despotic rule; yet long ago he had decided to introduce sweeping reforms when he came to the throne. Marie's rôle was one of encouragement. Her sharp intellect had not made her popular in St. Petersburg society but she had a firm friend and ally in the strong-willed, humanitarian Grand Duchess Elena, nick-named by conservatives "the Red Aunt." The jibe that these two ladies constituted "a petticoat government" was not wholly unjustified, as Alexander relied on feminine sympathy and support to keep his purpose steady. Soon after the Peace Treaty he lifted the ban on travel, lessened the censorship, and withdrew police control from the universities. For the first time students were allowed to hold meetings, form committees, publish their own magazines. In St. Petersburg and Moscow lectures were thrown open to everyone, and were crowded with middle-aged bureaucrats, women and priests. This led to Sunday seminars conducted by army officers who undertook to teach their soldiers how to read and write. Even more sensational was Alexander's determination to free the peasants. Echoing his father's words he told the Moscow nobility that serfdom must be destroyed from above, "otherwise it may well start from below." "Gentlemen," he said, "I ask you to consider my words and carry them back to the country."

Alexander's salvo marked the first shot in a fierce battle that was to rage for five years, for the landowners were just as determined to block emancipation now as before. They reiterated the arguments that it would bankrupt the country and produce anarchy. They obviously impressed Lord Granville for he wrote gloomily to Windsor that the serf question was of a very difficult character and would become even more complex as the wealth of the nation increased. "Indeed when that state of things occurs, it is more than likely that popular movements will take place, and it is frightful to consider the immediate results of a revolution in a country organised as this is at present. No country in Europe will furnish so fair a chance of success to Socialism. The reins of Government were held so tight during the last reign that even the relaxation which now exists is not altogether without danger."[3]

Nevertheless Alexander refused to be intimidated. Despite his autocratic powers it took five years of the whip-lash and the velvet glove, five years of arguing, pleading, threatening before emancipation became a reality. At times the problems seemed insoluble. Were the forty million serfs to be freed without land or with land? "With land," Alexander ruled. Who was to compensate the landowners? The State was not rich enough to buy all the land in Russia and give it away. And how were the peasants to farm with no capital? And who would own the crops and animals and houses in the period of transition? The public body set up by the Emperor was floundering hopelessly, so early in 1857 he supplemented it by a Secret Committee. But at the end of the year this, too, had failed to make progress. Alexander summoned the head of the Committee and handed him a Rescript for immediate publication. The Rescript dealt with peasant steading. Peasants were to have the right to buy an agreed amount of land, their huts and animals, by payments stretching over the years.

Things still moved at a snail's pace. "The business of liberation," Marie wrote to her brother in December, 1858, "goes on very slowly on account of the passive resistance of those in high places, and of the great prevailing ignorance. There has been a good deal of dispute in various local governments about it, and the majority is against it everywhere. The situation is serious, and the Czar's position very difficult, since people show little or no sympathy with him. But thank God he is not losing courage."[4]

The ignorance to which Marie referred was spread evenly between landowners and peasants. The peasants visualised themselves freed from all rentals, living a life of ease, while the gentry saw nothing but chaos ahead. The writer Saltykov depicted the fear and misunderstanding in his great work *The Golovlev Family*. The landowner, Arina Golovleva complains to her son:

" 'Now I have got thirty sluts in the maids' workroom alone. How can I keep them when nothing will be mine any longer? Now we have bread and meat, cabbages and potatoes, why, everything . . . But once freedom is granted, will it not be my business to run to the market every day and to pay hard cash for everything? An onion would not grow unless it is planted . . . How am I going to keep all these folk? Do I have to send them right away from the estate? What would happen to them? And what about myself? I can neither prepare food nor cook it nor serve it . . . I have not been bred to it.' "[5]

The Emancipation Manifesto was published in March 1861 and Russian Liberals hailed Alexander as the Czar-Liberator. On the Sunday that the proclamation was read in all the churches of the Empire, Alexander was in St. Petersburg. "At two in the afternoon," wrote General Cherbachev in his memoirs, "the Tsarina meadow was crowded . . . Suddenly the Emperor came riding back to the Palace from St. Michael's Riding School. At once hats and caps flew in the air . . . and it seemed as though the very ground under our feet was shaking—so thundering were the cheers and the hurrahs . . . No pen could describe the rapture of the people as the Czar rode past . . . I am happy to have witnessed such a moment . . . it beggars all description."[6] When the Emperor reached the Palace he went to the room of his little daughter, the Grand Duchess Marie, kissed her and said: "This is the happiest day of my life."

The word "liberal" was on every lip and soon became the most overworked adjective in Russia. Sometimes it was used in contexts which foreigners found odd. Alexander Kinglake, the author of a long, erudite *History of the Crimean War* was considered a Liberal because of the "daring manner" in which he spoke of Czar Nicholas I. "I heard Macaulay praised by Russians on the ground of his eminent merit as a 'liberal' writer," wrote an English journalist. "A Russian young lady, whom I recommended to read Christie Johnstone, wanted to know whether in that charming tale there were 'liberal opinions'."[7]

Even social customs were relaxing. Formerly soldiers had to stand, their heads uncovered, when an officer passed in the street; smoking in public was forbidden; only the lowest of the low would ride on an omnibus; a well-bred gentleman was expected to put on evening clothes before paying a morning call on a lady; the same gentleman not only was expected but required to wear evening dress when visiting the Hermitage picture gallery because it was in a palace. All these things were melting away. People even paid for their tickets on the Moscow-St. Petersburg railway instead of bribing the guard to give them free seats. But this last had less to do with the liberal tide than the fact that the railway had passed from the Government to private hands, and a strict scrutiny now took place.

Perhaps the greatest proof of the Golden Age was the changed circumstances of the secret police. They still existed, but not in such large numbers, and their social status was definitely on the wane. "A servant at Klee's Hotel, in St. Petersburg, where I was staying," wrote *The Times* correspondent, "informed me that the room next to mine had been taken by a police agent, who watched my going out and my coming in, and made notes as to the friends who visited me. One of the waiters told me that there was another spy who concealed himself under the principal staircase, and followed me whenever I went out. He spoke of this man with more pity than contempt. 'People of this class,' he said, 'are in a very sad position now, sir. I remember the day when that sort of work was done by perfect gentlemen, who dined at the *table d'hôte* and ordered their red wine and their champagne like the best in the land. Now they crouch under staircases and are glad to get a glass of vodka'."[8]

Many young noblemen celebrated the liberal régime by making friends with radicals, who would have been gaoled in Nicholas's day, and drinking to the toast: "Now we are all on the same side." One of these cheerful landowners, the handsome, ebullient Prince

Youri Golytsin, called upon Alexander Herzen a few months before the Emancipation Manifesto. He was completing a tour and arrived in England with a pet crocodile which he had acquired in Egypt, a young lady he had abducted in Voronëzh, and six serfs whom, he said, wished to see the world. Herzen was fascinated by his gaiety and charm, but appalled by his extravagance. Although he had very little money left and no hope of obtaining more from his father, the idea of altering his way of life did not occur to him. He rented a large house in Porchester Terrace and opened the doors wide. Outside stood a magnificent carriage permanently harnessed to a succession of fine greys in case he felt inclined to go for a drive. He had considerable musical talent and at one time had conducted a serf orchestra on his father's estate. Obligingly he composed a *pot pourri* of Russian folk songs for the evening Fantasia given by Herzen to celebrate the Emancipation Edict; and in order to appease his creditors launched a series of concerts. Unfortunately his habitual impulsiveness in inviting all the musicians to dinner devoured his profits. In the end he found himself in a debtors' prison. Once a week, however, the police allowed him to put on his white tie and tails and sally forth as a conductor. Under strict supervision he finally settled his bills.

The Golden Age was regarded as a permanency. Yet under the melting Russian ice the currents were dangerous. The peasants did not understand the responsibilities of ownership. They believed that the Czar had made them a gift; now they were told that they had to pay their own taxes for the first time, and, even worse, to make annual payments to redeem the land, far higher than their former rents. Although they were free men, their poverty had increased. It could not be what the Czar intended. They accused government clerks of trying to rob them; riots broke out in many parts of the country; and peasants murdered landowners and officials alike. Hundreds of arrests were made, and soon the rejoicing had given way to sullen disenchantment.

Even more disturbing, and wholly unexpected, was the revolutionary trend that began to develop in the universities. Russia possessed only eight universities with a total enrolment somewhere in the region of 5,000. Moscow University was the largest with nearly a thousand students, St. Petersburg next with 700. Most of the students were the sons of petty bureaucrats and impoverished landowners. Many were desperately poor, living in wretched conditions with barely enough food to keep them alive. "Steady progress" was a high-sounding phrase, but did it mean anything except a life-time of waiting? Emancipation was a case in point, a paper victory which had done nothing to improve the lot of the peasant.[9]

Worried by a future that seemed to offer only frustration and penury, they began to campaign for a revolutionary change in the whole system. They distributed Golden Charters to the peasants, and printed fly-leafs attacking the monarchy. Alexander lost his head, and despite the protests of the Empress, appointed Admiral Poutiatin as Minister of Education. Poutiatin was so reactionary that he suspected subversive tendencies in anyone who drank a glass of milk during Lent. He forbade student gatherings without the permission of the authorities and abolished the rule that allowed poor students to study free of charge.

These restrictions produced the inevitable result. In the autumn of 1861 several hundred students staged riots, first in St. Petersburg, then in Moscow. A story current at the time claimed that the Governor-General of St. Petersburg lost his head and telegraphed to the Emperor, who was in the Crimea, asking him what he should do. Alexander wired back: "Treat them like a father." But the words *kak atets* were interpreted as "Treat them like *my* father." No doubt this account is apocryphal; nevertheless the Governor called out the army and many students were seriously wounded. In Moscow the result was even worse, for although the police handled the rowdy processions themselves, they sent *agents provocateurs* dressed as workmen among the crowds lining the streets. These men whispered that the young demonstrators were planning to assassinate the Czar. The mob lost control and attacked the students, literally tearing some of them to pieces.

The Czar hurried back to the capital. He was furious with the police, and above all with Poutiatin whose clumsy direction had precipitated the affair. He sacked the Admiral on the spot and appointed in his place the lenient Golovnin who rescinded his predecessor's rulings. "There is nothing but a growing desire to tease authority," wrote the Slavophile, Youri Samarin. The trouble arose, he claimed, because the new middle-class intelligentsia had no roots in the land; atheism and materialism came naturally to such lost souls. "Their shrill voices frighten the Government which goes on making one concession after another."[10]

Nevertheless it was difficult to know how to deal with the new generation. No matter whether the reins were tightened or loosened, rebellion continued. A nineteen-year-old student, Zaychnevsky, wrote a pamphlet entitled *Young Russia* advocating wholesale nationalisation and "a bloody, ruthless revolution"; another young man, Pisarev, preached that "everything that could be smashed must be smashed" on the theory that what could not be smashed must be good. His doctrine swept the universities and became a craze. Young men let their hair grow long and wore unconventional dress; women cut their hair short and practised free love. Only science could be tolerated; all else, from social institutions to moral values, must be razed to the ground. In 1862 Ivan Turgenev published *Fathers and Sons* which gave the creed of total destruction a name which found its way into history.

> " 'What is Bazarov?' smiled Arkady.
> 'Would you like me to tell you, uncle, what he is exactly?'
> 'Please do, nephew.'
> He is a nihilist . . . a nihilist is a person who does not take any principle for granted, however much that principle may be revered.' "

Turgenev's hero, Bazarov, was studying medicine and had much more faith in dissecting frogs than in principles. Raphael was not worth a brass farthing, he said; a good chemist was twenty times more useful than a poet.

> " 'We base our conduct on what we recognise as useful,' Bazarov went on. 'In these days the most useful thing we can do is to repudiate . . . so we repudiate.'
> 'Everything?'

'Everything.'

'What? Not only art, poetry . . . but also . . . I am afraid to say it . . .'

'Everything,' Bazarov repeated with indescribable composure.

Pavel Petrovich stared at him. He had not expected this while Arkady positively glowed with satisfaction.

'However, if I may say so,' began Nicholai Petrovich, 'you repudiate everything, or, to put it more precisely, you are destroying everything . . . But one must construct too, you know.'

'That is not our affair . . . the ground must be cleared first'."

Turgenev's novel created a storm, for the author was attacked by both wings of opinion: the radicals, who claimed that he was ridiculing their cause by making Bazarov a caricature; the reactionaries, who claimed that he was encouraging revolutionary tendencies by allowing Bazarov to be so glamorous. Soon after publication of the book, mysterious fires broke out in St. Petersburg and began to spread, devouring whole streets of wooden tenements. The Apraxyn and Sennaya Markets ignited leaving thousands of small merchants destitute. When the timber yards off Fontanka burst into flames, threatening the Imperial Library and the Anitchkov Palace, it looked as though the whole city might be destroyed. The Emperor hurried to the capital from Tsarsko Selo and joined the firemen, working all day in the smoke and soot. Several large squares were transformed into refugee camps; the Grand Duchess Elena turned her palace into a canteen; and the Empress Marie and her daughter distributed food and clothing. "I returned to St. Petersburg," wrote Turgenev, "on the very day when Apraxyn Market was set ablaze and the word 'nihilism' was on everybody's lips. A friend I met on the Nevski said to me—'Look what *your* nihilists are doing! There is arson all over St. Petersburg'."[11]

To this day no one knows who was responsible for the fires, but the Imperial Family was convinced that it was the work of revolutionaries. "I want to give you a sign of life," wrote the Empress in June, 1862, to her brother Prince Alexander, "after the sad time we have been through with St. Petersburg bursting into flames at every corner. It appears that this was to be the beginning of a series of revolutionary acts that had been planned in London and that were to have been carried out simultaneously here and in Moscow, but which they refused to execute down there. A number of people have been arrested and if sufficient proof can be found, the ringleaders will be hanged, although we have neither gallows nor hangmen nor even the death penalty . . . What was most painful to Sasha was the arrest of five officers. One for inciting to rioting, three because they destroyed the pamphlets which a man was carrying who was being taken prisoner by some non-commissioned officers . . . Sasha is bearing this heavy burden without losing courage, but his heart is terribly torn. May God help him!"[12]

The Czar did not swerve from his course. Bold changes were needed to modernise the rusty bureaucratic machine and he remained faithful to his decision to carry them through. In 1863 a new Education Act was introduced, and in 1864 local self-government in the form of *zemstvo* institutions made its début, an innovation second in importance only to emancipation. That same year the Czar approved the reconstruction of the judiciary; public trials and the jury system were instituted and corporal punishment abolished. Financial reforms were carried out earlier; and a press reform dispensing with preliminary censorship became law in 1865. The War Ministry was instructed to start work on a reorganisation which would introduce competition and allow privates to rise by merit to officer rank.

In the midst of these great reforms the Polish people made a heroic attempt to free themselves from Russian domination. The rising was the most violent in Poland's long and tragic history. For a brief moment it looked as though England and France might interfere on the side of Warsaw, but in the end the Russians put down the insurrection at terrible cost. The brutalities on both sides were horrifying. The Poles butchered scores of Russian peasants including women and children. The Russians erected gibbets in the streets of Polish cities and conducted public hangings by the hundred. No one knows how many people died, but it was estimated that 100,000 Poles made the long march to Siberia. Russian feeling was so strong that for a while radical voices were silenced. Alexander Herzen championed the cause of the Poles from London. His paper, *The Bell*, which up till then had enjoyed an impressive readership in Russia, dropped in circulation from 3,000 to 500 and never recovered.

During these stormy years the Czar's joy and consolation lay in his wife. Marie appeared very little in public for she had never been strong, and preferred to devote her energy to her family. She adored her children—one girl and six boys—the last of whom, Serge and Paul, were born in 1856 and 1857. For a while Alexander was deeply concerned by her health as her cough appeared to be worsening but an Italian specialist assured him that there was nothing seriously wrong. "Since consulting Seanroni," he wrote to Prince Alexander of Hesse in 1863, "who set our minds at rest regarding dear Marie's condition, her health has improved visibly, thank God, and she is planning to go down to the Crimea in two or three weeks' time..."[13]

The doctor diagnosed Marie's trouble as rheumatism caused by the dampness of the St. Petersburg climate. Her eldest and favourite son, the Grand Duke Nicholas, was believed to be suffering from the same complaint, and Marie frequently took him abroad to Italy or the South of France. When she visited Prince Alexander at Darmstadt, however, she usually arrived with Serge and Paul who were nearer the age of her nephews.

Marie's devotion to her brother never waned. She had bought with her own money the beautiful estate of Heiligenberg, near Darmstadt, and presented it to him as a gift; and in 1859 she had persuaded her eldest brother, the Grand Duke of Hesse, to bestow the title of Battenberg on Alexander's children. Marie constantly lamented the fact that Alexander no longer resided in Russia and was obliged to serve in the army of so treacherous a country as Austria. Her loyalty to her husband was such that she could not forgive Austria its underhanded rôle in the Crimean War, nor England its open enmity. She indulged her dislike of the English by fastening on to malicious stories about the royal family—Queen Victoria in particular—and passing them on to her brother. However, in 1862, when the Queen's second daughter, Alice, married Marie's nephew, Prince Louis of Hesse, the Czarina controlled her prejudices and welcomed her as one of the family.

If Marie disliked the English, Queen Victoria could scarcely be described as entertaining warm feelings towards the Russians. The quarter of a century that had intervened since her brief, girlhood flirtation with Alexander II had washed away all traces of sentiment. Although she was glad that Alexander had replaced his terrifying father on the throne she was deeply suspicious of the Czardom. This was partly due to her eldest daughter, darling "Vicky," Crown Princess of Prussia, who complained endlessly about the behaviour of the Russian Grand Duchesses who flowed into Berlin to stay with their Prussian relations. During the first year of Vicky's marriage, the Grand Duchess Olga (the lady who had fascinated Alexander of Hesse) was intolerably rude to her. "When I went to see her," the seventeen-year-old Vicky complained to her mother, "she never asked me to sit down but sat at the table with her back turned to me, and condescended to ask me when I went away, whether I was sixteen. She is shockingly dressed, her things so crumpled and soiled and she herself, oh so *fanée* and worn; no remains of good looks . . ." Queen Victoria was very indignant and told her daughter firmly that she must not allow herself to be treated in such a manner; particularly since "our princes never admitted to the Grand Dukes of Russia having precedence over them; Romanoffs are not to be compared to the houses of Brunswick, Saxony and Hohenzollern."[14]

It was clear that the Queen's blood had been stirred, for in a later letter she referred to the Grand Duchesses in Berlin as "Wolves in sheep's clothing" and cautioned her daughter to have as little to do with them as possible. The Crown Princess never lost her dislike of the Russians, and was able to get her own back in 1861 when, on her mother's instruction, she was searching for a suitable bride for her brother, the Prince of Wales. She had seen pictures of the beautiful Princess Alexandra of Denmark, and marked her down as "just the style that Bertie admires." Then she heard a rumour that the Empress Marie was talking about the Danish Princess as a possible match for her own son, the Hereditary Grand Duke Nicholas. "It would be dreadful," she wrote to her mother in April, 1861, "if this pearl went to the horrid Russians." That seemed to settle it with the Queen as well. Without further delay a meeting was arranged between Alexandra and Bertie; and a year later the engagement was announced. The Grand Duke Nicholas had to content himself with Alexandra's sister, Dagmar, who had "A very plain face—all excepting her eyes which are very pretty."[15]

The story had a sad ending, for the poor Grand Duke Nicholas died before his wedding took place. He had gone to Nice to recover from a disagreeable bout of bronchitis, and was suddenly seized by what the doctors described as an attack of meningitis. His mother and father and Princess Dagmar hurried to his bedside, but he scarcely regained consciousness. When an autopsy was performed it revealed that he was suffering from tuberculosis of the spine. The Emperor was bowed in grief, the Empress distraught. Dagmar's future, however, was not much altered for she allowed her hand to be transferred to the new Heir Apparent, who would ascend the throne one day as Alexander III.

The wedding was celebrated on 9th November, 1866. Although Dagmar's sister, the Princess of Wales, was unable to attend the ceremony as she was expecting a baby, the Prince went without her. "Beside the pleasure of being present at Dagmar's wedding," he wrote to his mother, "it would interest me more than anything to see Russia." What he saw was fairly limited for he was so impressed by the charm of Russian ladies that he had time for little else. He set so many tongues wagging that his sister Alice felt obliged to give him a severe dressing down. He took her lecture, she reported, "most good humouredly."

That same year a student who had been dismissed from St. Petersburg University almost succeeded in assassinating the Czar. Alexander II returned to his carriage, after a walk in the Winter Garden, to find that a small crowd had gathered. Among the group was a peasant from Kostroma on the Volga, who was working in the capital as a hatter's apprentice. He was thrilled to see the Czar at such close quarters, but was disturbed by a youth who pushed roughly past him; a moment later the young man raised his arm and the apprentice saw the glint of a revolver. He struck at the man's hand, the bullet went wild and embedded itself in the pavement. After a moment of stunned silence spectators grabbed the would-be assassin, who made no attempt to escape, and handed him over to the police who soon appeared on the spot. Then they turned their attention to the hatter's apprentice. When word went round that he had saved the Czar's life the crowd, which by this time was considerable, lifted him shoulder-high, acclaiming him a hero. His fame increased, for the nobility fêted him and the Czar ennobled him, gave him a diamond ring, a portrait of himself, and a pension large enough to keep him in luxury for the rest of his life. The story had a disappointing end, however, for the apprentice took such a fancy to French brandy, which he had never tasted before, that he became an addict, and a few years later died of drink.

The capital was stunned by the attempt on the Emperor's life. When the deed became known huge crowds lined the streets leading to the Winter Palace and many people wept as Alexander passed. Although the police interrogated the Czar's assailant for weeks hoping to uncover a conspiracy, no accomplices came to light. The young man explained that he had tried to kill the Czar in order to draw attention to the plight of the peasants; in the end this explanation had to be accepted and the verdict was "unbalance of mind."

Nevertheless the bullet shattered the Czar's confidence in the path he was pursuing and brought Russia's golden era to an abrupt end. Alexander II was convinced that revolutionary thought in the universities was reviving. The new generation did not know how to use its freedom. Something must be wrong with the educational system. A few weeks later Alexander appointed the stupid re-actionary, D. A. Tolstoy, as Minister of Education; and a month later he issued a Rescript making it clear that the curricula of schools and universities would be altered. "Providence has willed to reveal before the eyes of Russia," the edict read, "what consequences we may expect from aspirations and ideals which arrogantly encroach upon everything sacred . . . My attention is now turned to the education of the youth. I have given instructions that education must be directed to respect the spirit of religious truth, the right of property, the fundamental principles of public order; and that in all schools the open and secret teaching of those destructive concep-tions which are hostile to the moral and material well-being of the people will be forbidden."[16]

The "materialistic" approach thrown up by nihilism and other revolutionary creeds, it was believed, sprang from the popularisation of natural science. Tolstoy decided therefore to use the classics to counteract the trend. Gradually the study of all subjects which stimulated independent thought, such as history, science, rhetoric, modern languages, and even Russian, were curtailed; instead the students were obliged to spend their time on Latin, Greek, pure mathematics and Church-Slavic. Discipline was the keynote.

As a result, thousands of frustrated undergraduates went abroad to Geneva and Zürich to sit at the feet of professional agitators. Some of them listened to Colonel Lavrov, a forty-year-old retired army officer, who could scarcely be described as an extremist for he preached evolution rather than revolution. Progress, he said, was "the development of the individual physically, mentally, morally and the embodiment of truth and justice in social forms." He encouraged the young to move into the villages and to try to win the confidence of the *moujiks*. This was easier said than done. Some students donned peasant dress, ate nothing but black bread and adopted the local idiom. But they soon tired of this experiment for the peasants regarded them as freaks and laughed at them.

Far more exciting was the teaching of Michael Bakunin, the anarchist who lived in Geneva and published a paper *The Cause of the People*. Bakunin advocated straight revolution, preaching that all forms of compulsion were evil and that the chief abomination was the State. Like the Nihilists, he argued that sentiment had no place in the new world and advocated the abolition of marriage, religion, maternal ties. The only things that mattered were those that were useful. In 1871 Alexis Tolstoy wrote a ballad based on this theme. A newly married couple were strolling in a garden on a glorious morning in May. "Is it not lovely to be with you here in the midst of all these flowers?" says the bride. "Indeed it is Paradise," sighs the groom. "But alas, turnips will soon be planted here . . ." "Their place is in the kitchen garden," the bride protests. "True, my love, but this beautiful spot must be ruined precisely because of its beauty, and the shrubberies from which the nightingales wake us at dawn will be cut down to the roots to make room for a poultry-yard, and nightingales will be driven away because of their uselessness . . ." "But this place is ours," she cries, "who are the people wicked enough to spoil what does not belong to them?" "Ah, my love, they think that everything is theirs to destroy. They are out to ruin everything for the sake of the future, and they call such destruction progress . . ." "You must be joking, my love, but if such people do exist, they should be shut up in a madhouse . . ." The groom shakes his head. "You would need too big an asylum for that, my dear one . . ."[17]

For a short while a new star in the revolutionary firmament eclipsed Bakunin. He was a twenty-three-year-old school-teacher named Nechaev whose dazzling personality had a hypnotic effect on people. He preached that the revolution could only be achieved by iron discipline, and conspiracy based on a hitherto undreamed-of ruthlessness. He was in fact, the first Bolshevik. His *Revolutionary Catechism*, which was studied by Lenin many years later, and became the accepted doctrine of Stalinist Communism was regarded, at the time, as one of the most chilling documents ever written and it has not grown less sinister with the passage of the years. His emphasis is on the debasement of every human value, the suppression of every human instinct. Here are a few extracts:

"The revolutionary is a dedicated man . . . He has torn himself away from the bonds which tie him to the social order and the cultivated world, with its laws, moralities and customs and with all its generally accepted conventions. He is their implacable enemy, and if he continues to live with them it is only in order to destroy them more quickly . . . For him, morality is everything which contributes to the triumph of the revolution. Immoral and criminal is everything that stands in his way. The revolutionary['s] . . . degree of friendship, devotion and obligation towards a comrade must be determined only by the degree of the comrade's usefulness in the practical work of complete and destructive revolution . . . Each comrade should have under him several revolutionaries of the second or third rank, i.e. comrades who are not completely dedicated. These should be regarded as portions of a common fund of revolutionary capital, to be expended as he thinks fit. He should expend them as economically as possible, always attempting to derive the utmost possible use from them . . ."

Nechaev gave precise instructions on how to deal with "liberals of various shades." "We shall pretend we are following their ideas and give them cause to think we are blindly conspiring with them, while in fact we take them under our own control. We shall root out all their secrets and compromise them to the uttermost, so that there will be no way out for them and they can be used to create disorder in the state."[18]

Nechaev created a cell system consisting of groups of five linked together by one person in each group. At the top was an executive committee consisting of himself alone. He blackmailed his companions by stealing their letters and terrorising them in every way possible. He insisted on obedience to the point of servility. One day in November, 1870, he ordered a member of one of his cells, a good-looking student named Ivanov, who was enrolled at the Moscow Agricultural Institute, to post revolutionary fly-sheets on the walls of the college dining-room and library. Ivanov refused, saying that it would only lead to a police raid and the arrest of innocent students.

" 'I tell you,' said Nechaev, 'the Society has ordered it. Are you disobeying the Society?'

'I refuse to listen to the Society when it tells me to do completely senseless things.'

'Then you refuse to submit to the Society?'

'Yes, when it behaves stupidly.' "

Nechaev departed, white with rage. A few weeks later he summoned the other four cell members and told them that Ivanov had "committed an act of treason" and was undoubtedly a police spy. He commanded one of them to summon Ivanov to a meeting in a grotto in the college grounds on the pretext that a printing press was hidden there. The others were told to attend and to bring a revolver, a knife and some rope. It was an appalling murder; the students pinned Ivanov to the ground, Nechaev sat on him, and shot him through the head. Afterwards his body was weighted with stones and thrown into a pond.

Five days later the corpse was discovered; four of the accomplices were arrested; and one by one members of Nechaev's network, known as *The Tribunal of the People*, were picked up. Nechaev himself escaped, slipping out of Russia disguised as a woman, and taking refuge with Bakunin in Switzerland. The trial of the *Nechaevsti*, eighty-four persons in all, took place in July, 1871. The *Revolutionary Catechism* was read in court and people talked of the mysterious "Nechaev monster." It took the Russian police another thirteen months to track down the wanted man. He was arrested in Zürich, extradited to Russia and tried in December, 1872. He was not sentenced to death but condemned to twenty years in Siberia. Many prisoners, however, had escaped from Siberia, while none had ever emerged from the Alexis Ravelin dungeons in the Fortress of St. Peter and St. Paul. So it was there that Nechaev was incarcerated. He died ten years later, faithful to his revolutionary principles. Dostoevsky based his novel *The Possessed* on the murder and was furiously criticised by radicals who claimed that he was trying to debase the movement.

Meanwhile the Empress Marie had started a stone rolling which was gathering momentum. It had begun over a cup of tea with three ladies-in-waiting, selected less for their beauty than their piety. Marie, whose religious fervour increased with the years, lamented the fact that the Great Powers had refused to recognise Russia as protectress of the Christian Slavs in the Ottoman Empire. The Princess Vassili Chikova, wife of a famous general, the Countess Protasova, wife of the Procurator of the Holy Synod, and Countess Antoinette Bludova, daughter of a former Procurator, decided to do something about it. They collected and sent large sums of money to Orthodox religious establishments in Adrianople, Constantinople, Prizren, Sarajevo, Mount Athos, and Orthodox monasteries in Dalmatia and Herzegovina. The Emperor took little interest in these activities, but his witty, sharp-tongued Foreign Secretary, Prince Gortchakov, did not conceal the fact that he found the Countess Antoinette Bludova a frightful bore. "That one," he said, "will not be content until she has placed her arse firmly on the cross of Santa Sophia."

The Countess, however, was not in the least perturbed by Gortchakov's patronising airs, and urged her intellectual friends in Moscow to start a committee of their own. Michael Pogodin, the History Professor, who had implored Nicholas I to look for allies among the foreign Slavs, and Ivan Aksakov, the Slavophile publicist, both responded; and later the Moscow Slavic Benevolent Committee came into being with the unenthusiastic permission of Prince Gortchakov. "I see no obstacle which would stand in the way of voluntary collections in Moscow for the benefit of Southern Slavs."

Charitable work, however, was not exactly what Pogodin or Aksakov had in mind. The Slavophiles of the forties had become the Panslavists of the sixties, just as Nicholas I had predicted. The Crimean War, they preached, had revealed the deep-seated hostility of the West and proved conclusively that Russia's destiny lay in Slavdom. In 1859 Aksakov brought out the first issue of a paper, *The Sail*, dedicated to promoting an international Slavic union. Unfortunately, the journal was closed down after the second issue for Aksakov made the error of printing a fiery criticism of Russian policy in Eastern Europe, written by his friend Pogodin. "For the sake of the balance of Europe," wrote Pogodin, "ten million Slavs must groan, suffer and agonise under the yoke of the most savage despotism, the most unbridled fanaticism, and the most desperate ignorance." But it was the bit about Austria that upset the Foreign Office most:

"In Austria there are five million Germans and twenty million Slavs who are alien to the former in language, creed and history ... Austrians cannot sleep a single peaceful night at home without making fast all the doors, without tightly closing all the windows, without posting sentries everywhere ... and it is this Austria, if you please, which feels an invincible vocation to gather into her arms ten million more Slavs in the East who are even more alien to herself ..."[19]

The censors castigated the article as "a caustic disparagement of our foreign policy... and forbidden interference by a private person in the views and deliberations of the government"; and at the same time ordered Aksakov to shut down the paper.

A fearful rumpus followed. The head of the Asiatic Department of the Foreign Office—which oddly enough controlled Balkan affairs—was an ardent Panslavist. He approached the Countess Bludova who, in turn, approached the Empress and asked her to intercede with the Emperor. Alexander II refused to lift the ban but the matter was raised at the Council of State. Although Prince Gortchakov had no objection to kindly ladies sending money to down-trodden Christian Slavs, he considered Panslavism fundamentally ludicrous. "I find it difficult to believe," he once remarked, "in the sympathy of the Slav people for autocratic Russia."

Alexander II could not make up his mind what to do about it. Before the complications leading to the Crimean War, his father would have punished Pogodin and Aksakov for advocating rebellion against a legitimate monarch. But at the end of his life even Nicholas had allowed the professor to inveigh privately against Austria. Although a public attack was more serious, in the end Alexander II decided that the movement was too insignificant for drastic action. The Moscow Committee numbered only 300 members and had almost no public following. Furthermore he did not want to quarrel with Marie who had become emotionally involved in the cause through the Church. She was so keen a supporter that she not only gave large sums of money to her Ladies' Committee but donated 300 roubles a year to the Moscow Society.

So in the end Aksakov was granted permission to start a new paper as long as it did not meddle in politics. *The Day* began publication in 1861 and continued until 1865. In that year Aksakov married Anna Fedorovna Tyutcheva, the daughter of the Slavophile poet who served as Marie's Court Chamberlain. He felt obliged to devote more time to earning money and therefore discontinued the paper, which ended its existence with a large deficit.

Nevertheless the movement had become strong enough to continue on its own. And in 1867 the Moscow Committee sponsored a meeting which was described as "an ethnological exhibition" but was, in fact, the first Panslavist gathering in Russia. Eighty-one Slavs, among them Czech and Moravian scholars from the Habsburg

Empire, Serbs from the autonomous states of Serbia and Montene-gro, and a solitary Bulgar from the Turkish Kingdom, attended. Public money was raised to entertain the visitors who were wined and dined to the point of exhaustion. In order to welcome them to the capital the ladies of St. Petersburg opened their own branch of the Slavic Benevolent Association and collected an imposing group of members; not just intellectuals but generals, ambassadors, judges and high public officials. The arts were represented by Feodor Dostoevsky whose views had come full circle. Although he had spent eight years in Siberia as a punishment for reading Belinsky's attack on Gogol—an attack inspired because Gogol had abandoned radicalism for religion, Dostoevsky had followed the very same course. Now a convert of the Church, he saw a dazzling future for Russia as leader of a Greek Orthodox Empire, breath-taking in its scope. Every honour was heaped upon him and his fellow Panslavs including a reception at Tsarsko Selo by the Emperor and Empress. "These gentlemen are for the moment the lions of St. Petersburg," wrote the Austrian Ambassador. "They are being dragged from one feast to another, and in the streets people run after their carriages in order to see 'the Slavs.' One would suppose that they had never seen any before, as though one had just discovered a new archipelago in Polynesia . . ."[20]

The Congress had moments of embarrassment. The Poles were conspicuous for their absence, which was scarcely surprising after the mutiny and terrible reprisals of 1863. "Where are the Poles?" cried Professor Michael Pogodin in a speech to a large banquet. "There aren't any," cried the audience. This gave Pogodin the opportunity to point out that "they alone of all the Slavs cast reproachful glances at us"; it also gave Alexander Herzen, in far-away London, the opportunity to point out that there were indeed Polish "guests" in Russia, only they were not at social gatherings but in Siberia, and instead of wearing the Czar's cross on a ribbon around their necks they were carrying it on their backs!

Before the Congress ended Tyutchev, whose grandiose ideas of a Russian frontier "from the Nile to the Neva, from the Euphrates to the Volga" had not diminished, wrote to a friend that "the goal would not be reached until the Slav visitors realised that they were one with Russia . . . that they were bound to it with a dependence, an organic communality . . ." But the Slav visitors came to no such conclusion. They would not agree on a common literary language; there was no serious talk of conversion to Orthodoxy; and political federation was not discussed. As a radical paper, the *Spark*, wrote jeeringly: "We had hoped to see our humiliated and injured brethren come to us to be instructed in mind and reason, to admire our greatness and power . . . We said to them: 'come, let us form one flock.' And they gave us their reply: 'We humbly thank you . . . but we do not wish to be members of a flock . . .' And our own knew us not."[21]

However, the Congress had set more in motion than it realised. The St. Petersburg Committee, with its powerful membership, had catapulted Panslavism into the very heart of the Establishment, while the government decision to encourage foreign Slavs to attend Russian universities would introduce Panslavism to the revolutionary movement. The repercussions of both would be felt in the following decade.

Meanwhile the Moscow Panslavists were deeply disappointed by the negative outcome of their Congress. They found it particularly galling when they looked abroad; for while Russians were talking about the unification of Slavdom, Prussians were bringing about the unification of Germandom. In the seven years between 1864 and 1871 Chancellor Otto von Bismarck launched the Prussian Army against Denmark, Austria and France in three swift, decisive wars. The aim was to draw all the German states into a federation under the hegemony of Prussia; and it was so successful that in 1871 William of Prussia, Alexander II's uncle, was proclaimed German Emperor, and a new giant bestrode the Continent.

Bismarck's achievement set the royal familie sof Europe at sixes and sevens. The two Danish Princesses, married to the heirs of the English and Russian thrones, were outraged at the annexation of the Duchies of Schleswig and Holstein, which, they said, "belonged to Papa," and managed to infuse their husbands with their indignation. On the other hand, Princess Alice, Queen Victoria's daughter, now Grand Duchess of Hesse, was delighted that her sister "Vicky" would wear an imperial crown one day, and voiced pro-Prussian sentiments at every opportunity. She infuriated Prince Alexander of Hesse (who had fought on the Austrian side during the disastrous Seven Weeks' War) when she took her husband, Louis, to Berlin in 1867. "No doubt," he wrote acidly to his sister, "Louis is going to apologise to the Empress for having done his duty as a Hessian prince in the last war." Marie, however, refused to take sides, for the Czar loved his Uncle William and hated Austria. And Prussia went out of its way to avoid offending Russia. Although Bismarck severely punished many of the small states which had taken up arms against Prussia (the King of Hanover, the Duke of Nassau and the Landgrave of Hesse-Cassel lost all their territories) he was careful not to offend those kingdoms with Russian connections. He let off very lightly Württemberg, where the Czar's sister, Olga, was Crown Princess; Baden, whose king was a favourite nephew of the Empress; Hesse-Darmstadt, the home of the influential Alexander.

This policy paid handsome dividends, for Bismarck was able to strike a bargain with Alexander II when Prussia attacked France in 1870. In return for Russia's neutrality the new Germany supported the Czar's repudiation of the clauses of the Treaty of Paris, imposed after the Crimean defeat, barring Russian ships from the Black Sea. It was announced casually that Alexander had resumed "his sovereign rights" in those waters; and although Queen Victoria fumed there was nothing she could do about it.

Most people believed that Prussia had met its match in throwing down the gauntlet to France, and were staggered by the success of the Berlin military machine. Even Prince Alexander of Hesse was forced to change his views. "The results are so astonishingly brilliant," he wrote two months after the German Empire had been proclaimed at Versailles, "that I suppose history can hardly produce a parallel." And although he had once declared that he would never again speak to William I, he now accepted an invitation to meet him. "For," he wrote in his diary, "he is after all, our Sovereign, and I must accept him if I do not wish to become a political exile."22

Although the Empress Marie continued to write spirited letters to her brother, expressing concern and solicitude for the Czar, she was deeply unhappy in 1872. Her doctors told her that she was suffering from tuberculosis of the lungs, but this was a mild blow compared to the stunning realisation that Alexander was passionately in love with another woman. The affair had been going on for five years, but Marie had refused to take it seriously. Alexander's infidelities were not rare but momentary, and Marie accepted them as part of the Romanov tradition. But when Princess Catherine Dolgorouky bore the Emperor a child in the spring of 1872 Marie was forced to recognise that this affair was different.

The Emperor had known the twenty-four-year-old Catherine as a child. He had seen her for the first time in 1857 when he was on army manœuvres in the region of Poltava. Prince Dolgorouky, the greatest landowner of the region and a friend of the Emperor, learned that Alexander was suffering from asthma and had been advised by his doctors not to remain in the open camp. The Prince, therefore, invited the Czar and his staff to take over his vast house. The Dolgorouky family moved out, and the children were told not to bother the imperial retinue. But the ten-year-old Princess Catherine appeared on the veranda one day when the officers were drinking tea and asked to see the Czar. Alexander laughed and took her on his knee.

The Dolgoroukys were one of the great families of Russia. Their lineage was older and more distinguished than the Romanovs, but the two names had been joined in 1613 when Marie Dolgorouky had married the Czar Michael, the founder of the Romanov dynasty. The Czar Alexander's host, Prince Michael Dolgorouky, was one of the richest men in Russia; yet two years after he had entertained his sovereign he died penniless, his fortune squandered in building schemes, women and horses. Out of respect for the family Alexander offered to take the children under his guardianship. The boys were put into a military academy and later given commissions in the Guards while the girls, Catherine and her sister Marie, were sent to the Smolny Institute, an exclusive finishing school in St. Petersburg founded by Catherine the Great and still under imperial patronage. The Empress Marie was its honorary head, but when she was unable to visit the school the Emperor often took her place. By 1865 sharp eyes could scarcely fail to detect the interest Alexander showed in the eighteen-year-old Princess Catherine Dolgorouky, who had grown into a beauty with an ivory skin and magnificent chestnut hair.

The Princess left the Smolny that year and went to live with her brother, Prince Michael, who was married to an Italian lady and had a house in St. Petersburg. One spring day when Catherine, followed by a maid, was crossing the Summer Garden which was still carpeted with snow, she ran into the Emperor who was taking his daily walk with an aide-de-camp. Alexander drew her aside into a more secluded part of the garden. "Then, to this inexperienced, ingenuous girl he addressed words so cajoling and so tender, so strange and disturbing, that she was filled with confusion. She would fain have asked him to stop, but the words she sought did not come, or stuck in her throat. They met fairly frequently in this way, either in the Summer Garden, or on the Islands of the Neva, in the winding avenues of Ielaghine, or again, after July, under the century-old forests which surround Peterhof. Each time he declared his love in vain; his great love pertinacious and passionate. She remained cold, hostile and reserved. Then for several months she succeeded in avoiding him; but he still followed her . . ."[23]

Marie knew nothing of her husband's passion. Her illness debarred her from playing a part in St. Petersburg society, and forced her to spend the winter in a warm climate. When she was at home she rested much of the day. She was withdrawing increasingly from the world, while the forty-seven-year-old Czar was in the prime of life, still regarded as the handsomest prince in Europe. The French writer, Théophile Gautier, who attended a Court Ball in 1865, found Alexander's features as perfect "as the cast for a bronze medallion" and his attire nothing short of sensational. He wore a uniform with "a sort of white tunic reaching half-way down his thighs, frogged with gold and trimmed at the neck, wrists and hem with blue Siberian fox, the breast being plastered with orders. Clinging sky-blue trousers sheathed his legs, and ended in close-fitting top-boots."[24]

Despite Alexander's devastating looks, the Princess Catherine resisted him for many months. Not until he narrowly escaped assassination was she shocked into the knowledge that she was in love with him, and consented to become his mistress. Alexander

was so bewitched by her that he could not bear to have a day pass
without seeing her. In St. Petersburg the lovers met in a small
apartment in the Winter Palace. In order that she should have easy
access he arranged a marriage between her sister and one of his aides-
de-camp. Later he had the temerity to appoint Catherine a maid-of-
honour to the Empress so that he could see her at Court functions
As he spent much of the year away from St. Petersburg he took a
house for her at Tsarsko Selo; another house near Livadia on the
Black Sea; and a third at Peterhof near Finland where he went for
a month in the summer.

The Princess was an unusual courtesan for she shunned society
almost as much as the Empress. She cared nothing for influence or
clothes or jewels. She seldom went out, and only appeared at court
when the Emperor begged her to do so, telling her how much he
liked to see her dance. She had very few friends, never entertained
and rarely attended the opera or ballet. She only saw members of
her family and lived for the hours that Alexander was with her.

Catherine's child was born in the Winter Palace, for the Princess
was spending the afternoon with the Czar when labour began.
Dr. Krasovsky and a midwife were summoned and sworn to
secrecy. The baby, a boy, was not born until the following morning,
a Sunday, and the delivery was scarcely over before the Czar had to
hurry to mass where the court was awaiting him. The child was
smuggled out of the palace to the home of Colonel Ryleev, a close
personal friend and a member of Alexander's police bodyguard. The
Colonel put the baby in the care of a Russian foster-mother and a
French wet-nurse. It was baptised George Alexandrovitch.

Despite the Emperor's efforts at secrecy the birth became widely
known. Not only did the Empress hear about it but the news ran
through the markets and before long crowds were collecting in
front of Colonel Ryleev's house to try and catch a glimpse of
the beribboned coif worn by children's nurses. "Colonel Ryleev
had gone to Tsarsko Selo," wrote a young Russian nobleman
to his mother. "His house in Mokhovaya Street is shut up. None
the less, it seems to excite great curiosity in herring-women and
pedlars."[25]

The Empress Marie's self-control was remarkable. The very fact that the Czar had bestowed upon the child the patronym of Alex-androvitch showed how serious the affair had become. She did not discuss the outrage with anyone, least of all her husband. She maintained such an impervious air that many people wondered whether or not she knew. Yet that summer, when Alexander of Hesse visited her in the Crimea, she poured out her anguish. She could forgive the insult to the Empress, she said, but not the cruelty to the wife.

Marie knew that the only way she could retain the shreds of her husband's affection was to continue to ignore the liaison, and behave as though her family life was unchanged. Alexander treated her with courtesy, even tenderness, but his thoughts were far away and he spent little time with her alone. On the other hand she always presided at his table and he still discussed political matters with her. By her incredible self-discipline she managed to create an agreeable aura for visitors. Lord Augustus Loftus, the British Ambassador, frequently dined with the Imperial couple *en famille*, and found the atmosphere friendly and informal. On one occasion, the Czar suddenly rose from the table and left the room. A moment later the Ambassador heard him cry, "Milord, Milord!" Lord Augustus put down his napkin and hastened after him, no doubt to the amusement of the Empress who was always ready for a joke. It is difficult to say who was the most embarrassed, the Emperor or the Ambassador, for the Czar was merely calling his pet dog whom he had named "Milord."

Although Marie accepted the bitter hurt of her husband's mistress, the affair split the family into pieces. The Czar's brothers insisted that the Sovereign was above criticism, but their wives were indignant at his behaviour. Four of Marie's five sons, the Czarevitch, Vladimir, Serge and Paul, sided strongly with their mother while Alexis refused to become involved. Their only daughter, however, the Grand Duchess Marie, worshipped Alexander II and could not find it in her heart to blame him for anything. Whereas the Czarevitch became reserved, Marie drew closer to her father, and tried to fill the void by accompanying him on walks and giving him the companionship she felt he needed. "The Emperor," wrote Lord Augustus Loftus, ". . . passed my house every day with his daughter,

followed by his sleigh, to the summer garden, without any atten-
dant."[26]

Alexander became so dependent on the sixteen-year-old Grand
Duchess that he could not bear the thought of her marrying and
living far away from Russia. When in the winter of 1871-2 he
received overtures from Queen Victoria on behalf of her son Alfred,
Duke of Edinburgh, he dismissed them instantly. Marie had met
Alfred the previous summer when staying with the Hesse-Cassel
family at Jugenheim. Apparently her flirtation had gone to considerable lengths for her mother (who backed Alexander in discouraging
the feelers) made her sit down and write a letter saying: "Although
the future may not unite us as closely as we hoped at one time, I
beg you never to doubt my cordial interest in your welfare."

The Queen wrote an indignant letter to her daughter Alice about
the "quasi-dismissal of Alfred by the Russians," and blamed her for
having instigated the affair. Alice loved fixing things. She had persuaded Alexander of Hesse to place his eldest son, Louis, in the British
Navy; and when her brother Alfred told her how much he admired
the attractive high-spirited little Grand Duchess, she decided to
promote the match. She began by persuading her mother that
Marie was very fond of Alfred and that the imperial Russian family
would welcome the idea.

No English prince had ever married a Romanov and the Queen
saw drawbacks in the Orthodox religion and the Russian upbringing. On the other hand England regarded Russia as her most formidable enemy and the union might help to ease the tension, if
only by putting the monarchs into correspondence with one another.
At that very moment the two countries were quarrelling over a
frontier. Ever since the Crimean War Russian troops had been
advancing in Central Asia. After completing the conquest of the
Caucasus in 1859, they moved forward in the area between Siberia
in the north and Persia, Afghanistan and India in the south. One by
one they had subdued and annexed the decadent Turcoman and
Tartar states. Turkestan was added to the Russian Empire in 1865;
Bokhara fell in 1866; Khiva and Khokand in the seventies. In
1872 England and Russia were disputing the Afghan frontier and
British newspapers were shrilly pointing out the danger to India.

Lord Augustus Loftus felt that the Czar was not to blame. "Where an enormous standing army is maintained," he wrote, "it is necessary to find employment for it. Every officer is anxious to gain the St. George or some such decoration, while both officers and men seek to enrich themselves. When a system of conquests sets in, as in Central Asia, one acquisition of territory leads to another and the difficulty is where to stop . . . Fresh conquests of territory are laid at the Czar's feet, gained by the prowess and blood of his troops. He cannot refuse them without offending his army; and troops so far distant . . . are difficult to restrain."[27]

Queen Victoria accepted this explanation with reservations for it did not explain Russia's urge to the Mediterranean nor her classic design on Constantinople. Like her daughter, the Crown Princess of Germany, she regarded the Muscovite Empire as a predatory animal. Darling Vicky did nothing to encourage the marriage as she still hated the Russians. Indeed she made mischief by writing to her mother that the Czar had been saying horrid things about Alfred. Meanwhile the Czarina was having second thoughts. "There is so little choice," she explained to Alexander of Hesse. "Marie didn't like the Prince of Württemberg, and the poor child is frightened about Strelitz because the Prince in question said himself that it was 'a dull little hole'."[28] Consequently, in July, 1873, a telegram was sent by the Empress inviting the Duke of Edinburgh to Jugenheim, and the couple were allowed to pledge their troth.

The Czar was not yet reconciled to the idea and when he received a letter written at Queen Victoria's insistence, asking him to bring his daughter to England to make the Queen's acquaintance before the engagement became public, he wrote "Silly old fool" in the margin, and sent a message saying that the long journey was completely out of the question. The Czarina tried to soften his refusal by offering to present her daughter to the Queen in Cologne, a city midway between St. Petersburg and London. Victoria was furious. She raged to Lord Granville about "Asiatic ideas of their Rank" and demanded of the sympathetic Vicky in Berlin: How could 'a Sovereign & a Lady' be ready in three days' time 'to run after her'? When Princess Alice was unwise enough to put in an oar urging her mother to make the trip, the Queen's wrath knew no bounds. "You have *entirely* taken the Russian side, I do *not* think, dear Child, that *you* should tell *me* who have been nearly 20 *years longer* on the throne than the Emperor of Russia & am the Doyenne of Sovereigns & who am a *Reigning* Sovereign which the Empress is *not—what I ought to do*. I think I know *that*. The proposal received on *Wednesday* for me to be at *Cologne* . . . to-morrow was the coolest thing I ever heard . . . How could I who am not like any little Princess ready to run to the slightest call of the *mighty Russians*—have been *able in 24 hours* to be *ready* to travel! *I own every one* was shocked."[29]

In the end Queen Victoria never met Marie until she arrived in London as a bride. But she greeted her daughter-in-law warmly and did everything she could to make her feel at home. "Dear Marie has a very friendly manner," she wrote in her diary, "a pleasant face, beautiful skin and fine bright eyes, and there is something very fresh and attractive about her. She speaks English wonderfully well."[30] She allowed her to take precedence over most of her daughters at court functions, but dug her toes in where Vicky, the Princess Royal, and the Princess of Wales were concerned. Even the hostile Czarina could not find anything to criticise in the welcome. The Queen, she wrote to her brother, "impressed our people as being kind-hearted and having delicacy of feeling, and they were touched by it." But that was as far as she would go. She delighted in passing on her daughter's disobliging remarks about England, and her own dislike of the Queen was as sharp as ever. "Marie has discovered that the Queen drinks whisky," she wrote to her brother two months after the wedding, "sometimes with water, generally without; and that she is afraid of Brown, who treats her like a small child . . . Between you and me, Marie thinks London hideous, the air there appalling, the English food abominable, the late hours very tiring, the visits to Windsor and Osborne beyond belief, but the English less dull than she expected . . ."[31]

The Czar visited his daughter in England that same June, and although nothing was spared to make the entertainment as magnificent as the occasion demanded, Providence seemed determined to preserve the tension between the two countries. Alexander's yacht ran aground at Dover, causing him not only to miss the gala luncheon arranged in his honour, but to arrive at the State dinner at half past ten at night. The Duke of Edinburgh could not help making jokes about the Russian Navy which got back to the Empress who angrily insisted that the British pilot ship was to blame. Instead of improving relations between the two countries the marriage only seemed to provoke gossip which turned pin-pricks into cuts. Queen Victoria had not seen her royal guest for thirty-five years and not a flutter of emotion remained. They met as total strangers and Queen Victoria wrote in her Journal that she found him "very kind but . . . terribly altered, so thin, and his face looks so old, sad and careworn . . ."[32]

There was good reason for Alexander to be tired and dispirited, for the wedding of his daughter and his trip to England coincided with a new wave of lawlessness inside Russia. Although the peasants still looked upon the Czar as a father-figure, socialists and anarchists pointed to the restrictions re-imposed on the universities after the failure of the liberalisation period, and insisted that the Czar was every bit as tyrannical as his father.

By the mid-seventies the doctrine of violence had once again become fashionable. Extremism seemed to appeal to something in the very depths of the Russian soul. The blood-bath and the martyr's crown fulfilled a yearning for heroic tragedy; anything short of this was tepid and unworthy. Michael Bakunin talked constantly of "a tornado of destruction," while even the level-headed Alexander Herzen shrilled that blood would "flow in streams." ". . . there will perish the world which oppresses these new men of the new time . . . Long live chaos, therefore, long live destruction! *Vive la mort* . . . We are the executioners of the past . . ."[33] It is not surprising that some years later Karl Marx cautioned Engels against the explosive nature of the Russian. "I do not trust any Russian," he wrote. "As soon as a Russian worms his way in, all hell breaks loose."

Nor is it surprising that the Czarist Government was bewildered as to how to control the tidal wave. When the sluice-gates were open the water poured through; when they were shut it flooded over the top. The hundreds of students who had been expelled from Russian universities for political activity had made their way to Zürich to sit at the feet of Bakunin and Prince Peter Kropotkin, and had turned the Swiss city into a hot-bed of revolutionary propaganda.

In 1873 so many pamphlets were being smuggled into Russia that the Czar finally adopted his father's methods and issued a decree demanding that *all* Russian subjects return home by January 1874. The students retaliated by going "to the people." Although earlier *narodniki*, under the inspiration of a young man named Chaikovsky, had formed a sort of Peace Corps and worked in the country as vaccinators, doctors, midwives and teachers, this new brand was far more aggressive and tried to incite the peasants to armed uprisings. The peasants did not like their over-bearing manners and city ways. They did not understand their literature and were bored to death by their mysterious talk of Karl Marx. When the police came into the villages the peasants eagerly denounced them. Over 700 persons were arrested in May, 1874.

Those who escaped detection decided that it was impossible to bring about a revolution without secret organisations. They formed a new society, *Land and Liberty*, and divided it into compartments. One section, "the heavenly chancellery," produced false passports; another section, "the disorganising department," undertook sabotage. Gradually this last group developed into Russia's first, fully-fledged terrorist society, known as the *Will of the People*. It was destined to meet with horrific success.

III

Fishing in Troubled Waters

<hr />

In the winter St. Petersburg presented a mournful picture. It had only four hours of daylight and icy winds kept the broad avenues empty of pedestrians. Paint peeled off the damp house-fronts, street lamps were dim and flickering and shops dispensed with window displays and barricaded themselves against the cold. The only touches of colour came from the spires and domes of the churches; the red shirts of the door-keepers which showed above their sheepskin coats; the occasional flash of a brightly decorated sleigh, pulled by fast-trotting horses and dominated by a bearded and padded coachman. "I had pictured St. Petersburg to myself as a second Paris," wrote a British diplomat, "a city glittering with light and colour, but conceived on an infinitely more grandiose scale than the French capital. The atrociously uneven pavements, the general untidiness, the broad thoroughfares empty except for a lumbering cart or two, the absence of foot passengers and the low cotton-wool sky, all gave the effect of unutterable dreariness. And this was the golden city of my dreams! This place of leprous fronted houses, of vast open spaces full of drifting snow-flakes, and of immense emptiness. I never was so disappointed in my life."[1]

Yet for the fashionable world the winter was the gayest time. Behind those sombre, flaking façades, in an atmosphere of warmth and luxury, Russian society laughed and talked and danced, almost without stop, for the whole of the ice-bound months. Ladies lived like hot-house plants, only poking their noses out of doors for an hour a day. They did not rise until two in the afternoon, received guests at four, dined at six; went to the opera or played cards at eight. Almost every night there was a ball which went on until the small hours of the morning with the guests still eating supper when ordinary people were having their breakfast.

Alexander II maintained the splendours of his father's court and added greatly to the pleasures of the season. What people liked best, however, were the small, more intimate parties he gave, known as *Les Bals des Palmiers*. On these occasions a hundred palm trees, specially grown at Tsarsko Selo, were brought to the Winter Palace in huge horse-drawn boxes. Around each palm in its tub supper-tables were built seating fifteen people. English guests invariably had a guilty feeling walking into the warm lighted palace and leaving their poor coachmen to wait all night in the freezing temperature. "That terrible cold!" wrote Sir Horace Rumbold. ". . . in the squares that adjoin the Winter Palace are iron pavilions, like great bandstands, where immense fires are kept up all night long for the coachmen and sledge drivers. In their long caftans wadded some three inches thick, and their fur capes and collars, they are really able to brave the cold with impunity, though one hears now and then of some poor wretch, with an overdose of vodka, having been frozen on his box. But once the Imperial threshold has been passed, it is the contrast with the cruelly bleak scene without that beggars all des-cription . . . The effect of the immense room is that of a tropical grove in some gorgeous fairy scene . . ."[2] At the *Bals des Palmiers* it was Alexander II's custom to make the rounds of the tables as soon as his guests were seated. As he approached, the occupants rose. He would say a few words to one or two of them, pick up a piece of bread or fruit and lift a glass of champagne to his lips. This was done in order that his guests might say that he had eaten and drunk with them.

Alexander was noted for his graciousness as a host; but in Novem-ber, 1875, he derived little pleasure from society for his mind was tormented by the political situation. A few months earlier a revolt had broken out in the Turkish-controlled, Slav-inhabited province of Herzegovina, (now part of Yugoslavia) which had sparked off frantic activity on the part of the Slavic Committees in Moscow and St. Petersburg. The rebellion had started in the summer when a group of peasants refused to pay the extortionist taxes demanded of them by their Moslem landlords. After attacking a number of Turkish

75

outposts, burning and slaying at random, they had set up head-quarters in the hills where they had a large store of arms. The British Consul in Bosnia, Mr. Holmes, entered the village of Nevesink, where the trouble had started, to find a Turkish boy's head blackening in the sun and a Turkish girl still breathing with her throat cut. In Constantinople the Grand Vizier had reacted in his usual leisured manner. He had sent emissaries to the scene to try to settle the dispute but the peasant chieftain refused to parley. The rebellion was still growing and some people claimed that it had already spread into neighbouring Bosnia.

When Alexander of Hesse visited Russia in January he was astonished at the bellicose mood of St. Petersburg society. Forgotten were student riots, reforms, revolutionaries. Instead people were quarrelling heatedly over whether or not Russia should go to the aid of her Slavic brothers. The hawks urged a Holy Crusade which this time, they said, would witness the birth of a Russian-Slav Empire with its capital in Constantinople, while the doves described the idea as "ludicrous" and remarked dryly that, if Russia did not mind her own business, she would find herself in another European war. Even the Emperor and Empress were in opposite camps. Marie could talk of nothing but the poor Christians while Alexander was desperately anxious to keep the peace.

Both Alexanders—the Czar and his brother-in-law—recognised the inflammatory character of the Panslav movement as they were well-acquainted with the slumbering ambitions of the Russian heart. The horizon was always limitless; no goal was too outrageous, no prize too extravagant for serious consideration. Only a Russian—in this instance Dostoevsky—could describe the vast Muscovite Empire as choking in its oppressive confinement, and talk of the "long-conceived necessity for a tremendous giant, such as Russia, finally to get out of his locked room in which he has already grown up to the ceiling—into free spaces where he may inhale the free air of seas and oceans."[3]

This imperialism, always latent among the Russians, had sprung to life in 1871 when the King of Prussia had been crowned Emperor and, overnight, a united Germany displaced Russia as the foremost power on the continent. Russian nationalists had looked around furiously for a rejoinder and found it, quite literally, at their finger-tips. Two Panslav books had rolled off the presses, one in 1870, the other a year later, which provided all the answers.

The books had two things in common, both of which differed from Michael Pogodin's dreamy Panslavism. They glorified war; and they preached that the Slav Federation must be brought under the domination of Russia. *Opinion on the Eastern Question* was a hard-hitting, ninety-eight page brochure written by General Fadéev, the son of a former governor of Saratov and a Dolgorouky, a relation of the Emperor's mistress. Fadéev had served for twenty years in the Caucasus and had been on the staff of the famous Prince Bariatinsky who had finally brought Shamyl to heel. Fadéev very nearly argued that Russian expansion was a primary law of the universe. "Russia cannot consolidate itself in its present state; political, like natural, history does not lend eternity to undefined, unfinished forms. All depends now on the evolution of the Slavic Question. Russia must either extend its primacy to the Adriatic Sea or withdraw again behind the Dnieper."[4]

The second treatise, *Russia and Europe*, was written by Nicholas Danilevsky, son of a general, who had studied botany at St. Peters-burg University and was now employed as a government inspector of Agriculture and Fisheries. Like Fadéev, Danilevsky argued for "a Slavic federation with Russia at its head, with the capital in Constantinople." His book was accepted as the Panslav Bible for he not only managed to incorporate the Slavophile mystique into his imperialism but to give it a scientific flavour, much in fashion, by defining history in terms of conflict between races and cultures. "A struggle with the West," he wrote, "is the only saving means, both for curing our own Russian cultural ailments and for develop-ing Panslav sympathies which would swallow up the petty quarrels among the various Slavic peoples and factions. The already ripening Eastern Question is making this struggle inevitable . . . despite anyone's wishes."[5]

Danilevsky envisaged a structure embracing 125 million souls. The Poles, Finns, Latvians, Esthonians and Lithuanians would con-tinue to be regarded as part of the Russian Empire; while the new structure would reach out to embrace, among others, the Czech-

Moravian-Slovak kingdom; the Kingdom of the Serbs-Croats-Slovenes and the Bulgarian Kingdom. The various states would be autonomous as far as their internal affairs were concerned, but dependent on Russia for defence and foreign policy; and a good many non-Slav states would be compelled to become part of the Federation because of the geography. "All these non-Slavic peoples (Greeks, Romanians, Magyars) which historic destiny has, for better or for worse, inseparably bound to us, wedging them into the Slavic mass, must willy-nilly also join the Panslavic federation."[6] The Greeks, he argued blandly, would be protected from the rapaciousness of the West; the Romanians from the ambitions of the Magyars; and the Magyars would simply have "to abandon their iniquitous lust for power." Meanwhile Russia's iniquitous lust for power would be purified by freeing Christians from Moslems, Slavs from Germans; above all by worshipping at Santa Sophia, the fount of Orthodoxy, and re-establishing Constantinople as the greatest city in Christendom.

The books set the breeze blowing and the Herzegovina revolt provided the first sparks. Even the Heir Apparent, the Grand Duke, joined the cause. The strength of the new Panslavic creed was that it held something for everyone: religion for Marie and her court ladies; conquest for the Heir Apparent and his army colleagues; intrigue for the diplomatists and their underlings. Even revolutionaries were beginning to infiltrate the ranks in order to work for the overthrow of the Turkish and Austrian monarchies; and to get a free passage to the scene of action. Although the right-wing Panslavists saw what was happening they shut their eyes to it, as they needed professional agitators to stir up rebellions abroad and to teach them how to organise subversive activities.

Meanwhile Ivan Aksakov was calling for volunteers from his Moscow office and opening new Associations in all the big cities of Russia. In St. Petersburg the Countess Bludova and other court ladies, with the powerful backing of the Empress, were raising funds through the Church. Although the rebellion was not religious in origin they saw it solely as a question of alleviating the lot of "oppressed Christians." They even took the unprecedented step of issuing an appeal through the *Zemstvoes*. This move was sharply countered by the Minister of the Interior who issued a Court Circular to all the Provincial Governors reminding them that the law expressly forbade subscriptions for anything but charitable purposes. No doubt Marie pleaded with her husband to intervene; for in a weak moment Alexander II suddenly proclaimed that money could be raised provided that funds did not go to the combatants, only to the wounded and destitute. But as one cynical observer remarked: ". . . in order to tend the wounded one must first procure them to tend. That will cost us half our money, the other half we will scrupulously employ in healing them."

By January 1876 Alexander II realised that a huge conspiracy was forming behind his back. The money being raised by Ivan Aksakov and the Ladies' Committee in St. Petersburg was not only being used for relief work in Herzegovina and Bosnia but to fan the flame of rebellion abroad. The master-mind was the Russian Ambassador in Constantinople, General Count Ignatiev. As one of the founder members of the St. Petersburg Slavic Committee, Ignatiev had embraced Panslavism, not for religious reasons, but as the best vehicle of Russian expansion. During the twelve years he had lived on the Bosphorus he had established a network of agents throughout the Balkans. He had even succeeded in organising Panslav committees in Austria which were now playing an important part in the rebellion.

Count Ignatiev was never short of helpers. Clandestine activities were as irresistible to Russians as candles to moths. The fact that Panslavs, working for the glory of the Czar, borrowed the techniques of home revolutionaries, working for the overthrow of the Czar, was overlooked in the patriotic surge. In December, 1875, Count Ignatiev's most important agent was Alexander Ionin, a member of the Russian Consular Service who had served for seven years as Envoy to the Prince of Montenegro, and was now stationed at Ragusa (renamed Dubrovnik), a small Austrian town on the Dalmatian coast within a mile of the Herzegovinian frontier. Ionin's job was to keep the rebellion going.* In the autumn of 1875 the Turks had proclaimed an amnesty and most of the insurgents had

* Indeed, it is not impossible that M. Ionin started the initial rebellion which was begun by Herzegovinian peasants who had spent some months in Montenegro.

gone back to their farms. Those who remained were short of money, food and arms and would have given up the fight as well if it had not been for the intervention of the Panslavists. "The soul of every enterprise, the centre of all the intrigues," wrote a Russian eye-witness, "was the Russian Consul-General, Ionin, at Ragusa . . . In January, 1876, the first officers actually serving in the Russian Army arrived at Cettinje and Ragusa, either to take part in the engagements or to watch the progress of the insurrection . . . the arrival of these gentlemen, the activity of the Slav committees . . . together with considerable help in money, provisions, arms, and ammunition, at once effected the desired change in the general state of feeling . . . Until that time the insurgents had been only peasants, malcontents, miserably armed Heiduks, patriotic brigands; they now became a corps of volunteers, well-armed and with some discipline, to whom the Montenegrins sent between 2,000 and 3,000 of their best warriors . . . the Prince of Montenegro, supported by the Russian Government, supplied with money and provisions by the committees which he well knew how to make the most of, threw aside the mask assumed till then, and took part, more or less openly with his oppressed brethren . . ."[7]

In March, the British Government, who had been warned of Ionin's activities, sent Edmond Monson, the Third Secretary at Vienna, to report from Ragusa. The town was filled with consular officials, newspaper correspondents, Russian military men and people who described themselves as "relief workers." Arms purchased from Austria were flowing into Montenegro through the port of Cattaro and being sent overland to Herzegovina. What astonished Monson most of all, however, was the brashness with which the insurgents came into the town to confer with Ionin, who appeared to have plenty of money at his disposal. Although the frontier between Austria and Herzegovina was supposed to be closed the Austrian officials, most of whom were Slavs, shut their eyes to what was happening. "It could hardly be possible for anyone not on the spot," he wrote to London on 25th March, "to believe in the freedom with which the insurgent chiefs visit Ragusa to confer with their friends; and in the worse than indifference with which these visits are regarded by the authorities."[7]

Edmond Monson, a young man in his twenties, wrote his dispatches on the thick, expensive, white paper used by the Foreign Service in those palmy Victorian days. His handwriting is clear and meticulous and his information almost dramatic in its laconic understatement. We see Ragusa swarming with adventurers; we see Russian Army officers rubbing shoulders with Russian revolutionaries posing as hospital workers. We see the Russian consulate as "a treasury into which Russian subscriptions are pouring," and the funds being expended not only on food but on arms and bribes. M. Ionin is not short of money for his personal use and frequently spends the day "swaggering about the town in Montenegrin costume; and the evening in boisterous champagne parties." "He receives a handsome salary and allowances and has a staff of *cavasses* who act as Government couriers; and a separate establishment of men and horses at Cattaro to facilitate communications with Cettinje."[8]

Ionin's assistant, Colonel Monteverde, was even more of a scoundrel, and kept permanent open house for the rebels. Madame Monteverde was a great beauty and not only had M. Ionin dancing to her tune (according to a story going the rounds), but had so attracted Pepe Pavlovitch, a handsome rebel leader, that he had promised to send her a Turkish head. A few weeks later she received an apology. He had plenty of heads, he said, but was at a loss to know how to get one through the Austrian Customs House.

Monson found *The Times* correspondent, Mr. Stillman, (an American by nationality), even more irksome than the Russians. This man spent all his time with the rebels and was such an open partisan that they gave a banquet in his honour. He pretended to write impartially for his paper but sent such outrageously biased accounts that Monson was worried about the harm he would do in England.

While Stillman claimed that the insurrection was spontaneous, Monson regarded it as almost wholly artificial. "It is not surprising," he wrote on 14th June, "that the large force of Turkish troops, badly officered, insufficiently clothed, half-starved during the winter and spring, and destitute as they are of a proper transport service, had been unable to suppress an insurrection which, in regard to its origin and to the number of *bona fide* insurgent combatants, may fairly be termed 'fictitious.' My own conviction is that had it not been for the money spent by Russia and by the Dalmatian Panslav Committees upon certain influential chiefs, the insurrection would have long since collapsed. The mass of the population of the revolted districts would probably from the outset have been contented if they could have obtained a hearing for the Agrarian grievances under which they undoubtedly have laboured.

"As it is a large proportion of them have not resorted to arms . . . In fact the purely agrarian population of the insurgent districts, comprising that portion whose grievances are well-founded, are almost entirely refugees; the combatants are from the districts coterminous with Montenegro and are by no means numerous, not exceeding, I should say, 5,000 men; their fighting strength made up, as occasion required, by reinforcements of Montenegrins and Dalmatians and directed by a few Russian volunteers . . . a great step in the suppression of the Insurrection would be effected if the Austrian Government would dissolve the Panslav Committees; enforce a strict surveillance of the frontier; and would absolutely forbid and put down the export of arms and ammunition to Montenegro."[9] The Austrian Government, however, feared that suppression would only drive the Panslavs underground and increase support for the movement; so no action was taken.

The Czar was bewildered by the defiance of his subjects, many of whom he looked upon as the very pillars of the autocracy. Nothing like it had ever happened in Russia before. The horse was running away with the master. While Marie lamented "sanguinary battles during Holy Week," Alexander was preoccupied with the storm clouds gathering in the West. If Russia attacked Turkey, Austria-Hungary would not stand aloof, as she not only coveted Bosnia and Herzegovina but had millions of Slavs under her own rule. Nor would Britain remain a spectator. English statesmen never tired of pointing out that Constantinople dominated the Turkish Straits, which led to the Mediterranean; therefore its integrity as part of the Ottoman Empire was "a vital British interest."

From the beginning Alexander had worked feverishly to restore peace through the impeccable channels of the Concert of Europe. Aided by his Chancellor, the vain, witty, aged Prince Gortchakov, he had collaborated with Germany and Austria, his partners in the League of Three Emperors, in drafting a note which had been signed by all the powers, demanding drastic reforms in Turkey. The Turks had already offered an amnesty and an armistice, and now agreed to negotiate on the basis of the note. But Alexander had been defeated by the Panslavists who had put pressure on the rebels to continue the insurrection, telling them that if they held out long enough Russia would be forced to come to their aid.

With official Russia seeking peace, and unofficial Russia inciting war, the situation was becoming grotesque. In May, 1876, Alexander, accompanied by Prince Gortchakov, travelled to Berlin to consult his uncle, the German Emperor, on a new diplomatic approach. "You ought to restrain your subjects," warned Uncle William, "otherwise they will lead you into war." Alexander replied gloomily that the movement was growing too strong for him. Although it was not a nationalist movement in the strict sense of the word—the peasants were scarcely aware of the agitation—it had caught the imagination of the bureaucracy. Men who were supposed to be serving the Czar winked at official instructions and pursued their own aims. The military were the worst of all. At that very moment Serbia was thinking of entering the conflict. The Czar had cautioned Prince Milan not to take the step, warning him flatly that Russia would not come to his aid if he got into trouble. But a Russian general, Chernayaev, known as "the hero of Tashkent," was rumoured to have offered his services to the Serbian Army. Chernayaev was the proprietor of the nationalist paper *Russky Mir*. As he was on the retired list of the army the Czar had no power to curtail his movements.

The German Emperor was shocked to learn that revolutionaries were joining the movement and a few months later tried to help his nephew by sending a memorandum to Queen Victoria. He referred to public meetings at which the Czar had been accused (by atheist revolutionaries) of ignoring the suffering Christians. "It cannot be known to Queen Victoria that on the occasion of these disturbances cries were uttered against the throne and the Emperor because he left his co-religionists in the lurch. It was thus evident that one can only *pity* the Emperor Alexander for the painful position in which he finds himself but one cannot *condemn* him."[10]

When Alexander left Berlin he went to Ems for a cure. There he received word that General Chernayaev had defied his wishes and assumed command of the Serbian Army in Belgrade. He was furious, for he knew that Europe would suspect him of connivance. "It's hard to say," Marie wrote to her brother, "what England's views are. But they are certainly hostile to us. That makes the Czar very anxious, on Marie's account too, and does not help the cure."[11] The Emperor broke his routine to spend a week with Prince Alexander at Heiligenberg. As soon as he arrived he sent for the Princess Dolgorouky, who was in Paris recuperating from the birth and death of her third child, Boris, who had lived only a few days in March. The Czar took a house for Catherine in the neighbourhood and every day after lunch rode over to see her. He did not seem in the least disconcerted by the fact that all the while he was accepting the hospitality of his wife's brother. Although Catherine was less than thirty and at the height of her beauty, she still led a rigidly secluded life, alone with her children, rarely going out, only living for the hours when her beloved was with her. Malicious people referred to her as "the golden-haired witch" and blamed her for the Emperor's indecision. She had become such an accomplished *amoreuse*, they said, that she had robbed him of all vitality and sadly impaired his will.

Catherine usually calmed Alexander's nerves, but this time she could not rid his mind of the English nightmare. Before he left Darmstadt he had a long talk with Princess Alice, whose husband was now the Grand Duke of Hesse-Darmstadt, and assured her that Russia had no ulterior motives in the Balkans. "Tell your mother again," he said, "that we are not able, nor do we wish to embroil ourselves with England. It would be mad to think of India and Constantinople . . ." "He had tears in his eyes," Alice wrote to Queen Victoria, "and seemed so moved, as if a dreadful weight was being lifted off his mind, so happy for the sake of Marie and Alfie too, that matters were mending."[12]

Queen Victoria saw no sign that matters were mending, and

received Alexander's protestations with reserve. She could not decide whether or not he was acting in good faith. Her Foreign Secretary, Lord Derby, did not think it mattered whether "the Emperor heads the movement or is dragged along by it."[13]

The reports flowing into London from Her Majesty's Ambassadors in Turkey, Russia and Austria and Her Majesty's Consuls scattered throughout the Ottoman Empire were far from reassuring. The Queen was well aware that Count Ignatiev was the villain of the piece. The Russian Embassy in Constantinople was like a military command-post directing a hidden army. Apart from Herzegovina, the only two Slav provinces of any size directly ruled by the Turks were Bosnia and Bulgaria. Panslav activities, therefore, fell into three categories: to keep the Herzegovinian rebellion going (which had been successfully accomplished); to spread the insurrection to Bosnia and Bulgaria (which was in the process of being done); and to persuade the autonomous provinces of Serbia and Montenegro to enter the conflict in aid of their brother Slavs.

Count Ignatiev had a genius for exploiting conflicting aims and using them for his own purpose. On his Panslav Committees he welcomed church-goers who could think of nothing but saving Christians; nationalists who fought against either Christian Austrians or Moslem Turks with equal impartiality; revolutionaries obsessed with overthrowing the dynasties. Ignatiev himself was working for a Russian-Slav Empire with its capital in Constantinople: and anything that helped to weaken the Ottoman or Habsburg Empires suited his book. "Much more like a Sarmatian grandee than a Russian general, with his high tenor voice, his mocking smile, his unabashed sleight of hand," Ignatiev made no secret of the fact that he "always had his own policy and tried to impose it on the Ministry." He had no loyalty towards his Foreign Office, considering himself "in the service of Russia and Russian Imperialism and not of the Russian bureaucracy."[14] He had an unlimited capacity for intrigue and specialised in playing off one embassy against another; in this he was ably assisted by his beautiful and seductive wife, a former Princess Golytsin, "whose face had the strength and grace of a ballerina" and who obligingly turned her charms on any diplomat who could be useful. The Austrian and Italian ambassadors were firmly in her toils.

The Count was such an inordinate liar that he was nick-named *Menteur Pasha*. A wit remarked that when he wanted to deceive, he told the truth. However, his personality was so flamboyant that even when he was caught red-handed in some dishonest act, he usually managed to extricate himself. Such an instance arose when Lord Salisbury, a member of the British Cabinet, visited Constantinople. Salisbury worked with Ignatiev and other ambassadors in redrawing some of the boundary lines in the Balkans. "As senior ambassador General Ignatiev had charge of the map upon which the decisions of the plenipotentiaries were officially recorded," wrote Salisbury's daughter and biographer. "On one occasion at a meeting of the preliminary conference, Lord Salisbury discovered that a frontier line which had been accepted at a previous sitting and traced upon this map had in the interval been subsequently altered in the direction desired by Russia. It is an embarrassing thing to charge a man of sharp practice to his face. Lord Salisbury pointed out the alteration and, with a feeling of irritated discomfort, prepared himself to receive as civilly as he could whatever improbable explanation might be offered. But the effort was not required of him. The implied accusation was not only recognised—it was accepted with the most perfect unconcern. A beaming smile—a shrug of the shoulders—and, '*Monsieur le Marquis est si fin—on ne peut rien lui cacher.*' The Englishman threw himself back in an uncontrollable burst of laughter in which both embarrassment and annoyance vanished."[15]

In the winter of 1875-6 Ignatiev's unrivalled position was due to the influence he exerted on the Grand Vizier, Mahmoud Nedim (nick-named Mahmoudoff) and even more remarkable, on the Sultan himself. Madame Ignatiev had opened this tightly shut door by making friends with the Sultan's mother, whom she visited regularly in the harem, bringing her gifts from Paris and captivating her with news of the latest fashions. Although the Sultan Abdul Aziz was still in his thirties he was the personification of the Sick Man of Europe, suffering from severe bouts of derangement. Sometimes he refused to read any document written in black ink, bringing his creaking administration to a halt until everything could be copied in red. Other times he pursued hens around the throne room, hanging round their necks the highest decorations in the Empire. He was insanely extravagant with the country's resources, placing orders in Britain for locomotives and men-of-war that could never be used because there were no tracks for the trains to run on, no sailors to man the ships.

Ignatiev was the only foreigner to have the Sultan's ear; and he did not scruple to give bad advice. When the revolt broke out in Herzegovina and the local Governor asked Constantinople for troops, Ignatiev persuaded Abdul Aziz not to comply, on the grounds that it would be a mistake to attract world attention by treating a small rebellion so seriously. And when, some months later, the Minister of War decided that an occupation of Serbia would be the best way of restoring order, the Ambassador used his influence with the Sultan to have the Minister removed. "The subterranean work," he wrote, "directed . . . against western and in general foreign influences on the Bosphorus, especially against Turkey and Austria-Hungary, had to be continued until . . . [we had formed] units of common blood and common religion, united to Russia by in-dissoluble bonds [leading to] the transfer of the Straits."[16]

The Count's most important activities, however, were not confined to the Sublime Porte. He corresponded with Ivan Aksakov in Moscow and the Countess Bludova in St. Petersburg. In Constantinople his house was thronged with spies and adventurers and contact men. At great risk to himself he preserved links with the revolutionary groups in the Balkans, passing the information to Russian consulates in sympathy with his views, and sending instructions to Panslav agents, directing, encouraging, advising. "I got in touch with all the Slavonic peoples," he wrote in his memoirs, "preparing them for independence . . ."[17]

The Count's most important agents in the winter of 1875-6 were the Ionin brothers. While Alexander Ionin was keeping the rebellion going in Herzegovina, Vladimir Ionin was operating at Bucharest and Giorgiuvo, a small Romanian town on the Danube, across from Bulgaria. His job was to organise a Bulgarian insurrection. The assignment suited him as he had spent a life-time fishing in troubled waters. He had retired from the Russian Consular Service in 1872 and since that time had worked for the Panslavs. He was a close friend of General Chernayaev who took command of the Serb Army in May.

Vladimir was financed by the St. Petersburg Slavic Committee and went to Romania in the middle of 1875. He worked through the Bulgarian immigrants in Romania, most of whom were members of the revolutionary committees. He supplied them with arms and infiltrated them across the frontier of their native country. Although. the "dour, slow-moving Bulgarian peasantry" was difficult to stir, Vladimir's agents claimed to have gathered together several hundred insurrectionists. When the hour struck, however, in the autumn of 1875, the enthusiasts faded away and not a single shot was fired. "When a nation doesn't want to free itself you can't make it, can you?" grumbled one of the insurgents, Stambulov, later Prime Minister of Bulgaria. "Lies, boasts, empty promises and nothing else; that's what one gets for wandering over these cursed mountains."[18]

The second attempt, in May, 1876, produced a rebellion, but it went off at half-cock two weeks before it was due. A number of villages rose, killed the local Turkish population, raising flags and dancing in the street. But their joy was short-lived for the Turks retaliated with unparalleled ferocity. Well aware that Bulgarian revolutionaries and Russian agents were being fed into the country, and that the first village to revolt was the home of Naiden Gerov, a notorious Bulgar who had been a founder member of the Moscow Slavic Association and now acted as Russian Vice-Consul at Philippopolis, they flew into a panic. An insurrection so near the capital, and one which might control the historic Adrianople-Philippopolis-Nish route, threatened the very existence of the Ottoman Empire. Instead of employing regular troops, they armed the local Moslem population, known as Bashi Bazouks, and the half-savage Circassians who had become residents of Bulgaria after being driven out of the Caucasus by the Russian conquest. These voluntary troops received no pay, but fought for loot. They put down the revolt by slashing their way through sixty villages, killing everyone in sight including woman and children. News of the massacre did not reach the outside world for some weeks. On the very day in June that a London paper printed the first report of the Bulgarian carnage, Serbia and Montenegro signed a military pact; the following week they declared war on Turkey.

The Czar returned to St. Petersburg to find the Slavic Benevolent Committee in a transport of joy. The Empress had accepted the Presidency of the Red Cross and was equipping hospital trains for the Balkans at her own expense. She had taken the three daughters of Prince Nicholas of Montenegro under her protection and they had already been placed in Russian schools.* Her court ladies jingled money-boxes on tram-cars and steamboats and did house-to-house canvassing. "The spectacle of the aged Countess Protasova, the Empress's mistress of the robes, and of the equally highly placed Countess Adlerberg publicly collecting money in the streets of the capital left no doubt that one section, at least, of the Court was doing its utmost to further 'the Slav cause'."[19] The Heir Apparent was equally bold in his activities. He kept in close touch with General Chernayaev through Zinoviev, his Marshal of Court; and in collusion with his confidant, Count Vorontsov-Dashkov, Chief-of-Staff of the Guards Corps, openly encouraged his men to volunteer. Largely due to his efforts a detachment of 120 Don Cossacks were fitted out. People whispered that the Czar was unable to control his wife and son because of his affair with the Princess. It was true that Alexander was at loggerheads with the Heir Apparent; but he did not attempt to argue with Marie as he was only too grateful that the Church obsessed her and made her less exacting as a wife.

In Moscow the excitement was even greater than in the capital. The Slav tricolour, red, white and blue, fluttered from many of the buildings, and Ivan Aksakov and his Slavic Committee ran their own recruiting office. Prince Dolgorouky, the Governor-General of Moscow, raised no difficulties about visas, and the railways doled out hundreds of free tickets. Commissioned men who volunteered for service in Serbia were forced to resign their commissions but were promised reinstatement. Altogether about 800 officers (many

* Two of these girls married Russian Grand Dukes, the third the King of Italy.

belonging to the best society in St. Petersburg and Moscow) and 5,000 men volunteered. Crowds assembled at the stations and waved them away like heroes.

Not everyone, however, felt like rejoicing. There were still plenty of people in Russia who deplored the whole adventure. "All of it is a typhoon of vapid sentimentality," wrote the poet, Prince Peter Wiazensky. "Our main trouble to-day is that we have begun imagining ourselves to be Slavs rather than Russians. Our Russian blood is all but denied, and Slavomania holds the stage . . . The Turks are Moslems and yet we expect Christian virtues from them. It is absurd! Chase them out of Europe if you can, convert them to the Christian faith if you know how to do it, if not leave them alone. . . . We irritate Turkey, send first aid to 'brother Serbs,' beat the drum, drink champagne to speed off the volunteers, and shout ourselves hoarse about nothing . . . Do these people imagine that Russia can grow stronger from the strength of the Southern Slavs? Or even win their friendship? There will be nothing but enmity and ingratitude from them in the end . . . Please keep this letter. I would like future generations to know that there were a few sober voices in an hour of Russian drunkenness . . ."[20]

Even the literary giants began to quarrel. Feodor Dostoevsky and Leo Tolstoy made their differences known to the public through works in the process of being serialised. "Constantinople must be ours," cried Dostoevsky in his Writer's Diary. By what *moral* right? "Precisely as a leader of Orthodoxy, as its protectress and guardian." Although political relations "must inevitably develop between Russia and all other Orthodox peoples . . . common unity under the protection of Russia is merely the assurance to each of his independent personality . . . a new exaltation of Christ's Cross."

Dostoevsky apparently did not feel that St. Petersburg was supporting the cause with sufficient enthusiasm for he administered a gentle rebuke:

"General Chernayaev had already sent word to Petersburg that the sanitary facilities throughout the whole Serbian Army are extremely poor: no doctors, no medicaments, insufficient care of the wounded. The Slavic Committee in Moscow has launched an energetic appeal throughout Russia for help to our insurgent brethren, and its members attended *in corpore*, in the presence of a huge crowd, a solemn Te Deum at the Church of the Serbian Hospice, held for the granting of victory to the Serbian and Montenegrin armies. In Petersburg there is beginning to appear in the newspapers letters from the public, accompanied by donations. Obviously the movement is expanding, even despite the so-called 'dead season.' But it is dead in Petersburg only."[21]

Count Leo Tolstoy, whose *War and Peace* had won national acclaim, was sickened by the whole affair. He was writing *Anna Karenina*, and in the eighth and last part of the book he depicted the Russian volunteers to Serbia as drunkards, misfits, or, like his hero Vronsky, men who felt they had nothing left to live for. "Thank God," said Vronsky's mother to a friend after Anna's suicide, "that the war should have happened to take my son's mind from that disaster . . ."

Tolstoy also made it clear that he did not consider "Panslavism" a national movement. His scene opens with the arrival of guests from Moscow; Levin gives them honey and cucumbers and seats them under the trees; they begin to discuss the Eastern question.

Sergey Ivanovitch: "The people have heard of the sufferings of their brethren and have spoken."

"Perhaps so," said Levin evasively, "but I don't see it. I'm one of the people myself and I don't feel it."

"Here am I too," said the old Prince. "I've been staying abroad and reading the papers, and I must own, up to the time of the Bulgarian atrocities, I couldn't make out why it was all the Russians were all of a sudden so fond of their Slavonic brethren, while I didn't feel the slightest affection for them. I was very much upset, thought I was a monster, or that it was the influence of Carlsbad on me. But since I have been here, my mind's been set at rest. I see that there are people besides me who're only interested in Russia, and not in their Slavonic brethren . . ."

"Personal opinions mean nothing in such a case," said Sergey Ivanovitch. "It's not a matter of personal opinions when all Russia —the whole people—had expressed its will."

"But excuse me, I don't see that. The people don't know any-thing about it, if you come to that," said the old prince.

"Oh, Papa! . . . how can you say that? And last Sunday in church?" said Dolly, listening to the conversation . . .

"But what was it in church on Sunday? The priest had been told to read that. He read it. They didn't understand a word of it. Then they were told that there was to be a collection for a pious object in church; well, they pulled out their halfpence and gave them, but what for they couldn't say."[22]

The editor of the *Russian Herald*, who was serialising Tolstoy's work, was a passionate Panslavist and had the temerity to return the closing chapters of *Anna Karenina* with numerous corrections and a letter saying that he could not print it unless the cuts were made. Tolstoy was "furious at the idea that a mere journalist should dare to correct his MS." and sent a sharp refusal to the editor which resulted in a breach. The *Russian Herald* had to wind up the story as best it could, giving a synopsis of the ending. Tolstoy published Part Eight as a pamphlet before the novel appeared in book form.

Count Leo Tolstoy was not the only person to decry the war. Ironically enough young, debt-ridden Prince Milan of Serbia deplored it just as deeply. ". . . the only thing he cares for are the pleasures of the table," wrote the British chargé d'affaires in Vienna in the summer of 1875. But the diplomat was wrong for the Prince cared very much for his luxurious fiancée, the daughter of a Bess-arabian landowner, especially selected by his mother for her beauty and her money. Milan was in Austria to complete his marriage arrangements, and the British chargé sympathised feelingly with his desire for distraction. "The life which this young Prince of twenty-three is forced to lead at Belgrade would perfectly account for his desiring to escape from it whenever an opportunity occurs for so doing—educated as he has been in Paris. He finds himself in his own country entirely cut off from any civilised intercourse, in hourly dread of assassination, seeing nobody but his ministers and his military aides-de-camp, and even these may be said to be but half-civilised, for the country possesses neither a proprietary nor a middle class; nothing beyond some 1,500,000 peasants, a few who have become Ministers; and a certain number of soldiers. ... Yet this is the State which aspires to be the 'Piedmont' of the Principalities, which has raised the nucleus of an army destined according to Serbian creed to march one day against Turkey and overthrow her and become the head of a Southern Slavonia, which is to absorb all the other Danubian and Austro-Turkish provinces of that race!"[23]

As Serbia had long ago flung off the Ottoman yoke and was an autonomous principality whose only obligation to Turkey was a formal acknowledgment of suzerainty, the issue was not freedom but nationalistic ambition. Although for months Milan had resisted the clamour of his semi-literate Parliament, he was worried that the Pretender to the Throne, Prince Karageorgevich, (the man who was always trying to assassinate him), was fast becoming a hero by fighting in Bosnia; and he was also worried by the bellicose speeches of his neighbour, Prince Nicholas of Montenegro, who ruled over a few hundred thousand tribesmen in a country even smaller and more primitive than Serbia, and was always looking for an opportunity to snatch away the lead from Milan.

The turning point came in March from unexpected quarters. A hundred Socialists carrying a red flag demonstrated in front of the Town Hall in a town not far from Belgrade, and shouted for a Republic. The police investigated, and reported that they had uncovered a plot to seize control of the country. Believing his dynasty at stake unless he could win the support of the militarists, Milan asked Chernayaev to command his army, and fell upon Turkey.

The war fulfilled his deepest misgivings for it was short and disastrous, lasting no more than five months. Not only were the soldiers badly led but supplies were inadequate, roads impassable. Serbian arms were inferior to those of the Turks, and as the Serbs were not horsemen they had no cavalry with which to consolidate their positions. Most surprising of all, however, was the fact that the Serbian peasantry showed no heart for the fight. While Montenegrin tribesmen cut magnificent figures in long white coats with jewelled knives stuck in their belts the Serbian peasants in brown jackets and red pantaloons looked bewildered and unhappy and had a disconcerting habit of running away. The Russian volunteers, numbering anywhere from five to nine thousand, did their best, but stories were soon circulating that many of them were being shot in the back while trying to lead their Serbian troops forward.

In August a twenty-year-old Englishman, Philip Salusbury, a former Westminster schoolboy, arrived in Belgrade looking for adventure. With English indifference to detail he flourished a letter of introduction to Prince Karageorgevich, the Pretender, whom he thought was ruling the country. This carelessness earned him a brief period in gaol; but he finally was bailed out and allowed to join a cavalry unit. As the only horses available were wild mountain ponies, and as no one in the unit knew how to ride except for himself, he decided that his chance of seeing action with this particular outfit was limited. He was fortunate enough to be invited by General Dotchtourov, a Russian sportsman who liked English horse-racing, to be his aide-de-camp. He found Army Headquarters swarming with Russians in the brilliant plumage of the Imperial Guards. The most spectacular figure, however, was Prince Milan's uncle who wore patent-leather boots to his thighs and carried white kid gloves.

Dotchtourov, who was appointed Chief-of-Staff to the Commander, General Chernayaev, took Salusbury to the front and gave him his baptism of fire. The day was unforgettable for the heavy shelling; the chilling cries of "Allah! Allah! Allah!" as the Turkish lines advanced; the panic and disorder of the Serbian ranks. Serbs were shooting off a finger of their left hand in order to escape the fighting; others collapsed at the first roar of the guns; still others turned and bolted. "Now was the time for our reserve to go to the rescue and Dotchtouroff gave the order to be 'up and at 'em'," wrote Salusbury. "Up they jumped, without waiting for any second order, and ran with great speed, firing off their guns and cheering loudly. There was only one fault to be found with them, and that was that they unfortunately ran and fired in the wrong direction! In vain Dotchtouroff shouted, in vain he swore, for they only ran the faster. I asked him to allow me to try and compel them, with the aid of my sword and revolver, to halt, front and charge the enemy. 'No, no,' said he; 'they are not worth wasting powder on. Nothing can stop them, and the day is lost'."[24]

The following week the Serbs lost the battle of Djunis. The Turks began streaming through the Morava Valley; the way to Belgrade was open; Milan and Chernayaev telegraphed frantically to Alexander II for help. The Czar responded, despite his earlier threats to leave the Serbs to their fate, and sent a forty-eight-hour ultimatum to Constantinople demanding an immediate armistice. The Turks, fearing war with Russia, complied.

Two-thirds of the Russian volunteers had been killed. Those who returned home spread terrible stories of Serbian treachery. At a speech to the Moscow nobility in November the Czar took the astonishing step of alluding publicly to Serbian cowardice. After praising the Montenegrins who had "shown themselves, as always, true heroes," he said: "Unfortunately it is impossible to say the same of the Serbs, despite the presence in their ranks of our volunteers, many of whom have paid with their blood for the cause of Slavdom."[25]

Ivan Aksakov told the Slavonic Committee in Belgrade that it merely went to show that it was impossible to fight an "unofficial war," relying solely on voluntary effort for arms, men and money. The campaign had been "an unheard-of phenomenon" but the war had begun with a lie which had weakened the effort. Russians talked about the "emancipation of the Slavs" instead of making it clear that they were fighting for the "acquisition of Old Serbia and Bosnia." Now Serbia must be forgotten and activity concentrated on Bulgaria. "It is much more important for us and for the future of Slavdom than Serbia."[26]

Alexander had moved a long way towards war. Before returning to Russia in July he had secretly squared Austria who—despite Aksakov's fine talk—was to be allowed to annex Bosnia and Herzegovina as the price of neutrality. Throughout September and October he had been at his palace in Livadia, near Yalta on the Black Sea. Under a deep blue sky, surrounded by vineyards and orangeries, he listened to a ceaseless flow of Panslav talk. The Empress and her ladies fluttered about burning candles, referring tirelessly to Russia's Holy Mission. Ignatiev arrived from Constantinople, and the

Czarevitch and the Grand Duke Nicholas (the Emperor's brother) from St. Petersburg. Although their aims were imperialist rather than religious they struck the same altruistic chord, particularly in front of foreigners. Count Voronzov, who entertained Lord Augustus Loftus in his wonderful villa a few miles from Livadia, told the British Ambassador that the whole of Russia from "the highest to the lowest" viewed the Eastern Question as "one of religion and humanity."[27]

This was far from true for, as Count Tolstoy had pointed out, one of the distinguishing features of Panslavism was the fact that it scarcely roused a ripple of interest among the peasants. Voronzov came much nearer the mark when he asserted that the Czar would not be able to resist Panslav pressure in the social and military hierarchy and that "no financial or other consideration would deter Russia from its course . . ." Count Reutern, the Finance Minister, was appalled when the Czar summoned him to discuss a war loan. Russia, Reutern insisted, was in no position to fight a war. At this very moment her gold reserves were being drained away and she was nearly bankrupt. To fight on credit, he declared, would mean sacrificing twenty years of reform and social progress. The future would hold nothing but trouble. "Even if we were victorious," he argued, "we would be greatly impoverished, and increased taxes and other hardships would play into the hands of the revolutionaries."[28] Alexander waved aside the objections and insisted impatiently that in a national emergency there must be a way. "Not at the treasury, Sir," replied Count Reutern crisply.

Nevertheless at Moscow on November 10th, the Czar told his audience that, although the six powers had agreed to hold a conference at Constantinople in a final attempt to wring lasting reforms from the Turks, he would act independently if the talks broke down. "I am convinced that in such an eventuality all Russia will respond to my appeal . . . May God help us to fulfil our sacred mission."[29]

Two days later Alexander gave the final order for the mobilisation of six army corps.

Meanwhile Britain was caught up in a gigantic political storm over the Turkish atrocities in Bulgaria. Sir Henry Elliot, the British

Ambassador in Constantinople had sent Walter Baring, one of his embassy staff, to investigate; and Baring's report, published on 19th September, described the massacre as "the most heinous crime of the century" and spoke of "a soil soaked and reeking with blood," "an air tainted with every imaginable deed of crime and shame." He put the number of villages destroyed at sixty, the number of people slaughtered at 12,000.*

Mr. Gladstone, the Liberal leader who had retired from politics the year before, anticipated the report. Informed of the contents, he spent three days writing a pamphlet which flayed the Turks with scorching invective and when it was published on 6th September had the effect of fork lightning. He referred to the "unspeakable Turk" and claimed that "there is not a criminal in a European gaol, there is not a cannibal in the South Sea Islands whose imagination would not arise and overboil at the recital of that which had been done."

"Let the Turks now carry away their abuses in the only possible way, namely by carrying off themselves. Their Zaptiehs and their Mudirs, their Bimbashis and their Yuzbachis, their Kaimakams and their Pashas, one and all, bag and baggage shall, I hope, clear out from the province they have desolated and profaned . . . If it be allowable that the executive power of Turkey should renew at this great crisis, by permission or authority of Europe, the charter of its existence in Bulgaria, then there is not on record since the beginning of political society a protest that man has lodged against intolerant misgovernment or a stroke that he has dealt at loathsome tyranny, that ought not henceforth to be branded as a crime."

The pamphlet sold 40,000 in a week; 200,000 by the end of the month. It not only raised an explosive Christian-Moslem controversy, but it cut across one of the main tenets of British foreign policy; that the integrity of the Ottoman Empire had to be preserved in order to prevent the Russians sweeping across South-East Europe and dominating Constantinople and the Straits. Liberals carrying the standard of conscience and Tories raising the banner of

* Baring's report was published as a supplement to the *Government Gazette*.

patriotism met in a head-on clash. Monster meetings were organised; professors and clergymen intervened; moral indignation,
so dear to the English heart, poured from every platform. The Prime
Minister, Mr. Disraeli, who a few weeks earlier had moved to the
Upper House as Lord Beaconsfield, was remarkably silent. "Generally speaking, when the country goes mad which it does every now
and then," he wrote to a friend, "I think it is best that one should
wait until everything is said . . ."[30] However, the Liberal leader,
Lord Hartington, demonstrated that English political life was still
sound by ignoring the fracas and sending Lord Beaconsfield four
brace of grouse from Bolton Abbey.

Queen Victoria initially was appalled by the Turkish outrages,
but as soon as the hated Mr. Gladstone entered the arena and began
to challenge the very basis of British defence, her attitude changed.
"Hearing as we *do* all the undercurrents," she wrote to her Prime
Minister on 28th September "and knowing as we do that Russia
instigated this insurrection, and *caused* the cruelty of the Turks . . .
the world *ought* to know that on *their* shoulders and *not* on ours
rests the *blood* of the murdered Bulgarians!"[31] And in October she
was reminding her Government that "the much abused policy of
upholding the Turkish Empire was merely to prevent Russia having
Constantinople." What were they going to do to prevent it? "It is
clear England *cannot fight for* the Turks, but we also cannot fight
against them."[32] She made a sensible suggestion, asking why the
Slav people could not constitute an autonomous country ruled over
by a Christian prince. Although this is roughly what happened in
the end, Lord Beaconsfield brushed it aside, explaining that primitive
countries could not be truly independent.

When the Liberals urged Britain to join forces with the Russians
in driving the Turks out of Europe the Queen's "blood boiled."
In December Mr. Gladstone sat on the platform with Madame
Novikov, a Russian lady whose brother had died fighting for the
Serbs. The meeting was chaired by the Duke of Westminster and
the Earl of Shaftesbury. Mr. Edward Freeman, the historian, brought
the house down by crying: "Perish the interests of England, perish
our dominion in India, sooner than we should strike one blow or
speak one word on behalf of the wrong against the right." The

Queen was wild with indignation. "She thinks the Attorney-General ought to be set at those men; it can't be constitutional," wrote Beaconsfield.

The Constantinople Conference, at which the European powers were demanding autonomy for Bosnia, Herzegovina and Bulgaria, did not seem to be progressing any better than people had expected. The Sultan Abdul Aziz was no longer on the throne. He had been deposed in May by his nephew, Murad, who turned out to be even madder and a dipsomaniac to boot. He, in turn, was overthrown by his half-brother, Abdul Hamid, of whom Lord Beaconsfield had hopes. "He has only one wife," he wrote to a friend, "a *modiste* of Pera; a Belgian; he was in the habit of frequenting her shop, buying gloves etc. and much admired her. One day he said 'do you think you would marry me?' and she replied: '*Pourquoi non?*' and it was done."[33]

The one wife, unfortunately, did not make the Sultan any more tractable than his predecessors. He neatly checkmated the European demands for autonomy by announcing that he had decided to grant all his subjects a democratic Constitution. No one believed a word of it, but the Sultan succeeded in his purpose and brought the talks to a close. "I wish they were all—Russians and Turks—at the bottom of the Black Sea," Lord Beaconsfield sighed.[34]

But there was no respite. In March the Russians made a last attempt to reach agreement by drawing up a protocol, calling on Turkey to implement immediately the promises she had made to the Christians and to carry out the administrative reforms already agreed. Count Ignatiev and his wife toured Europe getting the signatures of the powers, although no one felt that the protocol would be successful.

Although the British Government was taken aback at the prospect of meeting the notorious Panslav agitator in the flesh, Beaconsfield rose to the occasion and gave a banquet in his honour. The Prince of Wales led the Countess into dinner, while the English ladies who had heard "that Madame Ignatiev was even finer than themselves" were determined not "to yield without a struggle." "Lady Londonderry," wrote Lord Beaconsfield, "staggered under the jewels of the three united families of Stewart and Vane and Londonderry . . .

Madame Ignatiev had many diamonds and a fine costume but paled before this."[35]

The Count was too aggressive for English taste. When he visited Lord Salisbury at Hatfield he shocked two Liberal M.P.s by advising them how to attack the Government more effectively. They must have been incredibly pompous and prudish, for they appeared in Lord Salisbury's office a few days later and repeated the conversation, saying that they did not think it right for a man to intrigue against his host. He even succeeded in dismaying Lady John Manners but for different reasons. She had expected a man of the world; instead, when she asked him if he felt well after his long journey, he gave the nauseating reply: "I always feel well. My conscience is clear because I defend the Christians and so my wife and I are always gay."[36] Perhaps someone passed on this remark to the Queen for the next day she wrote to Beaconsfield criticising the protocol: "This mawkish sentimentality for people who hardly deserve the name of Christians, as if they were more God's creatures and our fellow-creatures than every other nation abroad, and forgetting the great interest of this great country—is really incomprehensible."[37]

The Sublime Porte rejected the Protocol on 9th April on the grounds that the supervision it would impose was unacceptable. On 21st April the Czar of all the Russias announced that his patience was exhausted and declared war on Turkey.

IV
Bitter Victory

QUEEN VICTORIA became so agitated about the supine attitude of her Parliament to Russian aggression that she threatened to abdicate. "If England is to kiss Russia's feet," she wrote to her Prime Minister, "the Queen will not be a party to the humiliation of England and would lay down her crown."[1] At the same time she sent a memorandum to her Cabinet emphasising that the crisis was not a question of "upholding Turkey"; "It is the question of Russian or British supremacy in the world!" What the Queen wanted from her Government was something that British Governments often decline to give: a firm declaration of intent. "Whatever we intend to do ought to be clearly explained to the other powers . . . there ought to be an understanding that we cannot allow the Russians to occupy Constantinople and that we must see that this is promised, or the consequence may be serious. To let it be thought that we shall never fight and that England will submit to Egypt being under Russia would be to abdicate the position of Great Britain as one of the Great Powers—to which she will never submit, and another must wear the crown if this is intended."[2]

Yet it seemed impossible to alter the obdurate views of Her Majesty's politicians. The Liberal Opposition was still so obsessed by the Bulgarian atrocities that many of them had become loudly pro-Russian to show how anti-Turk they were—although no one could pretend that Siberia and the knout were very liberal institutions. Even the Conservative Cabinet was weak and divided. Lord Salisbury, the Secretary of State for India, could not see the danger of a Russian occupation of Constantinople, arguing that, although Turkey controlled Egypt, Russia was too inefficient to establish itself as a Mediterranean power. Lord Derby, the Foreign Secretary, was willing to move to the brink of war but no farther. If a shot was fired he would resign; and so would Lord Carnarvon, the Colonial Secretary. As Lord Beaconsfield felt it essential to keep his Cabinet together, the weeks passed and Britain avoided taking the stand that the Queen thought imperative.

Meanwhile the Russian Army, under the command of the Czar's brother, the Grand Duke Nicholas, was meeting little resistance. It moved through friendly Romania in May and crossed the Danube into Bulgaria in June. Seventy newspapermen were attached to the Russian command and, despite Queen Victoria's complaints of apathy, the British public followed the campaign with intense interest. By July it looked as though nothing could stop the Imperial steam-roller, for a brilliant coup on the part of General Gourko had brought the front escarpment of the Shipka Pass into Russian hands. The Pass was the key to Turkey as it opened a route through the formidable Balkan mountains. Lord Beaconsfield decided that victory was only a question of days and ordered Her Majesty's Fleet to Besika Bay, at the mouth of the Dardanelles, "to protect British lives."

On 3rd August, however, the readers of the London *Daily News* were informed that the Russians had suffered a major defeat which had altered "the entire campaign." The Turks had built up a force of 60,000 men in the small town of Plevna, under the command of the brilliant general, Osman Pasha; as the Grand Duke Nicholas dared not advance and leave a strong enemy spearhead on his flank he ordered two of his commanders, Prince Shakovsky and General Krudener, to wipe out the Plevna salient. They underestimated the strength of Osman's feverishly constructed fortifications and heavy guns; also his fierce spirit of resistance. The fighting lasted six hours, "a chaos of stabbing, clubbing, hacking, clutching, shouting, cursing, screaming men in knots of two and three clinging to each other on the ground in their death agonies, above a surging mass of heads, the butt ends of rifles rising and falling, mounted men sweeping down their swords on the heads beneath, colours flying, horses charging, rolling over, burying men already mutilated beneath them, frantic faces streaming with blood; a mad-house . . ."[3]

In the end the Russians were routed, having lost 7,000 men, a quarter of their strength. Russian Headquarters were forced to retreat from Tirnovo and for the next twenty-four hours the civilian population was thrown into a panic. Osman Pasha was believed to be in hot pursuit and the cry "the Turks are coming" resounded through the Bulgarian countryside. Thousands of people stampeded across the bridge into Romania; and the Grand Duke Nicholas telegraphed to Prince Charles of Romania: "Come quickly to our aid. The Turks are annihilating us. The Christian cause is lost."

Archibald Forbes of the *Daily News* was the most famous journalist accompanying the Russian Army. While covering the Franco-Prussian War of 1870 and the Serbian War of the previous year, he had set a new standard for correspondents, proving that brawn was just as necessary as brain. It was comparatively easy to write an eye-witness report of a great battle; it was another thing to get the story on the wire before anyone else. After the battle of Plevna Forbes rode thirty-six hours (killing his horse on the way) to reach Bucharest. Here he had established a pony express, with fresh horses at ten mile points, to carry him the eighty miles across the Carpathian mountains to Kronstadt, in neutral Hungary, where he knew his story would not be mutilated. The dispatch cost £400 in cable charges but it was worth it, for it informed the world that the Russian set-back was serious, and could change the whole course of the war. The Czar's army could not advance until Plevna was taken.

Upon returning to Bulgaria and visiting Imperial Headquarters, Forbes was relieved to find that his story of the Russian defeat was not resented. Indeed he was congratulated on its accuracy. Headquarters was now at Gorni Studen, a mud-walled Bulgarian village without sanitation which suddenly bloomed with Kurdish tents and white pavilions that had sprung up in the night like a travelling fair. The scene was an unbelievable mixture of squalor and splendour. Grand Duke and Princess and high ranking officers squelched through the mud, past the rotting carcasses of dead animals, in highly polished boots and brilliant uniforms, while servants in Adriatic dress made them as comfortable as possible. The retinue included valets and cooks, and English grooms leading high-stepping horses, not to mention the indispensable coachmen sitting on top of their "staff-carriages" with peacock feathers in their hats. Indeed, eight locomotives were required, each pulling twenty-three coaches and baggage cars, to move the Headquarters Staff to a theatre of war. Every Russian general, wrote Forbes, had at least one, often two, carriages. "The larger proportion of field officers have vehicles too . . . there is a baggage wagon between every two officers, and a surprising number of miscellaneous vehicles besides. The chief of the artillery has a travelling chariot drawn by four horses, driven after the manner of a four-in-hand . . . Servants swarm and every servant contrives to find a place in or on a vehicle of some kind or other. The staff train is half a mile long if it is a yard, to say nothing of escort, marketenders (the Army sutlers) and the priest who rides in a vehicle of his own . . ."4

The Czar lived in a dismantled Bulgarian house, in a room with walls and floor of mud. He spent his days visiting the wounded and homeless, only appearing at meal-times to eat with his 200 officers in a huge marquee erected in a field. According to the British military attaché, Colonel Wellesley, the marquee was a splendid addition, for at the Emperor's previous headquarters the staff often ate in the open from plates crawling with flies "attracted by all the horrors of war." "On such occasions," wrote Wellesley, "we each of us had behind our chair a soldier with a branch of leaves with which he endeavoured to protect our food . . . it was indeed surprising that the persons responsible for the Emperor's health should not have taken even the most elementary precautions in the way of sanitation . . ."5

The Emperor was the fount of military honour and his all-seeing eye was supposed to discern every act of bravery. Almost every day at one o'clock an aide-de-camp followed Alexander into the tent, carrying a cushion bearing half a dozen orange and black ribands of St. George, and innumerable crosses. "The Czar's voice calls the chosen name, all make room for the envied man to pass; he comes blushing and flushed, receives the prize, bends low to kiss the Imperial hand, and retires bowing at every step, a made man for life, the admired and courted of all beholders. He is embraced and kissed on both cheeks by his friends, and he is so overcome with this mark of distinction that he walks about weeping with the prized decoration in his hand, half dazed."[6]

Alexander looked worn and haggard. Although he had been forced into the war by national fervour he had no real stomach for it, and was deeply worried by the turn the campaign had taken. "The great mistake," he wrote to the Princess Catherine Dolgorouky, "has been that General Krudener, knowing of the numerical superiority of the Turks, decided to attack them, as he had been ordered to do. By taking upon himself the responsibility of not carrying out this order he would have saved more than a thousand lives and a complete rout, for it must be confessed that such it was. Happily however the Turks did not pursue the remnants of our brave troops; otherwise few would have escaped."[7]

But it was not only the defeat that was worrying the Czar; it was the political situation and the ever-present possibility of British intervention. "I received more satisfactory news from London this morning," he continued, "following on the report from Wellesley. The language of the English had completely changed and they were quite ready to use their influence over Turkey to get her to sue for peace, on the conditions we should exact. Unfortunately, I fear that the disaster at Plevna may make them change their tone once more and may render the Turks still more presumptuous." Apart from these harassments, the Czar loathed the cruelty and suffering of war and wrote frequently to Catherine, "All these sights make my heart bleed and I find it hard to keep back my tears."

The Czar was not the only person to find the bestiality of war oppressive. At the outbreak of hostilities Prince Alexander of Hesse wrote to his sister, Marie, and asked if his second son, Prince Alexander of Battenberg, a dashing, handsome boy of twenty, known in the family as "Sandro," could serve in the Russian Army. It was a way, he said, of repaying some of the kindnesses the Czar had shown him during the past thirty years. Alexander II was delighted to have the young man and appointed Sandro aide-de-camp to the Grand Duke Nicholas. Sandro travelled to St. Petersburg in June and was received warmly by the Imperial family. He was allowed to choose three horses from the royal stables and wrote home enthusiastically of the hospitality showered upon him. He took a strong dislike to the Czarevitch, however, criticising his clumsy body and long whiskers; and he thought the Czarina (a sister of the Princess of Wales) "skinny and plain."

Sandro was attached to Headquarters for the crossing of the Danube and the march across Bulgaria to the Balkan mountains. "All the villages," he wrote to his father, "are inhabited by Turks and Bulgars. As soon as news of our approach comes, the Bulgars hurl themselves upon the Turks, murder them, plunder and burn everything. One consequence is that the Turks flee betimes and that wherever we come everything is laid waste." Sandro joined General Gourko's army and took part in the attack on the front escarpment of the Shipka Pass. He saw many days of fighting when the Turks counterattacked, finally regaining control of the defile. "We live amid blood and corpses," he wrote, "and see such horrible things that all our officers are disgusted with the war and would much rather go home." The country was magnificent, he said, "but the Bulgars are just as fiendish as the Turks."[8]

Sandro was struck by the disillusionment that had set in among the officers about the "moral purpose" of the war. Most Russians had visualised the Bulgarian people as poverty stricken and ill-used, groaning under the lash of their Turkish masters. Instead they found a land of milk and honey. For every mosque there were half a dozen churches while the fertile lands, the sleek animals, the tidy whitewashed houses breathed an air of prosperity unknown to the peasants of Russia, or for that matter, wrote Archibald Forbes, to many small-holders in England.

Forbes and Prince Sandro met at Headquarters and took an immediate liking to one another. They agreed about most things, particularly the inefficiency of the Russian Command. The card-playing generals were faithful servants of the Crown but were old and unimaginative and were fighting not the last war but the war before the last. Even the Czar's brother, the Grand Duke Nicholas, the Commander-in-Chief, seemed wholly inadequate for the task before him. Indeed, St. Petersburg society considered him more skilful in a lady's boudoir than on a battlefield. In St. Petersburg, his wife was forced to tolerate a pretty rival, who lived across the street and summoned the Grand Duke by placing a lighted candle in the window. When this happened a servant entered the room and announced to Nicholas that a fire had broken out in the capital. As the Grand Duke adored fires and always attended them whenever possible he felt no embarrassment in excusing himself and dashing off. Once guests were present and pressed to know the whereabouts of the fire. "Don't alarm yourself," the Grand Duchess intervened laconically, "it is only a candle that is burning."

Alexander not only clung to his inadequate brother as Commander-in-Chief but refused to allow any of the older generals to be set aside. The younger men would have to await their turn, otherwise the famous *tschinn* system would break down. Meanwhile the Russian Army could not advance to Sophia and Adrianople until Plevna was taken, and Plevna could not be taken until troops from Romania and reinforcements from Russia arrived. The date of the great assault, therefore, was fixed for the Czar's name-day, 11th September. Prince Charles of Romania was appointed Commander-in-Chief of the combined Russo-Romanian attack, a stipulation he had made before giving his assistance. Although the Turks had spent the intervening two months building trenches and parapets and fortifying redoubts for the artillery, the plan of attack was simple to the point of lunacy. The Russian Command decided to bombard the Turkish positions, then send waves of flesh and blood to take the fortified strongholds at the point of a bayonet. It was, in fact, the strategy that was to be used on a far more lavish scale in 1914.

Plevna was in a valley surrounded by undulating hills. A few days before the assault Russian sappers erected a platform on a slope out of the line of fire from which the Czar and the Grand Duke Nicholas and their staffs, (about fifty in all), could watch the battle. One half of the platform was in the open with a railing around it; the other half covered with a marquee under which was a table, laid with white damask, and spread with the choicest food and wine, reminding the British correspondents of a ducal lunch on the grouse moors. The battle began at three in the afternoon, after five days of bombardment. The Russians launched their attack from three directions. According to the military text-books, the first, second and even third waves of men might go down but the fourth, fifth and sixth would take the positions. This reckoning, however, belonged to an earlier decade. The Turks were equipped with Krupp artillery, steel breech-loading guns far superior to the bronze pieces of the Russians. Even their small-arms, Peabody-Martini rifles, made in Providence, Rhode Island, were far more effective than the old Krenck rifles of their adversaries. Apart from these considerations the advantage of entrenched positions was greater than the text-books indicated.

The Russian High Command watched a hideous scene of gallantry and carnage. The infantry advanced into a storm of shell and rifle fire; again and again the lines moved forward, only to stagger back and fall. At the end of three hours the battlefield was covered with dead and wounded. One redoubt was taken but there were no fresh reserves to follow up the victory; the next day the Turks attacked and after fierce hand-to-hand fighting recaptured it. Suddenly a Cossack officer approached the Czar's platform at full gallop. The Turks, he reported, had broken out of Plevna and their cavalry was already on the move. As it was unthinkable that the Emperor should be taken prisoner Alexander agreed to leave without delay—a move which involved no less than thirty carriages. Prince Charles of Romania (according to his biographer) was saddened "to see the Czar of all the Russias in retreat, the more so as it was later proved that the Cossack officer's report was a false alarm."

The true facts were scarcely more heartening. At the end of two days the Russians had lost nearly 25,000 men and not an inch of ground had been gained. Correspondents wrote of the madness of assaulting trenches defended by breech-loaders; and the Czar, shocked by the slaughter, ordered the assault to be abandoned. Plevna must be starved into submission. There were others, however, who wanted to break off operations until the spring. On 13th September a Council of War was held at Headquarters and the Grand Duke Nicholas urged an immediate retreat to the left bank of the Danube and a winter of recuperation in Wallachia. Snow blizzards, he pointed out, would start in November. The troops were inadequately clothed; food was running short; and fresh supplies could not arrive for another eight weeks because of the limitations of a single line railway.

Although the Minister of War, Milutin, had opposed the campaign before it started, he realised the consequences of a major retreat. So much blood spilled and nothing to show for it would arouse such anger in Russia that the army would never be forgiven. Furthermore, it would mean the ignominious end of the war. He therefore argued that the present position must be held whatever the cost. The Grand Duke Nicholas lost his temper and shouted at Milutin, asking if he intended the Balkans to be a tomb for the entire army. Alexander II intervened and said firmly: "There is to be no retreat." It was not an easy decision, for every fibre in Alexander's body cried out against the butchery of war. "My heart is bleeding," he wrote to the Princess Dolgorouky, "war is a mortal sin."

The repercussions of the Russian defeat echoed through Europe like a cannonade. The correspondent of the London *Times* wrote that, at Plevna, "a holocaust of mangled humanity was offered up to the inefficient helplessness of the General Staff Department of the Russian Army." People could scarcely believe that the Russian steam-roller, the bogey-man of the day, had been held in check by "decadent Turks" who were supposed to disintegrate at the first puff of cannon smoke. English Russophobes rejoiced wildly and Mr. Gladstone's "unspeakable Turk," in the person of the brave Commander, General Osman Pasha, became the hero of the hour. "Innumerable dogs, not a few cats, the son of an English peer, and a new type of lavatory-pan were christened 'Osman.' Thus England gave her accolade to the Defender of Plevna."[9]

The Czar, suffering from asthma and insomnia, looked more miserable and haggard than ever, while General Ignatiev, who up till now had been a key figure at Headquarters, was blamed by the Staff for not having warned them that the Turkish Army was so strong. In Russia itself criticism of the High Command, inflamed by foreign ridicule, burst through the censorship. The corruption and inefficiency of the army, it was alleged, was just as bad as in the days of the Crimea. The Grand Duke Nicholas was hopelessly incompetent; the Czarevitch not much better; and if the Czar could not bring himself to follow the customary practice of sovereigns and take command of his armies himself, why did he not return to St. Petersburg and at least ensure that the country was being properly governed?

Alexander bore these angry shafts with dignity. He not only refused to shield himself from the attacks but in the evenings frequently gathered together his staff and all the foreign military attachés and journalists and subjected them to "readings" from the world press. These meetings were referred to as *La Lecture* and no one dreaded them more than Colonel Wellesley, the British attaché. The London newspapers were so scathing that he found himself blushing to the roots of his hair. In his memoirs he gives a sample of some of the "English extracts."

> "Why is all that awful carnage at Plevna being wrought in the presence of the Czar, the Grand Duke and the Romanian Prince? We are assured that these eminent personages were gathered together on the field of action on Friday last when the conflict began, and there was especially prepared for the Divine Figure from the North a platform, or royal box, from which to survey the opening strife, wherein two hundred thousand human beings were to mangle and slay each other to the utmost extent possible, in the name of religion and philosophy."

and . . .

> "There is nothing more shocking in all the horrors of the 'crusade' than that at the present moment fresh butcheries are being prepared—not to gain territory, for it is too late, not to evangelise Bulgaria, for that pretence is exploded, but to soothe the august susceptibilities of the 'divine figure' and shed upon his return to the North even one solitary gleam of success from the fire of battle."

As these and other equally unflattering extracts fell on angry ears all eyes turned towards Colonel Wellesley, but the Czar did not forget his manners. "He simply smiled," wrote Colonel Wellesley, "and giving me a little bow after each particularly insulting passage said, 'Je vous remercie'."[10]

The press, of course, did not limit its attacks to Russia's policies, but pilloried the army for its defunct generals and clumsy strategy. Prince Alexander of Battenberg, who not only had spent weeks fighting with General Gourko in the mountains but had been attached in turn to the staffs of the Czar, Prince Charles of Romania and the Grand Duke Nicholas, secretly agreed with many of the things that were written. Young, idealistic and impulsive, he was outraged by the graft and hypocrisy that he saw on all sides. "You have no idea," he wrote to his father, "(1) of the levity with which the High Command does its work; (2) of the disorder *within* the army and *behind* the army; (3) of the robbery that goes on in the commissariat . . . Things are really so bad that it is a mercy we have only the Turks against us—all would have been lost long ago if we had had any other enemy . . . Instead of hearing about courts-martial we see nothing but St. George's Crosses and swords of honour! And who is victimised by all this? The Czar, the idealistic Czar, whose greatest virtue is his greatest fault. The Russians do not deserve his gentle kindness! . . . How gladly would I—unlike the Press—write nothing but good of the Russians! It is unfortunately impossible, and no one is sorrier about it than Your Sandro."[11]

Despite the world-wide mockery to which the Russians were subjected, Plevna was doomed. The town was now encircled by the Russian Army, every road was blocked, and it could only be a matter of weeks before starvation and disease forced Osman Pasha's capitulation. The Turkish soldiers were not yet aware that their fate was sealed, for the Sultan had promised to send a force to relieve them. But the truth was that the Turkish commanders dared not risk a single one of their scant divisions against the concentrated might of the Russian Armies, for defeat would leave the road to Constantinople wide open. They clung to the hope that, if Osman could maintain his position well into the winter, the Russians might be forced to abandon the campaign until the spring which would give them time to equip new divisions.

Osman's men held out for 143 days. By December British correspondents were sending back appalling stories of life inside the beleaguered town; no medical supplies, starvation rations, tainted water. With his men dying by inches Osman finally decided to attempt the impossible and try to break through the Russian steel ring. The battle began on 10th December in icy weather, and at one moment nearly 60,000 Turks and Russians were hacking each other to pieces in a hand-to-hand fight. The Turkish troops succeeded in penetrating several layers of the Russian defence but there was no real hope of springing the trap. In the end the great general, wounded in the knee, was obliged to raise the white flag and surrender his army.

The next day the Russians held a grand Te Deum in what was known as "Osman Pasha's redoubt." The Emperor and the Grand Duke Nicholas, accompanied by their staffs which numbered over 200 officers, then moved into Plevna. Colonel Wellesley, the British Military Attaché, was one of the company, and was not prepared for the surprises awaiting them. They suddenly came to two large wooden gates which opened as the Emperor approached. Inside was a long narrow yard, and at the end a white cottage with a veranda. Two trellis tables that ran the length of the yard were covered with white damask and groaned with wine and food.

The Emperor, accompanied by the Minister of War, disappeared into the cottage while the officers stood about interminably, eyeing the delicacies and wondering what was causing the delay. "After about an hour and a half," wrote Wellesley, "the ponderous gates of the yard again slowly opened, disclosing Osman Pasha, who had alighted from his carriage. With one arm round the neck of his Turkish servant, and the other round that of a Cossack, he was supported rather than carried into the yard.

"To the credit of the Russians, the moment it was realised that the wounded man they beheld was Osman Pasha, a spontaneous cry of 'Bravo, Osman!' arose from the entire staff. All rose to their feet and saluted the wounded foe as he passed, and what impressed me most was the fact that I did not see a single face among the Russian officers that was not moistened by a tear of pity and admiration ... Osman made his way slowly between the two tables laden with the wines which we were soon to drink in celebration of his fall, towards the Emperor's cottage, into which he was carried. It was not long before he reappeared having surrendered his sword to His Majesty who, I am glad to record, at once returned it as a mark of his respect for so brave an adversary. Our luncheon was then served, and as we sat down to it I could not but feel how great was the contrast between the luxury of this repast and the anguish, misery and starvation without."[12]

Unfortunately this old-world courtesy did not extend to the 43,000 Turkish prisoners. Although the Russian commanders had known for weeks that Plevna was bound to fall they had made no preparations for the unlucky men who would fall into their hands. The prisoners were marched back into Plevna and for ten days bottled up in a living hell. They were given nothing but a small piece of bread every other day; no fire-wood was allotted them; no help given to their sick and wounded. During the ten days in Plevna 4,000 men died. Even worse, the prisoners were forced to look on helpless as Bulgarian civilians searched the houses for wounded soldiers, many of whom had lost arms and legs, and killed them in their beds.

As it turned out the dead were fortunate, for the survivors were herded together for the long walk to Russia and treated in such a brutal manner that the western world was aghast. "In weather that became suddenly severe the Turks were marched off in rags and without shoes, although along their route thousands of empty transport wagons moved in the same direction. If a man fell by the wayside, he was left to freeze to death, his body to be devoured by the wolves. Between Plevna and Bucharest 5,000 men died; of the 43,000 who set out only 15,000 reached Russia, and only 12,000 returned home after the war. In all, some 50,000 Turks died in Russian captivity."[13]

The snows of winter did not deter the Grand Duke Nicholas, and by the middle of January his vanguard had reached Adrianople, only sixty miles from Constantinople. The British Foreign Office remained as complacent as ever, for the Emperor had assured the powers that geographical changes would be submitted to a European Congress. Queen Victoria, however, had no faith in Russian promises and once again verged on hysteria. Her distress was heightened by frantic pleas from the Sultan begging her to use her influence to secure an armistice. With the approval of her Cabinet she telegraphed to Alexander urging him to stop the fighting but the reply was barely civil—"unsatisfactory," "rude" and "vulgar" as the Queen described it. "The Commander-in-Chief of my armies in Europe and Asia," Alexander pronounced haughtily, "knows the conditions on which a suspension of hostilities can be granted."

This high-handed message confirmed Victoria's fears and increased her scorn at the pusillanimous attitude of her all-male Cabinet. "Oh! if the Queen were a man," she wrote to Lord Beaconsfield, "she would like to go and give those horrid Russians whose word one cannot trust such a beating."[14] "Oh! that Englishmen were now what they were!" she wrote to her daughter, the German Crown Princess, adding with forced optimism, "but we shall yet assert our rights—our position— & 'Britons will never be slaves' will yet be our Motto."[15]

She was right as usual. The Cabinet suddenly panicked: Russian success seemed to be producing a dangerous Russian arrogance. Admiral Hornby was instructed to take his six ironclads, which had been anchored at Besika Bay for six months, through the Dardanelles as a reminder that Britain wished to be consulted about an armistice. No sooner were the ships under way, however, than a telegram arrived from the British Ambassador in Constantinople reporting that the question of the Straits would be discussed by "the Emperor and the [European] Congress." On the strength of this conciliatory message the order to Hornby was countermanded and soon the ships were steaming back to Besika Bay. Alas, another telegram arrived altering the phrase about the Straits to "the Emperor and the Sultan."

"How we gnashed our teeth!" wrote a member of the Cabinet. The ships could not be turned around again without making Britain the laughing stock of Europe. However, it was not difficult to find another pretext. On 1st February the Turks and Russians signed an armistice. A week later rumours reached London (which turned out to be untrue) that the Russians were moving across the demarcation lines. The news caused a panic on the Stock Market, and gave Lord

Beaconsfield an excuse to set Admiral Hornby in motion again. This time the ships steamed through the Dardanelles and dropped anchor at the Island of Prinkipo in the Sea of Marmora, within sight of Constantinople.

Meanwhile a fierce conflict was taking place behind the scenes between Count Ignatiev, aflame with Panslav ambitions, and the Grand Duke Nicholas, commander of the Russian Army. Ignatiev had spent the first eight months of the war at Alexander's military headquarters, and when the latter returned to St. Petersburg after the fall of Plevna, Ignatiev went too. The wily Count was determined to remain close to the corridors of power, for the sweeping, sensational victory he was after depended on the Czar's nerve and resolve. Unceasingly he urged Alexander to seize Constantinople while the English were unsure of themselves; a *fait accompli* would call their bluff.

Alexander, however, could not rid his mind of the Crimean disaster. Although he longed for the crowning glory of Constantinople, he shrank from the nightmarish possibility of English intervention, and could not bring himself to give the decisive order. On 25th January he telegraphed his brother, the Grand Duke Nicholas, "to continue the advance but to stop before the walls of Constantinople," and "to occupy the heights of the Bosphorus" but not to conclude an armistice until Count Ignatiev, the Emperor's Plenipotentiary, arrived to negotiate a peace treaty.

It took Count Ignatiev nearly two weeks to reach Adrianople, and when he stopped for a night at the headquarters of the Czarevitch, near Bucharest, he learned to his shocked dismay that the Grand Duke Nicholas had signed an armistice despite the Czar's instructions. He hurried on, losing his baggage, falling in the mud, sliding down a precipice into a ravine. It is not surprising that by the time he reached Adrianople on 8th February he was in a furious temper. He upbraided the Grand Duke Nicholas like an angry schoolmaster, asking him why he had brought about the "untimely halt" and reminding him how often he had boasted of his intention to take Constantinople.

The Grand Duke explained uncomfortably that he had received

messages from Prince Gortchakov in St. Petersburg and Count Shuvalov, the Russian Ambassador in London, warning him that unless he concluded an immediate armistice England would intervene. Furthermore, the troops were tired and in a bedraggled condition, the roads were deep with mud, and the artillery had not been able to keep up with the advance of the infantry. He had not, he said, received the telegram to which Ignatiev kept alluding, instructing him to proceed to the walls of Constantinople.

Count Ignatiev as much as called the Grand Duke a liar. He said it was impossible that the Czar's telegram had not arrived in seven days by field telegram. He then told Nicholas that he intended to force the Turks to sign peace terms which were bound to be disagreeable to them, and in order to bring them to terms it might be necessary for the army to resume military operations. "God forbid!" shouted the Grand Duke. "Look here! Are you going to saddle us with another war with England? It's time to stop all these military operations and go home."[16]

Ignatiev traced the Czar's telegram and found that it had been delivered to the Grand Duke on the morning of the day on which the armistice had been signed. When he confronted Nicholas with this fact the latter replied lamely that it had arrived too late to alter the arrangements. This admission so angered the Count that it stung him into a frenzy of activity. He whirled about like a dervish, pulling every string, using every means at his disposal to force Nicholas to set his army in motion. His efforts provoked the Emperor into sending another telegram to his brother, ordering him "in view of the entrance of the British Fleet into the Sea of Marmora by some means or other, with or without the agreement of the Turks, to occupy their capital." The Grand Duke stalled. The shoes and uniforms of his army were in such bad condition, the morale so low, that he dared not risk a show-down with the English. On 24th February he found a way out. He occupied San Stefano, six miles from Constantinople, and informed the Emperor that it was "a suburb of Constantinople."

Meanwhile Count Ignatiev was using pressure on the Turks to sign a monstrous peace treaty, virtually giving Russia the hegemony of the Balkans. When the Grand Vizier refused, on 1st March, to put his signature on the document Ignatiev broke off relations with him and threatened war. At ten p.m. he stormed into the bedroom of the Grand Duke (who was already asleep) telling him that he must renew operations and seize Constantinople without further argument. "You have gone off your head," cried Nicholas excitedly. "You absolutely want to drag us into a war with England. That's what all your designs are leading to."[16] The Grand Duke threw on some clothes and summoned his Chief-of-Staff who argued with Ignatiev just as furiously as his master, insisting that the British Navy had only to move through the Bosphorus to seize Russian naval communications, and cut off supplies of food and ammunition to the army. It was a risk no responsible Russian Commander could take. The men parted at midnight and the argument was never resolved, for the next morning the Turks accepted Ignatiev's peace terms and the Treaty of San Stefano was signed.

The British did not learn the terms of the treaty for several weeks. During this brief lull a storm blew up over a personal incident which set the English and Russian royal families at each other's throats. Prince Alexander of Battenberg had returned to St. Petersburg after the fall of Plevna, but after a month or two of inactivity received permission to join the Grand Duke Nicholas's staff. He arrived at San Stefano shortly after Headquarters had been established. He was delighted with the small town on the Sea of Marmora, particularly as he was given a villa overlooking the Island of Prinkipo where Admiral Hornby's ironclads rode at anchor. One of these ships was commanded by Queen Victoria's son Alfred, Duke of Edinburgh, the husband of the Grand Duchess Marie; and even more exciting, among the serving officers was his elder brother, Prince Louis of Battenberg. "The Grand Duke Nicholas gave permission to all foreign officers to go into Constantinople to-day," Sandro wrote happily to his father. "And to me in particular he said that I might go and see Louis and stay as long as I liked. He would take the responsibility."

Sandro eagerly seized the opportunity, and with the help of the German Ambassador, Prince Reuss, arranged a meeting with Louis, who invited him aboard the *Sultan*. "A small boat," he wrote, "very soon brought us to the *Sultan* where I was received by Alfred and the whole ship's company with extraordinary friendliness. They all feel more Russian than the Russians and make no secret of it." Afterwards Alfred took Sandro on a tour of inspection of the newest ironclad, the *Temeraire*, and finally conducted him aboard the *Alexandra* and introduced him to Admiral Hornby.[17]

A few weeks later Britain was stunned to learn the terms of the San Stefano peace treaty which created a huge, swollen Bulgaria that stretched from the Ægean Sea to Albania, and virtually placed the whole of the Balkans under Russian control. Overnight the Foreign Office's policy of appeasement crashed to the ground and the firm stand advocated by Queen Victoria took its place. The change of heart occurred at the eleventh hour for the Russians were twisting and turning to find a way out of their promise that geographical changes would be submitted to a Congress of the Powers. Now Prince Gortchakov was saying that, although Russia would attend a Congress, she must "reserve the liberty of accepting or not accepting a discussion of the questions raised." England's Rip Van Winkle sleep was over. Votes of credit went whistling through Parliament; Indian troops were ordered to Malta; reservists called to the colours. Mr. Gladstone was hooted in the streets and the music halls rang to the ditty:

> *We don't want to fight*
> *But by jingo if we do*
> *We've got the ships, we've got the men,*
> *We've got the money too.*

At the height of England's patriotic fervour, Queen Victoria learned of the visit of Prince Alexander of Battenberg to the British Fleet, sponsored by no less a person than her own son Alfred. Her fury knew no bounds. She wrote an outraged letter to her daughter, Princess Alice, accusing the Grand Duke Nicholas of sending a "Russian spy" to the fleet. He had been "positively fêted aboard," she said, and had been shown all over the men-of-war and even allowed to inspect the mechanism of the newly invented torpedo. The Queen was so angry with her son, Alfred, that she ordered him to be relieved of his command for so long as the *Sultan* lay off Constantinople. As for Prince Louis he was transferred to another ship and sent back home.

Sandro was so dismayed when he heard of the unfortunate aftermath of his visit that he poured out his woes to his aunt, the Czarina. "The poor boy," she wrote to Alexander of Hesse, "that the Queen, crazy old hag, made him the pretext for persecuting Alfred, and more especially Louis. I was so indignant that at first my one idea was that he should leave the English service. But perhaps it would be a rash thing to do if there is really danger of war. But just because the danger threatens, I should be heartily glad for Alfred and Louis to be out of it, wouldn't you? . . . Marie says that if it is a question of treason, Hornby and the captains of the ships of the whole squadron are equally guilty." Gradually the Queen's anger subsided and in the end she did not carry out her threats. She bowed to the representations of the Admiralty and did not have the intended reproof conveyed to Alfred; and she asked for an announcement to be made that Louis's transfer was not a disciplinary move but part of the normal routine. The Czarina's anger, however, remained on the boil. "The insulting things that the Queen said in her letters to Alfred about the Czar and the Russian people," she wrote to her brother, "are worthy of a fish-wife."[18]

Count Ignatiev's tenacity was flabbergasting. In the quiet interval before the English discovered the terms of San Stefano, he once again begged the Czar to occupy Constantinople. Control of the Straits, he argued, would give Russia strategic advantages that she would need to possess when Britain learned what she had wrung from Turkey. He was so persuasive that he finally induced the Czar to send a telegram to Nicholas: "As a rupture with England is almost inevitable, it is necessary to occupy the shores of the Bosphorus with troops and no time should be lost in anticipating the arrival of British troops."

Alexander's message was a masterpiece of ambiguity, worded to escape blame if things went wrong. Nicholas, however, was no longer in a mood to try and duck the issue. He replied next day saying that he did not "refuse" to take Constantinople, but that he did not believe in the possibility of success and would have to be given a categorical "order." This order never came.

The truth was that Queen Victoria's policy of firmness was bearing fruit. The Russians did not take Constantinople because they feared British intervention. As a sop to the indignation of the Panslavs, Alexander recalled the Grand Duke and appointed General Totleben in his place. Nicholas, of course, was right in believing that the British meant business, yet he received nothing for his honesty except abuse. When his train pulled into St. Petersburg the Emperor met him in person, explaining dryly that he had done so to prevent him from being hissed by the crowds. Thus the victor of Plevna, Sophia, Shipka, Philippopolis and Adrianople was greeted. The Czarevitch refused to take part in the festivities in his honour; and General Loris-Melikov was present when the Emperor, who had shrunk from giving the decisive order, stormed at his brother "for his failure to take Constantinople."

The diplomatic struggle with England continued throughout April and May, accompanied by military preparations on both sides. Russia could not escape from the fact that she was morally bound to submit the San Stefano Treaty to a Congress of the Powers, as her acquisitions cut across the Treaties of 1856 and 1871 which bore her signature. Yet there was no point in convening an assembly unless England and Russia were willing to compromise. St. Petersburg knew that London was holding talks with Austria-Hungary, who not only objected to the San Stefano Treaty just as strongly as Britain, but for years had had her eye on the provinces of Bosnia and Herzegovina which she wished to annex. Count Shuvalov, the Russian Ambassador in London, recognised that Russia could not face the combined power of these two nations and urged the Czar to negotiate. Britain demanded that Ignatiev's inflated Bulgaria should be reduced in size and divided into two parts; in exchange she would support Russia's Asiatic conquests. Alexander vacillated and finally agreed in principle. "It does not matter if there should be one, two or three Bulgarias. It is of paramount importance that they should all be free of the Turks." This however did not reflect the views of his countrymen, as he was soon to learn.

The Congress met in Berlin in June with the celebrated Bismarck serving as "the honest broker." All the great men of Europe were present; every night there were banquets, and receptions, and opera galas. The Crown Prince and Princess acted as hosts, as the German Emperor was *hors de combat*, having been wounded by a would-be assassin a few days earlier. The suave, well-bred world of diplomacy, with its polished manners and calculated flatteries, was accustomed to dealing with explosive questions in an atmosphere of blazing chandeliers, brilliant uniforms and flashing jewels. The fact that war was still a possibility lent an air of excitement to the assembly far more stimulating than the champagne that flowed so freely.

Apart from Bismarck, the chief celebrities, of course, were the seventy-four-year-old Lord Beaconsfield who was suffering from gout, and the eighty-five-year-old Prince Gortchakov who travelled about in a wheel-chair. Beaconsfield, however, was not too crotchety to revel in the limelight and was particularly delighted to find how many ladies in Berlin were reading the novels of Benjamin Disraeli. He purred every time he was asked for an autograph, and exercised his powers as a writer by entertaining Queen Victoria to sharp-eyed observations. "At two o'clock the Congress met in the Radetsky Palace—a noble hall just restored and becoming all the golden coats and glittering stars that filled it," he wrote on 12th June. "Lord Beaconsfield believes that every day is not to be so ceremonious and costumish. Prince Bismarck, a giant 6 feet 2 in. at least, and proportionately huge, was chosen President. In the course of this morn Prince Gortchakov, a shrivelled old man, was leaning on the arm of his gigantic rival, and Prince Bismarck, being seized with a sudden fit of rheumatism, both fell to the ground. Unhappily P. Bismarck's dog, seeing his master apparently struggling with an opponent, sprang to the rescue. It is said that P. Gortchakov was not maimed or bitten thro' the energetic efforts of his companion . . ."[19]

Bismarck's rheumatism did not prevent him from keeping a firm hand on the assembly. As Britain and Russia were the only two countries liable to go to war with each other, he remarked, the bone of contention—Bulgaria—must come first on the agenda. The British proposed that in splitting Bulgaria in two, the northern half should be established as an independent principality, run as a constitutional monarchy with the right to elect its own prince; the southern half should remain under Turkish rule subject to stringent safeguards, cut off from access to the Ægean and renamed Eastern Romania. Although Prince Gortchakov was horrified by these proposals, Lord Beaconsfield threatened to break up the Congress if they were not accepted. As this could only mean war Bismarck pressed the Russians to accept, and after considerable heart-burning Alexander finally conceded.

None of the Balkan States was satisfied with the outcome of the assembly. The Bulgarians were angry at having their country divided; the Romanians indignant at having to surrender Bessarabia; the Serbs disappointed at acquiring so little new territory; the Bosnians and Herzegovinians furious at being placed under the administration of Austria. Indeed, the representatives of Austria and England were the only two men to leave Berlin satisfied with their work. The Turks, of course, were sickened at having lost most of their European possessions; and the Russians outraged at seeing the Balkans slip from their grasp.

If the Russians had fought the war for the reasons they professed—to free the Christian Slavs from Turkish rule—they would not have found the results of the Congress so humiliating. They had in fact all but pushed the Turks out of Europe; Romania, Serbia and Montenegro had gained independence in name as well as in fact; the great majority of the Bulgars were free to start a new life; Russia had recovered the parts of Bessarabia lost after the Crimean War. Furthermore, she had added Kars and Batuum and Ardaghan to her Empire, extending her Asian territory by thousands of miles. On the other hand, she had been denied access to the Mediterranean once again, which she had hoped to reach through the Bulgarian back door. And that, as Disraeli crowed to Queen Victoria, "was the real object of the late war." "Prince Gortchakov says," he added, " 'We have sacrificed 100,000 picked soldiers and 100 millions of money for nothing'."[20] This view was shared by every Panslavist in Russia who had dreamed of the double-headed eagle spreading its wings to the Mediterranean. Aksakov was so indignant when he got wind of what was happening at Berlin that he made a seditious speech which prompted the Czar to ban him from Moscow. In a vein of deepest irony he declared that the Czar must be ignorant as to what was happening. "The people are raging, grumbling, indignant, disturbed with the daily news from Berlin, and await like a blessed tiding, the resolution of the Throne . . . Its hope shall not be belied, for the Czar's words: 'The sacred cause will be brought to an end' shall not be broken . . ."[21]

What annoyed the Russians most of all was the fact that Britain managed to pick up Cyprus in the midst of the confusion. "Trust the Englishwoman," they said bitterly, "to land a fish from the troubled waters."[22]

V

The Killers

PEOPLE were shocked by the Czar's appearance for although he was barely sixty, anxiety had turned him into an old man. His hair was grey, his shoulders bent, his asthma worse than ever. Journalists commented on his "pale and mournful face" and claimed that he was suffering from "settled melancholia"; by comparison, they said, Prince Gortchakov presented a lively figure.

Alexander's gloom was not surprising for everything he touched seemed to turn to ashes. This was largely due to the volatile character of his people, whose opinions were so irrational that they frequently bordered on lunacy. Alexander loathed war, yet he had given way to the frenzied insistence that it was Russia's duty to free the Christian Slavs from the Turkish yoke. No sooner had this been accomplished than the same voices cried out that they did not care two figs what happened to the Serbs or the Bulgars. All that mattered was that Russia should keep possession of Count Ignatiev's swollen Bulgaria, which meant control of the Balkans and dominance of the continent.

The truth was that the Russian people were suffering from a bad attack of *folie de grandeur*. Their sweeping ambitions were not shattered at Berlin by bad diplomacy, but by the unpalatable fact that Russia was too weak to retain her perch at the top of the tree. Her treasury was empty, her army ravaged by typhus. When Britain turned nasty she had no alternative but to climb down and seek a compromise.

Russian opinion, however, refused to face reality, childishly preferring to delude itself that all had been lost through political ineptitude. People thrashed around for a scapegoat, complaining of English greed, Austrian cunning and Bismarckian duplicity, and finally blamed "the weakness of the Czar" for their undoing. The adulation they had heaped upon him after the fall of Plevna turned to sullen disenchantment.

The Nihilists were quick to exploit the situation, and early in 1878 shots rang out in St. Petersburg which revealed to the world the depth of the Russian *malaise*. In February a tall, dark girl from a well-known family, Vera Zasulich, succeeded in getting an interview with General Trepov, the Chief of the Gendarmes. No sooner had she entered his office than she pulled out a revolver and shot him twice. Her aim was so bad that he did not die but was seriously wounded. She made no attempt to escape and when her trial opened before a jury at the Central Assizes, she told the court that she had tried to kill General Trepov because he had broken the law by reintroducing flogging which had been abolished by the Czar's judicial reforms. Trepov, a dandy who wore scent and twirled a small blond moustache, had ordered a political prisoner, Bogolubov, to remove his hat when addressing him. Bogolubov had refused and Trepov struck him across the face. Trepov then ordered the man to apologise. Once again the prisoner refused whereupon Trepov gave instructions that he was to be whipped with a birch rod.

The verdict did not seem in any doubt until Vera's lawyer rose to his feet and delivered an impassioned plea which apparently touched the Russian soul to its very depths. He drew the picture of a pure young girl giving her life to avenge a comrade. Nobility, love, sacrifice, death were the chords he struck and soon the court was weeping in sympathy. Although the jury was drawn from the professional classes, Russian juries had a tendency to ignore the law and deliver verdicts from the heart. This was no exception. A pronouncement of "not guilty" drew the spectators to their feet, clapping and cheering. Vera was the heroine of the hour. She left the court-room surrounded by well-wishers to face a row of gendarmes drawn up outside the door. Several of them started towards her, as though to arrest her; a student let off a revolver, the police fired back, and several people were killed. In the commotion Vera vanished, and that same day was smuggled out of Russia.

Count Leo Tolstoy was fascinated by the Zasulich affair, but frightened and puzzled by the public admiration for lawlessness. ". . . it is open war," he wrote to his aunt on 6th April, 1878. "Every one of those who acquitted the assassin and every one of those who approved her acquittal know full well that for their own personal safety a murderer must not be allowed to go unpunished; but in their eyes the question is not who is right but who in the long run, will prove the strongest . . . Since reading the account of the trial and all this commotion about it, I can think of nothing else." The next day he wrote to a friend, "The Zasulich business is no joking matter. This madness, this idiotic capriciousness that has suddenly seized hold of people is significant. These are the first signs of something not yet clear to us. But it is serious. The Slavophil madness was the precursor of war, and I am inclined to think that this madness is the precursor of revolution."[1]

Tolstoy was right, although the revolution took the form of a long and sporadic guerrilla war. The blaze of publicity surrounding the Zasulich affair sparked off a series of outrages from one end of Russia to the other. Governors, civil servants and police officials were the main target. One of the most sensational murders was that of General Mezentsov, the head of St. Petersburg Third Section, who was summoned by the Czar after the attempt on Trepov and asked to recommend ways of holding the terrorists in check. Mezentsov's only solution was increased severity. Several months later when he was approaching his office at nine o'clock in the morning he was stabbed to death by a young man who plunged a sword into his stomach, leapt into a waiting carriage pulled by a fast horse and disappeared into thin air. It later became known that an intellectual named Kravchinsky, who had spread revolutionary propaganda in Serbia during the Serbo-Turkish war, boasted of being the killer. For many years this man made his home in England writing books and articles under the name of "Stepniak." But he was always terrified of the retribution of the Russian Secret Police. He lived in a one-storied cottage in St. John's Wood with a Russian lady who, people said, was not his wife. "This dreary residence was surrounded by a garden, carefully guarded by watch-dogs, who gave loud warnings on the approach of footsteps. The windows were protected by shutters which were bolted and barred, the doors were securely

fastened by bolts and chains, but there was a small peep-hole in it . . .
On crossing the threshold the visitor was made aware that the host
and hostess were armed to the teeth, and prepared to sell their
lives dearly . . ."[2] Stepniak's death was sudden and violent, yet very
different from anything he had ever imagined. In 1898 he was killed
by a train at a level crossing near Turnham Green.

Although the terrorists were estimated at no more than fifteen
hundred out of a population of fifty million, their blows were so
effective that by the end of the year Russia resembled a country in
a state of siege. When the Emperor made a trip to Moscow to plead
with the public to support the police in upholding authority,
elaborate security measures were taken. His nephew, the twelve-year-
old Grand Duke Alexander Mikhailovich, son of the Viceroy of the
Caucasus, travelled along the route a few days before the Czar.
"The four hundred miles between Moscow and St. Petersburg
were being closely guarded by soldiers. All along the route we saw
bayonets and uniforms; at night thousands of camp fires were light-
ing the way. At first we thought it had been done in father's honour,
then we learned that the Emperor expected to visit Moscow in the
near future and that extraordinary precautions had been taken to
protect his train from the attempts of the revolutionaries. The
revelation struck us all painfully. Things were coming to a pretty
bad pass if the Czar of all the Russias had to be guarded every inch
of the distance between his two capitals. Our father could not
disguise his worry."[3]

Some of the Czar's Ministers demanded bodyguards but Alexander
refused to have his private life under surveillance and would only
accept protection when others were travelling with him. At eight
every morning he left the Winter Palace and walked along the
Neva, and in the afternoons often strolled unaccompanied in the
Summer Gardens. He liked to drive about the capital in a small
sleigh or carriage with only one man on the box.

He was far less concerned about his own safety than that of the
Princess Dolgorouky who lived with her two children in a house
on the English Quay. In September she gave birth to her last child,
a girl who was christened Catherine. Soon after this event the
Emperor began to receive anonymous letters threatening her life.

For the first time he was thrown into such a panic he could not sleep or work. He finally decided that she must move with the children into the safety of the Winter Palace. A suite was prepared for her on the floor directly above the Emperor's apartment and a lift installed connecting the two. As the Emperor's rooms were also joined on the other side to those of the Empress Marie it was a *ménage à trois* in the literal sense.

The Emperor's sons, particularly the heir to the Throne, were incensed when they heard the news. It not only cut across the code of accepted behaviour, but seemed an act of cruel insensitivity in view of the fact that their beloved mother was fighting a hopeless battle against tuberculosis and had only a short time to live. Indeed the whole of St. Petersburg was shocked by the scandal. Yet Alexander could not help himself. He was devoted to Marie, but his passion for Catherine was so great that it tore him to pieces, and he could not rest unless he was assured of her well-being. Oddly enough, Marie minded less than her sons. She had long ago accepted Catherine as part of her husband's life, and refused to let this latest act embitter her. Alexander was still the centre of her invalid existence.

She was appalled in April 1879 when an attempt was made on his life. He was crossing the Palace Square at nine o'clock in the morning when a young man stepped coolly towards him and fired four shots, missing him each time. The people in the square ran towards the would-be assassin and overpowered him. He was a schoolmaster named Alexander Soloviev. He tried to swallow a pill on his way to the police station, but it was knocked out of his hand. When the Magistrate interrogated him he replied unrepentantly: "It's no use; you'll get nothing out of me. I made a complete sacrifice of my life a long time ago. Besides, if I confessed, my accomplices would have me killed . . . yes, even in this prison." "You can imagine how I feel," Marie wrote to her brother, dispersing any doubts about her loyalty to Alexander. "The first thing we did was to thank God on our knees for the wonderful escape. The Czar is marvellously well and cheerful . . . He is fully determined not to flinch before the severest measures . . . I admit that I feel broken and longing for a rest, which the Czar needs badly too. He feels it is so irksome never to be able to go out unless he has an escort of Cossacks, to which he has been with difficulty persuaded to agree. May God have mercy on us."[4]

The Czar's government was deeply shaken by the boldness of the attack and demanded a new machinery to deal with the terror. Six Governors-General with military power were appointed to take control of St. Petersburg, Moscow, Kharkov, Odessa, Kiev and Warsaw. From now on it was all-out war between Government and revolutionaries. Ten days after issuing his proclamation Alexander departed for Livadia, accompanied by the Empress, her face dangerously flushed and her eyes bright with fever. The Princess Dolgorouky had gone ahead and was already awaiting her lover at her villa, Buyuk-Serai, not far from the Palace.

Who were these young students who were terrorising the Empire? Although they were referred to in the foreign press as "Nihilists" they insisted that Nihilism was an old-fashioned concept, not applicable to themselves. Nihilism, they explained, had been the struggle for "absolute individualism"; the negation of the obligation placed upon the individual by society, family, and religion; a passionate and powerful reaction "not against the political despotism, but against the moral despotism that weighs upon the private and inner life of the individual."[5]

How were the young people of the seventies different? They claimed to be paving the way for a new system of society, although none of them gave much thought to how the new society should be organised. Political reform was the job of the Liberals, they said; but of course there could be no reform unless the revolutionaries provided a new framework by destroying the despotism.

The "framework," however, was nothing more than the creation of a political void, just as the Nihilists before them had tried to create a social void; and the weapon was murder. That the killing was much more likely to lead to less liberty, not more, did not seem to interest them, for they were drunk with egotism, dramatising themselves as the saviours of humanity. Foreigners found their disinterestedness in constructive ideas intensely Russian and intensely irritating. Lord Frederick Hamilton, a young diplomat who was posted to St. Petersburg in 1879, conducted exhausting conversations with the wife of a newspaper editor. "What struck me," wrote Lord Frederick, "was that behind the floods of vehement invective of Madame O—— [the editor's wife], there was never the smallest practical suggestion. 'You say, Madame O——,' I would hazard, 'that the existence of things is intolerable. What remedy do you suggest?' 'I am not the Government,' would retort Madame O—— with great heat. 'It is for the Government to make suggestions. I only denounce an abominable injustice.' 'Quite so, Madame O——, but how can these conditions be improved? What is your programme of reform?' 'We have nothing to do with reforms. Our mission is to destroy utterly. Out of the ruins a better state of things must necessarily arise; as nothing could possibly be worse than present conditions!' "[6]

It would be wrong, however, to think that the revolutionaries were incapable of thought, for they gave the deepest attention to their conspiratorial plans. The most effective terrorist organisation was *Will of the People*, an offshoot of *Land and Liberty* which once had contented itself with village propaganda. *Will of the People* was conceived by a wiry, saturnine, twenty-seven-year-old fanatic named Zheliabov, who came from a peasant family and had been educated at Odessa University. In June 1879 the group held a four-day conference in the province of Tambov under the very nose of the police. They formed an executive committee and decided that their first priority would be to murder the Czar. They voted to abjure such old-fashioned weapons as revolvers and knives and to make use of the military techniques of the Russo-Turkish war. Mines and bombs would be their means of destruction.

The Executive Committee numbered about fifteen people. Their most indispensable recruit was Nikolai Kibaltchitch, the son of a priest and a mechanical engineer by vocation. He had studied at the Institute of Civil Engineers and at the Medical Academy. He had been arrested in 1875 for spreading socialist pamphlets and had spent three years in prison. Shortly after his release he met Zheliabov who persuaded him to work as a chemist for *Will of the People*. He studied everything that could be found on the subject in German, French and English and was widely known as "the mechanic."

He had real talent and his bombs and mines soon won the reputation of being the best in Russia.

Although Zheliabov was the leader of the Executive Committee, his mistress, Sophia Perovskaya, was the dominating force. She was young and beautiful and came from a family long devoted to the service of the Czar. Her father had been a Governor of St. Petersburg and her grandfather a Minister of Public Instruction. She hated this side of her family, however, as her father was a noted disciplinarian, and disowned her when she became a revolutionary. On the other hand, she adored her mother whose devotion never faltered. The seductive Sophia was as merciless as a steel blade. Her energy and fanaticism were so great that occasionally she even managed to drive the monstrous Zheliabov to the brink of mental exhaustion. She demanded perfection and not only ordered cowards to be shot but once instructed a comrade to pay for a moment of weakness by committing suicide.

The first operation undertaken by the group was a triple plan to blow up the Czar's train when it returned to St. Petersburg from the Crimea in November. The Committee managed to plant members as signalmen and mines were laid along the route at Odessa, Kharkov and Moscow. Success seemed certain, for it was inconceivable that all three attempts could fail. Yet the Gods decreed otherwise. At the last moment the Czar's route was changed and Odessa eliminated from the itinerary; and although the train passed through Kharkov the mine failed to ignite due to an error in connecting the electrodes. Sophia was responsible for the third mine and her handiwork was faultless. When the Imperial train pulled into the Kursky Station at Moscow a terrific explosion blew the engine and three coaches off the track. Alexander II, however, was safely in the Kremlin. The train that had been damaged was the baggage train, which looked exactly like the imperial train and usually preceded it, but on this occasion had been held up at Kharkov because of engine trouble. When Alexander heard what had happened he exclaimed bitterly: "Am I such a wild beast that they must hound me to death?"

The people of Moscow were shocked by the attempt and that night everyone in the city seemed to be on the streets. Word went round that the plot had been organised by students, and police were called out to protect the University buildings from popular anger. The indifference towards the Czar, which had worried the authorities for months, had given way to a surge of indignation. "Those wretches are doing their best to ruin any case they might have," wrote Prince Nicholas Golytsin to his cousin in Paris. "You should have seen the streets of Moscow . . . The wrath of the people is beyond telling . . . There will be little for the police to do if, which heaven forbid, we have another such attempt . . . The Emperor insisted on driving to the Kursky Station as soon as he heard the news . . . His first question was—'How many killed?' None were, but several badly injured, mostly railway staff, poor, hard working people . . . Those demented scoundrels are so few and we are so many . . . It should be easy for the Government to stamp out the plague, and yet they do nothing except irritate those who are truly loyal."[7]

Sophia and Zheliabov were not discouraged by failure. After the railway fiasco they produced an idea which thrilled the Executive Committee with its daring. They proposed to blow up the dining-room of the Winter Palace when a maximum number of the Imperial family were gathered for dinner. Sophia had discovered from a family connection that Count Adlerberg, the Court Chamberlain, had disbanded the military labourers' colony which normally undertook Palace repairs on grounds of economy; recently he had hired a well-known building contractor to carry out extensive alterations in the basement. As the police had no jurisdiction over the Palace, which relied on its own gendarmes, the contractor was not forced to carry out a security check on the men he employed, and strangers were occasionally put on the payroll.

The project seemed perfectly suited to the talents of the Executive Committee, as one of the members, Stephen Chalturin, was a carpenter. He applied to the contractor for work and got it, not even being required to live in. He soon made friends with the watchman-gendarme who lived in the basement, by pretending to fall in love with the man's daughter. He had been supplied with a map of the palace and soon marked out the place in the cellar, directly below the dining-room, where he would lay his charges. The fact that a Finnish Infantry Regiment on Palace duty lived on an intervening floor did not deter him. Every morning when he came to work his tool chest was filled with dynamite which he hid in the cellars.

Sophia learned from one of her mother's friends that Prince Alexander of Hesse and his son were due to arrive in St. Petersburg on 16th February and would be dining with the imperial family that night. This seemed to be just the occasion for which they had been waiting. As palace dinners were always held punctually at 6 p.m. the bomb was timed for twenty minutes past the hour. On this particular evening, however, Prince Alexander's train was late; furthermore he asked the Czar's permission to see his sister who was now desperately ill, before going in to dinner.

The family were on the staircase on the way to the dining-room when a terrific explosion that could be heard on the left bank of the Neva shook the Palace. The gas jets went out and everything was enveloped in dust and smoke. Prince Alexander and the Czarevitch ran to the Yellow Salon and found the room a complete shambles, the floor covered with glass and china, a gaping hole in the wall, the air thick with fumes. They could hear cries and groans in the guard-room below, and there a terrible sight awaited them. Eleven men of the Finnish Regiment were dead, and thirty out of forty-four seriously wounded. The Emperor's first thought was the Princess Dolgorouky. He rushed to her apartment to see if she was safe. Finding her unharmed he hurried to his wife's rooms; but Marie had been given a heavy dose of morphia to relieve her pain and was fast asleep.

The fact that the Nihilists had been able to gain access to the palace threw the population into a panic. "All those who lived through those days," wrote Eugène Melchior de Vogüé, the French Ambassador, "will bear witness that no terms could be strong enough to portray the terror and prostration of every class of society. For the 2nd March, the anniversary of the emancipation of the serfs, we were promised mine explosions in various parts of the capital; the names of the threatened streets were given. Families changed their dwellings, others left the town. The police, convinced of their impotence, lost their heads; the action of the government was entirely devoid of initiative; the public, realising this, prayed for a deliverer."[8]

The deliverer came sooner than anyone expected. The Czar held a Council at the Winter Palace which was attended by the Czarevitch, a number of Ministers, including the Minister of War, and all the Governors-General of the Provinces, most of whom were soldiers who had distinguished themselves in the last war. The discussion seemed to be bogged down by argument and recriminations when the Heir Apparent suggested setting up a Supreme Committee with overriding powers in all parts of the Empire. Throughout the meeting General Loris-Melikov, who had taken part in the Asian campaign and covered himself in glory by the important capture of Kars, remained silent. A dark-skinned man in his late fifties, an Armenian by birth who spoke broken Russian, he did not intervene until the Czar asked him his opinion point-blank. Loris-Melikov said that he approved of the Heir's idea of a Supreme Committee as long as the Czar would make concessions to liberal opinion at the same time as he reimposed his authority. The next day Alexander gave his decision. A Supreme Committee would be established and its chief would be responsible to no one but the Czar. Then he turned to Loris-Melikov. "I appoint you to that post."

As soon as the General's task became known, Zheliabov and Sophia held a special meeting and pronounced the death sentence on the new dictator. There was no time for dynamite. A university student was sent to shoot him down. The boy fired three bullets at Loris-Melikov as he was coming out of his house, and all three embedded themselves in the thick hide of his fur collar. The assassin turned to run but the General sprang forward, knocked the gun out of his hand and threw him to the ground. As the youth was being led away he called out jeeringly: "Unfortunately I did not succeed but there are plenty more where I come from."

Despite this gruesome beginning, General Loris-Melikov referred to the new régime as "the dictatorship of the heart." He was determined not only to track down terrorists, but to try and remove the grievances that prompted sedition. He began by tightening up the security measures from one end of Russia to the other, abolished the hated Third Section and centralised the police under the Ministry of the Interior. He seconded army officers to help him and drew freely on military intelligence. He told Alexander that he owed it to the country to take proper precautions, and persuaded him to make use of the armour-plated carriage which had been bought from Napoleon III after the fall of the Second Empire. He introduced stringent regulations into the Winter Palace. Special passes were required for every visit; parcels could only be delivered at a certain gate where they were tested before being taken inside; sentries guarded every passage-way and even the servants were not allowed to move from one floor to another. Before these measures were introduced the palace was searched from top to bottom, so that the police should know of every door and every staircase; and once again it was noted that cows were living on the top floor, tended by the servants who availed themselves of the milk.

The police grilled suspects and made house to house checks through whole sections of the capital. Just before the New Year the Kharkov police had arrested an assassin named Goldenberg who had murdered Prince Kropotkin, the Governor of the Province. Goldenberg was transferred to St. Petersburg where the police interrogated him with such cleverness and sympathy that he repented of his crime and made a full confession. He revealed that he was a member of the Executive Committee. He named Zheliabov and Sophia Perovskaya, and told them how the Winter Palace explosion had been organised. News of his defection soon reached the Committee and after a hasty meeting Zheliabov ordered members of the group to go into hiding until the scare had blown over.

Meanwhile Loris-Melikov was pressing for greater freedom for the peaceful citizen. He sent Alexander a paper pointing out that the Czar's great reforms of the sixties had coincided with the rise of Socialism in Europe. This had caused Russian officials to recoil from the idea of freedom, instead of implementing the measures as they should have done. If the liberal concessions had been strengthened and expanded, he said, ". . . new shoots would have thrust their roots . . . and the coming struggle with Socialism would have presented no danger to the State."

Loris-Melikov began by sacking three or four of the Czar's most reactionary ministers—among them the Minister of Education—and appointing reformers in their place. He relaxed the censorship, introduced press conferences, and made an attempt to restore the authority of the *Zemstvoes*. By August there had been no terrorist activities for several months. He appeared to have effected such a change in the Russian climate that he told the Czar that the Supreme Committee was no longer necessary. He asked to be appointed to the post of Minister of the Interior which would give him all the power he required to continue his work

Although the Armenian dictator was popular with the public and had lifted an immense burden from Alexander's shoulders, the Austrian Ambassador, Count Kalnocky, was startled at the Czar's appearance when he saw him in September at manœuvres. He stared into space for hours at a time like a man "physically exhausted and morally broken." Nothing seemed to go right for Alexander; now he was tormented by the distress his personal life was causing, and the growing rift between himself and his children.

The sons felt that their father's frenzied infatuation for the Princess Dolgorouky was stripping him of all decency, and could not forgive his heartless treatment of their dying mother. Marie had such difficulty in breathing that her rooms were artificially impregnated with oxygen released from gas cylinders. While her boys rallied round and her daughter, the Duchess of Edinburgh, made a special trip from London to sit at her bedside, Alexander only found time for fleeting visits. In May he quit the capital altogether, pleading asthma trouble, and went to Tsarsko Selo where he could spend untrammelled days with Catherine. Although at this time the Empress was only conscious a few hours a day, she always called for Alexander in her lucid moments. He was seldom there. On 2nd June Marie died in her sleep; no one was with her and her death was not discovered until the maid entered the room in the morning to open the curtains.

Alexander II continued to cause deep offence. Although the

funeral took place with all the imperial pomp reserved for an Empress, he would not wait until it was over before bringing the Princess back to the Winter Palace. Countess Marie Vorontsov, one of Marie's ladies-in-waiting, told Alexander of Hesse, when he arrived in St. Petersburg, that "the Emperor's mistress had stood in the gallery of the palace watching the coffin being carried from the church to the fortress." "What boundless effrontery!" the Prince had written in his diary.[9] After the funeral the Emperor ordered the obsequies, which normally lasted a month, to come to a close.

A far worse shock was yet in store. A month after Marie's death the Emperor summoned his Court Chamberlain, Count Adlerberg, and told him that he had decided to marry the Princess Dolgorouky in a week's time; the ceremony would take place at Tsarsko Selo in the utmost secrecy. Adlerberg was so taken aback that he scarcely knew what to say. He pointed out that the Heir Apparent was abroad and asked the Czar if he would not wait for his son's return. Alexander replied glacially that the plans would go ahead as he had arranged.

The ceremony took place in an unused, unfurnished drawing-room in the Elizabeth Palace, specially chosen so that the suspicions of the servants would not be aroused. An improvised "field altar" was set up in the middle of the room and the only people present were Count Adlerberg, Generals Ryleev and Baranov and a female companion of Catherine's. The Archpriest of the Grand Church of the Winter Palace performed the ceremony. When it was over the Czar sent a secret Ukase to the Senate bestowing the title "Most Serene Highness" and the name "Princess Yourievsky" upon his wife.

The Heir Apparent was told of the event when he returned to St. Petersburg a few days later, and although he was sworn to secrecy his brothers and their wives were soon exchanging information in muted and shocked tones. Alexander did not inform his family officially until the autumn when he presented his morganatic wife to them, and bade Catherine take her place beside him at the dinner table. "I should certainly not have married again before the end of the year's mourning," he explained to his sister Olga, "if the times in which we live had not been so critical and if I had not every day to run the risk that a fresh attack would successfully put an end to my life. I am concerned therefore to secure as soon as possible the future of the being who has lived only for me during the past fourteen years, as well as the three children she has borne me. Despite her youth, Princess Catherine Dolgorouky preferred to forego all the pleasures and amusements of society, which generally mean so much to young people of her age, in order to devote her whole life to surrounding me with love and care. She therefore has every right to my affection, my esteem, and my gratitude. She has literally never seen anyone except her only sister, and never mixed herself up in anything . . ."[10]

The Emperor's sons had no alternative but to accept the marriage with as good grace as possible, but their wives observed an icy politeness which clearly conveyed their distaste. The Grand Duke Alexander, the fourteen-year-old son of the Emperor's brother Michael, later described the embarrassment of the Sunday night supper at which Catherine and her three small children were presented formally to the family. When the Czar entered the room with his thirty-three-year-old wife on his arm, the ladies nodded curtly and looked the other way. "Princess Yourievsky gracefully acknowledged the formal bows of the Grand Duchesses and sat down in the Empress Marie Alexandrovna's chair! Prompted by curiosity, I never took my eyes off her. I liked the sad expression of her beautiful face and the radiance of her rich blonde hair. Her nervousness was obvious. Frequently she turned to the Emperor and he patted her hand gently. She would have succeeded in conquering the men had they not been watched by the women. Her efforts to join the general conversation were met with a polite silence. I felt sorry for her, and could not comprehend why she should be ostracised for loving a handsome, kind and cheerful man who happened to be the Emperor of Russia."[11]

At the end of dinner the three children were brought into the room by the governess. The eldest, George, was a boy of eight. He climbed on to the Emperor's lap and played with his sidewhiskers. "Tell me, Gogo, what is your full name?" asked Alexander. "I am Prince George Alexandrovich Yourievsky," replied the child. "Well, we are all very glad to have made your acquaintance, Prince Yourievsky. By the way, Prince, would you care to be a Grand Duke?" "Please, Sasha, don't," nervously said the Princess.

"This joking reference to the possibility of legitimising their morganatic children made her blush," wrote the Grand Duke Alexander. This was scarcely surprising, as it was not a scene calculated to melt the disapproval of the Grand Duchesses. The thought of Princess Yourievsky as Empress was unendurable. On the way home, the Grand Duke Alexander's mother lashed out at her husband. "No matter what you do or say," she blazed, "I shall never recognise that scheming adventuress. I hate her. She is despicable. Imagine her daring to call your brother 'Sasha' in the presence of all the members of the imperial family."[12]

Alexander chose to ignore the family animosity and pushed the Princess to the forefront with the insensitivity of a being bewitched. "That this woman," wrote the wife of the Emperor's second son, Vladimir, to Alexander of Hesse, "who for fourteen years has occupied such a very invidious position should be introduced to us as a member of the family surrounded by her three children is more painful than I can find words to express. She appears at family dinners large or small, and also in the private chapel before the whole court. We are forced to receive her and visit her. The Czar goes on visits with her in a closed carriage, though not yet in a sleigh. Since her influence is very great, things go a step farther every day, so that one cannot see where it will all end. Since the Princess is very uneducated, and has neither tact nor intellect, you can imagine the kind of life she leads us. Every feeling, every sacred memory, is trodden under foot, we are spared nothing . . . You can imagine the conflict that agitates us all . . . My heart is so full that I cannot find the right words to give you an idea of the complete overthrow of everything one had hitherto regarded as rules of conduct . . ."[13]

Meanwhile the terrorists had come to life again, stung into action, oddly enough, by the *Zemstvo* of Tver, the most liberal organisation in Russia. This group declared that Loris-Melikov had justified the hopes of Russia by creating a new atmosphere between Government and people and that "a happy future was opening up for our beloved country." Such a prediction filled Zheliabov and Sophia with alarm, for if the Armenian dictator succeeded in winning the confidence of the Liberals it would make the work of the revolutionaries impossible. Something had to be done immediately to shock the public and shake their confidence in the Government. A constitutional, evolutionary process would spell the end of the violent upheaval to which the terrorists were dedicated.

Their aim remained the same: to kill the Czar. This time they decided to dynamite the capital in a dozen different places, choosing the routes most frequently used by the Emperor. Streets, bridges, intersections, squares were charged with mines, planted in the night. Some were discovered by the police, others exploded killing dozens of innocent people.

It is not surprising that the public took fright. Soon exaggerated rumours of all sorts of diabolical plots were sweeping the capital. When the Emperor attended an Opera Gala before Christmas the house was half-empty as no one wanted to share his fate. In January, 1881, Dostoevsky told the editor of the Russian *Times* that tragedy was in the air. "You said that there had been some clairvoyance in my *Brothers Karamazov* . . . Wait till you have the sequel. . . I shall make my pure Aliosha join the terrorists and kill the Czar . . ."[14]

The Emperor's family were caught by the panic. "To say that we lived in a besieged fortress," wrote the Grand Duke Alexander, "would be using a poor simile. In war-time one knows one's friends and enemies. We never did. The butler serving morning coffee might have been in the employ of the Nihilists for all we knew. Ever since the November explosion a servant coming to clean the fire-place was a potential bearer of an infernal machine."[15]

Neither public nor private fears were groundless, for Zheliabov and Sophia did not care how many innocent people they killed so long as they succeeded in murdering the Czar. In February they became more impatient than ever, for they got wind that Loris-Melikov was planning to take the first step towards representative government. For weeks they had studied the Czar's routine and knew that in the winter he was in the habit of calling on the daughter of the Grand Duchess Elena at Michael Palace, after reviewing troops on the Michael Parade Ground. They therefore decided to look for premises in the neighbourhood and to mine the street over which his carriage was likely to pass. The Palace lay between the Catherine Canal and Little Garden Street and they were lucky enough to find empty rooms on the latter. Posing as M. and Mme. Kobozev, Sophia and Zheliabov rented the lodgings by the month, explaining that they were planning to open a dairy but did not wish to commit themselves to a long lease until the business was established. On the ground-floor they sold cream and butter and cheese; in the basement they started digging a tunnel which passed under the pavement to the middle of Little Garden Street. Kibaltchitch set up the mine which consisted of eighty pounds of dynamite attached to a battery; all was ready except for joining two wires.

For several Sundays, however, the Czar's carriage passed along the Catherine Canal rather than Little Garden Street. Meanwhile the authorities had grown suspicious of the dairy. The doorkeepers, who regularly earned money by reporting to the police, noted that not many customers entered the shop, yet the proprietors never complained about lack of business. On 28th February the police knocked on the door, explaining that they had come to "make a sanitary inspection." They were not very thorough for all they saw were several large barrels and nine wooden boxes filled with cheese. If they had emptied any one of them they would have found earth under the top layer.

When the intruders finally departed, Sophia and Zheliabov were weak with nerves. They decided that there was not a moment to lose, for the police might easily have second thoughts and call again. The mine would have to be abandoned and the assassination done by throwing bombs. At lunch time Zheliabov "sounded a call" which, in revolutionary parlance, was an urgent summons for volunteers willing to sacrifice themselves. But that very evening Zheliabov was arrested for his complicity in the mining of the railway near Odessa, sixteen months earlier. He had been picked up as a result of Goldenberg's evidence.

A Polish revolutionary, a girl named Rina, saw Sophia Perovskaya, the day after her lover had been imprisoned. They met at the house of a man named Olenin. "White as a sheet she could scarcely drag one foot after another, and no sooner had she entered the room than she reclined on the sofa . . . She told us that she had spent her last farthing because she had been followed by a spy, and compelled to change her cab several times in order to escape. She added that she was not even sure she had succeeded, and that at any moment the police might come to Olenin's to arrest her. It was essential that Sophia should leave as quickly as possible . . . I had in my pocket a number of copies of *Narodnaia Volia*. Rather than let them be burnt Sophia took them with her, saying that if she were arrested with such things about her, it would not make any difference . . ."[16] Sophia's dejection was misleading as she had decided to carry out Zheliabov's mission.

On the morning of 12th March Loris-Melikov called at the Winter Palace with an official manifesto for Alexander to sign. It was an historic document declaring that delegates from the *Zemstvoes*, regardless of class or financial considerations, would be invited to enter a radically reformed Council of State. It was, as Sophia Perovskaya had feared, the first step toward parliamentary government. Alexander affixed his signature and gave permission for the document to be published in the Monday papers. Before leaving, Loris-Melikov informed the Emperor that the terrorist, Zheliabov, had been picked up by the police but that Sophia Perovskaya and several other dangerous revolutionaries were still at large, probably about fifteen in all. He begged the Emperor not to attend the Sunday Parade at the Michael Riding School, but Alexander laughed and said he could not remain a prisoner in his own palace.

The next day the Emperor left the Palace at a quarter to one in his armour-plated carriage. He was accompanied by an escort of six Cossacks and followed by two sledges carrying an equerry, Colonel Dvorzhitsky, and senior police officials. After the parade, he stopped to pay a short visit on his cousin, the Grand Duchess Catherine, who lived in the Michael Palace next to the parade ground. Then he gave orders to his coachman to hurry back to the Winter Palace as he had an appointment before 3 p.m. Four magnificent greys from the famous Orlov stable were pulling his carriage, and moved so fast over the hard-packed snow that the Cossack guard broke into a gallop. The carriage went down Engineers' Street which was patrolled by plain-clothes men, on orders from Loris-Melikov. But the coachman, knowing that the Emperor was in a hurry, took a short cut on his own initiative, suddenly turning right into Catherine Canal Quay. Sophia Perovskaya, disguised as a herring woman, saw the change in the route and signalled her accomplices by waving a handkerchief. The broad quay was deserted except for a small boy carrying a bread basket, and a young artillery officer. Another young man carrying a parcel suddenly appeared breathless from a corner and as the Emperor's carriage drew near him he threw his parcel in front of the horses. The explosion could be heard at the Winter Palace. When the smoke thinned out the little errand boy, two of the Cossacks and three horses were lying in a river of blood. The wheels of the Emperor's carriage were shattered, but Alexander climbed out unhurt. The police had leapt from their sledges and caught the assassin. People came running from all directions. The equerry and the coachman begged the Emperor to get into Colonel Dvorzhitsky's sledge and drive back to the Palace as quickly as possible. "Yes, yes, but these poor people must be seen to." "Thank God your Majesty is safe," said one of the police officers. "I am, thank God, but look at these . . ." "Rather too early to thank God," shouted a voice as Alexander was moving toward the sledge. A man raised his arm and threw what looked like a snowball at the Czar's feet. The second explosion was so loud it shook the quay from end to end. Smoke and snow blinded the crowd. When it cleared more than twenty people were lying on the ground, their blood staining the white road. The Emperor half-lay, half-sat, his back to the canal railings. His face was streaming with blood, his abdomen was torn open, his legs shattered. "Quickly. Home to the Palace to die," he murmured and lost consciousness.

Everyone at the Winter Palace knew what had happened before the sledge arrived, for they had heard the explosions. "We . . . started a mad race toward the Winter Palace," wrote the Grand Duke Alexander Mikhailovich, "passing on our way the Preobrajensky Regiment of the Guard doubling in the same direction with fixed bayonets. Thousands of people were already surrounding the palace . . . there was no need to ask questions; large drops of black blood showed us the way up the marble steps and then along a corridor into the Emperor's study . . . The Emperor lay on the couch near the desk. He was unconscious. Three doctors were fussing around but science was obviously helpless . . . He presented a terrific sight, his right leg torn off, his left leg shattered, innumerable wounds all over his head and face. One eye was shut, the other expression- less . . . Princess Yourievsky burst in, half dressed. Something or perhaps some over-zealous guard had detained her. She fell flat on the couch over the body of the Czar, kissing his hands and screaming: 'Sasha, Sasha!' " A few minutes later the Emperor was dead. The Princess dropped on the floor "like a felled tree." Her pink and white negligee was soaked in blood.[17]

By now the crowd in front of the Winter Palace numbered over ten thousand, many of the people kneeling bareheaded in the snow. The Grand Duke Vladimir came out on the balcony and announced the Emperor's death in traditional Russian fashion. Because of super- stition the word "death" was not used. "The Emperor has bidden you to live long," he cried, and the words conveyed their message.

Russia was numbed by the horror of what had happened. Even those who had been bitterly critical of Alexander cried out in misery. "Anguish, sorrow, shame—such are the feelings of every Russian heart," wrote Ivan Aksakov. "What were his failings compared to his virtues?" asked another critic, Sobolevsky. "Let us not argue about him . . . He lived by his resolve to do good for his people . . ." But it was Prince Golytsin who spoke the deepest truth. "The very lowest rag and bone pedlar of Okhotny Road knows himself orphaned." Even Rina, the Polish revolutionary, who had been hiding at Gatchina and travelled to St. Petersburg four days after the outrage, was forced to recognise the signs of sorrow. "The city, in mourning throughout, oppressed the mind," she wrote. "The lamps, the houses, the balconies, the windows, all were covered with mournful stripes of black and white."[18]

The Emperor's body lay in the Mortuary Chapel of the Winter Palace for five days before it was carried to the Fortress Cathedral. Morning and night priests chanted around the catafalque. "To-day," wrote the Procurator of the Holy Synod, "I took the service in the mortuary chapel. After the public prayers, and when everyone had retired, I saw the widow enter from the next room. She could hardly keep upright; her sister was supporting her; Ryleev led the way. She fell on her knees beside the coffin. The dead Emperor's face is covered with a veil which no one is allowed to raise; but leaning over she quickly pulled it aside and covered the brow and face with long kisses. Then, tottering, she went out. I felt very sorry for the poor woman."[19] Later that night, Catherine came back to the chapel. She had cut off her beautiful hair, and placed it in the dead man's hand as her last gesture.

The funeral blazed with candles and sombre pageantry and wonderful singing. A young French diplomat, Maurice Paléologue, who had just arrived in St. Petersburg for the first time, was counselled by the brilliant Eugène Melchior de Vogüé, to take a good look at the dead Sovereign; he was the man who had enfranchised the serfs, abolished corporal punishment, instituted the jury and established equality before the law. "He brought the eagles of Moscovy to the shores of the Propontis, the very walls of Constantinople; he delivered the Bulgars; he established Russian dominion in the heart of Asia. Finally, on the very morning of his death he was working on a reform which . . . would have launched Russia irrevocably along the track of the modern world: the granting of a Parliamentary charter . . . And the Nihilists have killed him . . . Oh, a Liberator's is a dangerous job!"[20]

Zheliabov was in prison at the time of the murder; Rysakov, the first bomb-thrower, a nineteen-year-old student at the St. Petersburg Mining Institute, had been captured at the scene of the crime; Grinevitsky, the actual slayer, a Pole who had answered the "call" and about whom little was known, had perished in the explosion; Kilbaltchitch, the chemist, was arrested a few days later; and so were Jessica Helfmann and Timofey Mikhailov, terrorists who had attended some of the early meetings. Only Sophia remained at large.

Rina, the Polish girl, had no idea that Sophia had taken part in the assassination. Four days after the killing she received an urgent message to meet her, and imagined that she wanted to be smuggled out of Russia because of the feverish activities of the police. They met at a friend's house and Rina saw that she was "enthusiastically excited by the terrible victory obtained by the Party." She had no wish to leave Russia; she wanted Rina to help her find out "something about the trial of the Czaricides." "The idea," wrote Rina, "was to go to a very great personage, an 'Excellency,' a man connected with the Superior Police, who undoubtedly would be able to give us some information respecting the trial, although the investigations were being carried out with the utmost secrecy. This man was not in regular communication with the Nihilists. It so happened I had known him personally for some years. That is why Perovskaya had thought of me. She was very anxious about it. The man she loved was among the accused. Although terribly compromised, it so happened that he had taken no direct part in the events of 13th March: and Sophia hoped . . ."[21]

The very fact that Rina, a revolutionary, could call on a high official in the confidence of the police, and get the information she was after, is revealing. The Excellency apparently received her warmly and told her that "the fate of Zheliabov, as of all the others, was irrevocably fixed. The trial was to be merely *pro forma* for appearance sake." Rina communicated the news to Sophia that same evening. "I did not see her face for her eyes were cast down," Rina wrote. "When she raised them I saw that she was trembling all over. Then she grasped my hands, sank down, and buried her face in my lap. She remained thus for several minutes; she did not weep but trembled all over. Then she arose and sat down, endeavouring to compose herself. But with a sudden movement she again grasped my hands, and pressed them so hard as to hurt me . . . 'His Excellency' had communicated to me many particulars respecting the proud and noble bearing of Zheliabov. When I related them to Sophia, I observed that her eyes flashed and the colour returned to her cheeks. Evidently it was a great relief to her. 'His Excellency' also told me that all the accused already knew the fate awaiting them, and had received the announcement of their approaching death with wonderful tranquillity and composure. On hearing this Sophia sighed. She suffered immensely. She wanted to weep but restrained herself. For a moment, however, her eyes were filled with tears . . ."[22]

The two girls parted at midnight; two days later Sophia was arrested.

The deeply religious Count Leo Tolstoy wrote to the new Czar and begged him not to execute the murderers. He had been horrified by the death of Alexander II. He had always opposed the use of terror and repeatedly told the long-haired youths who came to consult him (some of them from *Will of the People*) that their deeds, far from carrying the stamp of nobility, sinned against Christian morality. "The revolutionary and the Christian," he said, "are at opposite ends of an open circle. Their proximity is only apparent. In reality, no two points could be farther apart. To meet, they would have to turn around and travel back over the entire circumference."[23]

Tolstoy could not rid his mind of the nightmare of the Czar's death. A week after the killing, when he took an afternoon nap on his leather sofa, he had a dream: "in the courtroom, it was himself, not the murderers, who was standing trial; and he was the judge too; and Alexander III; and the executioner. He pronounced, carried out and was the victim of the sentence." He awoke in a cold sweat but he knew what should be done. Evil was destroying the structure of society; it was spreading everywhere, poisoning the minds of guilty and innocent alike. The new Czar Alexander III must return to the law of God and pardon his father's killers. His eyes brimming with tears, he wrote to the new Emperor, ". . . it is true that it is presumption and folly on my part to demand that you, the Emperor of Russia and a loving son, should pardon your father's murderers in spite of the pressure of those around you, returning good for evil. It is folly, yet I cannot do otherwise than wish it . . . These young revolutionaries aspire to heaven only knows what new order, or rather none at all, and, by the basest most inhuman method, fire and robbery and murder, they are destroying the structure of society . . . People have tried in the name of the State and for the welfare of the people, to suppress, deport and execute them; people have also tried, in the name of the same State and the same welfare of the people, to treat them humanely. The result has been the same in both cases. Why not try, then, in the name of God, to carry out His law, thinking neither of the State nor the people? . . ."[24]

Alexander III's advisers had warned him that some such appeal might be put before him. "Rest assured," he wrote firmly, "no one will dare to come to me with such a request and I promise you that *all six of them will hang.*" Tolstoy did dare. His letter was put on the Czar's desk by the Grand Duke Serge. Tolstoy was much too famous for the autocrat to lay a finger on. But the plea, needless to say, was tossed aside. The trial was conducted by "The Special Committee of the Senate for State Offences." There was no jury but the court was open, and the accused had counsel. Jessica Helfmann escaped the noose because she was pregnant; but Sophia and the four men, Zheliabov, Rysakov, Kilbaltchitch and Mikhailov, were sentenced to death.

The execution took place at nine o'clock in the morning of 3rd April at the Parade Ground of the Seminovsky Regiment. Several thousand people gathered to watch the spectacle. The prisoners were conveyed through the streets in two wooden carts to the sombre roll of drums; their hands and feet were strapped to their seats and on the chest of each was a placard with the word: Czaricide. The crowd grew noisy as the prisoners climbed the steps of the scaffold, a platform six feet high and twelve yards square bearing five gallows. A priest spoke to the condemned and held a cross to the lips of each; no one refused it. The hangman, a criminal released from prison for the morning, dressed in a red shirt, covered the heads of the prisoners with white shrouds. Kibaltchitch was hanged first, then Mikhailov, Perovskaya and Zheliabov. Rysakov was last. His legs shook as the hangman threw the noose around his neck. When the dreaded moment was almost upon him he tried to cling to the stool on which he was standing, and a macabre struggle took place until the hangman pulled it from under him. The corpses were cut down after twenty minutes, examined by a doctor, and placed in coffins with wood shavings at the head. Hundreds of people surged toward the gallows but two lines of Cossacks held them back. The movement was not a gesture of sympathy. It sprang from the widespread superstition that a piece of rope from the neck of a hanged man was lucky.

Sophia Perovskaya and her lover, Zheliabov, had made certain that

Russia would move into the twentieth century in a river of blood, for the assassination convinced Alexander III that the nation was not ready even for the mildest form of representative government. He tore up his father's Manifesto and informed his Ministers that he intended to rule with the same firmness used by his grandfather, Nicholas I.

VI

A Cousin's Vendetta

THE CZAR'S DEATH came as a stunning blow to the twenty-four-year-old Alexander of Battenberg, who lived in the precarious world underpinned by his uncle's power. The adventure had begun two years earlier with the decision of the Berlin Congress to establish an independent Bulgaria ruled by a prince of its choice. Alexander of Hesse had wasted no time in hurrying to the capital and putting forward the name of his son as a candidate. The Czar remarked gloomily to the Empress that he could not imagine anyone coveting the job, as the clash between Bulgarian nationalism and Russian imperialism was bound to be violent and prolonged. Marie repeated the Emperor's remarks to her brother and added, ". . . I feel the same. I should be wretched to think of one of my sons being in such a difficult position."[1]

Alexander of Hesse, however, refused to listen. Although he moaned that Alexander of Battenberg would have "to sacrifice his youth in the arduous task" he did everything to press his case. It was not easy to find a prince with the right qualifications, as Russian and Bulgarian nationals were frowned upon; yet it was desirable that the candidate have close ties with both these countries. Alexander of Battenberg was related to the Russian imperial family; had links with the German and English royal families; and, best of all, had served in the Russian Army which had liberated Bulgaria. He seemed the obvious choice. Lord Salisbury, the British Foreign Secretary, was certain the young man would eagerly grasp "the thorny crown" if it were offered him. With the arrogance of a *grand seigneur* he wrote to Queen Victoria that as Alexander "was

poor and nothing but a lieutenant he might look upon the principality of Bulgaria as a promotion."[2]

At the time of Alexander II's assassination Sandro had spent two
years as Prince of Bulgaria, almost every minute of which had been
a nightmare. Even his initial entry into the country had been far
from triumphant. Travelling by ship from Constantinople to Varna,
he had contracted dysentery, and the Russian Commissioner who
came aboard to welcome him, found him deathly pale, prostrate
in his bunk. The festivities had to be delayed four hours after which
the Prince made a supreme effort and went ashore to greet his
new subjects. The week's journey around his dominion was torture, and the sight of his capital such a shock that he had to go to bed
again.

Sophia, with a population of less than 18,000, was more a village
than a town. Although it was set on a plain surrounded by snow-
capped mountains, prompting some people to refer to it as "nature's
jewel," it was unbelievably squalid. There were no pavements, only
mud roads; the shops were roofless Eastern bazaars; the houses,
mostly Turkish, slatternly and thrown together in a jumble, only
the richest having glass windows. There was no gas, no light and
no drainage. The smell was appalling and very difficult to escape,
as Sophia was not linked to a railway and the roads were so bad that
no one travelled for pleasure.

The palace resembled a third-rate English inn. Built for the Russian Commissioner at the time of the Turkish war, the Prince
considered most of the rooms unfit to live in. "The disgraceful way
in which the few things that the Russians did here were carried out,"
he wrote to his father, "is shown by the fact that in three rooms and
in a passage the ceilings *fell in* with a crash like a cannon shot.
Thank goodness nobody was there at the time or they would certainly have been killed—In consequence a scaffolding has been put
up over my bed in case I should be flattened out one night. The
ceilings in *all* the rooms have to be taken down now, so that the
palace is in a horrible mess . . ."[3]

The political outlook was even worse than the domestic arrangements, as the Berlin Congress had not designed Bulgaria for the
Bulgarians but to meet the objections of the Powers. England and

Austria had persuaded the conference to divide the country into two sections to thwart Russian expansion; and Russia had countered by endowing the main principality with one of the most democratic constitutions in Europe. This was part of a cunning scheme to encourage the lost province, Eastern Roumelia, administered by a Turkish Governor, to start a movement for unification.

No one could pretend that it was easy to turn a peasant country, ninety per cent of whose inhabitants were illiterate, into a thriving democracy overnight. The Prince was appalled by the limitations on his powers. He discovered that, although he could appoint his own Cabinet Ministers, he could not enact laws or raise money without the approval of the National Assembly. Only two parties mattered; the Conservatives, who favoured more power for the Prince at the expense of the Assembly; and the Liberals, who favoured more power for the Assembly at the expense of the Prince. The Liberals had the overwhelming support of the country and commanded a large majority in the parliament; but as many of the elected delegates could not read or write it was almost impossible to find enough educated Bulgarians to take over the ministerial jobs without having to call on the Russians.

Yet it was clear to the Prince from the very start that if he wished to establish Bulgaria as the "autonomous province" envisaged by the Berlin Treaty, the Russians presented his greatest danger. Russian soldiers had been in occupation of the country while a Russian Governor-General, Prince Dondukov, drew up the Constitution. Although St. Petersburg had withdrawn its troops before the Prince's arrival, 200 Russian officers and a good many civilians had remained behind and installed themselves in all the most important civil and military posts. Despite the fact that Prince Alexander had the backing of the Czar these officials did not hide their resentment at the appearance of "a German ruler." Still smarting from the humiliation of the Berlin Congress many of them boasted that they would take a leaf from the Panslav book of 1876 and promote Russian interests in the way they saw fit. Indeed, the 200 officers had already set about it. As Bulgaria was not allowed an army under the Treaty they had accepted contracts from the Bulgarian Minister of War—a Russian national—to form and command a militia which would fill the military vacuum. They swaggered around the capital, as though they owned it. "Russian officers form the aristocracy of Sophia," reported an English journalist. "They roll about in carriages, and are looked at with no good will by educated Bulgarians. I was walking with the postmaster of Sophia, when one of these officers dashed past in his carriage with two horses. 'Ah,' said my friend, 'these fellows remain in Bulgaria because they are far better paid here than in their own country'."[4]

Indeed, Russians seemed to be swarming over the whole of Bulgaria, for St. Petersburg, far from reducing its commitments, was flooding the country with consulates, diplomatic missions and special agencies. As well as these officials, Russian business men, adventurers, and unemployed revolutionaries had flowed in looking for lucrative jobs. "All the scum of Russia has taken refuge here and has tainted the whole country," the Prince wrote to his father; "and the man under whose protection all this gang has collected is Dondukoff. Thanks to Dondukoff's dispensations the Russian system of bribery has actually been sanctioned, and every day I find myself faced with the painful necessity either of agreeing to the *most impudent* demands or being accused in St. Petersburg of treason . . ."[5]

The Prince felt the strain of his responsibility all the more acutely as the capital had few amusements. The Bulgarians never invited people to dinner as they felt their houses were not grand enough. There was only one public bar, the Café Chantant, which was packed with Russians who grew very drunk as the evening progressed. There were no tennis courts, not even a cricket pitch, which dismayed the English journalist. The only relaxation was the hot spring baths several miles outside the capital. But, as the journalist pointed out, they were not worth a trip to Bulgaria, so foreigners had best be content to read about them.

Even worse than the lack of amusement was the fact that the Prince had no friends in whom he could confide. He sensed the thick web of intrigue spun around him, but it was some weeks before he discovered that he was being kept under close surveillance. "Just think," he wrote furiously to his father, "the men the Russians left here for me as footmen, lackeys, etc., are *Russian agents*! I trust *nobody*, not even my friends; and you know how foreign that is to my character—how I love to be frank and open! . . . At times I feel I shall burst, because I am so longing to talk to somebody and cannot . . . Every party has its spies in the palace, because each is hoping to get some hold over me and have me at its mercy. Though I am so worried and anxious internally, I have to hide it under an air of great calm and assurance, and always be suave with everyone . . . My worst enemies are the Russians, and I have to be so desperately careful to save my own skin without injuring Czar Alexander."[6]

It was not surprising that the Prince soon acquired the reputation of being "anti-Russian." If Russian duplicity had shocked him in Turkey he found it even more distasteful in Bulgaria. What he minded most was the cynicism. Although Russian officers and officials complained that the Liberal party was filled with revolutionaries, they supported it quite cynically in order to thwart the Prince and to give the appearance of being "on the side of the people." Alexander refused to ally himself with the Liberals because they were pledged to whittle away his powers and he did not believe it was possible to rule without a strong executive. He flew in the face of public opinion by selecting all his ministers from Conservative ranks, except for the Minister of War who was foisted on him by St. Petersburg. Consequently the National Assembly became as noisy as a prize fight. Russian personnel were allowed to sit in the Chamber, and flowed on to opposition benches to take part in the debates. The pandemonium was so great ministers could scarcely make themselves heard. The Prince complained to the Czar that it was impossible to rule with such a farcical constitution. The people were too backward for a democracy and, unless the monarchy was strengthened, the country would fall into a state of anarchy. Alexander II, however, begged his nephew not to make difficulties and to get on as best he could.

Undoubtedly the Prince was right to denounce the constitution, but he was not without fault himself. He was young and impetuous and had a dangerous habit of blurting out what he thought. His lack of political experience made matters worse, for he knew nothing of dissimulation or even the art of persuasion. His education had been entirely military, first as a cadet in the Hessian Dragoons, then as a lieutenant in the Prussian *Garde de Corps*. Perhaps his greatest handicap was his German thoroughness and his insistence on the observance of protocol. He allowed a major quarrel to develop between himself and the Russian Army Officers because they addressed him as Excellency and not as Highness. He disliked the sloppiness of his Bulgarian bodyguard, modelled on Cossack lines, and tactlessly suggested the incorporation of German officers; and although he often remarked that he "worshipped his uncle, the Czar," he just as often spoiled it by adding "but Russia is not for me." His most implacable enemy was General Parsenev, the Minister of War, a cousin of the new Russian Foreign Secretary, M. Giers. Parsenev had been sent to Bulgaria to rebuild an army as a spearhead against Turkey. As St. Petersburg failed to send any guns and ammunition he was forced to train his men on captured Turkish material which did not lighten his task. Nevertheless he was so lax and inefficient that the Prince urged him to take Prussian officers on to his staff. This suggestion was received as a deadly insult, with the result that Parsenev wrote damaging reports about the Prince to his superiors at home, referring to him openly as "the German."

During the first year of his reign the Prince had only one supporter in the whole of Sophia, surprisingly enough the Russian Consul-General. This gentleman, M. Davydov, hated Bulgaria with a rare passion. He loathed the lies and corruption, the ignorance and primitive conditions. He begged Giers repeatedly to remove him from the awful backwater, writing that he would "go willingly no matter where and in no matter what capacity rather than stay here." When finally he was transferred—at the end of a year—he wrote joyfully: "I am finally out of that galley. All that I ask is that no one will ever mention the word Bulgaria to me again."[7]

Nevertheless he was a great strength while he remained, as he agreed with the Prince that the constitution was an impossible document. "It is," he wrote to Giers, "an absurdity in theory and an insanity in practice ... It is our duty to save this country from the consequences of a mistake that we have committed."[8] The Prince made several journeys to St. Petersburg to try and persuade his uncle to allow him to tear up the hated constitution and start again;

but the Czar was too concerned with the revolutionary terror inside Russia to give much attention to his nephew's problems, and his ministers advised against allowing the Prince to extend his own authority. On one of the visits to St. Petersburg, in February 1880, the Prince had no sooner set foot in the Winter Palace than the explosion took place which blew up the dining-room and killed so many Finnish Guards.

The following year, in January 1881, he wrote to the Czar that a crisis was bound to come, for his country was drifting into chaos. A month later Alexander II was dead.

The new Czar, Alexander III, had none of the charm of his father. A wooden-minded giant of a man who disliked society and, unlike his predecessors, was a model husband, his chief claim to fame was his fabulous strength. He could tear a pack of playing cards in half, bend a poker over his knee, and crush a horse-shoe in one hand. While his elder brother, Nicholas, who died of spinal tuberculosis at the age of twenty-two, had received the appropriate education for the Heir to the throne, Alexander had spent his youth in the army. In home affairs he was deeply Conservative. Upon his accession he sent for his old tutor, Pobedonostev, the procurator of the Holy Synod, one of the most reactionary men in the Empire, and asked for guidance. Pobedonostev, who later became known as "the black Czar", had an ascetic air, steel-cold eyes and a remarkable intellect. He stood for autocracy, anti-semitism and panslavism. He was appalled by the unsigned document lying on the dead Emperor's desk, introducing the first measure of representative government, and referred bluntly to some of Alexander's earlier reforms as "criminal." No one was surprised a few weeks later to learn that Loris-Melikov's manifesto had been scrapped; that the Czar had accepted the resignation of his father's liberal ministers; that not only would Alexander III's autocratic powers remain unimpaired but that a new *régime de sévérité* had begun.

Unlike his father, Alexander III responded to the entreaties of the police who had been complaining for years that it was impossible to maintain satisfactory security precautions in the capital. He moved his household from St. Petersburg to Gatchina Palace, forty miles westward. This vast building with 900 rooms had not been lived in since the days of Paul I. It lay in a huge park with a river and several artificial lakes. It consisted of two colossal quadrangles joined together by a narrow, curved, colonnaded wing of several floors, on top of which were two towers. Paul I, who died at the hands of a murderer, had slept in one of them and the bedroom was said to be haunted.

Apparently Gatchina's isolation made it easier to guard than any other imperial palace. Certainly every precaution was taken. "Round the wall of the park," wrote an eye-witness, "is stationed a chain of sentries placed at distances of twenty-five metres, who are changed every hour, in order that the surveillance may be vigorously applied. Entry into the park and Castle is not permitted, even to the servants and to the employees of the Imperial Cabinet, without presentation of a special card which is changed every week. Besides this, all persons residing at the Castle, whatever their rank and station may be, are forbidden to lock their doors either by day or night. General Richter, General Inspector of the Imperial residence, and General Tcherevin, Chief of the Police, are entitled to make investigations in the apartments of the Castle whenever they think proper. Gatchina is surrounded by a positively entrenched camp, and one would hardly believe, in passing it by on the railway, that a whole army was there simply to protect the life of one man."[9]

Alexander preferred Gatchina to any other palace for although he was ringed in by battalions of soldiers and servants the serene countryside suggested remoteness, and encouraged him to live as simply as he chose. He frequently referred to himself as "the moujik Czar" and maintained the strict personal discipline of his grandfather. According to his daughter Olga, he "was up at seven every morning, washed in cold water, dressed himself in peasant clothes, made his own coffee in a glass percolator, filled a plate with cracknels, and his breakfast eaten, he went to his desk and settled to the day's work. There was an army of servants to wait on him. He disturbed none of them. There were bells in the study. He did not ring them. Some time later his wife joined him, and a small table was brought by two servants. Husband and wife shared a breakfast of boiled eggs and rye bread and butter." Despite his many preoccupations he always found time for his children. He let the small ones patter into his study and sit under the desk; sometimes he allowed them to put the imperial seal, made of gold and crystal, on official communications. Frequently he took the two youngest, Michael and Olga, for walks in the forest, each carrying a spade, a hatchet, a lantern and an apple. He taught them how to clear paths in the snow, to cut down dead trees and to roast apples over a fire.[10]

A steady stream of ministers and diplomats travelled from the capital to Gatchina but the Czar's friends were few. Pobedonostev was one; so was General Tcherevin, head of the *Ochrana*; and for a short time Count Ignatiev, who became Minister of the Interior but was dismissed at the end of a year and went into retirement. Probably the man closest to the Czar was Count Vorontsov-Dashkov who had served with him as Chief-of-Staff of the Guards Corps. The Count had infected Alexander with his passionate Panslavism, and together they had worked to bring about the war with Turkey. Vorontsov-Dashkov had now become Minister of Court and remained the Emperor's confidant throughout the reign.

Although the Czar commanded the affection of his family, St. Petersburg society found him incredibly stiff and dull. He always spent several weeks in the capital in the winter and gave the balls and receptions expected of him, but made no attempt to rival his father's magnificence. As his wife, the sister of England's Princess of Wales, loved clothes and dancing he did just enough entertaining to keep her from complaining. Sometimes during a ball he sat in an anteroom playing bridge; other times he paced up and down looking at his watch. He had a habit of dismissing the members of the orchestra one by one. When a solitary man remained, usually the pianist, the Empress would turn reluctantly to the guests: "I suppose the Emperor wants us to go to bed."

As the Prince of Bulgaria was high-spirited and loved pretty women, he had always found his cousin remarkably uninteresting. The cousin, in turn, seemed resentful of Alexander II's affection for the Hesse-Battenberg family. Nevertheless the two men had established a pleasant, if restrained, relationship in the Russo-Turkish war. Sandro was well aware of his cousin's conservative outlook and at Alexander II's funeral predicted to his father that great changes were bound to take place under the new Czar.

It was not altogether surprising that Sandro decided to exploit the inevitable period of reaction by scrapping his own constitution. In April, two and a half months after his uncle's death, he convened his National Assembly and delivered an ultimatum. An election would be held in three weeks' time: unless a majority of the new delegates granted him special powers to revise the constitution he would lay down the crown.

If the Czar was nettled by the fact that Alexander had taken this action without consulting him he did not show it. "I ... have always held that this was the only solution for the disgusting situation in which the Prince found himself," he commented.[11] And when the Liberals appealed to him "to remind the Prince of his oaths to defend the constitution" he wrote on the petition: "I do not accept any telegrams from revolutionaries and these Liberals are not anything else but socialists. The Bulgarian people will support the Prince —for these are only a band of rowdies and cowards." The Prince rubbed his hands in glee, for Russian approval was all that was needed to tip the scales in his favour. When the election results were declared the Conservatives had won every seat except four, and the *Sobranje* speedily granted the Prince the powers he requested.

At this point all should have been well, for at last Sandro of Battenberg was free of Liberal interference. Yet the unexpected happened. Russia's diplomatic representative, M. Hitrovo, began to make difficulties over the railway issue. The Austrians were pressing the Prince to undertake his share of an international railway line —one of the provisions of the Berlin Treaty—which would run through Bulgaria from Vienna to Constantinople. The Russians, on the other hand, were eager to see the construction of an internal line which would start in the neighbourhood of Sistove on the Danube, cross the Balkan mountains and run along the Maritsa River Valley, more or less following the route taken by the Russian Army in its advance to Adrianople. The project offered no economic advantages to Bulgaria but would aid the Russians if they wished to move their troops to the Straits. Since Bulgaria could not afford two lines, the Prince asked the Czar if he would finance the Russian proposal but the answer was no. As Austria was backing a commercial venture that would enrich Bulgaria, it is scarcely surprising, quite apart from the Treaty obligation, that the Prince favoured the latter.

M. Hitrovo was furious. Undoubtedly he hoped to make money from the Russian line, for there is no other explanation for his unreasonable attitude. He rampaged around Sophia accusing the Prince of Austrian sympathies and stirring up all the dissident elements against him. He distributed bribes freely and even managed to subvert some of the Prince's Conservative ministers who agreed to adopt a policy of obstruction. Gradually the wheels of Government began to grind to a halt.

At his wits' end, Alexander was forced to the conclusion that he could not govern without the help of St. Petersburg. His hope had been to rule the country with his Conservative majority, independent of Liberals and Russians alike; now the only course open to him was to ask the Czar to send two Russian administrators who would take over the key Ministries of War and the Interior and keep their nationals in order.

His spirits were somewhat dampened, however, when he arrived in Russia in the spring of 1882 and discovered that all sorts of disgraceful stories were circulating about his doings in Bulgaria. The press was hostile, ministers evasive. The Czar was civil but detached; although he agreed to remove Hitrovo and to send two administrators he gave the impression of being too preoccupied with domestic affairs to take much interest in Bulgaria. Indeed, the Prince was shocked at how remote he had become, living most of the year at Gatchina, hemmed in by cordons of soldiers and police. He came to the conclusion that the Czar was a cipher and the government almost non-existent. "The press slanders me and finds willing listeners," he wrote to his father, "and nobody believes what I say because I speak as an interested party. I cannot get away until I have found ministers. St. Petersburg is a dreadful place. No Czar, no royal family, no government, nothing! Not a single theatre. I live here as I do in Sophia, and am melancholy and dispirited."[12]

Alexander III, however, was far from being a cipher. He knew

The Emperor Nicholas I of Russia, *engraved by G. Cook*

The Emperor Alexander II of Russia

Empress Marie of Russia, *after Winterhalter*

Princess Catherine Dolgorouky

The Battle for Plevna, 1877

Osman Pasha in 1880,
engraving by G. J. Stodart

The assassination of the Emperor Alexander II of Russia

The conspirators of March 1st, 1881, on the scaffold

The Emperor Alexander III of Russia

Sergey Nechayev

Leo Tolstoy in 1873
at the age of 45

Alexander of Battenberg

Princess Victoria of Prussia

King Ferdinand of Bulgaria, aged about 30

King Alexander of Serbia

Queen Draga of Serbia

E. F. Asev bathing with his mistress

The Emperor Nicholas II of Russia shooting,
with the Empress beside him

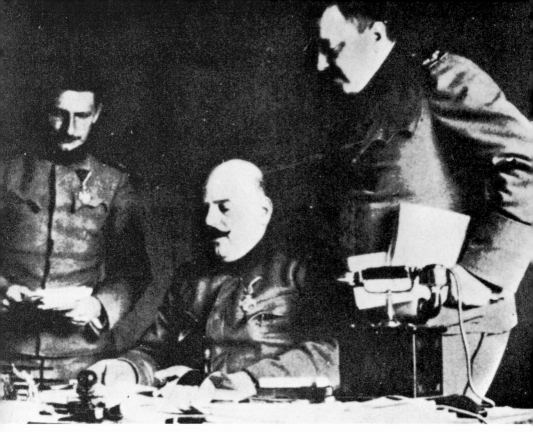

Colonel Apis

Gavrilo Princip

The arrival of Franz Ferdinand
at Sarajevo

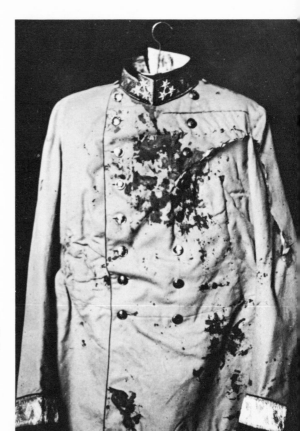

Franz Ferdinand's bloodstained jacket
after the assassination

The Emperor Nicholas II of Russia
with the Grand Duke Nicholas

exactly what he wanted. Although Russia was too impoverished to fight another European war he was determined to re-create the Greater Bulgaria that Count Ignatiev had sketched out at San Stefano. Such a country, dominated by Russia, would give militarists and Panslavs all that they desired; control of the Straits and access to the Mediterranean, not only by way of the Bosphorus but through a foot-hold on the Adriatic; and finally, by the acquisition of Macedonia (under Turkish rule and also lopped off by the Berlin Congress), a barrier to Austrian penetration and Russian mastery of the Balkans.

The Czar was not deterred by the fact that in 1881 his father had joined with Germany and Austria in reviving the Three Emperors' League and converting it into an alliance which, among other things, was pledged to observe the *status quo* in the Balkans. Open aggression was out of the question but there was no reason not to advance by stealth. The Panslav agitation of 1876 had set a new pattern of Imperialism; expansion by subversion.

Subversion, of course, required conspiratorial experience, but plenty of Russians had that. The Panslavs had taken a leaf from the revolutionaries' book, and now ordinary Czarist officials were studying the methods of the Panslavs. The object was to unite Roumelia with Bulgaria, in defiance of the Berlin Treaty, but to make it look like a spontaneous happening. As Roumelia was not allowed an army General Sobolev had visited the country and set up Gymnastic Societies whose secret purpose was drill and military training. Large supplies of Russian arms had been smuggled into the country and hundreds of agents, many of them members of Russian revolutionary groups, were engaged in organisation and propaganda. In 1882 one of these men conceived the brilliant idea of erecting a fortress under the very nose of the Turkish Governors. The intention was to build a church to commemorate a Russian victory in the last war. But when the Russians submitted the plan to the authorities, the British minister reported to London that the building had "walls of great thickness, cellars in which vast quantities of arms might be stored, and cells for monks which constituted a series of Block Houses, the cost of which edifice, it was estimated would amount to three million francs."[13] Needless to say the project was rejected.

The Czar's plans depended, of course, upon keeping Bulgaria firmly within the Russian sphere of interest. The loyalty of the Prince of Bulgaria was important, but Alexander III was not wholly dependent on him. He had another card up his sleeve. The Bulgarian militia, specified by the Berlin Treaty, had already swollen into an army; and the Bulgarian War Ministry, controlled by a Russian national, prohibited Bulgarians from rising above the rank of captain. All the higher grades were occupied by Russians; and by 1882 300 Russian officers controlled the Bulgarian forces. The Czar did not envisage using this army against its own people. But he was convinced that he could bring Bulgaria to heel whenever he chose simply by withdrawing his officers. The army would find itself leaderless and powerless; anarchy would follow; and Russia would have an excuse to send her own troops into the country to restore order. This ingenious plan was regarded by everyone, from the highest General to the Foreign Secretary, M. Giers, to be the ultimate weapon of control.

The Emperor was suspicious of his cousin and tended to believe the discreditable stories he heard about him, particularly the accusation that he favoured Austria to the detriment of Russia. He was more than pleased, therefore, when the Prince asked him to send Russian administrators to Sophia. He approved the appointment of two generals, Sobolev and Kaulbars. Both were thirty-eight years of age; both were veterans of the Russo-Turkish war; and both proved a disaster. The Czar instructed them to act decisively; and as neither knew the meaning of the word tact they arrived bragging of their wide powers. Sobolev became Minister-President and Minister of the Interior and Kaulbars Minister of War. They moved into their new jobs and began to rule as though the Prince did not exist, issuing strings of decrees, riding rough-shod over their officials, disputing the rôle of the police, making trouble over the railway issue. Sobolev, who was nick-named "the Vice-Prince," affronted his Bulgarian Cabinet colleagues by telling them they were in office "at his pleasure." What angered the population most, however, was the scorn for Bulgarian ability. "The open preference," wrote a contemporary observer, "for all that is Russian and all that comes from Russia, the appointment of Russians to such duties which Bulgars could perform, the sending of our young officers to Russia, the flooding of the country with Russian officers who are brought in daily . . . these are the reasons for the growing dissatisfaction with the Russians by the minute."[14]

The generals were aware of their unpopularity and blamed it on the Prince. He was, they informed St. Petersburg, in the service of Austria-Hungary; he had no loyalty or gratitude for the Imperial family and his one aim was to destroy Russian influence in Bulgaria. The only way the growing Habsburg influence could be checked was by "energetic measures and by a definite programme for the foreign and domestic policy of the principality."[15] No doubt there was a grain of truth in some of these accusations for Alexander had always been repelled by Russian intrigue and corruption, but it was wholly false to accuse him of working for Austria. His tragedy was that he was trying to rule his country in the best interests of the people and continually fell between two stools.

The Prince did not realise the harm the generals had done him until he attended the Czar's coronation in the spring of 1883. He hoped to convince the Emperor that these arrogant proconsuls were alienating the whole of Bulgaria and must be recalled without delay. He travelled to Moscow accompanied by his father, Prince Alexander of Hesse. They both rode in the Coronation procession which was done with traditional grandeur despite the fact that everyone was nervous of Nihilist bombs. Indeed, when a woman in the crowd dropped her umbrella just as the Czar was passing on his milk-white stallion, people jumped with fright and the Czar fixed his eyes reproachfully on the unhappy offender who was overcome with embarrassment.

It did not take the two German Alexanders long to discover that they were almost *persona non grata*. The Czar refused to grant Sandro an audience until at last he "forced his way unbidden to his presence," but the interview was a failure, the Emperor refusing even to discuss the Generals. Much to Sandro's anger he learned that General Kaulbars had been insolent enough to send a delegation from Sophia asking "in the name of the Bulgarian people" that Prince Alexander should be replaced by Prince Waldemar of Denmark. Although father and son were invited to the large functions they were not included in any family gatherings. At the Court Ball on 28th May Alexander of Hesse was outraged to find that he was being introduced only "to ladies of lesser degree," and sent home, as he put it, "dripping with sweat" while the Czarina entertained a large party at supper. "I'll be damned," he said, "if anyone ever sees me in Russia again on any ceremonial occasion."[16] And they never did, for it was, in fact, the last time he set foot on Russian soil.

Alexander III was enraged with his cousin, for he believed every word that the generals had written. Shortly after the Prince returned to Bulgaria the Czar dispatched an emissary to Sophia to convey his displeasure and to impress upon the Prince that Kaulbars and Sobolev would remain in office. He chose the notorious Panslavist, Alexander Ionin, to carry out the mission, the same man who while serving as Russian Consul-General in Ragusa, had masterminded the revolt in Herzegovina and helped promote the Serbo-Turkish war.

Ionin was a small, wiry little man who considered himself an expert operator. When the Prince received him in audience he began in an insolent tone of command: "His Majesty is greatly displeased with you, Highness, and your conduct since your return from Moscow, has offended the Czar very deeply . . . Consequently the Czar orders the following measures to be taken: retention of the Generals for at least another year; immediate dissolution of the chamber and unconditional agreement by the Prince of everything demanded by the Generals; final disbandment of the 'clique' surrounding you and complete renunciation of the Prince's legislative and plenary powers." After a pause Ionin added: "The Emperor gave you these and it is he who now takes them away because you have made wrongful and fraudulent use of them."

"You seem to forget to whom you are speaking," said the Prince.

"As M. Ionin I beg your pardon for the expressions I use, but as the Ambassador of the Czar I am forced to repeat them, as I received a formal order to use this phraseology."[17]

M. Ionin would not have dared to use such language unless he had been sure of his ground. He had already conferred secretly with the Liberal leaders. In return for their support he had offered them a restoration of the Constitution which the Prince had snatched away in 1881. Ionin called upon Alexander three times and on each occasion was more insulting than the last, snapping out his demands in the form of an ultimatum. The Prince stalled but was deeply dejected as he felt that the battle was lost. The Liberals were certain to sweep the country in a new election and Ionin and the generals would be in a position to force his abdication if he did not agree to their demands.

Alexander, however, had not reckoned on the widespread hatred of the generals and that mysterious force known as public opinion. Suddenly the most remote peasants in the most remote villages seemed to know that Bulgaria was facing a crisis which might end in Russian domination. Men and women in all walks of life began to pledge their support to the Prince, begging him to save them from becoming a vassal state. Even the Liberals, who longed for power and had every reason to dislike the Prince, were disillusioned and frightened. When the National Assembly opened in September all the delegates, Conservative and Liberal alike, arrived at the Palace and told the Prince that they would form a coalition Government to resist the Russians if he would give them back their old constitution. Alexander agreed and appointed M. Zankov, the Liberal Leader, Prime Minister. Then he issued a decree demanding the resignation of Kaulbars and Sobolev.

The Czar was completely taken aback by the news. Not only had he disbelieved the Prince's stories about the unpopularity of his generals, but his Foreign Office had assured him that the Liberals would support the Russians. Indeed, he had foreseen a long period of rule, obedient to his wishes, with the Prince of Bulgaria forlornly on the sidelines. M. Ionin was so mortified by the *coup* that he shut himself up in his house for three months, finally returning to St. Petersburg. The Generals also quitted Bulgaria to the joy of the population. "A deep gulf now yawns between the Czar and myself," the Prince wrote to his father a month later, "and I suppose it will never be bridged. Hatred and contempt are the feelings which animate this crowned fool, who is too cowardly to live in St. Petersburg, hides at Gatchina, imagines that he can impress the people by stirring up revolutions among his neighbours, and permits the newspapers to drag the names of his nearest relations in the mud . . ."[18]

Meanwhile at home the Prince had lost no time in mending his fences. Although the Liberals had agreed to the coalition, some of them found it impossible to overcome their animosity towards a ruler who had scorned them for so many years. When the Prince heard that Stepan Stambulov, the President of the Chamber, had caught a bad cold at the opening of the Assembly, and was lying in a room at the Hotel Bulgarie with a fever, he called upon him and asked if he could send him any fruit or delicacies, and perhaps help to defray his expenses. "The stubborn nature of the sick man, however, revolted even against such royal advances, and he answered that he had money enough to pay for all he needed, both tone and word being almost insulting. The Prince flushed scarlet with vexation, and, turning on his heel, left the room without a sound . . . 'I did not like him myself,' Stambulov later told a friend, 'but I supported him . . . because I saw that his personal beauty and chivalrous character were qualities likely to win the hearts of the Bulgarians and that when we should be able to gain him over to us, he would be a famous leader for our Nation.' "[19]

The Czar had never liked the Germans; and he liked them still less after his humiliating defeat at the hands of the Battenberg Prince. His anti-Germanism stemmed partly from the Slavophile doctrines imbibed in his youth from Pobedonostev; and partly from resentment that Germandom had managed to unite while Slavdom remained divided and quarrelsome. When the King of Prussia put an Emperor's crown on his head in 1871 Alexander, then Heir, had been so jealous he had fined anyone who spoke German in his presence. His father heard what he was doing and promptly addressed him in German, asking: "And are you going to fine me too?"

Despite the fact that Alexander III was almost wholly German himself with scarcely a drop of Russian blood in his veins, throughout his reign he pursued a policy of "Russia for the Russians." He instigated fierce Jewish pogroms and carried out a russification programme in Finland and Poland; yet the lash of his policy fell hardest on the German families residing in Russia. A ukase was issued prohibiting foreigners from inheriting or acquiring real property in the western provinces of the Empire, aimed at German manu-facturers and merchants who had built up large businesses. Many were forced to close down their factories and leave. Not only was the German language forbidden in the Baltic schools, but every sort of petty slight inflicted. A new military uniform was designed, eliminating all Prussian details, while German fashions were pro-hibited at Court. Even more drastic, every man with a German name who could be replaced by a Russian was dropped from Government service. When the Chief Astronomer of the Empire died, a man of German origin, Alexander III commanded that the job should be filled by a Russian with a fully Russian name. "To comply with the Imperial wishes the country was scoured for a Russian Astrono-mer, but . . . the only Russian Astronomer who was available was in the first place too young . . . in the second place was disqualified by the name of Kleber. There was no alternative but to bestow the office with its emoluments on a Russian general . . ."[20]

The result of this policy was to reduce greatly the efficiency of the Russian administration. No one was surprised that Kaulbars and Sobolev and Ionin had made a mess of things in Bulgaria; there was muddle and corruption everywhere. "Russia is not the most Eastern outpost of Western civilisation; it is the most Western outpost of the East," wrote Lord Frederick Hamilton, who was posted to the St. Petersburg Embassy in the eighties. "Russians have all the qualities of the Oriental, his fatalism, his inertness, and, I fear, his inate pecuniary corruption . . . The various German-Russian families from the Baltic provinces, the Adlerbergs, the Benckendorffs, and the Stackelbergs served Russia well. Under their strong guidance she had become a mighty power, but when under Alexander III the reins of Government were confided to purely Russian hands, rapid deterioration set in."[21]

The Czar was so obsessed by Panslavic ideas that he refused to alter his course. Although Ionin had made appalling blunders in Bulgaria, the fact that he was Alexander III's personal appointment, and Russian to boot, caused the Emperor to gush with praise. "I am *very satisfied* with all the energetic actions of Ionin," he wrote, "and

I *especially* value his decisiveness, firmness and his *taking upon himself responsibility* and not asking for instructions from Petersburg . . ."[22]

On the other hand, when he heard a rumour that the Prince of Bulgaria had taken upon himself the responsibility of becoming secretly engaged to Princess Victoria, the daughter of the German Crown Prince, his wrath knew no bounds. He stormed to his Foreign Secretary that he would never allow it; that such a marriage would involve Germany in Bulgarian affairs; that the whole thing was a plot on the part of Queen Victoria.

The truth was that Sandro of Battenberg had been trying to find a wife ever since he first set foot in Bulgaria. Provincial Sophia, over-laden with intrigue, was both oppressive and repugnant. The Prince was desperately lonely and wrote endless letters to his father complaining of his misery and asking for help in finding a wife. At one time he entertained hopes of the Grand Duchess Catherine, the Czar's niece, at another of the fabulously rich Princess Yussupov. But the prospects came to nothing, for fathers were not eager to see their daughters sharing the vagaries of the Bulgarian throne. Carmen Sylva, the Princess of Romania, adored match-making and suggested an Austrian Archduchess and any number of minor German Princesses, but although the Russian Government had no candidates of its own, it opposed every one. However, in 1882, when the Prince was returning to Bulgaria from St. Petersburg, he met the seventeen-year-old Princess Victoria, who had secretly been in love with him for four years, ever since she had first seen him in the dazzling uniform of the Prussian *Garde de Corps*. The Prince had no idea of the impression he had made upon the girl and gave her scarcely a thought, but the mother began to weave her plans.

The Crown Princess loathed the Russians with almost the same ferocity as Queen Victoria. Clever, strong-willed and emotional, she had been educated by her father, Prince Albert, as an English Liberal, and as a result had found herself at loggerheads with Bismarck ever since he came to power. Although she admitted the necessity of expediency, she resented his friendship with the Czar, for in her eyes the Russians were an Asiatic tyranny pushing their way into Europe and threatening the civilised world. She warmed to the attractive Sandro of Battenberg because he was fighting the enemy, romanticising him as a lone crusader against the monstrous incursion. She wrote to the Queen that his noble character reminded her of her father; no praise could be higher and it is not surprising to learn that she made up her mind to have him as her son-in-law.

When she confided her plans to the Crown Prince he was appalled. He did not regard the Battenberg Prince, a product of a morganatic marriage, as nearly grand enough for his daughter. Although she gradually talked him round, the obstacles in her way were still formidable. Bismarck had initiated a Three Emperors' Pact between Austria, Russia and Germany and he was not going to let anything interfere with it. Germany's policy was to keep out of the Balkan controversy, and to use her influence to prevent Austria and Russia from flying at each other's throats.

Although the Crown Princess was clever and erudite her impulsive nature was always plunging her into difficulty. With astonishing irresponsibility she wrote to Sandro hinting at a marriage between himself and her daughter. She flung the young couple together at every opportunity and in 1883 encouraged them to become secretly engaged. The sharp eyes of the courtiers saw what was happening and by 1884 Berlin and St. Petersburg were humming with gossip. That same spring Sandro's elder brother, Prince Louis of Battenberg married his first cousin, Princess Victoria of Hesse, a daughter of Princess Alice and a granddaughter of Queen Victoria; and later in the year the engagement was announced between another of Sandro's brothers, Henry, and Queen Victoria's daughter, Princess Beatrice. Thus the ties between the English royal family and the house of Battenberg were drawn with double tightness.

Sandro was naïve enough to hope that these events would make the Czar more amenable but of course they had the opposite effect; and the angrier that the Russian ruler grew the more anxious Bismarck became not to offend him. The latter took pains to see that his own Emperor was not won over to the marriage. Whenever he discussed the Prince with his octogenarian sovereign he referred to him as a "penniless adventurer," a "trouble-maker," a "climber." The Russian diplomats went further and in audiences arranged by Bismarck shocked the old man by hints of moral turpitude.

Sandro knew nothing of this and was encouraged by the Crown Princess to seek an interview with the Emperor William who, she assured him, was in two minds about the marriage. He was therefore completely taken aback by the sovereign's hostility. The old man was aggressive and disagreeable, opening the conversation by accusing the Prince of adopting a "disrespectful tone" in his letters to the Czar. Sandro replied heatedly that he had always observed the correct formalities; only in personal letters did he write confidentially as cousin to cousin. "Cousin, cousin," the Emperor cut in, "an Emperor is an Emperor. My own son signs himself from my 'most obedient servant' when he writes to me."

As the talk progressed the Prince refused to be intimidated, with the result that William I became increasingly annoyed and cutting. "I must tell Your Highness that I have heard that you are up to your eyes in debt and have had to humiliate yourself by taking a loan from European Jewry." This was touching the Prince on the raw, for Russia had promised to make funds available to him but had not honoured the agreement. "I beg your Majesty to remember," said Alexander, "that on entering Bulgaria I found next to nothing there in the way of a residence for a ruling Prince. I had to build up from nothing and, after all, the palace with its equipment and household, etc., will belong to the country and to my successor. If I had been prepared to become a Russian hireling I would have been spared the unpleasant necessity of applying to the Rothschild Bank."

"The former alternative would have been preferable," replied the Emperor.

"Besides, I also asked my father for a considerable loan and received it, so my family have certainly put plenty of money into the affair."

The Emperor did not like the tone of this impertinent young Prince and now began to fling at him accusations of immorality. "I have heard . . . that you are giving offence to your people and making it impossible for any decent woman to enter your house."[23]

This was the last straw. To be accused of sexual orgies when he had led such a dull life in Sophia was intolerable. He flared up angrily and threatened to leave Bulgaria for ever. "Very well, then, go, it won't worry me," said the Emperor, and the audience was over.

After this humiliating experience the Prince was given an interview with Bismarck who was no less hostile, but not so petty. The Chancellor immediately referred to the marriage question and when Sandro tried to dismiss the story as gossip, Bismarck said: "Well, as Your Highness appears to know so little about the matter, you will allow me to tell you there was serious talk of such a union, so much so that violent scenes took place in the palace; Her Imperial Highness, the Crown Princess, and the English Court are in favour of the marriage. His Imperial Highness, the Crown Prince, was *against* it; the Emperor and Empress have stated that they cannot agree to it. I, as Imperial Chancellor, have informed His Majesty that *Germany has no interest in Bulgaria, our interest is—Peace with Russia*. To ensure that, it is absolutely necessary that Russia shall be convinced that we are not actively interested in the East. On the day that a Prussian Princess becomes Princess of Bulgaria, Russia will grow suspicious and will no longer believe this assurance. In addition, *this marriage would interfere with my political interests*. This I will not permit and I have informed His Majesty that so long as I am Chancellor, this marriage will not take place; at the same time I have assured the Emperor that he would find no successor to follow such a policy.

"... In any case," Bismarck continued slyly, "I cannot understand why you want to marry a Princess ... I would advise you to marry an Orthodox millionairess; that would stabilise your position in Bulgaria, *for ruling in the East means bribery and that requires money*. Nothing can be done honestly there. Anyhow, I think it is time you made up your mind whether you are a German or a Bulgarian. Up to now you have been a German, but with your departure that chapter might be closed. In your case I might have remained a German, for I can understand that it must be repugnant to an honest, upright character like yours to have to deal with orientals. But if you wish to remain in Bulgaria you must submit to Russia for better or worse and even, if necessary, adopt an anti-German attitude..."[24]

When the Prince of Bulgaria told the Crown Princess of these two unpleasant scenes, and when she learned that her father-in-law, the Emperor, had forbidden him to communicate with his grand-daughter and had even refused to entertain him, she sailed into battle. She persuaded her husband to give a banquet in his honour, and arranged a clandestine meeting between the young lovers. By this time the Crown Prince was in full accord with his wife's views. At dinner he raised his glass surreptitiously and drank to Sandro with the whispered toast: "To the Pioneer of Germany in the East." Count Hatzfeldt, who sat next to the Prince, murmured: "Just as well that nobody heard that." Before Sandro departed the Crown Princess gave him a golden locket containing a picture of her daughter and a snippet of hair.

When the Prince arrived back in Sophia he learned that the Russians had started a new smear campaign. The Emperor, they said, had refused to give his consent to the Prince's marriage because the latter had contracted a venereal disease. Others were more fanciful, declaring that he was not interested in women but had "Turkish tastes"—that was why the Czar had recalled his two Russian aides-de-camp. "The cleft between the Czar and myself cannot be bridged," he wrote to his father. "I *hate* the Czar and shall never be able to forget what he has done to me . . ."[25]

The unhappy relations between the Prince of Bulgaria and the Emperors of Russia and Germany did not improve, and in the spring of 1885 an event took place which shook the whole of Europe. Eastern Roumelia announced a *coup d'état* against its Turkish administration; and the new Government proclaimed a union between itself and the principality of Bulgaria. Although Russia had worked to bring the two halves together for six years, the Czar was indignant to learn that the people of Eastern Roumelia were streaming through the streets crying: "Long live Prince Alexander!" The Russian press, however, congratulated the rebels and the Russian people rejoiced to think that the humiliating Treaty of Berlin had been nullified. At last Greater Bulgaria had sprung into being.

Only Alexander III sulked. He was furious that the union had taken place under the hated Prince of Bulgaria—so furious that after a few days of silence he decided to pull out the rug from under the Prince's feet. Impervious to the incongruity of the situation, he made a shock announcement reversing Russian policy. The union, he said, did not have his approval; and as a result he was withdrawing all Russian officers from the Bulgarian Army. This was the trump card. He felt certain that Turkey would react to the loss of Eastern Roumelia by launching an attack. By stripping Bulgaria of her defences at this critical moment he believed that the helpless country would be forced to call on Russia for protection.

Europe was astonished that the Czar could allow his hatred for his cousin to lead him to such lengths, particularly as the Prince had had nothing to do with the *coup*, even being abroad at the time. The fact that Alexander III was willing to see a state, which had been liberated by Russian arms, utterly crushed unless it was obedient to his will not only shocked the Bulgarian people but disillusioned idealists who had believed that Panslavism meant a "brotherhood" of the Slav people.

What was the Czar's explanation? M. Giers told Sir Robert Morier, the British Ambassador, that the educated Bulgarians were hopelessly tainted with anarchistic views which they had picked up at Russian universities. They attacked the Church and recruited their teachers from among Russian emigrants in Geneva, and finally organised the Eastern Roumelian revolt. The Czar, he said, "still lived, as it were, in the shadow of his father's murderers and he could put up with it no longer."[26] These arguments illustrated Russian ingenuity as the "scum" which Giers now castigated, was the very element that Russia had supported against the Prince for the past few years; and the revolt in Eastern Roumelia had been initiated by the famous General Sobolev and incited over the years by Russian agents and consular officials. "Russia behaves and has behaved shamefully," Queen Victoria snapped. "Her anger against Prince Alexander is merely because her plan of deposing him and uniting the two countries under a Russian prince ... failed."[27]

Meanwhile Alexander III waited for the inevitable consequences of his action. He was right in calculating that Bulgaria would be attacked but wrong in thinking the thrust would come from Turkey. It came from Serbia instead. King Milan was wild with jealousy at the sight of a huge, unified Bulgaria. Encouraged by Austria, which bore no personal ill-will towards the Prince but feared that sooner or later Bulgaria would fall under Russian domination, Milan launched an invasion. When the news broke most people felt that "the poor Bulgars" were doomed.

The Crown Princess lived in a state of permanent excitement. She had anticipated the war and some weeks earlier had written a twenty-eight-page letter to the Prince from Venice telling him that Vicky was sad "that in this decisive and momentous hour she cannot be at your side"; that "Vicky was inordinately proud of you and it was a source of great satisfaction to see your name in all the papers"; that "Vicky wanted to run away, disguise herself as a man and go to war with you"; that "Vicky wears your pearls and your first letter sewn up in a handkerchief close to her heart."[28]

The Czar not only gloated at the Prince's discomfiture but struck his name off the Russian Army list as the most insulting thing he could do; then placed the blame for the impending disaster squarely on his shoulders. "I was obliged," he wrote to Alexander of Hesse, "to censure an undertaking carried on without my consent, by revolutionary means that were bound to set the East ablaze and jeopardise the future of Bulgaria. Events have proved me to be only too right. The country is at war with the neighbours who should be its allies. The results of this act of folly are that the land is invaded, the capital threatened by an enemy, and the people ruined for years to come."[29]

When the Czar wrote his letter, he had not heard the news from Slivnica where the Prince had won a stunning victory. Alexander had countered the withdrawal of Russian officers by promoting non-commissioned men to captains and majors, and lieutenants to colonels and generals. Personally commanding his army, he had whipped up a fever of nationalist excitement, and after defeating the Serbs at Slivnica had penetrated deep into Serbian territory. "I thank God on my knees," he wrote to his father "that we have got through so well ... I was everywhere at once, in front, behind, right, left ... All that fortnight I never even washed and never *once* took my boots off so that I have got chilblaines and a bad cold on my chest. But otherwise I am well."[30]

A great strength to the Prince during these hectic days was the pugnacious Stambulov who gloried in a good fight and arrived at the Prince's Headquarters with a message from the Council on the eve of the battle of Slivnica. He found the Prince sitting in a litter of straw in his tent, surrounded with dead and wounded, over which a priest was performing the last rites. Stambulov joined one of the brigades as a private and fought throughout the war. "During this period," his biographer wrote, "he was in frequent contact with the Prince Alexander and the old misunderstanding between them was buried for ever . . . The ties which bound them were not those of master and servant so much as the affectionate respect on each side for the qualities of the other."[31]

The fighting ended almost as abruptly as it had begun. The Serbs sued for peace, the Powers intervened, and the Bulgarians withdrew to their own frontiers. "You must be very proud," Queen Victoria wired to the Prince's father. The Queen did not pretend to be neutral; indeed a few weeks earlier she had written to Lord Salisbury strongly urging the British Government to support the Eastern Roumelian-Bulgarian Union. Although Lord Beaconsfield had thought it prudent, she said, to divide the two territories, the situation was now completely altered; the Prince's courage in standing up to the Czar showed that Greater Bulgaria might be developed as a buffer against Russian aggression.

Russia was only too aware of the changed circumstances and at the Bucharest Peace Conference still refused to give her sanction to the Union. Germany and Austria would not defy her because of the Three Emperors' Pact, and Mr. Gladstone, who had become Prime Minister again, declined to take a firm stand. In the end Bulgaria emerged with no territorial gains, no financial compensation, and no recognised union. However, at the Constantinople Conference of Ambassadors a few months later, the Powers took notice of the *de facto* situation and approved a crippled form of collaboration which permitted the Prince of Bulgaria to serve as Governor-General of Roumelia for five years. "You will not achieve a real Union," the Russians crowed to the Bulgarians, "as long as you have the Prince . . ."

Nevertheless, the Czar of all the Russias had lost a good deal of face by his interventions. To recall his army officers, only to watch the Bulgarian Army win a smashing victory, was a humiliation that sank deep; and by the spring of 1886 his loathing for the Prince was almost pathological. If he could not rid himself of "this man we have raised from the gutter" in open political battle, other means would have to be employed. Despite his insistence to Giers that he would have nothing more to do with Bulgaria, and his bitter complaints about the revolutionary scum, he decided to harness this very element to remove his detestable cousin from the throne. Consequently, Colonel Sakharov, the Russian Military Attaché in Sophia, was encouraged to organise a *coup d'état* to force the abdication of the Prince.

Sakharov worked hand in glove with the Russian Counsellor in Sophia, Bogdanov. The latter ran the propaganda and provided the money for bribes. He cynically made his appeal to nationalist sentiment—the very element that Russia was determined to eradicate if she got control. The line was simple: as the Prince was the stumbling block to effective union, true Bulgarian patriots must sacrifice him for the good of the country.

Meanwhile Colonel Sakharov was busy subverting military men in key positions. As the Prince was the hero of the Bulgarian Army it did not look easy at first glance; nevertheless Sakharov was the right man for the job as he had served for some years as the head of the Cadet School. This meant that almost every officer had passed through his hands. He knew that the wholesale promotions made by the Prince when the Russians had withdrawn their officers had caused deep dissensions and jealousies among those who fancied that others had been given better jobs. He also knew the weaknesses of human nature and how to turn ambition to corruption.

He made four important recruits. The first was Captain Radko Dimitriev, a vain, drunken, thirty-eight-year-old officer whose aggressiveness had won him the name of "the little Napoleon" and who was working in the War Office. Dimitriev was an ardent Panslavist who wished to see Bulgaria in the Russian orbit, and therefore was easily won over. The second was Captain Benderev, aged thirty-two, who had done his military training at the *Akademiya Generalnavo Shtaba*, the Russian Staff College, and was acting War Minister due to the indisposition of his chief. Benderev had fought with the Prince at Slivnica, but was furious because Alexander had reprimanded him for exceeding his orders and had not given him the promotion he expected. The third was Major Gruev, aged thirty, who had also done his training in St. Petersburg at the Staff College; he was promised a high command in the Russian Army if he threw in his hand with the plotters. The fourth was Major Stoyanov, a Russian national, who had been born and bred in Russia but become a Bulgarian subject. He was Commander of the Strume Regiment but longed to secure a military transfer to his native country.

As the conspiracy began to grow, Prince Alexander was warned by anonymous letters that a kidnapping plot was afoot. He knew that there were plenty of people in Bulgaria who would like to see him out of the way. Indeed, that same August one of his servants handed him a headache powder that was straight poison. The Prince was suspicious of the smell and colour and pushed it away. A short time afterwards a Russian officer named Captain Nabokov was arrested and charged with conspiring against the Crown. The Prince was willing to admit that isolated plots were being hatched against him, but refused to believe that the army—his own victorious army— could be guilty of treason. "I do not wish to remain Prince of Bulgaria by force," he replied to one of his informants, "if they do not want me, then let them tell me so and I will go voluntarily."

The Prince therefore refused to concern himself with the stories that were gaining ground; whereas in Bucharest and Constantinople the possibility of a *coup d'état* was openly discussed. "It is the season of volcanic eruptions," a high Turkish official remarked to *The Times* correspondent in Constantinople; "and it is possible that we shall see one in the Balkan Peninsula."

Meanwhile the Russian Counsellor, Bogdanov, was keeping Giers and the Czar informed of every development. On the civilian front the conspirators had enlisted the services of Bishop Klement, a sort of Bulgarian Rasputin who had been trained for the priesthood in Russia but was known to be licentious and venal. The only politician who had wholeheartedly thrown in his lot with the traitors was the Liberal leader, Zankov, who had been in the pay of the

Russians for some time. For the past six months he had been in charge of the Russian subsidised paper *Svetlina*, and was committed to do everything in his power to bring Bulgaria into the Russian camp. The Prime Minister, Karavelov, knew about the plot but refused to have anything to do with it; on the other hand he would not warn the Prince as he maintained a pose of being "strictly neutral." Bogdanov, however, had long talks with both men, and assured them that Russia would protect Bulgaria from an outside attack if the Prince was removed. The head of the Asiatic Department of the Russian Foreign Office, M. Zinoviev, was worried for fear that Russian complicity would become known. "In such ticklish matters," he wrote to Giers in July, "it is necessary to be extremely cautious." He went on to point out that Sakharov must be warned to be "cautious" as his participation in the intrigue could "compromise us."[32]

At the end of July M. Bogdanov outlined to Giers the form that the *coup d'état* would take. It was scheduled for August. The Prince would be handed a memorandum giving false information about the imminence of a Serbian attack. If the ruse succeeded he would send his loyal regiments to the border, which would give the conspirators an opportunity of completing their plans. The dispatch ended with the sentence: "Sakharov [the Russian Military Attaché] asks that you transmit the above to Obruchev [the Russian Chief of Staff]." The Czar's conscience obviously pricked him at condoning a plot in which army officers were bribed to betray their sovereign prince for he wrote on the margin: "I am afraid that nothing decent will come of this."[32] Yet he did nothing to stop it.

The *coup*, however, went without a hitch. The Slav race, so inefficient in daily administration, had an undeniable talent for intrigue. The Russians had managed to enlist some thirty to forty officers eager for money or promotion. The anchor men performed their tasks without a flaw. Captain Benderev, the acting Minister of War, showered the Prince with false reports on the menacing movement of Serbian troops. The Prince agreed to strengthen his frontier forces and sent two battalions of his loyal Alexander Regiment from Sophia. Next, Major Stoyanov stepped in. His command, the Second Regiment, was already at the border. On the night of 20th August he informed his men that they were to carry out a "field exercise" which necessitated a march to Sophia. When the men reached the capital he told them that part of the exercise was to disarm the remaining battalion of the Alexander Regiment. When this was done the troops were posted at positions around the palace. The soldiers still did not know what was happening. The major did not allow them to enter the palace grounds as he was too uncertain of them. Instead, the teen-age cadets, under the command of the third key man, Major Gruev, were given the critical task of removing the Prince from the Palace. It did not occur to them to challenge their Commandant. They were told that they were being called upon to save Bulgaria from a ruler who was leading the country to ruin. They were brought into the palace yard, and instructed to form a cordon around the building.

At 3.30 in the morning the Prince's servant heard noises and footsteps outside and peering out of the window saw the garden filled with shadowy shapes. He ran to the Prince's room, handed the latter a revolver and cried: "For God's sake fly, Highness, they are going to murder you!" The Prince flung on some clothes and climbed to the roof where he saw that the entire palace was surrounded. As lights went on inside the building the rebels saw no further point in concealing themselves. Under orders from their officers, the cadets began firing their rifles into the air and shouting "down with him," "*dolu, dolu*!" The Prince realised he was in the presence of a well-organised revolt, alerted his brother, Prince Francis Joseph, (who had the misfortune to be on a short visit to Sophia), finished dressing, and went downstairs to the ante-room where he was immediately surrounded by officers and cadets. A tremendous tumult broke out, revolvers and bayonets were brandished wildly, while Captain Radko Dimitriev, by this time very drunk, demanded the Prince's abdication. "Our country is lost if you remain on the throne of Bulgaria," he said. "If I had known that there was anyone in the army who wanted that, I would have gone of my own accord," replied the Prince. Dimitriev then tore a sheet from the Visitors' Book and tried to write out the abdication form, but his letters were so illegible, a cadet took his place and put down the words dictated to him. The Prince barely read the document but wrote at the bottom: "God protect Bulgaria" and signed his name.[33]

The Prince was filled with deep disgust. Not only was he confronted by the treachery of officers whom he knew well, and had believed to be loyal servants, but he was given to understand that his entire army had turned against him. He felt that nothing worse could ever befall him and, overcome with repugnance, asked to be allowed to leave Sophia without further delay. His captors refused, telling him that he must first accompany them to the War Office. On the way Captain Benderev remarked scornfully to him: "This would not have happened if you had made me a major!"

At the War Office he was treated with scant courtesy and learned, with a sinking heart, that he was to be sent to Russia. At five o'clock nine phaetons, driven by four horses each, drew up outside. The Prince was assigned to one of them under the guard of a Captain Kardjiev, whom he did not know, while his brother, Prince Francis Joseph, rode in another with Captain Zafirov. The remaining seven carriages were filled with cadets. A number of officers stood on the steps and bade him farewell by flinging out insulting remarks. Captain Dimitriev stood grinning and munching an apple. Only Major Gruev gave him a military salute.

The dawn was just breaking, and people were still sleeping as the procession drove fifteen kilometres out of the city, then took a cross-country track leading to a monastery another fifteen kilometres away. The building had been occupied by Major Gruev's cadets, and the Prince and his brother, who had not been allowed to communicate, were given separate rooms, small, dirty cells guarded by soldiers. They were not allowed a moment of privacy and were subjected to a steady stream of abuse. Meanwhile the conspirators were organising the take-over of the Prince's yacht, the *Alexander*, which was at the port of Rahova on the Danube.

The journey continued next morning, and although Captain Kardjiev refused to tell the Prince where he was going or what fate lay in store for him, he did not mind discussing the rebellion. He informed his captive that the Russian Military Attaché had been the chief organiser of the plot; he, himself, had nothing against the Prince but, he added cynically, it was not something to take a stand about as no ruler could last long in Bulgaria. The people were too uneducated to appreciate merit, and the educated class too venal to be loyal.

All this while, the strictest watch was kept on the Prince who was told that he would be shot if he tried to escape. Villages were avoided so that the populace could not see what was happening, and even the overnight stop was not made until the local inhabitants were asleep. The yacht had been secured by terrorising the navigator and crew. When the carriages reached the port cadets swarmed aboard and the Prince and his brother were directed to the dining-saloon.

Alexander had been informed repeatedly that the reason for the close guard was to protect him from the wrath of his people. The whole Bulgarian Army had mutinied and many would like to see him strung up on the nearest lamp-post. His spirits were very low when one of the cadets crept into the saloon and gave him a different account. The conspirators were so unsure of themselves, the boy said, that they were directing the passage of the yacht at pistol point. They had taken the Prince along country roads and into darkened villages as they feared that if his subjects knew what was happening they would attempt a rescue. The population was ignorant of the kidnapping; and only a small portion of the army had rebelled. The Prince was being taken to the Russian port, Reni, where he would be handed over to the authorities.

Although this last piece of information filled Alexander with fore-boding, when the yacht reached Reni the Russian officials appeared to know nothing of the abduction. Not a soul was on the landing stage, and the conspirators drove into town to find someone to whom they could hand over their prisoner. The Russian Commander of the frontier station was absent and the cavalry captain doing duty for him said that he had received no instructions from St. Petersburg. When requested to take charge of Prince Alexander he replied in surprise: "How take charge?" "Why, he has been deposed and we have brought him here." "How brought him? A prisoner? How is he a prisoner? How could you do such a thing? What if I took you prisoner now?"[34]

Captain Kardjiev tried to explain to the cavalry captain that the army in Sophia had overthrown the Prince because he was a German working against the Czar. Finally the captain agreed to ask St. Petersburg for orders; but until he received them no one, not even the crew, might leave the ship. He did not have long to wait. Instructions came whistling back to Reni to allow the Prince to land and to set him free immediately to travel to Germany or Austria. This was surprising enough. He immediately took a train to Lemberg, arriving the following day, where even more astonishing news awaited him. A large crowd had gathered at the station, including the Austrian Chamberlain Baron Riedesel, who handed him telegrams informing him that the revolutionary régime had been overthrown, and that Stambulov, the Liberal leader, had formed a loyal government.

The Prince learned that much had been happening in the outside world in the seven days since the kidnapping. The story of the abduction had been released to the press on 22nd August when the rebels had proclaimed themselves the Provisional Government of Bulgaria. Queen Victoria, who was staying at Balmoral, branded it the work of "these Russian fiends." She wrote to her Prime Minister alluding to the "heroic, noble, young sovereign of Bulgaria," and referring to Russia's behaviour as "without parallel in modern history."[35] In a private letter to Prince Alexander himself she referred to the Czar as "your barbaric, semi-asiatic, tyrannical cousin." The British Ambassador in St. Petersburg had been instructed to make strong representations, while Prince Louis of Battenberg had been given leave from the Royal Navy to search the continent for his missing brother. He was not in the dark long, however, for on the afternoon of 25th August Alexander of Hesse received a telegram from his son saying: "Have to-day been delivered prisoner to the Russian police at Reni. Was released at the order of St. Petersburg, and am going by way of . . . Lemberg to Breslau, from where I will send further news . . . I am absolutely shattered by the fearful anguish I have suffered."[36]

Whatever the Czar originally had in mind for the Prince of Bulgaria, there is no doubt that he was disturbed by the reaction of the great powers, and completely taken aback by the news from Bulgaria itself. On 24th August, four days after the *coup d'état*, Stambulov had telegraphed to Alexander of Hesse: "The whole of the Bulgarian people and army have overthrown the revolutionary government in Sophia and beg their Prince Alexander to return wherever he may be." Queen Victoria and the German Crown Princess were beside themselves with joy. They both sent messages urging the Prince to hasten to Sophia; and this time, the Queen told her Foreign Secretary, "we must stand by him."

The Prince was so deeply despondent that he could neither eat nor sleep. The telegram that he had sent to his father describing himself as "shattered" was no exaggeration. The shock of dis-covering that trusted army officers had been capable of such perfidy was a traumatic experience from which he could not recover. Although modern historians sometimes cite the Prince's abduction as an example of Russia's moderation in the last century, Alexander had been handled roughly for any age, except perhaps our own. He had been forced to abdicate at the point of a gun; insulted, ridiculed, thrust into a carriage with no knowledge whether or not he was going to his death; refused all privacy; and finally told that he was being taken to the most dreaded place of all, Russia, perhaps to meet some awful end. Queen Victoria was incensed; she could scarcely imagine the indignity. ". . . being sent *without even a servant,*" she wrote to Lord Salisbury, "—as prisoners—and delivered over on Russian territory to a Russian gendarme, and condescendingly released by *orders* from St. Petersburg! . . . a common felon could not be worse treated . . ."[37]

The Prince seemed to have lost all interest in life, while the very thought of Bulgaria filled him with repugnance. Nevertheless the pressure was so strong from father and brothers, from Queen and Crown Princess, who saw the affair as a crucial battle against Russian Imperialism that he finally gave in. On 28th August he sent a wire to his father: "I am going to Bulgaria where I arrive to-morrow morning. May God help me." Accompanied by his brother Louis, the Prince travelled to Giurgievo in Romania where his yacht was waiting with Stambulov aboard. The new Prime Minister gave him a first-hand account of what had happened. The dissolute Bishop Klement had formed a Provisional Government the morning after the *coup*. He had conducted a Te Deum in the Cathedral to celebrate deliverance from "the Battenberg prince." People were dragged off the streets to attend, but once inside were given a *pour boire* of two francs. Word of this beneficence spread and soon the Cathedral was full although the peasant congregation had no idea what was going on. One young man cried out: "Thanks be to God, our Prince is being married to the Czar's daughter!"

Meanwhile Stambulov had raised the flag of counter-revolution. A young army officer, Captain Velcev, had responded to his appeal by winning over the Philippopolis garrison. Thus encouraged, Stambulov sent telegrams and messengers in all directions. When the provinces began to rally, he issued a proclamation calling on the people to defend Crown and Country, and informing Bishop Klement that if his ministers did not lay down their offices within twenty-four hours they would be shot. As news of loyal demonstrations began to flow in from all areas many of the traitors fled the country. Only the Russian officers in Sophia continued to resist; but when the Alexander Regiment, which had been dispatched to the frontier, marched into the capital and occupied the palace in the name of the Prince, the rebellion was finished.

The Prince looked pale and worn when he stepped on to Bulgarian soil. Thousands of people had gathered at Rustchuk harbour and greeted him in a delirium of joy. The Bishop of Rustchuk kissed him three times and clung to him as though he did not want to let him go; old people fell to their knees and thanked God for his home-coming; hundreds more surged round weeping and trying to touch him. Crowds lined the route to the palace, where a reception was being held in his honour, and strewed his path with flowers.

The Prince was taken aback to find the Russian consul, M. Shatokhin, present at the gala in full dress uniform. Shatokhin asked the Prince if he could have a few minutes alone with him. "I am instructed by my Government to inform Your Highness," he said in a half-apologetic tone, "that the Prince Dolgorouky is on his way from St. Petersburg to take over the Government of Bulgaria and Eastern Roumelia."

Although the message was fairly curt the Consul explained that it should not be taken too seriously for he was certain that the mood in St. Petersburg was undergoing a change. Otherwise the Government would not have permitted him to attend the Prince's reception. The time was ripe, he argued, for the Prince to make a generous gesture, to forget the past and hold out the olive branch.

The Consul's persuasiveness fell on fertile soil for the Prince could not believe that the Russians had played any part in the kidnapping. If so, why had the authorities at Reni released him so speedily? Furthermore, he was convinced that no matter how much animosity the Czar felt for him personally, he would not sanction treason; a military challenge to the crown must have outraged his instincts.

The Prince made the mistake of consulting his brother, Louis, rather than Stambulov who had gone to bed—his first good sleep in five days. Stambulov would have cautioned him not to believe the smooth-tongued Russian; Dolgorouky was not yet on his way; nor had the Consul received instructions from St. Petersburg to attend the reception.

The Prince was so weary that his wits seem to have deserted him. Eagerly he clutched at the notion that Alexander III had undergone a change of heart with the realisation that Bulgaria was whole-heartedly behind its ruler. In this hour of victory he could afford to be magnanimous. With the help of Louis he composed a telegram which he believed was "masterly in construction" as it offered the Czar "a golden bridge." "I thank Your Majesty for the attitude taken by your representative. His very presence at my reception showed me that the Imperial Government cannot sanction the revolutionary action taken against my person. I beg Your Majesty to instruct General Dolgorouky to get in touch with me personally as quickly as possible; I should be happy to give Your Majesty the final proof of the unchanging devotion which I feel for Your Majesty's illustrious person. As Russia gave me my crown I am prepared to give it back into the hands of its Sovereign. Alexander."[38]

The Prince travelled to Tirnova where the National Assembly was sitting; then to Philippopolis and finally to Sophia. He received magnificent receptions everywhere, but just before he entered his capital he was handed a reply from the Czar. The latter had been annoyed when the Prince's wire arrived. He read the last sentence several times, and could scarcely believe his eyes. So the Prince of Bulgaria was prepared to return his crown. Seizing on this truly remarkable offer he replied without delay. "I have received Your Highness's telegram. I cannot countenance your return to Bulgaria as I foresee the disastrous results it entails for that sorely tried country. General Dolgorouky's mission appears to be unnecessary. I will refrain from sending him in view of the unhappy situation to which Bulgaria is exposed as long as you stay there. Your Highness will appreciate what you have to do. I will reserve judgment about it in respectful memory of my father and in the interests of Russia and of peace in the East. Alexander."[38]

Stambulov was dumbfounded when he learned what had happened. The Czar not only had wired Alexander but had published the exchange of telegrams in the official Gazette so that all the world could witness the offer and the prompt Russian acceptance. What distressed Stambulov most of all was the Prince's statement that Russia had given him his crown. Bulgaria had elected the Prince herself, and did not relish being alluded to as Russia's vassal. How could the Prince submit so abjectly after the tumultuous events of the past ten days? "This is the man," Stambulov cried angrily to a friend, "for whom we have aroused the whole of Bulgaria, have put our necks in the noose and brother has raised sword against brother, and he takes such a momentous decision without even telling us beforehand; he throws his crown at the feet of a foreign ruler and keeps us in the dark about it."[38]

Queen Victoria was almost as agitated as Stambulov. "I am speechless and entreat you to cancel this step," she telegraphed. "After such triumphs this was unworthy of the great position you had won. You are being blamed for having telegraphed to the Czar instead of asking advice first."

The truth was that Prince Alexander had lost his will to fight. Buoyed by the hope of a reconciliation he had sent his telegram to the Czar in good faith. But now that it was clear that Russian hostility was as implacable as ever he had no wish to remain in Bulgaria. It was impossible to rule without the support of one of the Great Powers and he had no allies. Germany was afraid of offending the Czar; Austria was hand-in-glove with Serbia; Britain, for all her fine words, was only an interested onlooker. Russian intrigue combined with Bulgarian perfidy made the odds against him too great—particularly since he could never again trust his army. This last admission had broken his spirit. "I beg your Majesty to believe," he telegraphed to Queen Victoria, "that I have only come to the decision of abdication after mature deliberation. Three-fourths of all officers are mixed up in the conspiracy . . . The people and the soldiers are on my side, but supported alone by them I cannot govern. The whole clergy is implicated . . . the people demand a reconciliation with Russia . . . My remaining any longer would only cause a civil war . . . as soon, however, as blood flows Russia will . . . occupy Bulgaria, which Europe would not be able to prevent."[38]

Before the Prince departed from the country he set up a Regency with Stambulov at its head. Through Bogdanov, he received the Czar's assurance that Russia would respect the Regency and Bulgaria's independence. He then issued a decree bidding his people farewell. On the day of his departure crowds thronged around his carriage and followed him on foot for many miles. He drove to Loms where an Austrian steamer was waiting to take him away for ever from the country where he had suffered so much.

The Czar thought he had won a victory, but had not reckoned with the flame of Bulgarian nationalism kindled by the Prince. Russia broke its promise to respect Bulgaria's integrity and sent a general to Sophia demanding complete submission. The answer was given in a national election in which the pro-Russian party was smashed. The Czar countered by pronouncing the election null and void but Stambulov refused to take notice. The Russians then demanded that the men who had organised Prince Alexander's kidnapping should be released from gaol. When Stambulov refused this as well, the Czar sent Russian warships into the harbour. The Bulgarian leader finally gave way in order not to risk a Russian occupation, but public opinion had become so hostile that Russian officers were frequently accosted on the streets. In November, two months after the Prince's departure, Russia suddenly broke off diplomatic relations with Bulgaria. "Russia . . . feels that she has been made to look incredibly foolish in Bulgaria," wrote von Bülow, First Secretary of the German Embassy in St. Petersburg. "The Czar is embittered because even after the removal of his arch enemy Battenberg from Sophia everything there is going contrary to his expectations and wishes."[39]

The German Crown Prince, however, did not think that Russia's withdrawal should be taken as a sign that she had lost interest in the country: merely that she would work out another plan. "The Russians are masters of intrigue," he wrote to his mother-in-law, Queen Victoria, in January, 1887, "they will stop at nothing to gain their ends. Just as they once plotted against the life of Prince A. so they will now plot against the liberty of Bulgaria . . ."[40]

VII

Poacher Turned Gamekeeper

IN THE WINTER of 1887 three students from the University of St. Petersburg, one of them carrying a bomb, were picked up by the police on the Nevsky Prospekt. Another fifteen conspirators were rounded up; and after a brief trial five of them, including Alexander Ulyanov, a brother of Lenin, were found guilty of plotting to kill the Czar and were hanged on 20th May. The affair brought back memories of the outrage on Alexander II and convinced people that the terror of the seventies was beginning again. A year later, when the train on which the Imperial family was returning from the Caucasus went off the rails near the village of Borki, no one would believe that it was not the work of revolutionaries. Two engines were pulling twelve coaches when suddenly there was a violent lurch, the sound of splintering glass and breaking wood followed by a thunderous reverberation as some of the carriages careened down the embankment. The Emperor and Empress were in the dining-saloon with their children, having luncheon. The roof caved in and the floor buckled as the coach went on to its side. For once the Czar's Herculean strength proved of value for he freed himself from the broken timber and iron that was crushing him and managed to hold up the wreckage so that his wife, children, nannies and servants could crawl out. When he saw the Empress standing before him trying to smile, he was so unnerved that he clasped her saying: "Mimi, Mimi, are you sure that you are not hurt?" It was a terrible accident in which twenty-eight people were killed and over a hundred injured. The six-year-old Grand Duchess Olga had been thrown through the window and had tumbled down the bank. Although she was unscathed she was screaming hysterically: "Now they will come and kill us all!" Afterwards officials placed the blame on the decrepitude of one of the engines which went off the rails, pulling the coaches after it. Somehow that did not explain why the roof of the imperial saloon crashed in, and people continued to believe that bombs had exploded on the track.

Although the increased vigilance of the police had rendered the terrorists ineffectual throughout most of Alexander's reign, there was always a subterranean rumble which encouraged the Czar to keep the lid tightly fastened. "Liberalism" was no longer a fashionable word; universities lost their autonomy; even Alexander II's judicial reforms were curtailed in order that suspects might be picked up and tried without the bother of "legal red tape." The Czar himself was the most closely guarded sovereign in Europe; General Tcherevin, the head of the *Ochrana*, lived at Gatchina Palace and took his meals with the family. Troops not only surrounded the grounds, but a regiment of the famous Blue Cuirassiers were encamped in the park. Even the Anitchikov Palace in St. Petersburg, where the Emperor spent only a few weeks a year, looked like a building under siege. Although it faced a square and backed on to a canal the houses on both sides had been acquired and a huge moat dug, to prevent mines from being laid. Patrols of Grenadiers and mounted Cossacks circled the Palace continuously, while troops with fixed bayonets were always on duty in the small garden at the back where the children played and the Czar took his afternoon walk.

Occasionally, but not often, one of the Czar's trusted officials was found battered to death. Such was the demise of General Sudeiken, the St. Petersburg Chief of Police. He was killed by a revolutionary named Degaiev. This clever engineer had been caught by the police in Odessa, and blackmailed by General Sudeiken into working for the *Ochrana*. Apparently Degaiev served Sudeiken loyally but his game was discovered by his fellow revolutionaries; they, in turn, threatened to kill him unless he helped them to murder Sudeiken. Obediently he invited the police chief to his flat where several men were hiding, armed with iron mallets used for breaking ice. They battered Sudeiken to death, locked the flat and went out. Degaiev fled abroad and was never seen again.

Repression at home; expansion abroad. The Czar's armies moved forward steadily in Asia, adding thousands of square miles to the Empire and nearly clashing with Britain over Afghanistan in 1885. Coal production doubled; oil production increased fourteen times; railways were built; towns sprang up in the Donbas. Russians were as boastful as ever and irritated foreigners just as they had done in the days of the Marquis de Custine, with glorious plans for the future. China and India and the Persian Gulf had always been the basis of their Grand Asian Scheme. Now they talked happily of pushing through Norway to the North Sea; and of course, through the Balkans to the Bosphorus and the Mediterranean.

This last objective was the only goal that interested Alexander III. He burned with indignation if anyone dared to suggest that the great prize of the Russo-Turkish war had slipped through his fingers, for Bulgaria was still an essential part of his plan. Although in 1887 he informed the world sulkily that he had washed his hands of that ungrateful nation until the people came to their senses, the interested Powers did not imagine for a moment that Russian interference would cease. Only the methods would change. With the Czar's withdrawal of his officers from Sophia, the task of gaining control of the country would fall to Russian bureaucrats skilled in the art of deception. Ever since the Panslav activities of the seventies the Russian bureaucracy had operated at two levels; official and unofficial. Whereas under Alexander II unofficial policy meant "without the knowledge of the Czar," under Alexander III it meant "without the acknowledgment of the Czar." By the eighties unofficial activity had become so much a part of Russian foreign policy that the Eleventh Edition of the *Encyclopædia Britannica* made special reference to it. "The Cabinet of St. Petersburg confined itself officially to breaking off diplomatic relations [with Bulgaria] and making diplomatic protests, and unofficially to giving tacit encouragement to revolutionary activity."

Unofficial policy appealed to the Russian mind for it required a talent for duplicity which was not in short supply. "It is a well-known, if not quite intelligible fact," Turgenev once pointed out, "that Russians lie more than any nation in the world. But on the other hand there is nothing they esteem so much as truth, nothing for which they have so much sympathy." Observers usually explained Russia's schizophrenic nature by her East-West background, but Russians themselves had a way of reconciling the irreconcilable. They had resolved the paradox of Turgenev's axiom by the simple expedient of transforming deceit into a virtue. And this had produced a new man, a new creed, a new profession.

The new man had made his début as the Nihilist of the sixties and been tempered by the *Nechaevsti* of the seventies. He despised old-fashioned morality and used treachery to achieve his political aims, for the new creed proclaimed that the end justified the means. He lived in the twilight, excited by danger, exalted by the magnitude of his hidden power. He had a wide choice of objectives; at home he could conspire against the Czar or join the Czar's secret police; abroad he could work for revolutionary groups or give his services to societies which ranged from Slavic Committees to Foreign Office Intelligence. Although there was scope for every shade of opinion, every cast of mind, although he could be found in almost every place or profession from Grand Ducal circles to the factory workshop, the new man was easy to recognise. He was Russian to his fingertips and he did not shy from murder; political assassination was the new profession.

The new man operated Russia's unofficial policy in Bulgaria. In 1887 no one called it a cold war, but that is what it was. The headquarters was established in the Russian Legation at Bucharest and presided over by M. Hitrovo, the formidable Panslav operator who had made trouble for Alexander of Battenberg and had been dismissed by Alexander II. Now that the Prince of Bulgaria was in disgrace Hitrovo had been reinstated by Alexander III and given a new job of trouble-making for which he had already proved his capacity. The Asiatic Department of the Russian Foreign Office which controlled all Balkan countries provided him with a million roubles to carry out his campaign. His task was to find dissident Bulgarians who would organise a revolution to thrust Bulgaria into the Russian orbit.

Russia's most formidable opponent was Stepan Stambulov, the thirty-two-year-old Co-Regent of Bulgaria. This small, thick-set man with the beetle brows and close-cropped black hair, the son of a Tirnovo inn-keeper, knew every weapon in the Russian armoury, for he was poacher turned gamekeeper. As a young man he had attended Odessa University and become a Nihilist. When one of the revolutionary plots in which he was involved was discovered, he was expelled and sent back to Bulgaria. Then he joined the Panslavs and helped to organise the abortive Bulgarian risings which had triggered off the notorious Turkish atrocities. Stambulov knew the system of cells and secret committees, and he lost no time in setting up his own counter-revolutionary network.

Nevertheless, the country was so torn by faction that Stambulov was haunted by the fear of a *coup d'état*. No time must be lost in finding an occupant for the empty throne, as this alone would give the country the necessary stability. The Bulgarian Assembly invited Prince Waldemar of Denmark, a brother of the Empress of Russia and the Princess of Wales, to take the Crown, but the Czar vetoed the suggestion and the Prince declined. King Charles of Romania was approached but he also retreated before Russia's scowls. Finally Stambulov dispatched a three-man mission to scour Europe for a willing candidate. The first stop was Vienna, and soon a startled world learned that twenty-seven-year-old Prince Ferdinand of Saxe-Coburg, a cousin of Queen Victoria, had accepted the throne. "His affectations are innumerable," wrote Lady Paget, the wife of a British diplomat. "He wears bracelets and powders his face. He sleeps in pink surah nightgowns, trimmed with Valenciennes lace. His constitution is so delicate and his nerves so finely strung, that he only consults ladies' doctors. What an effect such a man will produce, after the handsome chivalrous Alexander, I don't know; but he is bent upon it. At all events, he will not arouse any jealousies."[1]

The Austrian Foreign Minister, Count Kalnocky, gave the enterprise exactly six months. "He has too much the air of a *vieille cocotte*," he told the British Ambassador, "to be any good as a successor to Alexander of Battenberg."[2] The Russian Czar on the other hand considered the rumours too grotesque to be true. "*La candidature*," he pronounced brusquely, "*est aussi ridicule que le personnage*." In spite of these reactions Stambulov refused to be disconcerted by the Prince's shortcomings. As no one else seemed willing to run the risk of being assassinated by the Russians, he felt that Ferdinand's effeminacy was a small price to pay for his presence; furthermore the prince was both rich and well-born. His mother, Princess Clementine, was the daughter of the French King, Louis Philippe, while his father was the son of a Coburg prince and a Hungarian heiress. Princess Clementine was a clever, politically-minded lady who doted on Ferdinand and had always believed that he was destined to wear a crown; and as the young man usually did what his mother wanted, he accepted the throne without demur.

Queen Victoria and the Crown Princess were dismayed and angry for they entertained secret hopes that Alexander might return to Bulgaria. When the Queen first heard the rumours of Ferdinand's candidacy she wrote to Lord Salisbury saying that "the absurd pretensions of this foolish young cousin of mine" should be "stopped at once"; that he was "totally unfit—delicate, eccentric, effeminate . . ."[3] The following summer, when the offer was a *fait accompli* she telegraphed curtly to Salisbury: "Trust it will be made clear that we have no hand in Prince Ferdinand's election. The *Standard* says Prince Alexander's refusal is for ever. That is quite false. His refusal is till Europe will support him, and till he would be independent."[3]

Alexander III was still enraged with Bulgaria, and Ferdinand's appearance did nothing to pacify him. As he continued to insist that the Bulgarian elections which had returned the Assembly were "illegal" he refused to acknowledge the vote of the Assembly which had confirmed Ferdinand as Prince. And as once again the other powers did not think it worth while to oppose Russia, the new ruler found himself very much on his own. "His haughty manner is said not to have pleased," the Queen wrote in her Journal in August, 1887. "He has gone to Bulgaria without the sanction of the Powers, who have not acknowledged him; therefore it is illegal, though the election in itself is legal, which the Russians do not admit."

There is no doubt that the rough Bulgarians, gathered in Tirnovo to watch the new prince take the oath, were astonished by his appearance. His tightly corseted waist was wasp-like; his hands and wrists were covered in rings and bracelets; his hair smelled of pomade; and his long robe, made of purple velvet and ermine was grand enough for an Emperor. "He needs a bodyguard more than a coronation cloak," growled Stambulov, while other Bulgarians laughed uproariously.

Ferdinand was tall and fair with a small pointed beard, piercing blue eyes and a huge Bourbon nose which soon became the delight of the cartoonists. Once, some years later, he confided to Princess Pauline Metternich that he was thinking of having an operation performed to alter a feature that was making him ridiculous; but the Princess insisted that a nose such as his must remain a permanency "like a cathedral."

Ferdinand was unabashed. He had no intention of adapting himself to Bulgarian ways; his subjects must bend to his. Although Sophia was a backwater, not even connected to the world by a railway line, the Prince travelled with a splendid retinue consisting of a Bulgarian diplomat and three French counts—de Bourboulon, de Forcas and de Grenaud. He bounced over the bad roads and ate the bad food without complaint. Even the palace, more dilapidated than ever, did not dismay him. In due course all would be changed.

Ferdinand was more French than German, fastidious, elegant, artistic. Although he found it difficult to ride a horse, he spoke six languages, talked amusingly, collected birds and butterflies and knew a great deal about gardening. His æsthetic tastes were disconcerting. "If I ever feel tired or depressed," he said, "I have only to look at a bunch of violets to become myself again." Indeed, a Bulgarian army officer, Major Popoff, never forgot his first meeting with the Prince. Ferdinand received him reclining on a couch, holding a Malmaison carnation, which he sniffed throughout the audience, pointing out the exquisite formation of the petals.

A month after the coronation a General Election was held and Stambulov's party swept to power with a large majority. Stambulov formed a Government which was to last seven years. Before he did so he made it plain to the Prince in the bluntest language that he would only accept the Premiership on the understanding that Ferdinand did not attempt to interfere in politics. The haughty Prince had no alternative but compliance.

Nevertheless his pride was stung, for he had enough to bear from the cold-shouldering of Europe. Although all the Powers sent Diplomatic Agents to Bulgaria, none was allowed to wear uniform or to attend official functions at the Palace. They were instructed merely to keep in touch with Stambulov and to report on the political climate. Ferdinand's uncle, the Duc d'Aumale, a son of King Louis Philippe, thought the situation so comical that he could not resist teasing his nephew. Once, in Paris, when Ferdinand was standing with his back to him, the Duke mistook him for someone else. "*Je suis comme les puissances, Ferdinand,*" he mocked. "*Je ne te reconnais pas.*"

The Prince swallowed his humiliation and occupied himself by studying Bulgarian, travelling around the country, buying himself palaces at Vrania and Euxinograd. Meanwhile his mother, Princess Clementine, arrived in Sophia and began the redecoration of the palace. Soon chandeliers hung from the ceilings; the walls were covered with silks and velvets; the floors with Aubusson carpets. The palace servants emerged in powdered wigs and knee breeches, the bodyguard in scarlet and gold. Chefs and wine-waiters were imported from Paris and before long Princess Pauline Metternich was describing Ferdinand's Court as "the most refined and exquisitely kept in Europe."

The elegance contrasted strangely with the atmosphere. Almost every man in the palace slept with a weapon under his pillow. "One night," wrote Princess Clementine's lady-in-waiting, "a zealous member of the household, Colonel von Dobner, Commander of the Palace, fell into a mood of active suspicion, and the rest of us could see him pacing up and down the badly lit passages with a loaded revolver at arm's length." Almost every evening officers and officials came to the Palace with alarming news—"a threatening discovery, some evil or other that meant a whole night's work of counter-action for the Sovereign and his staff."[4] "The position is not particularly brilliant," Ferdinand remarked cynically, "but where is a better one to be found? I am a reigning prince."

Stambulov refused to have a bodyguard and strode through the streets at will, but at home he, too, took precautions. His door had a peep-hole inserted through which his faithful servant, Guntcho, always peered before letting anyone in. "In interviews which he gave me in his private house," wrote Charles Hardinge, "he used to sit at a table with his back to the wall and a Winchester rifle leaning against a piece of furniture at his elbow."[5]

In view of the tension, the first overt move by a Russian national was almost comic in its amateurishness. An officer from St. Petersburg by the name of Captain Nabokov, who had organised an abortive rising against Prince Alexander a few years earlier, decided to undertake a "commando" operation against the town of Bourgas. He rallied two Orthodox priests and thirty-five Montenegrins from the slums of Constantinople. The expedition travelled in small boats to a point not far from the Turkish frontier and advanced inland, requisitioning arms from the villages through which they passed. A gendarme spotted them, not altogether surprisingly, and notified Bourgas. The Prefect immediately gathered a company of soldiers, telegraphed in all directions for reinforcements and set forth to meet Nabokov. He met the Russian party about twenty-five kilometres from Bourgas. After a short encounter in which several men were killed, Nabokov was routed. An hour later he was captured by a party of peasants who had tracked him into a wood. Although he asked for a trial, they found a letter upon him which they regarded as thoroughly incriminating. It was written by a Russian diplomat in Constantinople and addressed to Count Ignatiev, asking the latter to help Nabokov recruit an army of Montenegrins to overthrow the Bulgarian government. Without further ado the peasants shot down the intruder.

The Bulgarian press made great play of the fact that Nabokov was a son of the Russian Minister of Justice, and a relation of the Nabokov who later became Counsellor in London. The Russians denied the story, and said they knew of no Russian officer by that name. This provoked the Bulgarians into a macabre reply. "As it was winter," wrote Charles Hardinge, "when the ground was frozen hard they exhumed the body of Captain Nabokov, dressed him up in his uniform with his decorations and photographed his body leaning against the trunk of a tree. This photograph was sent to the Russian press as a *pièce de conviction* and I received also from the government a copy of this strange and gruesome photograph."[5]

The first serious attempt on the part of the Russians to promote a revolution came to a climax early in 1890, and was based on the defection of a Bulgarian officer, Major Panitza, a hero of the Serbian war and a boyhood friend of Stambulov. Panitza was a hard drinker, sometimes uproariously good-natured, other times excitable and quick to take offence. When, after Ferdinand's arrival, he learned that the Prince had persuaded Stambulov to promote a certain Major Petroff over his head to a Lieutenant-Colonelcy, regardless of seniority, he was enraged. He swore vengeance on the Prince to all who would listen; and a very willing listener was the Russian armament merchant, Novikov, who, as one might suspect, worked for the Russian intelligence service.

Novikov had come to Sophia, early in 1888, accompanied by M. Jacobsohn of the Russian Legation in Bucharest, to sell Berder rifles and revolvers to the Bulgarian Army. His intermediary was Lieutenant Kolobokoff, a Russian national who was serving in the Bulgarian Army. Kolobokoff immediately got in touch with Major Panitza and soon the commercial enterprise had swollen into a conspiracy. A code was invented which allowed the men to communicate freely between Sophia, Rustchuk and Bucharest, under cover of the arms deal.

The Asiatic Department in St. Petersburg was kept fully informed of developments through the Russian Legation at Bucharest. But the Department was cautious and, when the conspirators asked for money, spent months haggling over the sums. A year and a half passed before the plans were ready; and as the day drew close, the talkative Panitza, who spent late hours at the cafés, found it impossible to guard his tongue. He began to hint at "sensational events" which would spell the doom of the Prince. For once, Stambulov was caught napping. Knowing Panitza's boastful character he did not take the stories seriously. However, in January 1890, on the eve of the *coup*, one of Panitza's key conspirators, Colonel Kissoff, Commandant of the Sophia Garrison, lost his nerve and confessed to the Minister of War what was happening. The Prefect of Police, who was also in the plot, somehow learned what the Commandant had done, and rather than warn his colleagues hastened to save his own skin by making a clean breast to the Government.

When Stambulov heard the news he instructed his secret police to furnish him with details. This they did by terrorising Panitza's confidential messenger. The dimensions of the plot were far wider than he had imagined. He summoned his War Minister and another Cabinet colleague—the only two he could trust—and told them that he had decided to take Panitza into custody that very night. He hit upon the novel idea of sending the two defectors, the Commandant and the Prefect, to carry out the arrest. Despite their horrified protestations he assigned them six gendarmes and ten soldiers and ordered them to execute his orders without delay. But he took no chances. He instructed a second party, composed of five police commissioners and fifty soldiers to follow the first party and see that the mission was completed; if not, they were to arrest the lot. As Stambulov waited for a report he found the suspense so great that he finally went to Panitza's house himself. The arrest had taken place and his men were in possession of a large number of documents and codes.

Hundreds of officers were implicated—so many that it was impossible to make wholesale arrests. Apart from Panitza he did not dare to take other ring-leaders into custody until loyal officers had time to arrive from the provinces. The following night a Court Ball was held at the Palace, planned many weeks in advance. The rooms were banked with flowers from Vienna; silver and glass flashed in the candle-light; champagne flowed. The Bulgarians were introduced to the intricacies of the Cotillion and wonderful gifts from Paris were presented to the dancers. The room, of course, swarmed with traitors who knew that Panitza had been imprisoned. Many of them were almost sick with fright, wondering whether a mass arrest would take place before the evening ended. But the Prince gave no sign of displeasure. "Of course," wrote an eye-witness, Madame Anna Stancioff, "he was well aware of the foreign intrigue which had sown hatred and treason in all these young inexperienced heads . . . he surveyed the scene attentively and indicated each conspirator with a glance at Princess Clementine who stood by his side."[6]

The trial took place in May and brought hundreds of journalists swarming into Sophia. Panitza and the Russian officer Kolobokoff were the two main defendants, for Stambulov had allowed many traitors to go free, in order to prevent the world from seeing how deep the disaffection had gone. The prosecution relied chiefly upon the documents seized at Panitza's house, and the famous "Jacobsohn letters." These letters were alleged to be dispatches between St. Petersburg and the Russian Legation in Bucharest, stolen by the clerk Jacobsohn, who had accompanied Kolobokoff to Sophia. It was claimed that he had sold them to Stambulov for a large sum of money.

The Russian Government indignantly denounced the incriminating correspondence as a forgery; and historians are still arguing about them. But the best-informed journalists of the day believed that they were "too near the truth to be disregarded." "I learned later," wrote the correspondent of the London *Standard*, Hulme Beaman, "that . . . Jacobsohn had copied out the numbers and the résumés of contents, which are very fully given in Russian Chancelleries, with the dates and names of senders and recipients, and with these materials he had constructed the dispatches which, from his knowledge of the official style, and from his aptitude in invention, doubtless very closely resembled and fairly represented the originals."[7]

The verdict was delivered at the end of May. The Russian merchant Kolobokoff was sentenced to imprisonment but handed over to his own government. Panitza was condemned to death. No one believed that the execution would be carried out, but Stambulov had not a moment's doubt where his duty lay. The Prince signed the death warrant on board his yacht at Lom Palanka, before leaving for a trip abroad. The documents were brought back to Stambulov, who was acting as Regent, and the execution was carried out without delay. Panitza was taken to the camp at Bali Effendi, tied to a willow-tree and shot.

Sophia swarmed with journalists, while Europe waited anxiously for Russian retaliation. Everyone gathered at the Café Panachoff; Cabinet Ministers, officers in white duck trousers, diplomats, opposition leaders working on the great Bulgarian dictionary. "In the cool of the evening," wrote an American journalist, "the newspaper 'specials' could be seen giving their Barb ponies gentle 'breathers' on the plain beneath snow-crested Mount Witosh, preparing for the hour when the news that the world was awaiting would come, that Stambulov was assassinated, that Ferdinand had abdicated, that the independence of the principality had been declared, or that the Russians were crossing the Danube . . . Strange signs and symbols appeared on the political horizon, but the great event hung fire."[8]

And nothing happened—at least not for the moment. The Russian Government was relying on hired assassins to settle the score. "The experience which I have gained of Oriental affairs during my seven years of office," Giers told the German Ambassador in July, 1890, "is valueless if I am incorrect in my conviction that this action will wreak its vengeance on Stambulov."[9] What Giers left unsaid was that Russian bribes would make certain that men were found to do the job. Eight months later Stambulov joined his friend, Beltcheff, the newly appointed Minister of Finance at the Café Panachoff. Shortly after eight they strolled home in the dark. Beltcheff was on Stambulov's right, but as Stambulov was carrying a heavy stick he crossed to the outside. A few moments later a pistol shot rang out. Stambulov bolted like a horse at the starting post. "Run, Beltcheff, run after me," he shouted. But Beltcheff turned into a nearby garden, hoping to hide in the bushes; instead he ran into the hiding place of the killers. Two more shots rang out. "He's dead!" cried a voice. "Stambulov is dead!" There was a shuffle as the murderers departed, then silence.

As no trace of the villains could be found Stambulov arrested every suspect in Sophia, and instructed the police to use "any method" to get the facts. One man died under "examination." Finally, four Macedonians, youths in their teens, were brought to trial. None were executed. One escaped and the other three were sentenced to penal servitude. Although Stambulov was deeply affected by the murder, he continued to stroll about Sophia accompanied by his servant

Guntcho, a squat dark little man, quick on the draw, who served as his only bodyguard. He commissioned an oil painting of the murder, which proved to be a difficult assignment. The result was an almost wholly black canvas, dotted with white specks. The large specks were the faces of Stambulov and Beltcheff; the small specks revolver flashes. The picture hung in Stambulov's drawing-room in his little house at the edge of the town.

Meanwhile Alexander III sat on his Olympian pinnacle and pretended to be wholly divorced from the sordid intrigues of the Balkans. How deeply he was involved emotionally was clear, however, by the pathological hatred with which he continued to pursue poor Alexander of Battenberg. The fact that he had driven the Prince from the Bulgarian throne was not enough. Although there was no longer any reason why the young man should not marry the Hohenzollern princess, Victoria, he passionately opposed the union. The German Royal family was split in two. The Princess's mother, who had become an Empress and a widow in 1888, all in the space of three months, continued to side with her daughter. Her son, the new Emperor, the nervous volatile William II of World War fame, supported Prince Bismarck and the Czar in opposing the marriage. His purpose, of course, was to keep on good terms with Russia, but he offended his mother and sister so deeply, the family rift never healed. While the quarrel was at its height, Alexander of Bulgaria fell in love with a Viennese actress, Joanna Loisinger, and married her in 1889. Their happiness was brief, however, for Alexander, now known as Count Hartenau, died of peritonitis in 1893, only thirty-six years of age, and was buried in Sophia. Princess Victoria, on the other hand, never recovered from her unhappy romance. Although in 1890 she dutifully married Prince Adolph Schaumburg-Lippe, the antithesis of the dashing Alexander, she continued to nurse a broken heart. The Prince died during the First World War, and in 1927 the Princess, aged sixty-one, scandalised her friends by running off with a Russian waiter half her age who abandoned her within a few months. She died two years later, sad and penniless.

No doubt William II and Bismarck were right to placate St.

Petersburg at the expense of Victoria and Alexander, for they were well aware of Russia's hostility towards Germany and feared an alliance between Russia and France. When the Three Emperors' League expired in 1887 the Czar did not renew it but offered Germany a bilateral treaty which Bismarck accepted. This "Re-insurance Treaty," as the Chancellor called it, guaranteed neutrality if either power found itself at war with a third power. The signatories also pledged themselves to observe the *status quo* in the Balkans, but emphasised Russia's "right to a decisive influence in Bulgaria and Eastern Roumelia."

Bismarck was proud of the juggling feat that enabled him to keep on reasonable terms with two such snarling dogs as Russia and Austria. But William II managed to upset the act. In 1890 he sacked Bismarck and refused to renew the Re-insurance Treaty which, he said, was incompatible with the German-Austrian alliance. This freed the Czar to take the step so long dreaded by Bismarck. He reached across Germany and made an alliance with France. From that moment onwards the struggle between Slav and German stood out in naked clarity.

Now not only Russia but Austria kept Bulgaria under close scrutiny. M. Giers tried to play his hand very coolly, aping his master's majestic indifference. "We regard Bulgaria," he snapped, "as a flea which although it bites and annoys, is otherwise harmless. We spit on Bulgaria." Spitting on Bulgaria, however, was not synonymous with detachment. Although Giers belonged to the old school of diplomacy, and certainly was not one of Russia's new men, he was too weak to put a stop to the cloak and dagger games in the Balkans. "M. Giers had always been averse . . . to our perennial interference in political affair in the Slav states of the Balkan Peninsula," wrote Baron Rosen, one of Russia's ambassadors. "This interference . . . was, however, favoured for reasons of its own by the General Staff and patronised by the Slavophile and ultra-nationalist press, and Giers was not strong enough to resist them, and was perhaps too good-natured to deal with subordinates whom ambition prompted to rely on powerful outside backing rather than on approval of their chief."[10]

Nevertheless it had the approval of the Supreme Chief. What

was curious about Alexander III was his failure to see any connection between terrorism in Russia and terrorism in Bulgaria. His grandfather, Nicholas I, had argued that subversion was an epidemic. If you encouraged it abroad, you could expect it at home. Alexander III, however, barricaded the doors of his fortress palace and allowed his Foreign Office to plot the downfall of brother monarchs who stood in Russia's way. Indeed the two movements acted as a spur to one another, like two competitive firms who stole each other's ideas and personnel. On the whole the Foreign Office put forward the most fanciful ideas. Whereas revolutionaries posed as shopkeepers, cab-drivers and even beggars, imperialist agents frequently used the Church as cover. The Russian monastery at Mt. Athos in Greece was known to be an espionage centre and was flooded with monks, many of whom were agents. The Empress Frederick comments, in a letter to her daughter, the Crown Princess of Greece, on rumours that the Czar is trying to buy the Greek island, Paros, as a base for his fleet and refers to the fact "that the Russians have already a strong hidden arsenal at Mt. Athos."[11] At the same time Mijatovich informs us that Russian icon sellers were swarming over Serbia in an effort to start a revolution.[12] The Russian Foreign Office could also claim successes in the art of propaganda and press leaks; and it was proud of the fact that it had hit upon the scheme of paying people to make "spontaneous" demonstrations which it found very useful in influencing opinion in democratic countries.

Yet, by the summer of 1892, no one could pretend that subversive efforts in Bulgaria had chalked up any spectacular successes. The Russian Asiatic Department and the Russian Legation in Bucharest were not in line for medals. The Panitza revolution had been organised on a grand scale and the attempt to murder Stambulov had been bold enough, but both had failed. The only successful *coup* had been the murder of a completely harmless individual, Dr. Vulkovitch, the Bulgarian Agent in Constantinople, who was attacked out of frustration more than anything else. None of these acts had advanced Russia's cause in the Balkans and it was clear that the time had come to make a reappraisal. It was no secret that Prince Ferdinand smarted under the ruthless authority of his dictator. Whereas Ferdinand longed to be recognised by the Great Powers—which meant Russia

—Stambulov was Russia's implacable foe. If a wedge could be driven between the two, Ferdinand might remove Stambulov himself and bring Bulgaria into the Russian orbit.

The new strategy had much to commend it, for although Ferdinand accepted Stambulov as a necessity he did not like him. Indeed, it would be difficult to imagine two men more different. Stambulov cared nothing for appearance. He lived in a semi-detached house, wore his clothes to shreds, fought his enemies with their own weapons, and spoke his mind bluntly. Ferdinand, on the other hand, was the epitome of nineteenth-century refinement. Proud, sophisticated and devious, style was almost as important to him as performance. He recoiled from Stambulov's coarse manners and complained that it was intolerable to be patronised by a rough peasant who regarded his Prince as nothing more than an ornament. Stambulov did not even trouble to hide his views from foreign journalists. "I confess I was a little surprised," wrote an American correspondent, "when the semi-barbarian Stambulov went on to speak of his sovereign, Prince Ferdinand, the grandson of Louis Philippe, descended from a long line of mighty kings, in much the same tone that a millionaire merchant might refer to one of his clerks who was diligent in small things, and for the moment useful, but who could easily be replaced. There was not a suggestion of personal loyalty to the young Prince who, at his urgent request, and after many others had refused, had embarked on the Bulgarian adventure. The only thing he seemed to dwell on with satisfaction was the fact that, thanks to the generosity of Princess Clementine, his devoted mother, Ferdinand was spending a great deal of money in the principality, and he congratulated himself and his people on the fact that, come what might, much of this would remain."[13]

During the first five years of his reign Ferdinand realised the futility of opposing Stambulov, detached himself from politics, and devoted himself to civic improvements. Under his supervision Sophia's crumbling Turkish houses and muddy streets were transformed by stone buildings, wide avenues and spacious parks. Harbours, factories and railways were under construction, the forests which the Turks had destroyed were being replanted. But

Ferdinand's artistry was best seen on his own property. "He turned an old half-ruined monastery at Euxinograd, near Varna, into a magnificent estate, with a park full of rare and precious shrubs and trees," wrote the daughter of the British Minister. "His little summer palace at Vrania, near Sophia, was set in an exquisite garden, which he himself had planned and laid out. His private zoo was the most perfect of its kind . . ."[14]

Ferdinand's obsession with dress was perhaps excessive, but at least it was a royal failing. He had uniforms designed for every festive occasion. On Easter Day he wore crimson velvet; on St. George's day blue velvet slashed with silver; on Independence Day the Bulgarian national costume made from the finest silks that Paris could produce. He even appeared as an Admiral of the Bulgarian Navy, which some people thought was going too far.

Although the Diplomatic Agents of the Great Powers were not permitted to attend official functions, there was nothing to stop them from dining informally with the Prince. As Ferdinand was not only one of the most entertaining of conversationalists but a gourmet as well, they vied with each other for invitations. "It always amused me greatly to meet him," wrote the British representative, Charles Hardinge, "as he was very witty and loved to joke about the ways and habits of his Ministers and Court officials. I remember well his telling me how a military official at his Court had in the middle of dinner taken off his boot and brought it above the table to see what it was that was hurting his foot, and his description of the incident was as good as a play. He was very French in all his thoughts and ways . . . and prided himself greatly on being the grandson of King Louis Philippe."[15]

Ferdinand's wit, however, was sometimes too sharp to be appreciated. When his mother's French lady-in-waiting became engaged to one of his Bulgarian secretaries, he sent her as his only wedding present a box of chocolates with a black ribbon around it. With it came a card: *"Toutes mes condoléances. Ferdinand"*! Occasionally he shocked diplomats with his startling candour. When, years later, the French Ambassador referred to the "devotion" the Bulgarian people felt for their ruler, Ferdinand interrupted. "Devotion? Is that the right word? . . . The truth is they detest me!"[16]

Indeed, Ferdinand was so fearful of assassination that in 1892 he told his Prime Minister that he had decided to secure the dynasty by marrying without further delay.

Stambulov approved of this move but where could a princess be found willing to risk the dangers of Sophia? Like Alexander of Battenberg, Ferdinand decided to tour the capitals of Europe. His first stop was London, where Queen Victoria received him sympathetically and wrote in her diary that he was "improved." "He cannot go about without an escort," she noted, "since the two murders, of one of his Ministers, and of his Minister at Constantinople, Dr. Vulkovitch, both instigated by the Russians; and the murderers though convicted are not given up by them but still at large."[17]

Although the Queen added that the Prince was devoted to his country, political reasons made it impossible for her to give her consent to a marriage with an English princess. Ferdinand's next stop was Berlin where William II flatly refused to receive him; then on to Munich where he was told firmly that he would not be allowed to approach a Bavarian princess.

He arrived in Vienna, exasperated and resentful, but the Emperor Franz Joseph was more helpful. Although an Austrian Archduchess was out of the question, the Duke of Parma, who represented the Italian branch of the Bourbon family, had a marriageable daughter, the Princess Marie Louise, and was open to persuasion.

After much bickering the Duke finally agreed to the betrothal of the princess on condition that Ferdinand would give his solemn promise that children born of the marriage would be brought up as Roman Catholics. This was a tall order, for the Bulgarian constitution expressly decreed that royal children must be baptised in the Greek Orthodox faith. Stambulov, however, was convinced that the marriage was essential to Bulgaria's stability and assured Ferdinand he would amend the constitution. Although this required considerable political skill he was as good as his word. The wedding took place in the spring of 1893.

Scarcely were the festivities over before Ferdinand declared war on his Prime Minister. The first Stambulov knew of it was when the results of the General Election were declared. The dictator had given instructions to his party not to rig the elections (as was usually the case) for he wished to gauge truly the measure of his popularity. The results were a triumph as only sixteen members of the Opposition were returned. Although he immediately wired the Prince he did not receive a reply for five days; and when the congratulations came they were worded in the coldest language.

Stambulov knew at once that Ferdinand had decided to get rid of him. Now all the pieces fell into place. For some months the Prince had been coquetting with notorious, pro-Russian Bulgarians, wining and dining them at the palace. The *éminence grise* was Colonel Petroff, the man whom the Prince had promoted over the head of Panitza, sparking off the mutiny. For some time Stambulov's intelligence service had informed him that these men were trying to cause a breach between himself and the Prince. They pretended to be outraged by the dictator's "reign of terror," although they well knew that Stambulov was merely using the same methods to protect Bulgaria's independence as the Russophiles were using to disrupt it. Every newspaper article and cartoon that could make mischief was brought to Ferdinand's attention. Some of the cartoons depicted the Prince with tears trickling down his huge, Bourbon nose, in his "prison-palace"; others showed him hiding ungallantly behind the burly figure of Stambulov. They whispered that if it were not for the futile hatred against Russia stirred up by his Prime Minister, Ferdinand and his bride not only could live in peace, but win the friendship of St. Petersburg and the recognition for which the Prince had always longed.

Stambulov grimly prepared himself for battle. Gratitude was not a Balkan characteristic, therefore the turn of events did not surprise him. He was confident that Ferdinand could not do without him, and felt that he could play his hand as skilfully as the Prince. Then he got wind of a rumour that Ferdinand was planning to summon him to the Palace late one night and, at the point of Colonel Petroff's gun, demand his resignation. Four times he received night summonses and four times he went, but Ferdinand was charming and nothing happened. Finally he decided to end the farce, and confronted the Prince with the story he had heard. Ferdinand denied the accusation. Stambulov pulled a piece of paper from his pocket and said quietly: "Your Highness has not learned in seven years to know me if you think I could be forced into signing anything. You might cut off my hands and feet, but you could never compel me to do what I now do voluntarily, and of my own free will. Here is my resignation, signed and undated. Take it, and keep it by you if you think it will help you . . ." Stambulov saluted, turned on his heel and departed.[18]

Ferdinand was deeply unhappy. He could not bear the atmosphere of uncertainty in which he lived. The threats of assassination were more numerous than ever—no doubt a reminder from the Russians that he could expect no peace as long as Stambulov remained. Even the poor bride, who in January, 1894, gave birth to a son and heir, Prince Boris, was the recipient of sinister communications. "It is a wonder her nerves are not more shaken," wrote the widowed Empress Frederick to her daughter, Sophie, "as the whole time before the baby was born she received threatening letters from Panslavist agents, telling her she would be murdered with her child, she would be assassinated if she had a son, one dagger was to pierce them both, which was not very pleasant for the poor thing."[19]

Indeed, the Princess was so frightened and ill that Ferdinand took her abroad to recover, not returning to Bulgaria till April. Meanwhile the Minister of War died and Ferdinand tried to persuade Stambulov to give Colonel Petroff the job. Instead, the dictator appointed his own friend, Savoff. Petroff retaliated by making mischief which had results far more startling than anyone could have imagined. Everyone knew that Savoff had a young wife of whom he was madly jealous. In order to provoke a public scandal Petroff spread the rumour that the wife was having an affair with one of Savoff's Cabinet colleagues. When Savoff heard the story he lost his balance and challenged the "lover," who needless to say was innocent, to a duel. Stambulov intervened and forbade the encounter on the grounds that there was not a shred of proof against the accused, whereupon the unhinged Savoff promptly turned round and challenged Stambulov to a duel. The dictator accepted, but the seconds refused to let the meeting take place on the grounds that Savoff's honour had not been impugned. Savoff wrote a pitiful letter to the Prince begging him to protect him from Stambulov's wrath, which Ferdinand forwarded to the dictator. He also asked for his passport, and left Bulgaria for Vienna. This, of course, once more left the Ministry of War vacant. Again the Prince pressed for Petroff. The latter even called upon Stambulov and begged him to give him a chance, swearing to serve the Prime Minister loyally. Stambulov, no doubt hoping to heal the breach between himself and the Prince, finally gave in. It was a fatal mistake.

Stambulov's downfall came far more swiftly than anyone imagined. The members of the Opposition were so emboldened by the inclusion in the government of such a severe critic as Petroff that they launched a virulent attack on the dictator. Stambulov fought back through the columns of his own newspaper, the *Svoboda*, and was inclined to treat the whole affair with indifference until the Opposition press began to accuse him of cowardice in not fighting Savoff. He lost his self-control and retaliated by publishing Savoff's cringing letter to the Prince. When Ferdinand heard the news he sent an angry telegram *en clair* from his holiday resort referring to his First Minister as "a vulgar churl." On the day of Ferdinand's return to Sophia Stambulov sent yet another resignation to the Palace. He expressed the hope that Ferdinand would find a minister "if not so devoted to the country's interests, at least not so *gemein* and more courtly and refined . . ."

Stambulov had fallen into a carefully laid trap through the most lethal of all human weaknesses—vanity. First he had made the error of permitting Petroff to become Minister of War. Second he had allowed himself to be pin-pricked into resigning.

Undoubtedly Stambulov believed that Ferdinand would be forced to recall him; but he forgot that the sovereign who commands the army commands the country—particularly a wily prince like Ferdinand. The latter formed a new Cabinet consisting of half a dozen Russophiles; then he encouraged mass demonstrations against Stambulov to destroy the myth of the latter's impregnability. At the same time he sent Stambulov a Rescript couched in glowing terms and thanking him for his services. No acknowledgment was due but the Prince would be pleased if Stambulov would call upon him at the Palace.

This was another trap, for Ferdinand knew how to be cruel. He once said he had learned his Oriental tricks from his Hungarian grandmother, the Kohary heiress. Stambulov went to the Palace and talked to Ferdinand for two hours, while a mob gathered outside the building. "When he went out," wrote an eye-witness, "Stambulov saw a rabble nearly one thousand strong, but composed mainly of youths and street urchins ... a yelling, seething mass crying 'Down with Stambulov! Down with the tyrant! Down with the usurper!' Accompanied only by his faithful Guntcho, Stambulov walked coolly forth. Some of the ragged crew spat upon him, others took muddy water in their mouths and squirted it at him, but he smiled contemptuously on his ignoble assailants, and now and again acknowledged some insult by a bow and a sweep of his hat. Opposite the public library a man leaped out with a knife, but in an instant Guntcho had covered him with his revolver and he fell back. When Stambulov reached home he was mad with rage and told me that he held the Prince responsible for allowing his guests to be treated so beneath his windows; a treatment which the wildest Albanian would never permit his guest to suffer, even if he were his most deadly enemy . . ."[20]

Sentinels were posted round Stambulov's house and for two months he rarely went out. The police had orders not to allow any one to leave or enter the house between 9 p.m. and 9 a.m. On the tenth of August, when the Prince returned to Bulgaria from one of his many trips, Stambulov wrote to him: "If I have been guilty of any crime, arrest me and try me; but do not put my wife, my mother, my family and my friends under a general arrest in my own house." But the latter received no answer and when Mr. Dering, the British Representative, raised the subject, Ferdinand replied mockingly: "Ah! I dare say *they* are worrying him a little on account of the manner in which he attacks *them* in his paper; that is all."

Stambulov's temper was not improved by remarks such as these, which were always repeated to him. Even more offensive was the interview which the new Prime Minister, M. Stoilov, gave to a certain Herr Kanner, the correspondent of the *Frankfurter Zeitung*. Stoilov talked about Stambulov's "brutal methods" and even hinted at peculation. When Kanner came to interview Stambulov it is not surprising that he found the latter in a vindictive mood. "The Prince's policy," he told the journalist, "is to be recognised by Russia. It is an *idée fixe*, almost a kind of malady. His object, I believe, is to get a thoroughly Russophile Chamber elected, so that he can meet the objections of the army on the concessions he must make to Russia by contending that he is obeying the will of the people." Then he dealt with Ferdinand himself:

"The Prince is undoubtedly a clever man, but he wastes his cleverness on petty matters. He is nervous and excitable. He reads everything that is written about him, perhaps some fifty newspapers a day, and tears one into pieces if it contains disparaging remarks. I have often told him, 'Do not read so many newspapers but study public affairs. Get a French or an English colonel to teach you the elements of military knowledge so that you may be able to understand your Minister of War.' I used to speak to him just as freely as I speak to you. But he thinks of nothing but his Court, his uniforms, etc. Even with regard to his recognition his great object is to be able to travel abroad as a reigning Prince, to show himself in his Bulgarian uniform, to be received at railway stations as a general."[21]

The interview was printed all over the world, and everyone who read it knew that Ferdinand would never forgive Stambulov, for the latter not only had attacked the Prince but made him ridiculous. Now the gloves were off, and the two men would fight to the death.

The Palace counter-attack came a week later. Stambulov was summoned to Court and charged with defamation of character. His lawyer argued that he could not be held responsible for an article by a foreign journalist. Although legally the judge could not produce a case against him, an enormous bail was demanded. The friends who had accompanied him to Court produced the money and he was freed. Outside a mob of paid trouble-makers had assembled. When Stambulov appeared the crowd hesitated; then one of them, a Police Commissioner of all things, shouted: "What are you waiting for?" picked up a stone and threw it. Soon everyone was hurling stones and brickbats. "Had it not been for the presence of mind of Guntcho who was sitting on the box," wrote an eye-witness, "the hired ruffians would probably have torn Stambulov from his seat, and finished with him; but when Costa Pavlov (one of the mob) and another made at his master with sticks, he drew from his pocket a penknife in a wash-leather case, and holding it as if it were a pistol, made pretence of aiming at Costa's head, whereupon he dealt a furious blow at Stambulov, and fell back into the crowd . . . It was proved afterwards that Costa Pavlov . . . on his departure for Rustchuk was the recipient of a present of two thousand francs. The only inquiry ever made into this riot was that Guntcho was brought up for having made his threatening demonstration with a penknife in its case . . ."[22]

In the spring of 1895 Ferdinand sent a delegation to Russia to discuss the terms of recognition. "As you know," Stambulov wrote to his friend, Hulme Beaman, ". . . the Prince . . . is ready to make any concessions if only the Czar will recognise him. And so the independence and freedom of our poor Fatherland finds itself in deadly peril, through the wretched Russophilism of our government. . ."[23]

Meanwhile every trace of the Stambulov régime was being erased from the country. Hundreds of police officials, magistrates, mayors and heads of local committees, believed to be sympathetic to the dictator, were systematically replaced by Russophiles. Stambulov had only one weapon left, his newspaper *Svoboda*, edited by his friend M. Petkoff. Under a column headed "Anarchy" he launched biting attacks on the government. The arrows went home, for the Prince frequently tore the papers to shreds and racked his brains for new ways to make the fallen minister's life disagreeable.

Of course, Stambulov's printing press was confiscated but friends got hold of another and the paper was printed in secret. Soon all sorts of petty persecutions were taking place. His bank account was confiscated, and the trees on his small property in the north of Bulgaria were cut down. Although soldiers still paced beneath his windows, he was free to come and go as he pleased between 9 a.m. and 9 p.m. The Diplomatic Agents called on him regularly and he talked as indiscreetly as ever. But in the summer of 1895 he fell ill with diabetes, and applied for a permit to go abroad, which was refused. Ferdinand had other plans for the great Bulgarian patriot.

Most diplomats felt in their bones that Stambulov was doomed, and Stambulov shared their apprehension. His only recreation was to walk along the broad leafy avenue from his house to the Union Club a few hundred yards away. "This is the street on which I will die," he remarked lightly to a friend. "Right here," he said waving his arm, "on this little stretch." An ominous sign was the release from jail of the professional killers who were alleged to have murdered Beltcheff and Vulkovitch. They were allowed to roam the streets of Sophia freely and for a time were housed next door to the man they were stalking. Yet Stambulov's spirit remained unbroken. Ill and persecuted as he was he still knew how to fight, even to laugh.

In July, 1895, the Government paper, the *Mir*, printed a hysterical attack on the fallen dictator, calling him a spy and a traitor and advocating that "his flesh should be torn from his bones." Two nights later Stambulov went to the Union Club accompanied by his friend M. Petkoff, and his farouche and loyal servant Guntcho. "I left him in good spirits," Sir Arthur Nicolson, the British Diplomatic Agent, reported to London, "full of vivacity and on the point of returning home . . . His house is in the same street as the Club, a broad open street with many people about, it was a beautiful summer's evening, and the sun still shining brightly."[24]

Stambulov's hired cab was waiting outside and he climbed in with Petkoff while Guntcho mounted the box next to the driver. He had not travelled more than twenty yards before a shot rang out. He leapt from the cab into the roadway crying: "We are to be assassinated, Petkoff. Jump out." He started running in the direction of the Club only to be confronted by three men with *yatagans*. The hired cab-driver instantly whipped up the horses and the carriage went careering down the street. Petkoff and Guntcho managed to throw themselves off and fell heavily to the ground. Meanwhile in the bright sunlight, with people strolling nearby, the three men fell upon Stambulov. As he felt for his revolver he received a slash across his right wrist which nearly severed his hand. He raised both arms to protect his head and the fingers of his left hand fell to the pavement. Another blow cleft open his head and he sank to the ground in a pool of blood. By this time Guntcho had picked himself up and was firing from two revolvers. He wounded one of the men and all three took to their heels with Guntcho in pursuit, firing and crying to everyone to arrest them, but an Inspector of Police and two gendarmes, who had been standing at the corner, pretending not to see, blocked his way and arrested him, to give the murderers time to escape.

Stambulov was carried home, not yet dead. His forehead was criss-crossed with cuts; his one eye was nearly out; and his arms so mutilated that both had to be amputated. He regained consciousness for a short time and instructed his wife not to reply to the telegram of condolence which would certainly come from Ferdinand. He died three days later.

Europe was appalled by the hideous attack. Madame Stambulov openly accused Ferdinand of the crime. Most diplomats secretly shared her opinion. "It is . . . incredible," Nicolson wrote to London, "why the police never stirred and that the only man arrested was the servant who was pursuing the assailants."[24]

Ferdinand's government was not abashed. Although the Prince hotly denied complicity the funeral was the scene of terrible disorder. As the procession passed the place where Stambulov had been cut down Petkoff began to deliver an oration on the greatness of his dead leader. "His opening words," wrote Nicolson's son and biographer, "were interrupted by a volley of rifle-shots, and mounted police, debouching from two side streets, charged at the procession with drawn swords. A stampede followed. The roadway was littered with wreaths, umbrellas and top-hats. Nicolson lost his temper. Escaping down a side-street he proceeded at once and on foot to the house of M. Stoiloff. He found some difficulty in gaining admittance. The door eventually was half-opened by the Prime Minister himself, who held a revolver in his hand. Nicolson, for a space of twenty minutes, was able to tell Stoiloff exactly what he thought."[25]

Although the scented, bejewelled Ferdinand now acquired a sinister reputation, his goal was almost in sight. With Stambulov's death the last obstacle to recognition was out of the way. Russia laid down but a single condition; that Ferdinand's heir, Boris, should be converted to the Greek Orthodox faith. As the Duke of Parma had refused to consent to the betrothal of his daughter, Marie Louise, until Ferdinand had pledged his word that children of the marriage would be brought up as Roman Catholics, some people thought that an *impasse* had been reached. But not Ferdinand. He travelled to Rome and begged the Pope not to oppose the conversion. But the Pope replied angrily: "Abdicate, monseigneur, abdicate!"

This was a vain request. Despite the anger of the Parma family, and the misery of his wife, who left the country for many months, the conversion of Boris took place in February, 1896. "A man who is capable of such infamy," gasped the Emperor of Austria, "is capable of betraying everyone and selling his best friend."[26] A few days later, the official emissaries of the Czar arrived in Sophia with Russia's recognition of Ferdinand in their pockets. "I will never allow Russia," said Franz Joseph, "to keep the only hand on Bulgaria."

VIII
Uneasy Lies the Head

In October 1894, sixteen months before Ferdinand's reconciliation with Russia, the Imperial yacht *Polar Star*, with a dying Emperor aboard, dropped anchor at Yalta. Alexander III was suffering from dropsy which some doctors thought had come from internal injuries not detected at the time, received at the Borki train disaster. Although the physicians knew that the end was only a matter of weeks they recommended the soft air of the Crimea. Alexander had never liked the lovely palace at Livadia, with its orangeries and oleanders, built for his ailing mother, Marie, but he was too ill to ignore the doctor's advice. The crowds that gathered at the port were shocked by his appearance; the giant frame was bones, and the ghostly skin and sunken cheeks wore the look of death.

The Czar was in great discomfort for his legs swelled so badly he could not sleep. He spent most of the day in a wheel-chair gazing at the sea. The Imperial family began to assemble one by one. The beautiful Princess Alix of Hesse arrived from Darmstadt in response to a telegram from her fiancé, the Hereditary Grand Duke. The Prince and Princess of Wales were also summoned by the latter's sister, the Empress. When they changed trains *en route* at Vienna the British Ambassador met them and they asked anxiously: "Are we too late?" He nodded his head, for Alexander III had died that day.

In the Crimea the guns were booming out a salute for the new Czar, twenty-six-year-old Nicholas II. The shy unassuming young man was suddenly overcome with terror. He sought out his sister Olga, flung his arms around her and sobbed: "I'm not ready for it. I don't even know how to receive my ministers." "Even Alicky could not help him," the Grand Duchess told a journalist many years later. "He was in despair. He kept saying that he did not know what would become of us all, that he was wholly unfit to reign ... Nicky had been trained as a soldier. He should have been taught statesmanship and he was not. It was my father's fault. He would not even have Nicky in a Council of State until 1893. I can't tell you why ..."[1]

The funeral took place in St. Petersburg. The open coffin lay in state in the cathedral of St. Peter and St. Paul for two weeks before the burial. All the powers, great and small, sent representatives; and the royal mourners had to undergo the ordeal of kissing the dead Emperor's lips. "As he lay uncovered in his coffin," wrote Lord Carrington, a member of the Prince of Wales's suite, "his face looked a dreadful colour and the smell was awful. He was not embalmed until three days after his death."[2]

All the visiting rulers and celebrities were eager to gauge the mind and character of the new Czar. Would he follow in his father's autocratic footsteps; and would he pursue an expansionist policy in Asia and the Balkans? The Prince of Wales had more opportunity to form a judgment of Nicholas than any other visiting Royalty as he and his wife stayed with the Dowager Empress in the Anitchikov Palace; and so did the Czar. The Prince was amazed at the control the widowed Empress exercised over her son. Ten days after Alexander III was laid to rest, court mourning was suspended for a few hours so that Nicholas could marry his princess, who became known in St. Petersburg as "the funeral bride." Yet his mother refused to allow him to have even the briefest of honeymoons. Dutifully the Czar brought his bride back to the palace where they lived in the rooms which Nicholas had shared with his brother George. The Prince of Wales told Lord Carrington that the young couple came down to breakfast after their bridal night "as though nothing had happened."

It is not surprising that the Prince of Wales came to the conclusion that Nicholas II was "weak as water." The poor young man had no firm views on anything and allowed himself to be swayed like a tree in the wind. He did not try to conceal his apprehension at the thought of ruling 133 million people, twice the number as in his grandfather's day. He acknowledged the brilliance of Sergius Witte, his Minister of Finance, who had started life as a station-master and had until recently been responsible for communications. In 1894 Russia was enjoying a minor industrial boom, due to the fact that Witte had built a network of railways linking the great centres; even a Trans-Siberian line was in the process of being con-structed. But although Russia was one of the world's largest pro-ducers of oil and metals and was supplying herself with locomotives, rolling stock and argicultural machinery, the peasants were poorer than ever. The Treasury still relied on grain exports for the bulk of its revenue and the world price had fallen sharply. As a result dis-content was spreading; political controversy bubbled dangerously beneath the surface and people in all parts of the country were calling for parliamentary government and a free press.

No doubt the Prince of Wales touched upon representative government, for he told Lord Carrington that he was disturbed by Nicholas's autocratic ideas and lack of worldly sense. Carrington remarked gloomily that a revolution was inevitable but the Prince replied tartly that nothing was inevitable if only the Czar would move with the times. Perhaps Nicholas toyed with the idea of reform. Some people think he did, for when he received the dig-nitaries of the Empire at the Winter Palace confusion surrounded the speech that he had promised them. It was delayed an hour while rumours flew about that the reactionary Pobedonostev was persuading him to tear up one address and substitute another. At any rate, when he finally made his pronouncement it fell on the ears of the assembly like a clap of thunder. He rejected the mildest form of representative government as a "senseless dream" and made it clear that he would "maintain for the good of the whole nation the principle of absolute autocracy as firmly and strongly as did my late lamented father." From that moment onward every liberal element in the country joined battle against him.

Nicholas was a dangerous ruler. He had the same grandiose am-bitions, the same insatiable appetite as all his ancestors. The only difference was that he could not make up his mind how to tackle his ventures, swinging like a pendulum between one idea and the next. "This 'charmer,' without will, without aim, without imagination, was more awful than all the tyrants of ancient and modern history," wrote his enemy, Trotsky. "He is not treacherous but he is weak. And weakness fulfills all the functions of treachery," commented his second cousin, Kaiser William II. "Show your own mind and don't let others forget who you are," his wife scribbled across his diary.

Nicholas longed to be strong, for he dreamed of glory just as his grandfather, Nicholas I, had done. "I told Witte," wrote General Kuropatkin, the Minister of War, "that our Czar has grandiose plans in his head: to capture Manchuria for Russia, and to annex Korea. He is dreaming also of bringing Tibet under his dominion. He desires to take Persia, and to seize not only the Bosphorus but the Dardanelles."[3] The question of the Bosphorus arose in a particularly amateurish way two years after Nicholas ascended the throne, in the winter of 1896-7. The young Czar became almost childishly excited about a hare-brained scheme presented to him by M. Nelidov, the Russian Ambassador in Constantinople. As the Turks once again had outraged European feeling by carrying out massacres—this time against the Armenians—the Ambassador argued that the time was ripe for Russia to seize the heights of the Bosphorus above Constantinople. His proposal envisaged a bold *coup de main*, a sort of lightning commando operation, which would be an accomplished fact before England or any of the other Great Powers realised what was happening. The Czar would dispatch 30,000 troops on warships and transports from Odessa to the Upper Bosphorus and land them on both sides of the straits. The arrangements were astonishingly amateurish. Nelidov was to return to Constantinople; and when he deemed the time propitious would give the signal for the descent of the Russian landing force by a telegram: "Long without News."

Nicholas held a secret Ministerial Council at which he won the support of the President of the Council and the Ministers of War and the Navy. Luckily Sergius Witte was appalled and finally stopped the undertaking by convincing the Czar that the result would be a European War with Turkey, Austria and Britain lined up against him. The feckless Nicholas was not in the least disconcerted, for his moods changed overnight. He merely switched his attention to an attractive alternative. For months Kaiser William II had been trying to interest him in the Far East, as he knew that a clash between Russia and Austria in the Balkans would inevitably involve Austria's ally, Germany. William talked tirelessly to Nicholas about the "Yellow Peril" and urged him to become the civilising power in the Orient. As a result, when the Emperor Franz Joseph arrived in St. Petersburg in the summer of 1897 and asked Nicholas to sign a Treaty with Austria, pledged to observe the *status quo* in the Balkans, the Czar agreed with equanimity. The document was hailed by the powers as "putting the Balkan Question on ice."

This did not mean, however, as so many historians suggest, that Russia turned her back on the Middle East. "This misconception," wrote the American scholar, Sidney Fay, "arose largely from the inspired Russian Press and from misinformed persons who believed that the Russian Bear had shifted his appetite completely to the plains of Manchuria. In reality, although the Czar and his Ministers talked of Port Arthur, they were at the same time thinking of Constantinople."[4]

They were also thinking of the Balkan countries. In his own handwriting the Czar later summarised his policy as "not to take our eyes off the East but to pay the greatest attention to the West."

The Western country that most gripped Russian attention at this time was Serbia. Ferdinand of Bulgaria had worked his passage back to Muscovite favour but the twenty-two-year-old King of Serbia, Alexander Obrenovich, was becoming increasingly troublesome. The Russian chargé d'affaires, M. Mansurov, and the Russian military attaché, Baron Taube, who worked together closely, were uncertain how to handle the situation until they learned, in the autumn of 1897, that Alexander had fallen madly in love. They were not slow to see the possibilities of re-establishing Russian influence by gaining an ascendancy over the King's mistress. And this prompted them to promote a policy which ended in one of the most ferocious royal murders in history. "I frankly accuse Russia," wrote M. Mijatovich, the Serbian Ambassador in London, "of having planned deliberately . . . the ruin of the Obrenovich dynasty. And I will show that to accomplish that object the Russian official and unofficial diplomacy did not hesitate to apply methods of such Asiatic Machiavellianism that the mind and morality of Western Europe can hardly realise that such actions would have been possible at the end of the nineteenth and the beginning of the twentieth century."[5]

The threads of this gruesome tragedy stretched back twenty years to the time when Alexander's father, Prince Milan, was on the throne. In the mid-seventies the Russians talked of a "Greater Serbia" and Milan dreamed of the day when his small kingdom of two and a half million peasants would include the Serb-populated provinces of Bosnia and Herzegovina under Turkish rule. Needless to say, Milan was a passionate Russophile; and so was his beautiful black-eyed seventeen-year-old bride, Nathalie, the daughter of a rich Bessarabian landowner. Indeed, Nathalie often confided to friends that "in her innermost heart she never ceased to be Russian."

Milan felt unable to ignore the frantic pleadings of the Russian Panslavs; and in 1876, against the wishes of the Czar, he plunged Serbia into war with Turkey on behalf of Bosnia and Herzegovina. The fact that his peasants dropped their guns and ran so annoyed the Czar that he publicly rebuked Serbia for cowardice; and overnight Panslav enthusiasm veered from a Greater Serbia to a Greater Bulgaria.

This change of allegiance suited Russian diplomacy for Bulgaria was the gateway to the Turkish Straits; and control of the Straits still dominated official thought. Consequently, at the Berlin Congress following the Russo-Turkish war, Russia used Serbia as a bargaining counter against Austria. While Bulgaria nearly doubled its territory Milan was left almost empty-handed. Bosnia and Herzegovina were assigned not to Serbia but to Austria who was allowed to occupy and administer them, although formally they remained under Turkey's suzerainty.* And as the final cynicism, Russia aban-

* This was the result of a secret arrangement made between Russia and Austria in 1876 to ensure Austrian neutrality in the Russo-Turkish war. Russia had gone even further in 1881, agreeing that Austria could annex the provinces when it suited her.

doned Serbia to Austria's "sphere of influence." Milan was so outraged that he opened negotiations of his own with Vienna and three years later signed a secret pact which bound him still further to the Habsburgs but elevated Serbia to the status of a Kingdom.

Milan's hatred for Russia never altered and he remained an implacable enemy until his death. But St. Petersburg knew how to wait. Officially, at the level of Czar and Foreign Secretary, Russia did not interfere in Serbian affairs. Unofficially, at the level of Legation secretaries, Panslav enthusiasts and secret agents, she worked to promote Russian control. Milan was well aware of her methods. As a Slav himself, he felt that he understood the mind and character of his adversaries. No matter how many promises Russia made, he knew she would not surrender an inch of the Balkans to her archrival Austria if she could help it. From his own bitter experience he recognised her genius for intrigue, and attributed every misfortune that befell him to her malign influence.

There were plenty of opportunities for mischief-making as Serbia possessed two dynasties. The Karageorgevich family had ruled the country from 1842 to 1858 and the present claimant, Prince Peter Karageorgevich, had never given up hope of retrieving his father's throne from the grasp of Milan Obrenovich. He spent much of his time in St. Petersburg and in 1883 strengthened his ties with Russia by marrying Princess Zorka, a daughter of the King of Montenegro. As Zorka's two sisters were married to Russian Grand Dukes, King Milan was not wrong in interpreting the union as a strategic move. It could scarcely have been a love-match, he insisted, for Zorka was the image of her father; and as the British Consul had pointed out: "His Majesty's features are so masculine and his complexion so dark that they can scarcely be reproduced to advantage under a feminine form."[6]

Prince Peter was enough of a problem; but in the eighties a new party, the Radicals, sprang into being, subsidised by Russia and led by Nikola Pashitch. Whatever the King did, the Radicals opposed. When he instructed the police to collect the small arms from the peasants—in order to prevent disorder—the Radicals incited them to rebellion. Although the revolt fizzled out in four days the leader—

Nikola Pashitch—and hundreds of frightened villagers fled into Bulgaria. The Russian Panslavs sent them money and several Russian newspapers praised Peter Karageorgevich and hailed his possible assumption of the throne. King Milan knew enough about Alexander III's autocratic rule to appreciate the fact that these voices would not be heard if they displeased the Czar.

Unfortunately the King's domestic affairs were even more unsettled than his political life; and Serbia, a simple little country with a peasant population that still believed in evil omens, were-wolves and vampires, was transformed suddenly into a tempestuous Ruritania, supplying the European press with a steady stream of gossip and scandal. Milan was not without ability; but he succumbed too easily to pretty women and found the Monte Carlo Casino irresistible. Although he had married for love he soon drifted away from the Queen, complaining ungallantly that she was frigid in bed. Out of bed Nathalie was a tiger of a woman, jealous, strong-willed, with a liking for public scenes. Once at a State Dinner the King and his Foreign Secretary were deep in conversation when the Queen inquired across the table: "What are you discussing in so lively a fashion?" "Madam," answered the Minister, "His Majesty is discoursing on education." "Then I pity you," snapped the Queen, "for you are talking of education with a man who has none."[7]

On another occasion Nathalie caused a scandal at the Easter reception. It was customary for the Queen to kiss the wives of dignitaries and foreign diplomats. When the wife of the Greek Minister approached, Nathalie turned her face away. Everyone knew that Milan was pursuing this lady and watched with bated breath. The Chamberlain coughed and Milan made the mistake of moving forward and remonstrating with the Queen. Some people say that Nathalie indulged in a flow of invective; others that she slapped her rival's face.

It is not altogether surprising that the King sought consolation in a mistress. Unfortunately his choice fell upon Nathalie's best friend, Madame Artemesia Christich, the wife of his private secretary. People whispered that she was a Russian agent, particularly when Milan began to talk of divorcing Nathalie to marry her.

"Bear your trial as I have borne mine," Prince Rudolph of Austria cautioned the King. "I can sympathise with your fate but you must avoid any further scandal, or you will lose all."[8]

At times Milan grew so depressed that he talked of abdicating. Not only was his personal life unsatisfactory, not only was he harassed by Russian intrigue, but he found the treachery of his own people contemptible. "We must support each other," he wrote in 1884 to Prince Alexander of Bulgaria, "for *the peoples of this peninsula have a tendency to change rulers like their shirts*. They are Slavs and that explains everything . . ."[9] Unfortunately Milan, far from supporting Prince Alexander, made the mistake of attacking Bulgaria to prevent her from seizing territory in Macedonia. Once again he was defeated—this time at Slivnitza—and his throne rocked dangerously.

Milan now made an effort to patch things up with the Queen, but he could not free himself from Artemesia and the quarrels were worse than ever. "The Castle is in utter confusion," wrote an officer stationed in Belgrade in October, 1886. "One scandalous scene succeeds another; the King looks ill and as if he never slept. Poor fellow! He flies for refuge to us in the guard-house and plays cards with the officers. Sometimes he speaks bitterly about his unhappiness at home. The army is devoted to him; the defeat in Slivnitza is forgotten. Card-playing, however, is his worst enemy; it will work his total ruin. He loves it passionately, and plays excitedly for high points, and never wins."[10]

The only link that bound Milan and Nathalie was a mutual adoration of their only child, Crown Prince Alexander. However, in 1886 Milan received reports that convinced him that Nathalie was plotting with St. Petersburg to force his abdication and set herself up as Regent. His dislike flamed into hatred and he became obsessed with the idea of expelling her from the country. Finally he resorted to a trick. In 1887 he persuaded her to take the Crown Prince to Germany for six months' schooling; and at the end of the period refused to allow her to return. He told her that he was applying to the Church for a divorce; and, furthermore, that he was sending two officers to Germany to bring Prince Alexander back to Belgrade. The scene that took place riveted world attention. When the Serbian officers arrived in Wiesbaden Nathalie refused to hand the child over to them. Instead she telegraphed for help to the Emperors of Russia, Austria and Germany. No one wished to get mixed up in the affair. Finally Kaiser William II ordered the German police to assist the Serbian Emissaries and remove the Crown Prince by force. When the police officers entered the Queen's suite the ten-year-old Alexander fled screaming to his mother's arms. She stood pointing a loaded revolver at the door. "Advance and I fire!" Luckily the police officer was tactful. "Your Majesty cannot be in earnest," he said gently. "I have my orders. Your Majesty knows an officer must obey orders."[11] Finally, the weeping Queen surrendered and twenty-four hours later the Prince was back in Belgrade.

Meanwhile Milan had decided to abdicate. Weary of the hazards of kingship he longed for a life of irresponsibility in the sophisticated capitals of Europe. But the thought of Nathalie as an influential Queen-mother was unbearable. First he persuaded the Church to give him a divorce; then he formed a Regency consisting of three statesmen who pledged their solemn word that they would not allow the Queen to enter Serbia without Milan's permission; finally he extracted two million dinars from the Rusisan Government in return for his abdication. In the autumn of 1889 he departed happily for Paris accompanied by Madame Artemesia Christich. Some people said that Artemesia had acted as a Russian agent in persuading Milan to abdicate; others, that she did so in the hope of marrying her royal lover. Whatever her reasons, Milan tired of her after tasting the glittering society of France and she faded into the mists of time.

Alexander was only twelve years old when he became King. He was not an attractive boy. As a child he had surprised people by his heartlessness, and now he was colder than ever, for the quarrels of his parents had left him silent and withdrawn. Although he showed no emotion when told that his father had abdicated, he wept when he was instructed to put away his toys. From that time onward his only companions were grown-ups.

Alexander was forced to endure more anguish, for Queen Nathalie defied Milan's proscription and arrived in Belgrade determined to take up residence with her son. She was told that it was out of the question; that she could not even see the King unless she signed a paper agreeing to limit her incursions to two short visits a year. But Nathalie was fighting for the right to supervise Alexander's education, and refused to comply. She was not allowed to enter the Palace, and the King grew ill pining for his mother. The Regents finally telegraphed Milan who reluctantly gave his consent to a meeting between the two.

Nathalie drove about Belgrade every day in a carriage drawn by white ponies and received an enthusiastic welcome from the populace. But she made the mistake of inveighing against Milan and the Regents and encouraging the King "to break away from his leading strings." She fed malicious stories to the Russian press and invited prominent Panslavists to dinner—all in the hope of furthering her objectives. In the end the Regents ordered her out of the country, and once again she was removed by force. She was escorted to the harbour at six in the morning by a military detachment and put on a steamer for the Hungarian frontier-town of Zimony. She was so angry that she turned on the commanding officer and reminded him of the defeat of Slivnitza.

Although the Regents issued formal decrees of banishment, first on Nathalie, then on Milan, they were forced to withdraw them by pressure of public opinion. And during the next three years the ex-King and the ex-Queen whirled in and out of Belgrade, one arriving when the other was departing, both pouring out advice to their son.

In April 1893 the boy King astonished everyone by taking matters into his own hands. He invited his Regents and Ministers to dinner at the Palace. As the evening was drawing to a close he addressed the company. At that very moment, he said, a proclamation to the people was being posted on the streets of Belgrade, announcing that he, Alexander, had declared himself "of age" and was taking over the reins of government. His Regents and Ministers must spend the night in the Palace. They could remain as his guests or, if they preferred, as his prisoners. The doors of the drawing-room were flung open and the astonished group saw that the passages were lined with troops, their bayonets drawn.

Europe was startled by a *coup d'état* on the part of a seventeen-year-old King. Alexander had planned it with the connivance of his tutor Dr. Lazar Dokich, who was very keen to become Prime Minister. Dokich had his wish and made the mistake of persuading the King to sack his father's Liberal Ministers, all of them staunch supporters of the Obrenovich Dynasty, and to appoint Radicals in their places. For a while this party referred emotionally to their King as "Alexander the Great."

Russia, of course, looked upon the young Serbian ruler with favour for putting the Radicals in power. And when, the following year, Alexander Obrenovich travelled to St. Petersburg for the funeral of Alexander III the Foreign Office made a great fuss of him. The Prince of Wales, however, told Queen Victoria that the Grand Dukes snubbed him because of his lack of polish; and the Czar wrote in his diary how sad it was to forgo an hour of "his wifey's" company in order to receive the King of Serbia.

Alexander Obrenovich did not enjoy Russian political favour for long. Soon after the King's *coup d'état* the death occurred of his tutor-Prime Minister, Dr. Dokich, and "Alexander the Great" lost control. The Radicals proved even more oppressive than the Liberals, impeaching the ex-Ministers and sweeping out of office all Liberal adherents. As most of these men were loyal supporters of the dynasty the King protested; but the Radicals "resented his remonstrances . . . they took every day less account of his wishes and opinions, and even told him that he could attend the Cabinet Council only when they requested him to do so."[12] Once again Alexander resorted to illegal means to assert himself. He suspended the new constitution and substituted an old one which allowed him to dismiss his government and form a "neutral Cabinet."

This happened in 1897—the year that St. Petersburg and Vienna signed their pact to observe the *status quo* in the Balkans. It was also the year that Russia began the intrigue that swept Serbia along its murderous path. The Russians were outraged by the news that their implacable enemy, ex-King Milan, was returning to Belgrade as an adviser to his son. "The Russian intrigue to get Serbia into her power," Milan wrote to Mijatovich in 1897, "is so persistent, great and dangerous that I consider it my duty to return to Belgrade to be at the post of danger, and to help this poor and friendless young man."[13]

King Milan was not imagining things. Baron Rosen, the Russian diplomatist who served as Minister in Belgrade in 1896, deeply disapproved of the machinations of his countrymen. He blamed the military influence at the Russian Legation, which was not subordinate to civil policy but assumed "the part of an independent branch of the Government, entitled to have a policy of its own and to pursue it in foreign countries through its own regularly credited agents." Baron Taube, the Russian military attaché, wrote Rosen, "had been working for years hand in glove with my predecessor actively supporting one of the political parties in Serbia supposed to be devoted to Russian interests . . ." Rosen also criticised St. Petersburg's lack of Government control and "the tendency of ambitious subordinate agents to indulge in playing politics on independent lines." "If one adds to this the innate, somewhat anarchistic tendencies of the [Russian] mentality, generally rather refractory to the idea of discipline, one easily realised how difficult it may be for a Minister of Foreign Affairs to keep his agents abroad under proper control and to prevent their striking out on lines of policy of their own, sometimes even in direct opposition to the policy of the central authority."[14]

However, by 1897 Count Muraviev had taken over the Foreign Office, Baron Rosen had left Belgrade, and Russian plots could no longer be attributed to "undisciplined underlings." The "unofficial policy" that had been a hall-mark of Alexander's III reign once again became an integral part of Russian diplomacy, and Baron Taube and M. Mansurov worked together with the full approval of St. Petersburg. For instance, when King Milan returned to Belgrade in 1897 to advise his son, and accepted the appointment of Commander-in-Chief of the Serbian Army, the Russian Foreign Office immediately sent Zhadovsky to Serbia with instructions to discredit the ex-King in all ways possible. "Zhadovsky did not hesitate to denounce and calumniate King Milan to every Serbian politician or citizen with whom he came in contact," wrote Mijatovich, "calling him the most opprobrious names. He went even so far as to insult King Milan, taking no notice of him when they met in society, and refusing to salute him in the streets of Belgrade. He expected that such conduct would prove to the Serbians that Milan was a man of no consequence to Russia, that he was hated by the Czar and that they would do well to drive him away."[15]

When these tactics did not work, more drastic ones were recommended. The Prime Minister, Dr. Vladan, intercepted dispatches sent by Zhadovsky to St. Petersburg inveighing against Milan's influence on his "weak-headed son." ". . . it is necessary in our own interests that this evil [Milan] should be cut down as soon as possible," he wrote.[16] Not long afterwards an attempt was made on Milan's life. The ex-King was driving to the Palace in an open Victoria. A young man fired four revolver shots at him, one of the bullets grazing his shoulder. The youth was captured, gave his name as Knezevich and said that he came from Bosnia. He told the police that he had been taken to a house in Bucharest and paid £400 to kill Milan. He was shown a picture of the residence of Colonel Grabov, the head of the Russian Secret Service in the Balkans, and identified it as the place he had visited.

Meanwhile other members of the Russian bureaucracy were working on a plan more subtle than murder. Everyone knew that King Alexander Obrenovich had fallen in love with his mistress, Madame Draga Mashin. He had met her at his mother's villa at Biarritz. Queen Nathalie had taken an interest in the attractive, impoverished widow, particularly when she learned that Draga was descended from a swine merchant who had been a close friend of the first Obrenovich ruler. She had invited Draga to become her lady-in-waiting and to live with her in France.

Draga was nine years older than Alexander, voluptuous, sophisticated and said to be "careless with her favours." Up till now Alexander had worried his parents by his lack of interest in women. Some people said that he was malformed and could not perform the sexual act; others that he did not have the right genes. His father and mother were relieved to have proof of his normality and raised no objections when he invited Draga to return to Belgrade with him in the autumn of 1897.

The King installed her in a pretty little house, and soon her salon was crowded with all the most influential people in the capital. Milan did not like Draga and was worried by the number of Russians who attended her evening receptions. He learned that, when she had stayed in the Tyrol with his son, Alexander Isvolsky, the Russian Minister to Bavaria, had spent four days with them. Soon there were rumours that Draga had placed herself "unreservedly" at the service of the Russian cause. The Russian military attaché, Baron Taube, was a frequent guest in her house; and so was M. Neklidov, the secretary of the Russian Legation; and M. Mansurov, the chargé d'affaires.

Only a few months after Draga had moved to Belgrade ex-King Milan pressed his son to think seriously of securing his dynasty by marrying a suitable princess. Alexander agreed and the Austrian and German ambassadors were asked to find a wife for him. It was not easy, as Alexander stipulated that his bride must be "young, beautiful and lovely, so as to win his love; further she ought to be politically well-connected, and at least have family relations with one of the first-class courts of Europe; further she ought to be a highly cultured and gifted woman; and last, but not least, very wealthy."[17] The Austrian Foreign Secretary asked M. Mijatovich to tell King Alexander that both the Austrian and German Emperors would join in the effort to find him "a suitable princess," but that a princess who possessed all his requirements "could do better than marry King Alexander of Serbia and spend her life in Belgrade." However, the Austrian Foreign Secretary finally came forward with a photograph of the Princess Alexandra von Schaumberg-Lippe. Although she belonged to a minor princely family and had nothing much in the way of a dowry she was far from ugly. Alexander told his father that he liked her picture, but must have time to think things over. Milan stressed the political urgency of the marriage but Alexander refused to be hurried. Not until the spring of 1900 did he come to a decision. He urged Milan and his Prime Minister to leave Belgrade and complete the foreign trips they were planning. When they returned in August he would travel to Germany with his father "to see my princess and if God so wills give her the ring; and certainly by the end of the year, if not sooner, you will see me a married man." Milan was overjoyed for he believed that the marriage would cement Serbia's relations with Germany and Austria. Unfortunately Alexander only wanted to get Milan and the Prime Minister out of Serbia so that he could proceed with a plan which he knew that neither would tolerate.

A month later the acting Prime Minister, M. Vulkashin, was leaving his office when the Home Minister stopped him and in an agitated voice told him that "something dreadful," "something fateful for Serbia" was going to happen. "I have wired in cipher to King Milan, that a great misfortune for him personally, for King Alexander, for Serbia, and for us all is in preparation and have asked him to come at once to prevent that misfortune if possible."

The Home Minister advised Vulkashin to go to the Palace at once, as he had taken an oath not to repeat what he knew, but "perhaps the King will tell you what is going on." Vulkashin lunched at the Palace the next day and afterwards the King took him into the elegant room known as "Queen Nathalie's Boudoir." Alexander began by saying that the eternal quarrel between his parents had embittered his life and undermined his health. As a result he had never had any ambition, not even the ambition to reign as a King. "I wear the Crown not because I love it but because it is my duty to do so." Then he came to the point. He had decided to bow to the wishes of his Cabinet, and to marry. But, he added, as none of the great sovereign Courts would provide him with a wife he had made up his mind to marry a Serbian, "a daughter of my own people." "There already exists a woman," he said, rising to his feet, "whom I love more than anyone or anything in this world, the only woman with whom I can be perfectly happy, and only then can I consecrate my whole life to the interests of the people if she becomes my wife . . ."

"And who is that woman, Sire?"

"Madame G. Draga, the daughter of the late Panta Lunyevitza."

"Draga Mashin . . . No, Sire, that cannot be—that ought not to be."

The King's eyes filled with rage. "He who tries to hinder me is my enemy." Vulkashin handed the King his resignation but before leaving made a final plea. "It is hard for me to believe that you mean to marry Madame Draga. Do you not see, Sire, that such a step is nothing less than suicide of the dynasty? Putting aside anything that could be said against that lady, her known sterility would be quite sufficient to prove what I have just said. But other circumstances of the case ought not to be overlooked. Madame Draga is much older than yourself. She does not enjoy a good reputation—rightly or wrongly—and as it often happens in common life, a good mistress does not make always a good wife. The Pretender Peter Karageorgevich would gain, in consequence of such a marriage, much more than if he had distributed a million gold pieces to the agitators against the Obrenovich Dynasty. You ought to know, Sire, that after such a marriage not a single European Court will receive you; you will be boycotted by all the Sovereigns in Europe. The entire intelligence of the country will rebel against it, and will never be reconciled to it. Not only your Majesty, but Serbia will lose the esteem which it now enjoys in the world, and will soon become an object of irony and contempt. Believe me, Sire, I would gladly sacrifice my life if I could but save you from this fatal step . . ."[18]

The King had told other ministers of his resolve and all had implored him to reconsider his decision, but he replied that he could not live without Draga. That same day he telegraphed the news to his father and issued a proclamation to the public. All over Belgrade people gathered on street corners and in cafés to discuss the news. Soon the lowest street sweeper knew that Draga's father had died in an insane asylum, that her mother was a dipsomaniac; that Draga herself was a woman with a shady past, nearly ten years older than the King. The fact that Draga had had no children by her first marriage obviously meant that she was barren. Who could find anything good to say of the monstrous indignity Alexander was inflicting on Serbia? The women were particularly shocked and declared that they would never recognise such a woman as their Queen.

Meanwhile the King had ordered the wedding rings, engaged the priests and summoned his ministers to luncheon. Two ministers went to Draga's house and begged her to give up the King and leave Serbia. This she promised to do, but instead went to a friend's house and sent a message to Alexander. When his Cabinet Ministers arrived for luncheon and handed him a joint resignation he tore it up. "Gentlemen," he said, "I have the right as a man to be happy. That lady is the only condition for my happiness and I wish to take her unto myself. No one can deter me from that course. Neither in youth nor in adolescence did I have anyone who loved me. This woman understands me completely and I wish to share both good and evil with her. I want to give her a ring. Of you I have the right to demand that you perform your duties. That right has been given to me by the Constitution."[19]

Despite this appeal, the Ministers refused to take back their block resignation. The King shouted at them and some shouted back. Before the guests had departed Alexander rushed off to Draga's house. He placed "a beautiful diamond ring" on her finger and became "formally engaged to her."

The Ministers were stunned and puzzled by the fact that nothing they said or did had any effect upon the King. What they did not know was that Alexander had told M. Mansurov, the Russian chargé d'affaires, of his wish to marry Draga three months earlier; and that Mansurov had promised to help him if he would follow a pro-Russian line and work with the Radical Party. Mansurov had conferred with the Radical leaders who made the following conditions; the restoration of constitutional government; an amnesty for imprisoned Radicals; and most important of all, the banishment of ex-King Milan from Serbia. Alexander agreed to all their provisions.

Meanwhile Milan had replied to Alexander's telegram. He resigned his post as Commander-in-Chief of the Serbian Army and gave a copy of his letter to Alexander to the world press.

"My dear Son,—With the best will to oblige you, I cannot give my consent to the impossible marriage for which you have decided. You ought to know that, by doing what you intend, you are pushing Serbia into an abyss. Our dynasty has sustained many a blow, and has continued to live. But this blow would be so terrible that the dynasty could never recover from it. You have still time to think it over. If your decision should really be, as you say, inflexible, then, nothing remains for me but to pray to God for our Fatherland. I shall be the first to cheer the Government which shall drive you from the country, after such a folly on your part.—Your father, Milan."[19]

King Alexander managed to persuade the President of the Court of Appeals, a judge with no political standing, to form a Cabinet. Yet he was far from happy. No statesman of reputation would agree to serve him; and the army, if possible, was even more hostile. Not a single general would accept the post of War Minister. Military circles were clinging to the faint hope that Milan would return to Belgrade and lead a *coup d'état*.

For the first time King Alexander was depressed and uncertain, realising at last that he was sitting on a powder keg. His anxiety did not last long, however, for on 14th July, five days after the proclamation announcing his marriage intentions, Russia came to his rescue. M. Mansurov announced to the Serbian people that Czar Nicholas II had sent his congratulations to King Alexander and Madame Mashin—whom he referred to as "Her Serene Highness"—on their approaching wedding. Four days later the public was stunned to learn that the Russian Czar had agreed to serve as King Alexander's best man; and had commanded Mansurov to represent him in this capacity.

Russia had knocked the wind out of the opposition. People were so surprised and confused they did not know what to think. For a while they meekly accepted the situation. Alexander regained his confidence and instead of contenting himself with a modest wedding, celebrated his marriage on 23rd July with spectacular festivities.

The Russian Legation was now the political centre of Belgrade. By facilitating the marriage between Alexander and Draga the Russian chargé d'affaires, M. Mansurov, could claim to have broken the links between the King and his father, and with one blow smashed the pro-Austrian orientation of Serbia. It was a formidable *coup*, particularly as no one could accuse the Russian Foreign Minister of behaving in a dishonourable way. He could still smile blandly and assure the Austrian Foreign Minister that Russia was observing the *status quo* agreement of 1897 with meticulous care. That was the way "unofficial" Russian policy worked.

St. Petersburg was delighted with the turn of events; and so, of course, was the King. A few weeks after his marriage Draga told him that she believed herself to be pregnant. She was examined by a French doctor, M. Collet, who confirmed her hopes. The King was so excited that he announced the news publicly at the end of August. As the baby was not due until April many people felt that his proclamation was so premature as to be indecent. Others refused to believe it. Draga, they insisted, was sterile. What trickery was she up to? The fact that her sister was pregnant was sufficient to start a rumour that the Queen was planning to palm off the latter's baby as her own when the time came.

Meanwhile Alexander devoted all his efforts to making Draga a popular figure. He named regiments and villages and schools after her. He turned her birthday into a national holiday and even struck a Queen's Medal to be given to women of outstanding merit. He presented decorations to writers and artists in her name and declared an amnesty for all those suspected of hostile acts against ex-King Milan. For a while his efforts drew a gratifying response. The Court was flooded with gifts from grateful families; three newspapers took up the Queen's cause; and the City of Belgrade gave the couple a yacht costing 120,000 dinars.

Unfortunately Queen Draga was both power-thirsty and foolish. No matter what the King did for her, she demanded more. Her brothers and sisters were continually at Court and she even allowed them to take part in audiences. She begged the King to punish her enemies and reward her friends. In order to please her he went to extreme lengths to vilify the ministers who had served in his late government. Posters appeared all over Belgrade attacking them for incompetence and venality. The Prime Minister and several of his colleagues fled the country. But the hostile attitude of the army rankled most with the Queen, and she urged Alexander to carry out a purge among the higher officers. Four generals and numerous colonels and majors—among them Draga's former brother-in-law, Colonel Mashin—were pensioned off, and their places filled by officers said to be friendly to Draga. The secret police was increased, denunciations encouraged, and hundreds of people sent to gaol on suspicion alone.

Alexander had a terrible foreboding that his father might suddenly reappear, rally the army, and effect a lightning *coup d'état*. He became so frightened that he enlisted help from the head of Russian intelligence in the Balkans, Colonel Grabov. Grabov instructed his agents in Vienna and Budapest to keep an eye on the ex-King. The Serbian borders were heavily patrolled and orders given to "shoot him down like a mad dog" if he made any attempt to cross the frontier.

But King Milan had lost all interest in life. In January, 1901, he fell seriously ill of influenza. At first his son made no move to go to him. However, when Alexander learned that his father was likely to succumb, some sentiment moved him, for he instructed his minister in Vienna to visit the ex-King and to wish him a speedy recovery. Milan, broken and disillusioned, asked the Serbian diplomat to thank his son for his thoughtfulness. A few days later Milan was dead. During the last days of his life he had confided to the Emperor Franz Joseph that he did not wish to be buried in Serbia, but in a Serbian monastery in the town of Srem in Austria. Thus, in a way, he had the last word.

As April approached—the month that the royal birth was expected—the rumours of trickery on the part of Queen Draga began to multiply. Undoubtedly Queen Nathalie had written about her scathingly in letters to Russia. She now hated Draga even more than Milan had done, if such a thing were possible. She sent a postcard to a friend in Belgrade calling her a whore. The censors had shown the card to the King who had gone to the length of announcing in the Official Gazette that future intrigues against the royal house would be treated as treason, citing Nathalie's card as an example.

Not only had Queen Nathalie voiced her suspicions about Draga's pregnancy to St. Petersburg, but Colonel Grabov had done the same thing. The Queen, however, did not demur when Russia offered to send two doctors to be present at the accouchement. They arrived in Belgrade early in April and after an examination announced that Draga was not pregnant after all, but was suffering from "a tumorous condition." The news had to be broken to King Alexander in small doses. He was beside himself with mortification and anguish, banging his fists on the table, threatening to arrest all the doctors, sending to Vienna for specialists in the hope that they would upset the diagnosis.

Some historians insist that Draga was play-acting all the while, hoping to substitute another baby for her own. Apparently she had pretended to be pregnant on other occasions; once with a French lover; once with Alexander to prod him into marriage. However, one is inclined to believe Mijatovich who was convinced that this time the Queen was genuine in thinking herself pregnant. After all, the French doctor had signed a statement verifying the fact; and the Queen had not remonstrated against the arrival of the Russian doctors. But the public would not believe that she had been mistaken. It was all a sinister plot, people insisted, to deceive the Serbian people and build a dynasty of her own.

At this time, in the summer of 1901, a new Russian Minister, M. Charykov, appeared in Belgrade. Alexander suspended court mourning for King Milan in order to give the Czar's representative the finest welcome possible. Soon Charykov was the most influential figure in the capital. He interfered in all matters, both domestic and foreign. He mediated between the Radical Party and the Crown; and on the Czar's name-day gave a huge reception at the Russian Legation which was attended by everyone who held an official position. Many members of the Russian intelligence service were present as they worked closely with Charykov in foreign policy.

Alexander was putty in the hands of the Russian Minister for he realised only too well the damage done by Draga's false pregnancy. Popular discontent was spreading; only a gesture on the part of the Russian Court could put things right. If the Imperial family would receive Alexander and Draga the calumny would stop. Hysterically he badgered Charykov to arrange the matter for him. The Minister promised to bring an invitation from the Czar when he returned from his leave in November. Although he came back empty-handed he assured Alexander that the matter was in hand; and a few months later Count Lamsdorff, the Foreign Secretary, informed the Serbian Government that the royal couple would be received at Livadia in the autumn. The trip was featured in the Serbian press, but on 4th September, 1902, Lamsdorff telegraphed that the reception would have to be postponed because of the illness of the Empress.

What was happening in St. Petersburg? Lamsdorff referred to "feminine influences." He had in mind the two "Black Pearls," the Montenegrin Princesses married to Russian Grand Dukes. They were busy informing the shocked Empress of the scandals surrounding Draga, for they hoped that the time was coming when their brother-in-law, Prince Peter Karageorgevich, might regain the Serbian throne.

The truth of the matter was that as far as the Russian Foreign Office was concerned Alexander had served his purpose. He had smashed Serbia's ties with Austria so completely there was little possibility of restoring them. It was no longer important whether or not he retained his throne, as his only successor was the pro-Russian Karageorgevich. Now that Alexander had outgrown his usefulness even the Russians were willing to admit that he was a despicable prince.

Alexander saw the red light flashing and made frantic efforts to patch things up with Austria. He took Draga on a trip to Vienna and had the temerity to place a wreath on his father's grave. This act, far from mollifying the Emperor's ministers, sickened them. Viennese society smirked and said that he was hoping to present Draga at Court. But the King had wider aims. In the autumn of 1902 he sent a secret emissary to Vienna, offering to sign a pact that would make Serbia completely dependent on Austria in return for safeguards that would guarantee his throne. For once the Austrians did not respond. The Foreign Secretary had become so disillusioned by the King's behaviour that he had begun to look upon his abdication as inevitable and had even reconciled himself to seeing the Pretender take his place. In the spring of 1903 Alexander again approached Vienna, this time angling for an invitation to army manoeuvres. Any sign of recognition, no matter how small, would strengthen his position, but even this request was ignored.

Meanwhile a conspiracy to kill Alexander and Draga was gathering momentum. The plan was first bruited in 1901 by a young army officer, but it did not harden into a plot until the following year. Mijatovich dates its true inception to the autumn of 1902 when Colonel Mashin returned from Russia. This was about the same time that the Russian Court excused ·itself from receiving the Serbian King and Queen. Colonel Mashin, a brother of Draga's first husband, blamed the Queen for his dismissal from the army and hated her with an almost pathological intensity. Apart from Mashin another key figure emerged that same autumn—a twenty-six-year-old army lieutenant by the name of Dragutin Dimitrievich, known to his friends as "Apis," the Egyptian for Bull-God, because of his massive frame and Herculean strength.

Apis was a born leader and a born conspirator. Quiet, charming and sympathetic he exercised such a fascination for his fellow officers that he could do anything he liked with them. He had been educated at the Belgrade Lycée and the Military Academy, and had graduated from both with distinction. He needed no persuasion to join the murder plot, for he had made several trips to Russia where his imagination had been fired by the exciting and perilous life of the revolutionary. He was romantic and ruthless and had already vowed to dedicate himself to political killing.

From the moment he joined the plotters things began to move. In the autumn of 1902 only nine officers and three civilians were fully committed to the conspiracy. Apis made them sign the following oath which he kept hidden in his house:

"Anticipating certain collapse of the state if the existing situation continues even for the shortest time, and blaming for this primarily the king and his paramour Draga Mashin, we swear that we shall murder them and to that effect affix our signatures. In place of these dishonourable individuals, we shall bring to the Serbian throne Peter Karageorgevich, grandson of the Leader and the legitimate son of Prince Alexander Karageorgevich."[20]

Events played into Apis's hands, for in November the King dismissed his Government and formed what he called "a neutral Cabinet" which was merely an attempt to re-establish personal rule. In March 1903 students and shop assistants demonstrated in Belgrade, calling for a return of parliamentary rule. The police fired into the crowd and a number of people were wounded. After this Apis had no difficulty in recruiting for the conspiracy. By April, 1903, 120 army officers were sworn to act.

In the autumn of 1902 an ex-army secret service agent, designated as "Count Y," called on Mijatovich, the Serbian Ambassador in London, and told him that "a certain Power" and "a certain Pretender" had made a pact that would "seal the doom" of King Alexander. Although Mijatovich did not place much credence in the story he reported the incident to the King.

Other letters, some signed, some anonymous, were beginning to trickle into the Palace warning the King of a conspiracy. But it was not until the spring of 1903 that he learned to his consternation that many army officers were involved in the plot. Alexander's Prime Minister refused to believe the reports. The police, he said, were deliberately trying to discredit the army. Officers who had taken an oath to the king could not be guilty of such treachery.

Nevertheless the King and Queen were deeply apprehensive, for they felt in their bones the stories were true. Some months earlier Draga had been much agitated when a Belgrade newspaper had run a serial based on "The Black Prophecy." This prophecy, made many years before by a peasant woman known as Mata of Kremna, foretold the end of the dynasty by assassination. The royal couple could not get this terrible prediction out of their minds, but they did not know what to do or to whom to turn. In April and May they received so many warnings that they cancelled their engagements one by one and never left the Palace. They would be cut to pieces at the military and religious service on Palm Sunday at the Belgrade Fortress; they would be murdered when the King laid the foundation stone for the Home of Arts in Belgrade; they would be shot down at the opening night of the circus; they would have a bomb dropped in their carriage from the balcony of the Foreign Office. "Never," wrote Mijatovich, ". . . have a King and Queen undergone a more terrible penalty; during, at least, the last five months of their lives, they suffered as though they had been stretched and tortured on the rack."[21]

The Queen poured out her heart to a faithful friend of the dynasty, M. Todorovich, a newspaper editor. "There is something that wears and exhausts us more than the danger," she confided, "—it is the uncertainty . . . We have asked ourselves all these months: Can it be true? Is it possible that the Serbian officers thirst for the blood of their King and Queen? This uncertainty paralyses the King's usual energy and decisiveness and cripples his action. When we consult our devoted friends about it, we find that everyone has some special opinion of the matter. Some friends come and exclaim in great alarm: 'For God's sake, why are you waiting? Do you not see that you are in imminent danger of your lives?'. . . The moment the King prepares to act, other not less faithful and trusted friends rush in: 'For God's sake, Sire, don't. You will strike innocent men and then you will provoke a terrible misfortune.' Some cry: 'Don't wait,' others again: 'Do wait!' The King gets perplexed . . .

"The King himself," the Queen continued, "is sometimes cheerful; but of late that is less and less frequent. There are days and nights in which he is overwhelmed by sadness, anxiety, and something like fear. Some nights he sits in his working-room the whole night, lost in deep thought. I go to him, and try to cheer him up, and to induce him to go to bed. But it is of no use. Often in the morning, I find him sitting, fully dressed, in his arm-chair. Sometimes he comes to my bedroom, draws a chair near the bed, takes my hand in his, and sits pale and silent for a long time . . ."[22]

King Alexander was not stupid, but he was cruel and deceitful. Throughout his reign he had not hesitated to sacrifice his friends for gains that had appealed to him. The only true emotion in his life was his passionate love for Draga; and for her he had committed the most foolish acts of all. He had shocked people by his behaviour to his father and betrayed all the most loyal supporters of his dynasty. Finally, he had reached a point of no return by severing his ties with Austria. His feverish efforts to make Draga respectable only seemed to worsen the situation, for now rumours were sweeping the capital that she was plotting to make one of her brothers the King's heir.

The conspirators were almost as nervous as Alexander and Draga

for by May, apart from the officers actually involved in the plot, probably another hundred people knew about it. Each time they were
ready to make an attempt the King and Queen failed to turn up.
This prompted them to work on an alternative scheme which they
had been considering for some time: to storm the Palace and murder
Alexander and Draga in their beds. The plan necessitated the support
of key men in the inner circle of the Court. One such man had
joined the ranks of the traitors in April: Lt.-Col. Naoumovich, the
King's aide-de-camp, who held a high position at the War Ministry.
His motive appears to have been money. He was a clever officer
but a man of debauched tastes, a heavy drinker and gambler. Early
in May the King had given him £800 to pay off his debts, and he
had accepted it despite the fact that he was already supplying the
conspirators with information.

The force that the rebels would have to overcome inside the
Palace consisted of a bodyguard of three officers and forty-five
cavalrymen; an infantry guard of twenty men; and a gendarmerie
detachment of one officer and six men. There was always an adjutant
on duty, as well as the King's first aide-de-camp, General Lazar
Petrovich.

The conspirators planned to surround the Palace with troops,
isolating it from the rest of the city. As the officer commanding
the Sixth Regiment was one of the rebels no problems were envisaged. In May two more key men joined the group, Captain
Kostic, who commanded a company of Guards inside the Palace,
and Lt. Peter Zivkovich, the youngest and newest cavalry recruit.
If Captain Kostic could arrange for Zivkovich to be on duty on
the night of the murder the latter would put opium in the drinks
of his fellow officers and open the outside gate of the Palace. Lt.-Col.
Naoumovich then would release the huge wooden gate that led
into the building itself. With inside help it was estimated that no
more than twenty-eight officers would be needed to seize control
of the Palace.

The Russian Minister, Charykov, had many agents operating in
Serbia and was well aware of the conspiracy. But he was determined
to remain detached, as the Russian Foreign Minister, Count Lamsdorff, had instructed him at the end of 1902 "not to meddle with the

internal affairs of Serbia," but "to take care that its foreign policy continued to be in complete harmony with that of Russia." As these exhortations were not necessarily compatible the interpretation was "not to meddle *as long as* Serbia's foreign policy remains harmonious . . ." Charykov, as the reader will see, carried out this order with meticulous care.

Quite apart from Charykov's foreknowledge, on 25th May Alexander Weissman, the head of the Russian Secret Police in the Balkans, arrived in Belgrade from Sophia, and informed the King that a military rebellion was imminent. Why should Charykov remain silent and the Russian *Ochrana* warn the King? The explanation lies in the fact that Weissman's loyalties were not wholly with Russia. He was in the pay of Austria-Hungary and had penetrated the top rung of the Russian police. When St. Petersburg discovered this disquieting fact several years later the Sophia Bureau was disbanded, and the Balkan *Ochrana* Headquarters moved to Paris where it was reorganised.

King Alexander thanked Weissman for his information, but told him that he had already been informed of the plot by King Ferdinand of Bulgaria. That night, according to Mijatovich, he had a scene with his Prime Minister demanding that the key traitors be arrested without any further delay. Apparently the Prime Minister asked for another forty-eight hours to check the lists with the Belgrade police, in order to avoid mistakes. Colonel Naoumovich overheard the conversation and called a hurried meeting of the conspirators. Colonel Mashin, the leader of the revolt, decided that the plan must be put into operation without any further delay.

On the evening of 28th May the King and Queen had audiences which prevented them from dining until 10.30 p.m. Lt.-Colonel Naoumovich was the equerry on duty. Although he was in full-dress uniform, he had not shaven and he looked ill. As the King passed him on the way to the dining-room he said: "Naoum! What is the matter with you? You look so unwell." "I am ill, Your Majesty," answered the Colonel in a trembling voice. "Why have you then not asked to be relieved of duty to-night?" asked Alexander sympathetically, not waiting for a reply. At that very hour in the Guard House, Lt. Zivkovich was offering wine, which had been drugged, to the loyal officers of the Guards.

It was a hot sultry night and the beer-gardens of Belgrade were full; particularly the restaurant opposite the National Theatre. This place was filled with officers who were drinking heavily. Repeatedly they called for "The March of Queen Draga." At eleven o'clock, one of the officers, a Colonel, left the room. He went to the fortress and ordered the Sixth Infantry Regiment, of which he was the Commander, to take up a position on the narrow street that ran between the Russian Legation and the front garden of the Palace. At the same hour Colonel Mashin put on the army uniform that he had not been able to wear since his forcible retirement at the instigation of the Queen. He went to the Headquarters of the Seventh Regiment, where one of the traitors, the Commander of the 1st Battalion, introduced him as the new Divisional Commander. Colonel Mashin ordered the entire regiment under arms, and marched it to the Palace. The troops surrounded the northern, southern and eastern sides. Meanwhile the Police Commissioner, surprised at seeing troops emerging from the Fortress at midnight, had telephoned the Prefect of Police. This gentleman peevishly ordered the Commissioner to address himself to the Central Police Station. As fate would have it, the young officer on duty that night had abandoned his post and gone out to enjoy himself, leaving a clerk in his stead. The clerk did nothing.

The troops were told confidentially that they had been called out by command of the King, who had decided to send Queen Draga away. About twelve-thirty twenty officers appeared at the iron gate leading from the street to the Courtyard of the Palace. One of them gave a low whistle and Lt. Zivkovich opened the gate. They made such a clatter as they walked up the carriage drive that the sergeant of the Guards shouted to his comrades "To arms!" The soldiers grabbed their rifles, but one of the conspirators fired at the sergeant and killed him on the spot. Lt. Zivkovich sprang forward, drew his sword and cried: "Stand still!" Soon the company was at attention. "The King's orders," said the Lieutenant, "are that you do not move from here no matter what takes place around you." The revolver shot that had killed the sergeant brought the King's loyal aide,

General Lazar Petrovich, hurrying to see what was happening. One of the conspirators fired at him, wounding him in the arm.

The officers then rushed to the entrance door of the old Palace. Lt.-Colonel Naoumovich had agreed to open this huge wooden door, but he had fallen into a drunken sleep and did not wake. The besiegers had to destroy the door with dynamite cartridges. It was exactly half past twelve and the detonations were heard all over the town bringing many people out into the street. Even Naoumovich woke up and ran forward to meet his fellow conspirators. No one knows why Dragutin Dimitrievich—Apis—shot him dead. Some people say that his wife was Apis's mistress; others (and this seems more plausible) that Apis was so enraged at his negligence, and suspicious that he had changed sides, that he killed him without more ado. Apis then rushed into the interior guard-room and was fired upon and wounded. He carried three bullets in his chest for the rest of his life. This was almost the only mishap suffered by the conspirators, for Captain Kostic rounded up the guards, told them that he was acting on the King's orders, and marched them to the Palace gendarmerie where they took control of the police.

Someone had turned off the Palace lights and no one could find the main switch. A group of officers groped their way through the darkened rooms trying to find their way to the royal bedchamber. Many of them were drunk and swore and blasphemed to give themselves courage. They forced one of the servants to bring them candles and to lead them to the King's bedroom. Although the bed had been slept in there was no trace of the King or Queen. The traitors began slashing at the curtains, thumping the walls, looking under sofas and in cupboards. They ordered the wounded General Petrovich to be brought in and told him they would spare his life if he told them where the King and Queen were hiding. He replied that he did not know, whereupon they manhandled him, shouting abuse. "You have not been to the New Palace," he said. "Perhaps they are there."

This sent them hurrying away. But when they reached the courtyard their commander, Colonel Mashin, stopped them. "What on earth are you doing?" When they explained Mashin cried angrily: "You fools! Do you not see that this rogue is only making dupes of you to gain time. Back at once to the Palace and we will go with you.''[23]

Meanwhile King Alexander and Queen Draga were hidden in a small alcove off their bedroom. The secret door which led into this hiding place was cleverly disguised with paper and impossible to see. The alcove had a window overlooking the courtyard and facing the Russian Legation. The Queen saw an officer pacing up and down in the courtyard. She recognised him as Captain Kostic of the Royal Guard. She must have thought God had answered her prayers as she flung the window open and cried at the top of her lungs: "Your King is in danger. For God's sake, to the rescue, to the rescue!" The Russian Minister, M. Charykov, was standing at the lighted window of his Legation, peering into the darkness of the Palace yard, aware that he was witnessing the terrible scene that had been plotted for so many weeks. "Suddenly," he wrote in his memoirs, "a window was opened in the lower storey of the Palace facing the street, and we heard the Queen's voice calling to the soldiers outside for help. We also heard one of them answer, 'Fear nothing, Majesty'."[24]

Draga's despairing cry had sealed her doom, for now Captain Kostic knew where she was. He ran up the staircase and told the enraged conspirators, who were still in the bedroom, swearing and smashing the furniture, that he had seen the Queen from the court-yard standing at a window. They then knew that she was hiding in a secret alcove off the bedroom, but still were unable to find the door. They called for an axe and were about to smash in the wall when General Lazar stepped forward. "Gentlemen, will you give me your word of honour that you will spare the life of the King?" Several voices answered "yes" and Lazar knocked on the papered wall. "Sire, Sire," he shouted. "Open, open, I am your Lazar. Here are your officers."[25]

The door opened and the King and Queen stepped out, only half dressed. They found themselves facing a room dense with officers. The King moved in front of the Queen to protect her and said: "What is it you want? And what of your oath of fidelity to me?"

There was a moment of complete silence. Then one of the officers cried: "What are you standing gazing at? Here is our oath of fidelity to him!" He fired his revolver at the King who sank into the arms of the Queen. Then other officers began to fire at both of them and continued to fire as they lay bleeding and groaning on the floor. One of them drew his sword and began to slash at the bodies. More swords came out and soon they were cutting Draga to pieces. "I cannot describe the horrible, disgusting and ferocious conduct of some of those murderers," wrote Mijatovich. "They seemed to emulate the exploits of Jack the Ripper on the dead body of the woman who was their Queen. As I write these lines I feel utter shame and humiliation that Serbian officers could have conducted themselves with such brutal cruelty."[26]

Now one of the officers suggested that they throw the two mutilated bodies out of the window into the flower garden so that the soldiers surrounding the Palace could see that the King and Queen were dead. This was done while the officers shouted in chorus: "Long live Peter Karageorgevich, King of Serbia!"

In his memoirs the Russian Minister lamely excuses himself for standing at his window, not lifting a finger to intervene. He recalls his instructions "not to meddle in Serbian affairs." "I do not believe," he writes, "that under the prevailing circumstances even my personal intervention as the representative of Russia could have saved the lives of the Royal couple. The conspirators would not have been satisfied with their mere abdication. My duty was to obey to the end the orders I had received, and to safeguard the interests of my country, leaving all responsibility to Count Lamsdorff. My attitude in this crisis was approved by my Government . . ."[27]

Nevertheless, at four in the morning, after the naked bodies had lain in the open for two hours, Charykov crossed the street from the Russian Legation and entered the garden. Colonel Mashin stepped forward and saluted the Czar's representative. "For God's sake, gentlemen," said the Russian, "carry their bodies inside the Palace. Do not leave them here in the rain exposed to the public gaze." Sheets were brought from the Palace and the corpses were carried into a room on the ground floor. Meanwhile the officers, drunk with wine and success, had been looting the Palace. They stole all the royal jewellery they could find, and £8,000 which they discovered in the King's desk. Other officers, on orders from Colonel Mashin, were engaged in more killing. They had already murdered the faithful General Lazar; now they went out into the night, tracked down the Prime Minister and shot him; next the War Minister; and finally the Queen's two brothers.

Europe was so appalled by the ferocity of the assassinations that only two countries would recognise the new Serbian Government: Russia and Austria. King Edward VII of England, who remembered his meeting with King Alexander at the funeral of Czar Alexander III, had strong views on the subject. Not only was he deeply shocked by the fate of the Serbian rulers, but he looked upon regicide as an insult to his profession. Some years later he told the Italian Ambassador that he "could not overlook the brutal murder of a fellow member of his craft"; and that he could not recognise Serbia until all the regicide officers had been placed on the retired list.

Edward VII's stand was reminiscent of the attitude of Nicholas II's grandfather, Nicholas I, who had always believed that monarchs should support one another. But for the past forty years Czarist Russia had been following a different—and more dangerous—line.

IX
Protectress of all the Slavs

ON A HOT summer day in August 1904 a smart brougham drawn by two horses, its curtains tightly drawn, moved briskly along a tree-lined avenue in St. Petersburg, conveying the Minister of the Interior V. K. Plehve, to his weekly meeting with the Czar Nicholas II. The Minister's carriage passed a vehicle in which was riding E. J. Dillon, the English correspondent of the London *Daily Telegraph*, and a scholar of international repute. "Suddenly," wrote Dillon, "the ground before me quivered, a tremendous sound as of thunder deafened me, the windows of the houses on both sides of the broad street rattled, and the glass of the panes was hurled on to the stone pavement. A dead horse, a pool of blood, fragments of a carriage and a hole in the ground were part of my rapid impression. My driver was on his knees devoutly praying and saying that the end of the world had come. I got down from my seat and moved towards the hole, but a police officer ordered me back, and to my question replied that the Minister, Plehve, had been blown to fragments . . ."[1]

Plehve's murder was front page news all over the world. It is difficult to imagine how much greater the sensation would have been if the public had known that the architect of the murder was none other than one of the dead Minister's own trusted, hand-picked police operators, Ievno Asev, probably the most successful double-agent of all time. Asev had drifted into his hazardous occupation through lack of money. Born of poor Jewish parents in the province of Rostov on the Don, he had hankered after a university education. This he had achieved by the unlikely means of becoming a travelling salesman for butter. He cheated his employers by selling his consignment privately, and absconded with the funds to Germany.

He entered the Polytechnic in Karlsruhe and began studying for a degree in engineering. He tried to make friends with the Russian revolutionary émigrés living in the town, but they were so repelled by his appearance that they rejected his overtures. Everything was wrong with Asev's face. His forehead was low, his lips thick, his ears protruding, his nose flat, his eyes bulging and shifty. However, his quietness and modesty, and, above all, his eagerness to serve the revolution, soon broke down their reserve. There was only one fly in the ointment; Asev's money began to run out. Soon his fat body had fined down, his clothes were shabby and his face drawn and white. One day he picked up his pen and wrote to the Russian secret police, the *Ochrana*, and gave them details of the revolutionary organisations in the town. He offered to supply information regularly for a fee of fifty roubles a month. The police investigated his background and enrolled him as an agent.

By the turn of the century Asev was a power in the revolutionary movement. At that time there were two main revolutionary parties in Russia; the Social Democrats and the Social Revolutionaries, known as the S.D.s and the S.R.s. The S.D.s embraced Marxist Socialism and were split into two factions, Mensheviks and Bolsheviks. The S.R.s, no less rabid in their opposition to capitalism, resisted the view that revolution could be achieved only through industrial workers. They were the children of the *Narodniks* and believed that the new Socialist order would spring from peasant revolt. Although the two parties were on close terms, frequently exchanging members, Lenin, the leader of the Bolsheviks, concentrated on propaganda and strikes while the S.R.s maintained that terror was the only effective weapon. They had inherited the mantle of the *Will of the People*, the group that had killed Alexander II; and in 1902, after successfully carrying out the murder of M. Sipyagen, the Minister of the Interior, (Plehve's predecessor), they created an inner society known as *The Battle Organisation* whose sole purpose was assassination. A year after its inception Asev became its chief.

Asev had climbed the ladder by his organising ability. He had co-ordinated scattered groups and knitted them into a strong unit. His diligence had won him the confidence of Gershuni, the Party's leading terrorist, and when the latter was arrested in 1903 his comrades found that he had left a letter recommending Asev as his successor. Asev immediately informed the *Ochrana*, and asked what he should do. Up till now police agents who succeeded in penetrating revolutionary organisations were forbidden to accept executive positions. But the matter was referred to the new Minister of the Interior, the tight-lipped, ruthless, all-powerful V. K. Plehve who surprised his subordinates by giving his consent. Why? He must have known that Asev would be obliged to render his revolutionary colleagues considerable service in order to hold his job. The only logical explanation is that Plehve was thinking of his own security. As one of the most feared and hated men in Russia, almost every terrorist in the country had contemplated killing him at one time or another. With Asev operating as chief of *The Battle Organisation* Plehve would not only be forewarned but protected.

At first things worked out as Plehve expected. On several occasions Asev informed the *Ochrana* of plots to murder the Minister which resulted in arrests. He also put the police on the trail of secret printing presses, explosive arsenals, propaganda depots. He gave them the names of provincial revolutionary societies and, on his travels to Berlin and Paris, kept them informed about émigré conspiracies. But Asev only told the police what he wanted them to know. He protected terrorists who were helpful to him, and threw the *Ochrana* off the track when he felt that disclosures would be harmful. He worked solely for money. He received a large salary from the police and, as he also controlled the funds of *The Battle Organisation*, was able to live in luxury.

Needless to say at the end of Asev's first year as chief the morale of *The Battle Organisation* was at a low ebb. The terrorists had planned a dozen murders, but the police had an uncanny way of always being on the spot. Although there was no shortage of volunteers, many arrests had been made and nothing had been achieved. Asev was shrewd enough to know that he could not continue indefinitely like this, and must do something to impress his revolutionary comrades. As he was a man with a flair for drama he decided to kill Plehve. No doubt Asev was influenced by the fact that the Minister had instigated a series of pogroms against his co-religionists, the Jews. Furthermore, Plehve had become careless about his safety. Recently an acquaintance had found him walking alone on the Aptekarsky Island. He asked the Minister how he ventured to run such a risk when everyone knew that the terrorists were plotting against him. "Oh, I shall know about all these plans in good time," he smiled.

While Asev was working out the details of his *Attentat* a rival organisation, headed by a woman terrorist, appeared on the scene with the same purpose in mind. Asev did not have a moment's hesitation in betraying her to the police, who managed to run down every member of her group. He knew that if she succeeded in bringing off the *coup* he might lose control of *The Battle Organisation*— and the funds. His own plan did not go into operation until the summer of 1904. News of Plehve's assassination reached Geneva a few hours after it had taken place. On the borders of the lake a Congress of Social Revolutionaries living abroad was being held. Suddenly a member burst into the room waving a telegram. "For several moments," an eye-witness wrote, "pandemonium reigned. Several men and women became hysterical. Most of those present embraced each other. On every side there were shouts of joy . . ."[2] Asev not only had re-established his position, but had become the hero of the Party.

What explanation did he give to the police? He upbraided them for not having paid more attention to his early warnings, insisting that this last attempt had been made impulsively without his knowledge. Did the *Ochrana* accept his story? M. Lopuhin, the Director of Police, insists that he did not know about Asev's complicity until 1908, but his assertions must be treated with reservation, for Sazonov, the man who threw the bomb, although mortally wounded did not die at once. He lay delirious in the hospital with police detectives at the foot of his bed. He mentioned the word "Vilna" several times, a town that Asev had visited shortly before the murder; and even more damaging, the word "Valentine," which the police recognised as one of Asev's revolutionary code-names. Some historians, such as E. J. Dillon, the English witness to the murder, insist that both police and government officials were aware that Asev was responsible, but that Plehve was so unpopular no one regretted his loss;

furthermore, since Asev had regained the confidence of his comrades, his value to the police could be greater than ever. As the *Ochrana* did not press for an investigation and allowed the whole matter to drop, this cynical interpretation is probably correct.

For the next six months Asev served the police diligently, but in February, 1905, he repeated his tactics by master-minding the blowing-up of the Czar's brother-in-law, the Grand Duke Serge, Governor-General of Moscow. After preparing the plan Asev left for Paris. Here he received the news of the Grand Duke's death. Suddenly he was overcome with terrible fear that the *Ochrana* would discover his complicity. He could not lift himself from his couch. For days he lay, white-faced and trembling, moaning and staring at the ceiling. Nearly a month passed before he could summon enough courage to return to Russia. When he did, the *Ochrana* greeted him warmly and seemed to be devoid of suspicion.

Meanwhile Russia was undergoing a convulsion. In 1904 the ambitious Nicholas II had plunged the country into war with Japan over Korea. As usual everyone thought Russia would win, and as usual everything went wrong. The Japanese had sunk the Russian fleet and inflicted heavy losses on the Russian Army. Once again Russian disorganisation and corruption became glaringly apparent. "This country has no real Government," wailed the British chargé d'affaires in St. Petersburg. ". . . each Minister acts on his own, doing as much damage as possible to the other Ministers . . . It is a curious state of things. There is an Emperor, a religious madman almost—without a statesman, or even a council—surrounded by a legion of Grand Dukes—thirty-five of them and not one of them at war at this moment, with a few priests and priestly women behind them. No middle class; an aristocracy ruined and absolutely without influence, an underpaid bureaucracy living, of necessity, on corruption. Beneath this, about 100 million of people absolutely devoted to their Emperor, absolutely ignorant . . . gradually becoming poorer and poorer as they bear all the burden of taxation, drafted into the Army in thousands . . ."[3]

Trouble abroad was matched by trouble at home. In January, 1905 (a month before the assassination of the Grand Duke Serge), a woolly-minded priest, Father Gapon, sparked off a chain of events which ended in a minor revolution. He led 200,000 workers to the Winter Palace to deliver a petition to the Czar. Nicholas, however, deliberately left the capital, and the army was ordered to fire on the crowd; they killed and wounded over a thousand people. "Bloody Sunday" shocked the country and provoked a series of demonstrations which finally turned into a general strike, supported by all shades of opinion and completely paralysing the city. Nicholas was busy signing a humiliating peace with Japan; and now he was forced to give his reluctant consent to the establishment of a Duma—Russia's first Parliament—a consent which he never ceased to regret and spent the rest of his reign trying to nullify.

Terrorist activity was increasing. Although the *Ochrana* had welcomed back Ievno Asev, and showed no sign of suspicion, they had taken the precaution of infiltrating a second police agent into the Social Revolutionary Party—a man named Tataroff whose job, among other things, was to report on Asev. This agent informed his superiors that an important meeting of *The Battle Organisation* was due to take place, presided over by "Valentine," Asev's code name. Asev was fortunate enough to learn what Tataroff had done and denounced two members of his organisation in order to retain the confidence of the police. Meanwhile Tataroff had put the *Ochrana* on the trail of a terrorist who was planning the murder of Plehve's successor, M. Bouligin, and as a result a dozen men were arrested.

Asev soon found himself caught between two fires. In September, 1905, a trusted senior official of the *Ochrana*, M. Menstchikov, turned traitor, due to the shake-up which had taken place in the police department following the Grand Duke's death. M. Lopuhin had been dismissed and a volatile character, Ratchkovsky, appointed in his place. Menstchikov was worried about his own job and decided to try and get into the good books of the revolutionaries. He sent a mysterious, veiled lady to the Headquarters of the St. Petersburg Social Revolutionary Party with the warning that their organisation contained two spies, "a certain T. . . . an ex-convict," and "the engineer Asev, a Jew, who had recently arrived from abroad." The letter gave details of their betrayals.

Asev was shown the letter that same day. "T. . . . that can only be Tataroff, and the engineer Asev, that must be myself," he said coolly, and left the room in a display of contemptuous indignation. Although the letter caused a sensation, the revolutionaries refused to believe in Asev's guilt. They accepted his explanation that it was a trick on the part of the police department to discredit him. Tataroff was guilty; he was the real villain of the piece and Asev recommended that he be executed without delay. *The Battle Organisation* knew that Tataroff had gone to Warsaw where his parents lived. One day in April, 1906, a terrorist knocked at his door. The father refused to admit the caller as he knew that his son was in trouble. There was a scuffle and Tataroff came into the hall. The visitor pulled out a revolver and fired, but the father knocked the weapon out of his hand. The man then produced a dagger and stabbed Tataroff to death. He escaped and was never caught.

Asev made it a policy to show no mercy to traitors. That same year he encouraged *The Battle Organisation* to kill Father Gapon, the priest who had led the procession on "Bloody Sunday." Gapon had joined the revolutionaries after the débâcle at the Winter Palace, proclaiming to the people: "We no longer have a Czar . . . Take bombs and dynamite. I absolve you!" But the priest was weak and vain. After touring the capitals of Europe for some months, where he was fêted as a hero, he returned to Russia and soon fell under the spell of the new police chief, Ratchkovsky. The latter turned the priest's head by declaring that "Russia has need of men like you." If Gapon would serve the *Ochrana* and help to stop the terror, the Government would willingly improve the conditions of the workers. Gapon finally agreed. He told the police all he knew about *The Battle Organisation* and gave detailed information on the part that Asev was playing. He promised to try and persuade his friend, the engineer Rutenberg, who was an active member of the Organisation to work for the police; and for this service he demanded the exorbitant sum of 100,000 roubles. The matter was referred to Count Witte, the President of the Cabinet, who advised the *Ochrana* not to bargain too much.

Gapon called upon Rutenberg and after a long and muddled conversation told him the truth and offered him 25,000 roubles to betray his comrades. Rutenberg reported the matter to *The Battle Organisation* and Asev's indignation knew no bounds. "He thought," Rutenberg later recalled, "that Gapon should be killed like a snake. I was to arrange an interview with him, take him out to dinner, and after dinner, while driving back through a wood in a sledge belonging to *The Battle Organisation*, stab him and throw his body out."[4]

Gapon, however, was killed in a different manner. Rutenberg took him to a deserted villa on the Finnish frontier to discuss, he said, the final terms of payment. Several members of *The Battle Organisation* were concealed in an adjoining room. "What are you dilly-dallying about?" asked Gapon. "Twenty-five thousand is good money!" Rutenberg protested that many of his comrades would be hanged if the police caught them. "Well, what of it! It's a pity of course but we can't help that. You can't cut down a tree without the splinters flying." Rutenberg went to the door, opened it, and his fellow-revolutionaries burst into the room. Gapon fell on his knees begging for mercy, but the men silently placed a noose around his neck and attached it to an iron hook on the wall. A few minutes later he was dead. The police did not discover his body for several weeks.

Meanwhile because of Gapon's disclosures Ratchkovsky had decided to have done with Asev. Indeed, he thought him better dead. One night when Asev was walking home a number of ruffians set upon him and tried to stab him. He was wearing a thick fur coat which saved him. He recognised the men as members of *The Black Band*, Ratchkovsky's hired killers who were employed to remove troublesome individuals. However, six months later, in October 1906, P. A. Stolypin, who later became Prime Minister, was made Minister of the Interior. He dismissed Ratchkovsky and appointed Gerassimoff in his place.

Dillon, the English historian who lived in Russia and was on close terms with many members of the Government, declares that both Stolypin and Gerassimoff were aware that Asev had masterminded the murders of Plehve and the Grand Duke Serge but that they considered him too valuable to dismiss. In his memoirs Gerassimoff denies any such knowledge, but his disavowal is difficult to accept in view of the denunciations both of Tataroff and Father

Gapon. Furthermore, Gerassimoff admits that he suspected Asev's complicity in the attempt to kill Dubassoff, the Governor-General of Moscow, in 1906. Although the *attentat* did not succeed, the Governor's aide-de-camp, Count Konovnitzin, was killed and the Governor himself so badly wounded that he was forced to go on prolonged leave and never resumed work. Asev's explanations, Gerassimoff wrote in his memoirs, were "unsatisfactory"; but he excuses his conduct on the grounds that Asev was not on the police payroll at the time due to his break with Ratchkovsky. Gerassimoff gives the impression that he regarded it as quite natural for an ex-agent of the police to pass the time of day killing government servants.

Stolypin virtually ran the *Ochrana* himself, using Gerassimoff as his chief-of-staff. The latter employed new tactics with Asev. He treated him with deference, requesting weekly reports which he sent to Stolypin, and sometimes even soliciting the agent's opinions on political matters. Above all, Gerassimoff concerned himself with Asev's safety, promising not to make any arrests without the latter's consent. He had other new ideas; the best way to destroy *The Battle Organisation*, he argued, was by a programme of failure. He suggested that Asev should excite his comrades by undertaking the assassination of Stolypin. Every attempt, of course, would be balked by the police and after months of frustration the Organisation would fall to pieces. At first Stolypin did not like the plan for he had a premonition that something might go wrong, but finally gave his assent.

Gerassimoff's psychology was not correct, for after two months of abortive attempts a number of terrorists broke off from *The Battle Organisation* and formed a group of their own, the *Maximalists*. Without informing Asev, two of them went to Stolypin's home at the hour when he received official callers. The guards refused to let them pass beyond the hall so they threw their bombs where they stood. The explosion destroyed the guards, the terrorists, twenty or thirty callers and the greater part of the villa itself. Stolypin's small children were severely injured, although the Minister himself, who was in his study, escaped without a scratch. Asev was so fearful that Stolypin would hold him responsible that he forced *The Battle Organisation* to issue a statement deploring "the methods of the *Maximalists*." As their methods were no different from the methods of other terrorists his comrades were puzzled. Asev tried to counteract the failure of Gerassimoff's scheme by arguing with the Central Committee of the Party that the time had come to dissolve *The Battle Organisation*; its tactics—and explosives— were too old-fashioned to be effective against a streamlined police force. He counted on the support of Natanson-Bogrov, one of the members of the Committee, and a close friend; but Natanson believed in "terror" and refused to support him. As a result Asev not only failed to convince the Party, but could not carry the majority of his terrorist colleagues with him. Nevertheless Asev insisted on handing in his own resignation, and *The Battle Organisation* split into several sections, each one operating on its own.

Asev went abroad; and the *Ochrana*, denuded of informers, stood by powerless as a spate of killings took place. The agent returned, however, in time to tip off the police about two plans; one to kill the Czar, the second to blow up the State Council. The *Ochrana* made sweeping arrests and Stolypin was able to claim credit in the Duma for the efficiency of the security system.

Asev now resumed his double rôle. He stood so well with the *Ochrana* that he could afford to help the other side; he would thrill the revolutionaries by assassinating the Czar himself. Throughout the winter of 1907-8 he played cat and mouse, drawing up plans with his comrades, and at the same time informing the police. But in the spring of 1908 he applied his mind seriously to the problem. In the Vickers' shipyard at Glasgow a new Russian cruiser *Rurik* was being built. A skeleton crew had been sent from Russia to supervise the work and to acquaint themselves with the new design. Both revolutionary parties—the Social Democrats and the Social Revolutionaries—had sent people to make contact with the crew and to do propaganda work among them. Asev arrived in Glasgow in the middle of July and got in touch with the naval engineer who was known to be sympathetic to the revolutionary movement. Asev worked out a plan by which two members of the crew would shoot the Czar at the Naval Review scheduled to take place in Russian waters in October. He supplied the engineer with revolvers and left his right-hand man, Savinkoff, to find the volunteers. Savinkoff was successful and in September sent Asev a farewell letter written by one of the recruits: "I can now realise the significance of the task entrusted to me . . . One minute will decide more than whole months."

The plan went off without a hitch. The two would-be assassins met the Czar face to face. One of them was even asked by Nicholas to bring him a glass of champagne. But nothing happened. Savinkoff explains the failure simply as "loss of nerve."

Asev was disappointed, for once again he was in serious trouble with the revolutionary comrades. A number of *Ochrana* agents, who had lost their job when the department was reorganised by Stolypin, had begun to take their revenge by betraying police secrets. One such man had written to the well-known revolutionary Burtzeff, the editor of a historical review, *Byloye*, and given him a disturbing account of Asev's activities. Burtzeff began to investigate and the further he went the more convinced he became that Asev was a traitor. But the evidence was circumstantial and he knew he would not be able to convince his colleagues without proof. So he contrived to board the same train from Cologne to Berlin on which Lopuhin, the ex-Director of Police was travelling. As Lopuhin was responsible for Asev's recruitment to the *Ochrana*, he listened with interest to Burtzeff's account of an astonishing "double-agent." And before the two-hour journey was over Lopuhin had given the revolutionary the necessary evidence by admitting that he knew Asev in an "official capacity." Why did he do this? Because he had an old score to settle. He suspected that the man who had displaced him from his job had encouraged Asev to murder Plehve, and he wanted to get him into trouble.

The Revolutionary Committee confronted Asev, but in the middle of the night he fled to Vienna. He never returned to Russia. After a "honeymoon" trip with one of his many mistresses to Greece and Egypt he disappeared from sight. He was, in fact, living in Berlin under the name of "Alexander Neumayer," and earning his living as a stockbroker. His double life did not catch up with him for many years. Retribution when it finally came, however, wore an unexpected guise. Twelve months after the outbreak of the World War he was arrested by the German police and imprisoned as "a dangerous revolutionary." He was released at the end of 1917 but died a few months later. On the whole, he confided to a friend—or so it is claimed—his sympathies were with the police.

The revolutionary movement had a profound impact on the Russian character. Just as Count Tolstoy had feared, its creed of violence and treachery was poisoning the whole structure of society. The Englishman who witnessed Plehve's murder was alarmed because he "met nobody who regretted his assassination or condemned the authors. This attitude towards crime, although by no means new, struck me as one of the most sinister features of the situation . . ." He expanded this theme in an article in the English *National Review* in May, 1905. "In that connivance at lawlessness," he wrote, "lurks a danger the insidiousness of which few people realise. Personally I fear that unless its progress be speedily stayed it may lead to the moral paralysis of the nation."[5]

By 1908 the moral paralysis was nearly complete. The debasement of human values, begun by the Nihilists and Nechaevsti fifty years earlier, had continued so relentlessly that now the public looked upon murder with indifference and state servants betrayed and ruined each other with the utmost unconcern. In his memoirs, Lopuhin, who was almost as perfidious as his employee, Asev, exposed the confidence of almost everyone who had dealt with him. He accuses Count Witte, the President of the Council, of urging the police to murder the Czar in the hope that the latter's brother, the Grand Duke Michael, would come to the throne. Witte, on the other hand, claims in his autobiography that the Holy League, an aristocratic assassination society organised by the Grand Dukes, tried repeatedly to murder him for having forced the Duma on the Czar. Treachery had gained such a hold on Russian life that it was estimated that at least ten per cent of the members of revolutionary parties were police agents; and probably the same proportion of police agents were revolutionaries.

Again Russian diplomacy reflected the recrudescence of lawlessness at home. Not just professional conspirators, but individuals in all walks of life were contaminated by the moral anarchy. And Isvolsky, the Foreign Secretary, was no exception. In 1908 he diverted attention from the Far East and brought it back to Europe with a dramatic flourish. Isvolsky was vain and ambitious, almost a caricature of a diplomat, a man who "strutted on little lacquered feet . . . wore a pearl pin, an eye-glass, white spats and . . . left behind him, as he passed onwards, a slight scent of *violette de parme*."[6]

M. Isvolsky had new worlds to conquer and was not in the least discouraged by the fact that Europe was now neatly divided into two camps—the Triple Alliance consisting of Germany, Austria and a doubtful Italy, and the Triple Entente composed of Russia, France and a hesitant England.

Any number of cross-currents swept the two opposing groups. England and France had no quarrel with Austria but feared Germany; Russia on the other hand got on reasonably well with Germany but regarded Austria as an intolerable obstacle to Panslav ambitions in the Balkans.

Isvolsky decided to end the Austro-Russian stalemate by sweeping the pieces from the board and starting the game afresh. At a secret Ministerial Council in February, 1908, he told the Czar that Russia could not afford to remain a passive spectator. If she allowed the Balkan Question to remain indefinitely "on ice" she would lose "the fruits of her century-long efforts, ceasing to play the rôle of a great power, and falling into the position of a second-rate State to which no one pays any attention."[7] Nicholas II apparently agreed with the argument for he minuted one of the papers: "God helps those who help themselves."

Isvolsky was not contemplating force. Russia was too weak for that. He was thinking of a deal with Austria which would result in a glorious Russian *coup* and make up for the ignominious defeat in the war with Japan. Indeed, he had already dropped a hint in the ear of the Austrian Foreign Secretary and had been pleased by the reaction. "Russia," he told Baron Aehrenthal, "has lost Manchuria and Port Arthur and thereby access to the sea in the East. The main point for Russia's military and naval expansion of power lies henceforth in the Black Sea. From there Russia must gain an access to the Mediterranean."[8]

In the summer of 1908 Isvolsky was even more explicit. The "Young Turks" had seized power in Constantinople and the country was in a state of disorganisation; the time had come to act. He sent an *aide memoire* to Baron Aehrenthal proposing that Russia should settle the Straits Question by securing the right to send Russian warships through the Bosphorus and the Dardanelles; Austria in return, could strengthen her position in Bosnia and Herzegovina by converting her thirty-year-old occupation into a direct annexation. Although both these moves would constitute an infringement of the Treaty of Berlin, Isvolsky was convinced that an agreement between Russia and Austria would pacify the Great Powers.

Perhaps it was not astonishing, but at least it was surprising, that both the Czar and the Foreign Secretary were wholly out of touch with Russian opinion. The question of the Straits had been receding steadily into the background over the past decade, while the idea of a federated Slavdom, simmering since the 1870s, had been gaining support. The isolation of the Czar, who shut himself away at Tsarsko Selo and rarely visited his capital, is more understandable than the Foreign Minister's ignorance; although later it was said that Isvolsky had spent so many years abroad as an ambassador that he had lost touch with his own country.

Nevertheless it is difficult to explain why neither of them bothered to brief themselves on developments inside Serbia. When King Peter Karageorgevich mounted the throne after the murder of Alexander and Draga, Russian influence moved into the ascendancy. In order to widen the breach between Serbia and Austria-Hungary, Russian diplomats revived the vision of a Greater Serbia which would include Bosnia and Herzegovina, perhaps even Montenegro, and a large slice of Macedonia. This future not only enthralled the government of Pashitch, but thrilled the regicides, many of whom held important posts. It also pleased the Russian Panslavs who secretly envisaged Greater Serbia as a puppet state and, even more important, the Russian General Staff who had always argued that Austrian influence must be eroded in order to open the way for Russian expansion in south-eastern Europe.

Isvolsky's bland suggestion to the Austrian Foreign Minister, of converting the occupation of Bosnia and Herzegovina into an annexation, therefore ran completely counter to the line being taken by Russian ministers in Serbia. Aehrenthal, of course was delighted with the proposition and invited Isvolsky to a meeting in September at Count Berchtold's castle in Moravia. The talks went smoothly, although later the participants quarrelled over what was said, provoking bitter recriminations. At the time, however, Isvolsky was in high humour. When he left the castle he set forth on a leisurely tour of Europe to win the support of the Powers. On 23rd September he wrote to Aehrenthal saying that he had sent a memorandum to the Czar for approval; and two days later he told the German diplomat, Baron von Schöen, whom he met in Berchtesgaden, that he expected Austria to announce the annexation during the first week in October. He saw no problem with England over the Straits; after all Russia had signed a Treaty of Friendship with Britain, and Isvolsky had been careful to eliminate Balkan complications by gaining Austrian support. He reached France on 3rd October, and although Austria did not announce the annexation of Bosnia and Herzegovina until the 6th, a leak occurred and the French press carried the story on the 4th. The Serbian Legation in Paris was in an uproar, but Isvolsky dealt firmly with them:

"You Serbians surely cannot be thinking of driving Austria-Hungary out of Bosnia and Herzegovina by force of arms. And we Russians, on the other hand, cannot wage war on Austria on account of these provinces . . . I have foreseen this step of Austria-Hungary's, and it did not surprise me. For that reason I made our acceptance of it dependent upon her renunciation of her rights to the Sanjak of Novi Bazar; and then will follow the revision or alteration of the Treaty of Berlin, which we shall demand; upon this occasion Serbia, too, will be able to present her wishes as regards the rectification of her frontiers . . . I do not understand your state of agitation. In reality you lose nothing, but gain something—our support . . ."*

The blow fell when Isvolsky reached London. He found the Government steaming with anger over Austria's high-handed breach of

* Report of Vesnitch, Serbian Minister in Paris, of conversation with Isvolsky, 5th October, 1908; quoted by Bogitchevitch, *Causes of the War*.

the Berlin Treaty. Although as far as Russia was concerned the British Foreign Secretary was all smiles, things did not go as he expected. Of course, Sir Edward Grey assured him, he understood Russia's desire for a free passage through the Straits; he regarded it as "fair and reasonable" and was not against it "in principle." Nevertheless it could not be a one-sided arrangement; if the Straits were opened to Russia they would have to be opened to all the Powers. This, of course, was the last thing that Isvolsky intended. Freedom of the Straits meant Russian warships; not foreign warships which might sail into the Black Sea and bomb Odessa. Isvolsky argued, implored, threatened and wept, but the British were adamant.

Meanwhile a wave of indignation was sweeping Russia. The Foreign Minister had made a complete fool of himself; he had been duped by Aehrenthal, and even if his plan had succeeded, were the Straits worth the sacrifice of Bosnia and Herzegovina, the two provinces selected to be the core of Great Serbia, Russia's springboard into the Balkans? Unanimously the Press accused Isvolsky of swopping the provinces for "a mess of potage"; and some papers asked sarcastically why he was so concerned to open the Straits to Russian warships when most of them, thanks to the Japanese Navy, were lying at the bottom of the sea.

Isvolsky saw the spectre of a shattered career arising before him; disgrace, ridicule, ruin. So he began to lie. He regaled everyone who would listen, including Edward VII, with accounts of Baron Aehrenthal's "duplicity." He flatly denied that he had concluded a bargain, insisting that he had expected Austria's annexation claims to be placed before a conference of the powers. He had been double-crossed by Aehrenthal's premature announcement, and he referred to the Foreign Secretary as a "half-Jew" and "certainly no gentleman." King Edward, who had played an important part in concluding the Anglo-Russian accord, was not in a mood to blame Russia for anything. He was gullible enough to believe Isvolsky's story and wrote to his Foreign Secretary describing Aehrenthal as "nearly the Devil incarnate."

The British Foreign Office, however, had a shrewd idea that Isvolsky had committed himself to Aehrenthal much further than he was willing to admit. "Directly I began to speak to him his eyes became very dull and defensive," wrote Sir Edward Grey. Isvolsky went about wringing his hands and saying that, if he were dismissed by the Czar, the Russian Government might fall and "reactionaries" move in. "We must do our best to support him, such as he is," the Foreign Office instructed the British Ambassador in St. Petersburg. As an opening move it was decided that King Edward should write to Nicholas II singing Isvolsky's praises. "You know how anxious I am for the most friendly relations between Russia and England, not only in Asia but also in Europe; and I feel confident that, through your M. Isvolsky, these hopes will be realised . . . etc., etc."[9]

Isvolsky was saved but Bosnia and Herzegovina appeared to be lost. Nowhere was excitement greater than in Serbia. The small kingdom behaved as though its own territory had been invaded. War credits were voted; mobilisation plans drawn up; irregular armed bands formed; a National Defence Society established. What was Russia, the Protectress of the Slavs, going to do? The answer was nothing; Russia was too weak to lift a finger. Finally, after some months of crisis and indecision, Germany intervened and in a peremptory manner advised Russia to acknowledge the annexation. Isvolsky had no option but capitulation. "There is no doubt whatever," Sir Charles Hardinge wrote to Edward VII, "that Aehrenthal has in his pocket a paper in which Isvolsky has thoroughly compromised himself, and had promised to recognise the annexation of Bosnia, provided that Austria would agree to the opening of the Dardanelles. He is terrified lest Aehrenthal shall some day publish this document; and it is the threat of this document which has made him cave in in such an ignominious manner to the Germans . . . He is a very unscrupulous and unreliable man."[10]

The annexation crisis prepared the stage for the Great War; therefore it is important to examine it a little further. From the emotions aroused one might have supposed that Russia and Serbia had some prior claim to Bosnia and Herzegovina. The opposite was the truth. Not only had Austria been occupying and administering the provinces for years but in countless secret clauses, right up to Isvolsky's assent, the Russians had affirmed the Monarchy's right of annexation. Apparently Nicholas II was as ignorant of these proceedings as he was of his own public opinion. "... there is something else which is really most distressing and which I had no idea of until now," he wrote to his mother in March, 1908. "The other day Chirekoff [Charykov Russian, Ambassador in Constantinople] sent me some secret papers dating back to the Berlin Congress in 1878. It appears from them that, after endless controversy, Russia consented to a possible future annexation of Bosnia and Herzegovina ... What an awkward situation! ... and what an embarrassing position we are in ..."[11]

If any country had a claim on Bosnia it was Turkey, the suzerain power; and if any country had the right to object it was Bosnia. However, Austria managed to square the Turks by paying compensation "for the loss of crown property"; and only a handful of people in Bosnia and Herzegovina protested against what most people regarded as a paper transaction, a switch from *de facto* to *de jure* occupation.

However, the Russians had a gift for propaganda and a genius for distorting facts that convinced many people—including themselves—that they had suffered some grievous personal injury. The only blow, of course, was to their expansionist plans. But Isvolsky was not a man of scruples, and when Berlin intervened in the crisis he changed his tactics and began to talk of German imperialism. Germany, for once, had no axe to grind, and was trying to keep the peace. When Austria responded to Belgrade's war-like moves by carrying out a partial mobilisation and sending troops to the Serbian frontier, the Kaiser was alarmed. The Austrian Chief of Staff, Conrad von Hötzendorff, made no secret of the fact that he wished to invade Serbia. By a "preventive war" now, he argued, "the dangerous little viper" could be crushed once and for all. Never again would Austria have such a favourable moment for averting the "Greater Serbia" menace which could only spell the destruction of the Habsburg Monarchy.

The Kaiser was determined to keep on friendly terms with the Czar. He had known nothing about Austria's annexation plan and had been furious when Vienna had announced the *fait accompli* without consulting Berlin. Now, with Serbia leaping into the breach and Austria mobilising its troops, he was determined to put an end to the uproar. So he restrained Austria and confronted Russia and Serbia with a mediation proposal; acceptance of the annexation with no further delay; yes or no, otherwise Germany would draw back and allow Austria to deal with Serbia on her own. Affirmative answers arrived within twenty-four hours, and the Czar wired the Kaiser thanking him personally for preserving the peace.

Isvolsky, however, soon upset Nicholas II's composure. Conveniently forgetting the part he himself had played, he now presented the sequence of events as a deliberate Austro-German plot to subjugate Slavdom. The mediation proposal had been nothing but a harsh ultimatum. "This affair," the impressionable Czar wrote to his mother on 18th March, 1909, "which has been going on for six months, has suddenly been complicated by Germany's telling us we could help to solve the difficulty by agreeing to the famous annexation while, if we refused, the consequences might be very serious and hard to foretell. Once the matter had been put as definitely and unequivocally as that, there was nothing for it but to swallow one's pride, give in and agree. The Ministers were unanimous about it. If this concession on our part can save Serbia from being crushed by Austria, it is, I firmly believe, well worth it. Our decision was the more inevitable as we were informed from all sides that Germany was absolutely ready to mobilise. Against whom? Evidently not against Austria. But our public does not realise this and it is hard to make them understand how ominous things looked a few days ago: now they are willing to go on abusing and reviling poor Isvolsky even more than before."[12]

"Poor Isvolsky" not only succeeded in deceiving the Czar, but the British Ambassador, Sir Arthur Nicolson, as well. He told the ambassador that "the whole Austro-German plan had been skilfully conceived, and the right moment chosen"; and the next day we find Nicolson echoing his words in a private letter. "My firm opinion is that both Germany and Austria are carrying out a line of policy and action carefully prepared and thought out."[13] Many years later Sir Arthur's son and biographer explained: "Nicolson was not at the time aware of the blackmail being applied by Berchtold and quite sincerely believed that Russia was being faced by an ultimatum. It is possible that Isvolsky exaggerated the German action in order to distract attention from his own secret commitments to Austria."[13]

The annexation crisis was the first taste that European diplomacy had of "the big lie," a technique that was to become increasingly popular as the century progressed. Isvolsky's vanity was too great for the humiliation he had suffered. He became almost pathological in his thirst for revenge and spent the rest of his life working for the down-fall of Germany and Austria. Indeed, when the Great War finally came he remarked exultantly to the British Ambassador in Paris, "*C'est ma guerre!*"

After accusing Berlin of playing a sinister rôle, Isvolsky went a step further and declared excitedly to anyone who would listen that "a war with Germandom was inevitable." His warnings fell on receptive ears, for France was worried by Germany's huge army, and Britain apprehensive of Germany's growing navy. And the Kaiser's megalomaniac attitudes did nothing to ease the tension. When William II visited Vienna in 1909 he omitted to tell his listeners how shocked he had been at the news of the annexation: instead he boasted that Germany had stood beside her ally, Austria, "in shining armour." Now not only the Czar and Sir Arthur Nicol-son accepted the Russian Minister's predictions; soon all the Great Powers were racing to increase their armaments.

Isvolsky did not neglect Serbia which had become the lynch-pin of his cold war against Austria-Hungary. Although for half a century Russian diplomacy had promoted subversive activities in support of its foreign policy, Isvolsky studied revolutionary techniques and gave the game fresh impetus. He appealed to the younger gener-ation of Serbs with his talk of "a future reckoning" and advised the Belgrade Government not to disband its patriotic clubs and irregular bands but to take them underground. Although the Serbs had been forced to "renounce their attitude of protest and opposi-tion" and had promised "to live on good neighbourly terms" with Austria, Russian money and arms flowed in to Serbia and Bosnia to stimulate preparations for "the day of liberation." At the end of March, 1909, the Serbian Government informed its Minister in Vienna that Serbian National propaganda would be directed in future by Panslav organisations financed by Russia. The revolutionary propaganda would emanate "from St. Petersburg and from golden Prague. We shall also promote this activity through connections which . . . the General Staff [will] maintain."[14] A few weeks later the Panslav Conference in St. Petersburg issued a secret circular to Slav organisations in the Balkans assuring them of generous financial support for their military needs. "Certainly within two or three years at the most, the time will come when the Slav world under Russian leadership must strike the great blow."[15]

One of the most inflammable young men in Belgrade was the Heir Apparent, Prince Djordge, the eldest son of the sixty-eight-year-old King Peter Karageorgevich who had mounted the throne after the horrible death of King Alexander. Djordge was a wild youth who had been educated in St. Petersburg in the *Corps de Pages*, and was almost more Russian than the Russians. He created a stir by burning the Habsburg flag after the announcement of the annexation, and picking a quarrel with the Austrian military attaché in the streets of Belgrade. However, if Isvolsky counted on the Prince's support he was doomed to disappointment for Djordge removed himself from the political scene by murdering his butler. This caused such a scandal in the spring of 1909 that he was forced to abdicate in favour of his brother, Alexander. Apparently Djordge had discovered the butler reading his mail, and had delivered him a fatal blow by kicking him in the stomach. The family relationships were certainly unusual, for some years later Alexander tried to persuade a group of officers to murder Djordge. At the last minute one of the assassins changed his mind and upset the poisoned coffee before the Prince drank it. However, when old King Peter died and Alexander ascended the throne he put Djordge into solitary confinement and kept him there for twenty years.

There were plenty of Serbs to fulfil Russia's purposes but most of them were left-wing students. The fact that Czarist Russia was locking up its own left-wing students did not cause the Foreign Office the least embarrassment. Ever since the seventies it had been accepted policy to encourage revolutionaries abroad and to suppress them at home. Indeed, for years the most conservative Russian Panslavists had seen nothing odd in working hand-in-glove with foreign revolutionaries. Yet the game was growing dangerous, for the advance in twentieth-century communications made it impossible to keep the two groups apart. They were borrowing each other's techniques, provoking and nourishing each other's ambitions. Russian diplomacy, however, was incapable of perceiving the perils, and fanned the flames outside their frontiers in the belief that they were serving the Czar's interests.

The key organisation through which Russia worked in Belgrade was the *Narodnaya Odbrana*, the para-military defence society which had sprung into being over the annexation. Administered by an Austrian major, Pribicevitch, who had been forced to flee from Vienna because of revolutionary activity, the *Narodnaya Odbrana* made a pretence of transforming itself into a "cultural" society. In reality it became an agency for espionage and subversion throughout southern Austria. When the Major was approached by Bosnian students who were studying at Vienna University he encouraged them to organise cells, based on the Russian revolutionary system of groups of fives, which would link the villages of Bosnia and Herzegovina; this, he explained, would enable the *Narodnaya Odbrana* to distribute literature and "prepare the people ideologically." "The new secret society in Vienna also decided to come into contact with 'all . . . progressive and revolutionary—elements which understand our national aspirations,' particularly with 'revolutionary, anarchistic and nihilist organisations in the world.' One of the members left for Russia in January, 1909, in order to contact 'Russian revolutionaries and learn their methods of secret work'."[16]

One of the leaders of the Young Bosnians was Vladimir Gatchinovich who was destined to play a decisive rôle in inciting the murder of the Archduke Franz Ferdinand at Sarajevo. This thin, sharp-featured youth was the son of an Orthodox priest. The father hoped that the boy would follow his calling, but unfortunately sent him to the High School at Mostar in Herzegovina which had become a hot-bed of anarchism. The teachers glamorised Russian revolutionaries and soon the boys were reading Nechaev, Bakunin and Kropotkin. They were thrilled by the *panache* of the Russian terrorists who struck down their victims mercilessly and paid the penalty with their lives. Sophia Perovskaya became a sort of Jeanne d'Arc to them. They talked about "the cult of the individual deed" and quoted Mazzini to prove that they had found a new religion. "There is no more sacred thing in the world than the duty of a conspirator, who becomes an avenger of humanity and the apostle of permanent and natural laws." They had nothing but contempt for the older generation who insisted upon legal methods of opposition, sneering at them for submitting to Austria at the time of the annexation. "Our fathers," wrote Gatchinovich, ". . . are real tyrants who want to drag us along with them and want to dictate to us how we should lead our own lives."[17]

During the annexation crisis Gatchinovich went to Belgrade and joined one of the guerrilla groups. He enrolled at Belgrade University but spent more of his time organising a revolutionary movement than in study. The Serbian Government rewarded him by sending him on a subsidy to Vienna University where he occupied himself in the same way. In 1910, when his school-friend, Zherajitch, responded to his incitement by firing five shots at the Governor-General of Bosnia (all of which missed) and then committing suicide, Gatchinovich wrote a pamphlet entitled *The Death of a Hero* calling upon Serbdom to avenge the martyr by imitating him. He spoke of the dead boy as "a type who opens an epoch." "Young Serbs, will you produce such men?" About this time he joined the *Narodna Odbrana* and undertook the task of distributing his eulogy in Bosnia. "He speaks," wrote one of his friends, "wakes people up, and again disappears like a shadow, as if he were swallowed up by the earth, feeling himself followed by the foot-falls of Austrian agents among whom were to be found some Serbians also."[18]

Nevertheless Gatchinovich apparently longed for more exciting activity than distributing propaganda and in 1911 he found it. He joined a sinister, newly-formed organisation, *Union or Death*, which came to be known as *The Black Hand*. Its aim was "the union of all the Serbs" and it stated in Article II that it preferred "terrorist action to intellectual propaganda, and for this reason must be kept absolutely secret from non-members." Its leading spirit was none other than the notorious bull-like Dragutin Dimitrievich—"Apis," who had organised the murder of King Alexander and Queen Draga.

Apis had done well in the intervening eight years. As Professor of Tactics at the Belgrade Military Academy he had acquired great influence. His views were passionate and dangerously political. In 1911, at the age of thirty-four, he was a full-fledged Colonel and a power in Serbian politics. "One saw him nowhere, yet one knew that he was doing everything ..." a friend wrote. "There was no Minister of War who did not have the feeling of having another, invisible minister next to him."[19]

Colonel Apis was not quite as invisible as his friend liked to imagine. Early in 1911 he gathered together a group of officers—most of them fellow-regicides—to urge the Government to resume the revolutionary agitation in Turkish territory which had been suspended after Constantinople's proclamation of a constitution. The Prime Minister refused; and this provoked him into setting up his own organisation—*The Black Hand*—with the object not only of conducting the forbidden terrorist activity himself, but of exerting strong political pressure on the Government.

Colonel Apis had no difficulty in attracting followers for he had a mixture of charm, ruthlessness and modesty which people found fascinating. "Although he was a soldier with ambitions," wrote the historian Slobodan Jovanovitch, who knew him well, "he was indifferent to his career. He never spoke about his own personal merits and successes ... When he would recall the *coup d'état* of 1903 he would tell everything except his own rôle ... As all fanatics he esteemed more the success of a cause than the lives of men ... Friends for Apis were at the same time very dear and very cheap. His friendship had a dangerous quality; but this made his personality very attractive. When he wanted to draw his friends into a conspiracy or some other adventure, he behaved like a seducer."[20]

The Black Hand was controlled by a Central Committee of eleven members. Five of the founders were officers who had taken part in the 1903 regicide. Members were grouped in cells, and referred to by numbers. Discipline was based on the *Revolutionary Catechism* of Nechaev who had lived in the sixties and became the subject of Dostoevsky's novel *The Possessed*.

Joining *The Black Hand* was an irrevocable act. No one was allowed to resign and Article 30 stated: "Each member must realise that in becoming a member of this organisation the individual loses his

273

personality; he can expect no glory, no personal benefits, material or moral. Any member, therefore, who attempts to misuse the organisation for his personal, class or party interests will be punished. If the organisation suffers any damage from him, he will be punished by death."

The initiation ceremony had a Ku-Klux-Klan atmosphere. The novitiate was led into a semi-dark room and made to stand before a table on which lay a revolver, a dagger, a cross. A man dressed in a long black domino with a hood over his head entered and asked for the oath of allegiance which resounded with such phrases as "by the Sun that warms me," "by the Earth that nourishes me," "by the blood of my ancestors."

Shortly after the creation of Apis's organisation, the Serbian General Staff set up six frontier posts, three on the borders of Bosnia-Herzegovina and three on the frontier between Macedonia and Turkey. Colonel Apis managed to get *Black Hand* members appointed to all of them. Thus from the very beginning he was able to control the movements of agents, to infiltrate irregular bands into neighbouring territories and to build up his own espionage service. At the same time he set up a school to train terrorists near the Orthodox bishopric in Nish. Here students received instruction in shooting, bomb-throwing, bridge-blowing and espionage.

In the early days King Peter of Serbia's second son, Prince Alexander Karageorgevich, was on excellent terms with *The Black Hand* and gave a substantial sum of money to Apis to found the journal *Piedmont* which became the mouth-piece of the organisation. The Minister of Foreign Affairs, Milovanovitch, was also enthusiastic. When Apis told him about the society at the end of 1911 he replied: "My young friend, put your *Black Hand* at my disposal and you will see what Milovanovitch will manage to do in a short time for the Serbian cause."[21]

The Czar's Government still worked in water-tight compartments. One hand never seemed to know what the other was doing. This confusion was increased by Nicholas II, who had such a mania for secrecy that he refused to have a secretary and wrote letters to his Ministers in his own hand. The Ministers only met sporadically when a Crown Council was held. Otherwise Nicholas dealt with them one by one and often failed to keep his Prime Minister advised about decisions reached with the Foreign Secretary or War Minister.

Although Nicholas II had an agreeable smile his heart was made of ice and he cared for no one apart from his family. He always received his Ministers with meticulous politeness, never argued, never raised his voice. "The Minister would take his leave," wrote the head of the Court Chancellery, Mossolov, "delighted at having, to all appearance, carried his point. But he would be sadly mistaken. What he had taken for weakness was merely dissimulation. He had forgotten that the Czar was absolutely without moral courage; that he loathed making a final decision in the presence of the person concerned. Next day the Minister would receive a letter from him . . . a letter of dismissal . . . The Minister had ceased to give satisfaction . . . nobody could say how or why."[22]

Nevertheless, by 1911 people were beginning to understand the influence exerted on the Czar by his wife. The Empress was a religious fanatic. She loathed the Duma and believed that her husband's autocracy stemmed directly from God.

To complicate matters still further rumours were sweeping St. Petersburg that she had come under the spell of a dissolute monk, Rasputin, whom she believed to possess holy powers. At that time no one except members of the Romanov family knew the reason for Rasputin's hold. The Czar's only son and heir, born in 1905, suffered from the incurable bleeding disease, hæmophilia. Rasputin had been brought into the Imperial circle shortly after the child's birth by the two Montenegrin Grand Duchesses (the Black Pearls) who were wildly superstitious and believed in table-tapping and spiritualism. On several occasions Rasputin seemed to have stopped the hæmorrhages and relieved the terrible pain. This bound the Empress to "Gregory," as she called him, with tigerish ferocity. She hated anyone who criticised him and did everything she could to destroy the calumniator's influence.

This was the basis of her dislike for Stolypin, the Czar's Chief Minister. A tall, stiff man with a dead white face and a dead black beard, Stolypin had headed the Cabinet since 1908, and was widely regarded as the best Prime Minister Russia had ever had. "He was, in my opinion," wrote the British Ambassador, "the most notable figure in Europe. Although he was ruthless in crushing terrorism, he was equally determined when the revolutionary movement had been suppressed to introduce reforms generally, and to satisfy, as far as possible and prudent, all the legitimate demands of the people."[23] In 1906, when Stolypin's children had been wounded in the terrorist attack on his house, the Czar had sent Rasputin to the Minister. But Stolypin had been appalled by the man's filthy appearance and repelled by his attempt to hypnotise him. Early in 1911 police reports reached the Prime Minister concerning the monk's sexual orgies and his drunken evenings with the gypsies. The fact that his name was coupled with the Empress and her children did not stop the Prime Minister from doing his duty. He persuaded the Czar to banish the man from St. Petersburg and ordered an investigation of his private life. The report corroborated the stories of venality and lasciviousness and was given to the Czar. The Empress, however, managed to convince her husband that it had been concocted by Gregory's "enemies" and that not a word of it was true. From that moment onwards she hated Stolypin with every fibre of her body.

On 1st September, 1911, the Imperial family attended a Gala Opera in Kiev. The Prime Minister was also present, but was ignored by the Court who did not even bother to assign him a carriage to drive him to the Opera. "Stolypin and I had seats in the first row, but rather far apart," wrote Kokovtsov, the Minister of Finance. "During the first intermission I went into the foyer to see some friends and, during the second, I made my way to Stolypin to say good-bye, explaining that directly after the following intermission I was going to leave . . . I went to bid the Afanasevs adieu and to thank them for their hospitality. But I had scarcely spoken a few words to them when there resounded two muffled detonations like those made by firecrackers.

"At first I could not understand what it was. A group of men in the left aisle close to the front row were struggling with someone on the floor. There were shouts of 'Help' and I ran towards Stolypin, who was still standing near his seat. His face was white, and a small stain of blood was beginning to appear on the lower part of his chest. There was general confusion but I remember seeing General Dediulin with a drawn sword near the Imperial box. Stolypin turned unsteadily in that direction, made the sign of the Cross over the box, and sank slowly into a chair, in which he was carried towards the entrance. The man with whom I had seen the group of men struggling was led away. And immediately crowds surged into the aisle. The Czar and his entire family appeared in their box, the curtain was raised, and there sounded the strains of the national anthem sung by the entire ensemble."[24]

It was ironical that Stolypin, who had encouraged Asev's work as a double-agent, should have been shot down by a man of the same ilk. His assassin, Bogrov, had worked as a police agent for some time, then secretly joined the revolutionaries. He told the Kiev *Ochrana* that he knew the details of a plot against the Czar. Security precautions were tightened and no one was allowed in the Opera House who was not identifiable and safe. On the night of the Gala Bogrov entered the theatre on the pretext of having a message for Lieutenant Kulyabko, Chief of the Kiev Special Police.

Stolypin lived for three days. His friend Kokovtsov, who spent most of his time at the hospital, says that the Imperial family not only did not visit the dying man but sent no message of condolence. Only when the Prime Minister was dead did they pay their respects. Kokovtsov succeeded Stolypin as Prime Minister. A month later, when he met the Empress, she said to him: "Find your support in the confidence of the Czar . . . the Lord will help you. I am sure that Stolypin died to make room for you, and this is all for the good of Russia." Kokovtsov was shocked by her coldness. ". . . a month after Stolypin's tragic end he was spoken of with perfect calm; only a few gave themselves the trouble to think of him at all; he was profoundly criticised, and hardly a soul expressed a word of sorrow that he had gone."[24]

Thus Russia began the year 1912. Kokovtsov was able and scrupulously honest, but he was new to his job and was astonished to find that even as Chairman of the Ministers' Council he had difficulty in discovering what Ministers were doing. Russia's foreign policy, he learned, was concentrated wholly on the struggle against Austria to gain control of the Balkans. The Foreign Secretary, Sazonov, did not hide his Slavophile leanings and not only encouraged the Serbs to take their para-military organisations underground but to penetrate Austrian territory, particularly Bosnia and Herzegovina, with subversive societies. He was not a man of strong character and allowed his ambassadors great latitude in promoting Russian interests. When Isvolsky asked for a large sum of money with which to bribe the French press he supplied it.

More important, as far as world affairs were concerned, Sazonov encouraged the formation of a Balkan League. Conceived by Isvolsky in 1909, the League sprang into being in 1912 as the work of the Russian Ambassadors in Sophia and Belgrade—Nekliudov and Hartwig. The basis of the League was a *rapprochement* between Serbia and Bulgaria, hitherto hostile as both coveted the same territory in Macedonia. The Treaty was considered a great *coup* for Hartwig who, it later transpired, persuaded *The Black Hand* to use pressure on the Serbian Foreign Minister. The Balkan League meant war, and this was what *The Black Hand* wanted. "We do not say that this war between Serbia and Austria is declared yet, but we believe that it is inevitable," cried Colonel Apis's journal, *Piedmont*, in May 1912. "If Serbia wants to live in honour, she can do so only by this war. This war is determined by our obligation to our traditions and our culture. This war derives from the duty of our race which will not permit us to be assimilated."[25]

When M. Poincaré, the French Prime Minister, visited St. Petersburg in the summer of 1912 and learned for the first time the details of the Serbo-Bulgarian Treaty he was deeply disturbed. "I did not conceal from him [M. Sazonov, the Russian Foreign Minister]," he wrote, "that I could not explain to myself why these documents had not been communicated to France from Russia . . . The Treaty contains the germ not only of a war against Turkey, but a war against Austria. It established further the hegemony of Russia over the Slav Kingdoms, because Russia is made the arbiter of all questions. I observed to M. Sazonov that the convention did not correspond in any way to the definition of it which had been given to me; that it is strictly speaking a convention for war . . ."[26]

The war, when it came two months later, was against Turkey,

not Austria. Montenegro and Greece scored swift and unexpected victories, finally driving the Turks once and for all out of Europe. The peace was uneasy, however, for Serbia began to quarrel furiously with Bulgaria over Macedonia and threatened to attack her. Once again, Colonel Apis swung his weight on the side of war. The Russian Foreign Minister, however, did his best to distract Belgrade by offering her other tempting fruits. "Serbia's Promised Land," he wrote to Hartwig in Belgrade, "lies in the territory of the present Austria-Hungary, and not where she is now making efforts and where the Bulgarians stand in the way. Under these circumstances it is of vital interest to Serbia to maintain her alliance with Bulgaria on the one hand, and on the other to accomplish with steady and patient work the necessary degree of preparedness for the inevitable struggle of the future. Time works on the side of decay. Explain all this to the Serbians! I hear from all sides that if any voice can have full effect at Belgrade it is yours."[27]

The Austrian militarists were only too conscious of "signs of decay." At the end of 1912 the fire-eating Baron Conrad von Hötzendorff had been reappointed Chief of the Austrian General Staff. He had been urging a preventive war against Serbia ever since 1909, warning the Government that if it remained inactive the dissolution of the Habsburg Empire would take place before its eyes. He talked repeatedly about the necessity of invading Belgrade to put an end to the Russo-Serbian subversive societies now honeycombing southern Austria.

Once again the spectre of a European war arose; and once again Germany intervened. Early in 1913 the Kaiser wrote to the Archduke Franz Ferdinand begging him to use his influence for peace. At the same time the German Chancellor, Herr von Bethman-Hollweg, sent urgent dispatches pointing out the folly of aggression: "Only insistently can I warn against the idea of wanting to gobble up Serbia, for that would only weaken Austria . . ."[28]

The British Ambassador in Vienna, Sir Fairfax Cartwright, felt that Serbia was to blame and sent a prophetic warning to London: "Serbia may some day set Europe by the ears and bring about a universal conflict on the Continent," he wrote to Sir Arthur Nicolson in January, 1913. "I cannot tell you how exasperated people are getting here at the continual worry that little country causes Austria under encouragement from Russia. It will be lucky if Europe succeeds in avoiding war as a result of the present crisis. Next time a Serbian crisis arises I feel sure that Austria-Hungary will refuse to admit of any Russian interference in the dispute and that she will proceed to settle her differences with her neighbour *coûte que coûte*."[29]

In the end it was Bulgaria, not Serbia, which launched the surprise attack. The second Balkan war broke out in June 1913 over Macedonia, and lasted eight weeks. Serbia emerged triumphant. The two wars had doubled her territory and swollen her population from three to four and a half million. Now she was fired with self-confidence and talked about seizing Bosnia and Herzegovina as the first step towards a Greater Serbia.

X

Who Planned Sarajevo?

IN THE WINTER of 1913-14 everyone in St. Petersburg knew that the War Minister, General Soukhomlinov, frequently referred to as "the Czar's favourite minister," was protected by Rasputin. No more unlikely person to command the respect of Nicholas II and his deeply religious wife could possibly be imagined. Not only was Soukhomlinov unprincipled and venal, but he had been mixed up in one of the most scandalous divorce cases of the decade. In 1908, at the age of sixty, when he was serving as Governor-General and Commander-in-Chief of the Kiev District, he had fallen madly in love with an ambitious married woman of twenty-five, Madame Ekaterina Boutovitch, who was eager to improve her station in life. When this lady asked her husband for a divorce M. Boutovitch was thunderstruck and in great agitation went to the Palace of the Governor-General where he had a violent altercation with his elderly rival. "Soukhomlinov refused any explanation," he wrote, "and spoke in such a tone that I challenged him. He refused to fight, saying that a duel would injure his prestige. I struck out at him, but he dodged me. Then I spat in his face and left."[1]

Soukhomlinov did not take no for an answer. He engaged a number of agents, among them Bogrov (who three years later murdered Stolypin), and applied every pressure to Boutovitch, ranging from enticement to threats of prison and banishment. The wretched husband refused to give way until his wife pretended to commit suicide. She told him she had swallowed poison and would only take an antidote if he signed a paper consenting to the divorce. Broken-hearted he agreed, and later discovered that the document not only pledged him to release his wife but fleeced him of thousands of roubles.

Soukhomlinov married Ekaterina in 1909 and that same year was appointed to the post of War Minister. How did he get the job? We know that Prince Andronnikov, a disreputable adventurer who lived by blackmail and extortion and who made a point of cultivating persons of power, was his strong backer. We also know that Prince Andronnikov was a friend of Rasputin. Undoubtedly pressures were used on the Czar, for it is inconceivable that Nicholas II on his own initiative would have selected Soukhomlinov at this particularly unsavoury moment in his career.

Soukhomlinov's infatuation for Ekaterina was expensive, as his wife was wildly extravagant; as Minister of War he controlled the army contracts and before long was deep in graft and corruption. Kokovtsov, who succeeded Stolypin as Chief Minister in 1911, was shocked by the huge sums he demanded for rearmament, particularly when there was so little to show for the money. In 1912 when the Balkan Wars broke out and Austria sent four divisions to protect her frontiers, Soukhomlinov recommended that Russia declare a partial mobilisation. None of the Ministers was informed of this decision until they arrived at a Crown Council. "I wish to stress particularly the fact that this partial mobilisation refers exclusively to our Austrian frontier," announced the Czar, "and that we have no intention of taking any steps against Germany. Our mutual relations leave nothing to be desired, and I have every reason to hope for the support of the Emperor William."[2]

The Council was appalled by the very mention of the word "mobilisation." "Only the presence of the Czar restrained us from giving vent to feelings which animated all of us," wrote Kokovtsov, "I stated frankly that the Minister of War and the two Commanders apparently did not perceive what danger they were preparing for Russia in planning this mobilisation—a danger of war with Austria and Germany, and at a time when in consideration of the state of our national defence every effort should be made to avert this catastrophe."[2] In the end both the Czar and Soukhomlinov climbed down; but afterwards Kokovtsov confronted Soukhomlinov angrily and said: "Don't you understand even yet where you very nearly pushed Russia? Are you not ashamed to make such a game of the fate of the Czar and your country?" The War Minister defended himself by pointing out that he had taken the precaution of calling a meeting before sending the mobilisation orders. Then he added, "But we shall have a war anyway . . . The Czar and I believe in our army and know that a war would bring us nothing but good."[2]

Despite the apprehension of his colleagues the War Minister continued to take a belligerent line, declaring repeatedly that it was high time Russia "stopped cringing" before the Germans. He was encouraged by the chauvinistic Grand Duke Nicholas Nicholaevitch who became Commander-in-Chief of the Russian Armies on the outbreak of the World War. The Grand Duke was a man of marvellous appearance. Six feet five inches tall, handsome, erect, he looked every inch a soldier, but unfortunately he was scarcely more competent than his fire-loving father who had led the Russian Armies in the war against Turkey in 1877. Although the Grand Duke had a powerful voice in military affairs as head of the Council of National Defence, this body was so incompetent that for five years it had not succeeded in moving "a single matter from a dead point" and, according to Stolypin, was "no better than Bedlam."

The Grand Duke's wife, the daughter of the Prince of Montenegro and sister-in-law of King Peter Karageorgevich of Serbia, was a passionate Panslav and longed for her husband to play a political rôle. She pressed him continuously to grasp the leadership of the "patriotic" forces in the country; and as a result he kept Panslav fever at a high pitch throughout the Balkan Wars by organising "Slavic banquets" which "were arranged as a means of arousing general sympathy for the Balkan Slavs and of bringing pressure on the Government for a more aggressive policy . . ."[2] Although the Balkan League had launched an unprovoked and aggressive war against Turkey, the banners referred to Russia as "the Protectress of all the Slavs"; others read "A Cross on Santa Sophia" and "From Scutari to Montenegro."[2]

In 1912 the Grand Duke succeeded in securing the appointment of a new Chief-of-Staff, a relatively young and undistinguished officer, General Yanoushkevitch, who was pliable and conciliatory and understood the importance of pleasing the Grand Duke. This was not a good way to select high officers, yet the Czar had an even less desirable method. When he asked Soukhomlinov whom he would like as Assistant War Minister the latter was not ready with an answer. " 'Very well,' said the Czar, 'we'll see what luck will do for you.' And with these words he opened the Army List at the generals' section, and at random laid a finger on the page. 'There you are,' he added, looking at the name beneath his finger— 'General Vernander! How does he suit you?' "[3]

In the last days of 1913 a storm broke when the Russians learned that Turkey had invited Germany to send a high military officer to Constantinople to reorganise her battered army; and that Berlin had responded by appointing General Liman von Sanders to command a Model Army Corps. Not that Russia had a leg to stand on. She had conjured up the Balkan League and encouraged it to attack Turkey. Surely Turkey had the right to invite a friendly power to send technicians to her aid in peacetime? Indeed, a British admiral was already streamlining the Turkish Navy. Russian gall, however, was not in short supply and Russian indignation was real. The excited protests did not spring from fear, but from fury that the German presence might block future plans of expansion. This was something of a *volte face* for only five years earlier, in the autumn of 1908, the Russian press had lambasted Isvolsky for being prepared to give up "Greater Serbia" in order to control the Straits, and had even referred to the Straits as "a mess of potage." Since that time, however, the appetite of the Russian Bear had grown; and now it was no longer a question of "either/or" but of both.

Soukhomlinov and the Grand Duke Nicholas led a furious campaign against German imperialism which resulted in a Crown Council where the question of war was discussed. Luckily Kokovtsov, the Prime Minister, was a cool-headed man. At the meeting he asked: "Is war with Germany desirable and can Russia wage it?" The Foreign Secretary, Sazonov, replied "no" to the first part of the question. Then Soukhomlinov and General Yanoushkevitch plunged in and "declared categorically the complete readiness of

Russia for a duel with Germany, not to speak of one with Austria."
They went on to add that "such a duel is, however, hardly possible;
those powers would be much more likely to have to deal with the
Triple Entente [Russia, France and England]."[4]

The German Kaiser was worried and subdued throughout 1913.
He met Russia's objections by altering the rôle that General von
Sanders would play. Instead of commanding an Army Corps he
would serve in the more sedentary capacity of an Inspector-General.
The Czar declared himself satisfied, emotions subsided, and the
British Annual Register for 1913 gives the Kaiser the main credit
for having preserved the peace of Europe.

However, in March 1914, much to everyone's surprise, the War
Minister, Soukhomlinov, dictated an article to the *Petersburg Bourse
Gazette* entitled "We are Ready," repeating what he had said at
the Crown Council; Russia not only was capable of defending itself
against an aggressor but sufficiently strongly armed to launch an
offensive war against the combined might of Germany and Austria.

Needless to say this article created a sensation throughout Europe.
According to Kokovtsov (who had been dismissed in January
and replaced by the seventy-three-year-old Gorémykin, "an old fur
coat being taken out of camphor") Soukhomlinov was convinced
that if a European war broke out it would last only a few months;
and almost all the Ministers except Kokovtsov had an "implicit faith
in the might of the Russian people to meet any national crisis."[5]

Against this background of growing hostility between Slav and
German, the crime took place that finally set Europe ablaze, producing the terrible holocaust known as the First World War. On
June 28, at Sarajevo in Bosnia, the middle-aged Archduke Franz
Ferdinand, heir to the Austrian throne, and his wife, Sophie,
were shot dead in what has been called 'the perfect political
murder'. The names of the young Bosnian Serbs who threw
the bomb and fired the shots are known; the name of the organisation who directed the operation and supplied the weapons—*The
Black Hand*—is also known, yet the story reads like an unfinished
thriller. For even to-day, sixty years after the event, the affair is still
veiled in mystery and historians continue to quarrel over the

motives of the killers. "The world will presumably never be told all that was behind the murder," wrote Sir Edward Grey, the British Foreign Secretary, in memoirs published in 1925. "Probably there is not, and never was, any one person who knew all there was to know."[6]

Some people knew a great deal but they are dead; and with the passage of time truth has been suffocated beneath an avalanche of tendentious statements, contradictions, lies and omissions. Was the crime a nationalist outrage or a deliberate attempt to start a European War? What rôle, if any, was played by Russia—official or unofficial, Czarist or revolutionary? All we can do is to lead the reader through the tangled forest, pointing out the disputed turnings and unexplored trails. He must choose his own path.

So let us return to Vladimir Gatchinovich, the priest's son, whom we left in Belgrade in 1911 newly enrolled as No. 217 in Colonel Apis's organisation, *The Black Hand*. Although Gatchinovich still spoke of himself as a student he was nearly twenty-one and had not yet completed the fifth grade of the gymnasium. His real occupation was that of a full-time agitator. Subsidised by *The Black Hand*, he spent his time "organising *kruzkoks* and secret links from one village to another for the gathering of military intelligence to benefit Serbia."[7] The cells were on the Russian model, small and isolated, with only one central link.

Gatchinovich worked exclusively through students as they were the most inflammable material. He established the master-key for Bosnia in the house of Danilo Ilitch in Sarajevo. Ilitch was the son of a cobbler who had died some years earlier and was studying to become a teacher on a scholarship provided by the Austrian Government. He was a quiet, rather gloomy youth "always in a dark tie as a reminder of death." He spent most of his time reading revolutionary literature and translated the books he liked best—Bakunin's *The Paris Commune and the Idea of The State*; Andreyev's *The Dark Horizon*; Gorky's *Greetings to the Liberated Humanity*.

Ilitch's mother earned a living by accepting schoolboys as boarders. In 1911 Gavrilo Princip, the seventeen-year-old son of a postman, who lived in a small village in a wild and mountainous region near the Dalmatian coast, was put in her care and entered at the

Sarajevo High School. Princip had a frail, consumptive body and the burning blue eyes of a fanatic. He devoured revolutionary ideas with a fervour that delighted Ilitch and despite the difference in ages the two youths soon became bosom friends. They travelled to Belgrade together and joined *The Black Hand*. Apparently this experience further stimulated their ardour, for when they returned their house became famous as the pulse of Bosnia. "Through it passed all that was most revolutionary," wrote a Serb historian. "It was, in a way, the leading organ of all the nationalist currents in the country. Its relations, direct or indirect, with the émigrés in Belgrade was very close."[8]

Some time in 1911 Gatchinovich went to Switzerland. Undoubtedly he was sent there by Colonel Apis to make contact with the Russian revolutionaries. Apis liked to throw his net wide, and already had links with revolutionaries in Bulgaria and Austria. Gatchinovich arrived with such impressive credentials that he was at once taken under the wing of Natanson-Bogrov, a member of the Central Committee of the Russian Social Revolutionary Party.

As the reader may recall, Natanson had worked closely with the double-agent, Asev, until 1906 when the latter tried to persuade the Central Committee to disband *The Battle Organisation*, on the grounds that its methods had become so hopelessly old-fashioned that it was doomed to failure. As Natanson was a fierce advocate of the use of terror he had thrown his weight against Asev. Indeed, he had been one of three men appointed by the Party to address a mass meeting of terrorists in an effort to strengthen their resolve. He was so successful that *The Battle Organisation* resumed its work despite Asev's resignation. Incidentally, Natanson could never bring himself to believe wholly in his friend's treachery. Even after Asev had fled to Berlin he continued to hope that some miracle would occur to establish his innocence.

Although Vladimir Gatchinovich was young and naïve his passionate belief in political murder must have commended itself to Natanson. For several years Vladimir had been preaching that the bullet fired in the name of the people was an act of the highest nobility, and that life was "a mission that could only be fulfilled by the ultimate sacrifice." At any rate, Natanson opened wide the doors of revolutionary society to his young guest. Although he himself was a "left wing Social Revolutionary" he had many Social Democratic friends and Gatchinovich was able to discuss the current theories and deviations to his heart's content. As the S.D.s had embraced Marxism and had an irritating tendency to insist that it was not possible to be a nationalist and a socialist at the same time, Gatchinovich found himself drawn toward Natanson and the S.R.s.

Natanson showed sympathy for his young visitor's contention that the foreign yoke must be broken and the Serbs united before Socialism could be put into practice. At the same time he took pains to lecture him on Russian Populism and the peasant society of the future. "How much I have lived these last few days," Gatchinovich wrote to a friend in Bosnia. "One whole faith has collapsed and withered away and in its place is growing a new ideology which is seething chaotically in my mind, an ideology vigorous and intense, but still obscure and imprecise."[9]

Two years later Gatchinovich moved permanently to Switzerland. As he was an Austrian subject and had failed to reply to his military call-up papers, he could not remain in Bosnia without danger of arrest. Once again he enrolled in a university, this time Lausanne. The Propaganda Department of the Serbian Foreign Office arranged his entry and paid his fees. Why we do not know. *The Black Hand* supplemented the allowance.

This time Gatchinovich not only renewed his friendship with Natanson but identified himself completely with the Social Revolutionaries—"if not actually a member, since he was not a Russian, then a co-opted member. With such a position he had contact with many Russians, exchanging letters, frequenting their meetings and lectures and even contributing to the Russian socialist press."[9] Gatchinovich struck up an acquaintance with Trotsky who referred to him as "my young friend" and occasionally wrote forewords to his articles; and according to his brother, he also met Lenin.

Despite his new life he was still in the service of *The Black Hand* and remained in charge of the Bosnian network. He kept in close touch with his friends, Ilitch and Princip, and continued to preach the necessity of terror from his conveniently remote terrain. Considering all the propaganda he had done, he had met with remarkably little success. In the past four years only one student, not a Bosnian but a Croat, had succeeded in murdering anyone; the victim was the rather humble Croat Secretary of Education.

In the spring of 1913, Gatchinovich summoned Ilitch to Switzerland. The latter made the journey on foot and was thrilled to find himself surrounded by Russian revolutionaries. What the purpose of the trip was, we do not know, except that he returned to Bosnia with a message from Gatchinovich that "the heads of some of the leading dignitaries of the Empire must fall."[10] Whether this clarion call was inspired by *The Black Hand* or whether Natanson and his terrorist friends had prodded Gatchinovich into action is also a mystery. In 1912-13 the Russian revolutionaries were having a thin time. Lenin wrote mournfully that he did not expect to live to see the revolution; and early in 1913 he confided in a letter to Gorky: "A war between Austria and Russia would be a very useful thing for all of Eastern Europe, but it is not likely that Franz Joseph and Nikolasha [Nicholas II] will give us that pleasure."[11]

That summer Bulgaria attacked Serbia, and Serbia emerged the victor; the "promised land" was visibly closer. The Governor of Bosnia, General Potiorek, saw trouble ahead and declared a state of emergency. He closed the Mostar High School, banned meetings and refused to allow Serbian newspapers to circulate in Bosnia. Gatchinovich wrote indignant letters to his friends and finally, in December 1913, arranged a rendezvous in France between himself and two young Moslem students whom he had persuaded to join *The Black Hand*, personally administering the oath to them. As one of the youths, Golubic, was studying in Toulouse, it was decided to hold the meeting there. The other boy, Mehmedbasitch, raised the money for his journey with difficulty but turned up on the appointed day. The three conspirators foregathered at the Hotel St. Jerome, rue St. Jerome.

Many years later Golubic declared that the conference ended with the determination to "prepare an outrage against the Archduke Franz Ferdinand followed by others against important civil and military personages in various parts of the Austro-Hungarian Monarchy, including Vienna. It was hoped by these means to incite the Slav element in Austria-Hungary to revolt and even to cause a general European war." After the meeting, Gatchinovich wrote to Gavrilo Princip in Sarajevo urging him to come to Lausanne with Danilo Ilitch so that they could plan the details of the outrages. Princip went to Belgrade to ask *The Black Hand* to sanction the journey; but Colonel Apis's adjutant, Major Tankositch, replied that the trip was unnecessary because "it had been decided at Belgrade to assassinate the Archduke."[12]

Meanwhile Mehmedbasitch was returning from France preoccupied by a plan to murder General Potiorek. Gatchinovich had told him that it was "urgently necessary" and entrusted him with the mission. "A dagger was chosen as the surest weapon, especially if poisoned beforehand," he wrote many years later. "Gatchinovich gave me a little bottle of poison with which I was to moisten the blade of the dagger before doing the deed. From Toulouse I went to Marseilles and there embarked for Ragusa. At Ragusa, I took the train but noticed that the gendarmes were searching the compartments for something. Fearing I was the man they wanted I threw away the dagger and poison in the lavatory. I afterwards found that it was a petty thief they were after. When I reached Stolac I wrote Gatchinovich and pending his reply, did nothing more about carrying out the outrage.

"Some weeks later I received a letter from Ilitch asking me to go to Mostar in an important matter. I went. Ilitch told me that Franz Ferdinand was to visit Sarajevo, that the plot against Potiorek took a second place since the attack on the Heir Apparent was far more important, that Belgrade was of this opinion and would provide us with the necessary means; bombs and revolvers. He asked whether I would take part. I said I would, but reminded him that I had definitely promised Gatchinovich to kill Potiorek. I must therefore inform Gatchinovich and get his consent to the change of plan. We both wrote the letter and a few days later came the reply: 'Forward Lions,' giving his approval."[13]

The reader can see from this sketchy and unsatisfactory narrative how many theories were bound to arise concerning the origin of the outrage. Even the accounts of the two Moslems—both of whom were present at the Toulouse meeting—differ. Whereas Golubic claims that the assassination of the Archduke came first on the list—although it was to be followed by attempts against other high dignitaries—Mehmedbasitch insists that General Potiorek was the primary target.* As a result some historians argued that the decision to murder the Archduke did not originate at Toulouse but with the "young Bosnians"; others pointed to Gatchinovich as the chief culprit.

After the war, however, Golubic and other members of *The Black Hand* stated categorically that the murder was instigated by Colonel Apis and Major Tankositch, and that Gatchinovich acted on their orders. To-day the weight of historical evidence supports this claim, although some distinguished scholars still doubt the veracity of the witnesses. Two facts, however, are incontrovertible; the assassins received encouragement and help from *The Black Hand*; and no one can say whether the crime would have succeeded otherwise. Colonel Apis, therefore, must bear the prime responsibility.

The Colonel kept himself in the background and worked through intermediaries. Danilo Ilitch was instructed to direct preparations in Sarajevo while Gavrilo Princip was summoned to Belgrade to recruit more volunteers and to familiarise himself with the weapons. Princip found the capital overflowing with émigrés from Bosnia, ex-partisans of the Bulgarian war, young, poor and restless. They spent hours each day at the Green Garland coffee house talking about their military exploits and prophesying the next round against Austria. Princip persuaded his two closest friends to join the conspiracy. They were nineteen-year-old boys like himself, both from Sarajevo—Grabez and Chabrinovitch. Colonel Apis delegated Major Tankositch to look after them; and Major Tankositch delegated Milan Ciganovitch, a twenty-six-year-old Bosnian who had

* Both of these assertions may be true. At the time of the Toulouse meeting it is unlikely that the conspirators knew of the Archduke's intention to visit Bosnia, which was not announced until March, 1914. An assassination in Vienna would have required months of preparation whereas an attempt against Potiorek could have been made immediately. There is no reason to suppose that one plan invalidated the other. Colonel Apis learned of the Archduke's trip through secret channels some weeks ahead of the published date, but probably not as early as January.

served with him in the Bulgarian war and was one of the early members of *The Black Hand*, to instruct the boys in the use of bombs and revolvers. Meanwhile a message was sent to Ilitch in Sarajevo to recruit three more youths locally in order to distract attention from Belgrade and to make the whole affair as Bosnian as possible. He enlisted the Moslem boy, Mehmedbasitch, but the other two were high-school boys of seventeen and eighteen who scarcely knew what the affair was about.

At the end of May, a full month before the Archduke's visit, Ciganovitch gave Princip and his companions their weapons—four Belgian automatic revolvers and six bombs manufactured in the Serbian State Arsenal, the latest model, weighing only $2\frac{1}{2}$lbs. each. He also gave them vials of potassium cyanide which they agreed to swallow immediately after the attack.

The three boys travelled by boat down the river Save until they reached the border station at Sabac. Here they presented a letter to the frontier officer, a member of *The Black Hand*. He passed them along to a second frontier officer, who arranged the crossing into Austrian territory. They travelled to Sarajevo by means of the *Narodna Odbrana* "tunnel," a route peopled by reliable agents who would give them food and shelter. Princip left the guns and bombs wrapped in a neat package with one of *Narodna Odbrana*'s "confidential men," a cinema director who lived in Tuzla, a small town not far from Sarajevo. When they reached the city he went to Ilitch's house where he remained for the next few weeks. His companions retreated to their own homes, one in the centre of Sarajevo, the other a few miles outside.

Ilitch took charge of the operation, although at one point he lost his nerve and for several days tried to persuade his fellow conspirators to abandon the project. Once more resolved, he travelled to Tuzla, picked up the package, returned home and hid it under the couch in his bedroom. He spent hours studying the Archduke's itinerary and planning where the conspirators would take their positions. Franz Ferdinand would arrive in Bosnia on 25th June, spend three days at Ilidze attending army manœuvres, and motor to Sarajevo on the morning of the 28th. He would drive along the long straight avenue bordering the river, known as the

Appel Quay, and attend a ceremony at the Town Hall. Ilitch decided that all seven of the assassins must take up places on the Quay, so that if one missed another might succeed.

On 26th June he sent a telegram to Mehmedbasitch summoning him to Sarajevo. The latter arrived the next morning and booked in at the local hotel. That same day Ilitch collected his two innocent schoolboys, took them to the park and gave them lessons in shooting. Firing off two practice shots he remarked: "Anyone getting this bullet, he's done for." On the eve of the crime Ilitch, Princip and Mehmedbasitch sat up talking until three a.m. They sent a joint postcard to Gatchinovich in Switzerland, their last communication with the outside world before the event. Early the following morning Ilitch joined Grabez and Chabrinovitch at a Turkish coffee shop. They were the only two who had not yet received their weapons. He handed Grabez a revolver and a bomb, and Chabrinovitch a bomb. Now the time had come to take up their stations.

The twenty-eighth of June was a beautiful day. The streets were bedecked with flags and crowds began to assemble early to see the procession pass. The Archduke arrived in Sarajevo from Ilidze about ten in the morning. After reviewing local troops his small cavalcade of four cars headed for the Town Hall. A police car led the way, followed by a motor carrying the Archduke, arrayed in his full-dress uniform, his wife who sat beside him wearing a large picture hat, and Governor Potiorek on the seat facing them. Two cars followed carrying the Governor's staff.

Ilitch and his three Bosnian recruits (Mehmedbasitch and the two schoolboys) were standing within a few yards of each other near the Cumurja Bridge. All four of them seemed frozen with fear and stood motionless as the Archduke passed. The fifth assassin, however, Princip's friend from Belgrade, Chabrinovitch, was standing on the other side of the bridge. He knocked off the cap of his bomb on a post, stepped forward and threw it. The chauffeur saw him and accelerated. The bomb fell on the folded hood of the open car, bounced off and exploded in the street. It detonated loudly, damaging the car behind, seriously wounding one of the Governor's aides and a number of bystanders. Chabrinovitch jumped over the wall and ran towards the river. He swallowed his poison but it did not work. Police agents bounded after him and caught him. The Arch-duke behaved impeccably. After making sure that the wounded had received all possible aid he remarked coolly, "Come on. The fellow is insane. Gentlemen, let us proceed with our programme."

The royal guests remained at the Town Hall for about half an hour. In view of the attempt on the Archduke's life, the Governor decided not to risk a drive through narrow streets on the return journey. Instead of turning off the broad Appel Quay half-way down, as originally planned, they would keep straight on; a quick visit to the hospital to inquire about the wounded officer and then to the Governor's residence for luncheon. If the chauffeurs had understood their instructions the assassination might never have taken place. Princip had moved to the corner of the narrow street joining the Appel Quay where he expected the Archduke's car to turn. The Mayor's car was leading and instead of continuing straight led the way along the Quay and swung into the side street. The Archduke's chauffeur followed. "That's the wrong way," cried Governor Potiorek. "Drive straight down the Appel Quay." The chauffer stopped and began to back the car. Princip was standing only a few feet away. He stepped forward and fired two shots at point-blank range. The first hit the Archduke in the neck, causing blood to spurt from his mouth. The second embedded itself in his wife's abdomen. "Sophie, Sophie, do not die," cried the distracted prince. "Live for our children." Within an hour both were dead.

Princip, meanwhile, had swallowed the poison but it did not have any more effect than Chabrinovitch's. He was roughly handled by the crowd and finally taken into custody by the police. When he was questioned he denied knowing Chabrinovitch; he said he had acted alone and was not a member of any group. His story was spoiled by Ilitch who was arrested later in the day because Princip was known to have stayed in his house. Although the police had nothing against him and it was only a routine round-up, Ilitch lost his head and tried to make a deal with the judge. He admitted his complicity and asked for leniency in exchange for a confession. He named his five companions and many of those who had aided the conspirators on their way to Sarajevo. The police picked up the lot within the next ten days, except for Mehmedbasitch who managed to hide and eventually crossed into Montenegro.

Ilitch was more discreet when it came to *The Black Hand*. He and three of his accomplices—Princip, Grabez and Chabrinovitch—the only four who knew any details of the organisation—took pains to throw their interrogators off the scent. They insisted that the idea of the murders had originated solely with themselves; they wished to kill the Archduke because he was an enemy of the Slav people. They mentioned the *Narodna Odbrana* which had not been officially involved; named Milan Ciganovitch (who was safely in Serbia) as the man who had supplied the weapons; and pretended that Major Tankositch, whose name came up inadvertently, was almost a stranger, despite the fact that he had given some of them revolver practice. Although the Austrian Government knew of the existence of *The Black Hand* and even possessed a partial list of alleged members, their information was scanty. They looked upon the society as a military conclave, hostile to the Serbian Government, and concerned with internal affairs. Time was short; the assassination was being overtaken by a rush of momentous events leading to the world war. If the Austrian Ministry of Foreign Affairs had not been so rattled it might have seized the clue of Tankositch's name and connected the crime to *The Black Hand*; and *The Black Hand* to Colonel Dragutin Dimitrievich-Apis. As it was, Apis was not mentioned.

Even so, it is surprising how close the Judge came to the truth:

"The Court regards it as proved by the evidence that both the *Narodna Odbrana* and military circles in the Kingdom of Serbia in charge of the espionage service, collaborated in the outrage . . . There is no doubt that both the *Narodna Odbrana* and military circles on the active list of the Kingdom of Serbia knew of the aims of the outrage and were prodigal of all possible assistance and all possible protection to the perpetrators for whom they actually procured the means of carrying out the assassination . . ."[14]

Meanwhile Austria was in a state of fury and excitement. Demonstrations took place in many parts of the country. Serbian flags were burned, Serbian property looted and destroyed. In Sarajevo the damage ran into millions of kronen. The Austrian Government led by Count Berchtold, the Foreign Secretary, was certain that Belgrade had countenanced, if not actively encouraged, the crime. Judge Pfeffer's report suggested as much but was too vague to be of use. In a fevered effort to fill in the crucial gaps Berchtold dispatched to Sarajevo Dr. Friedrich von Wiesner, the legal adviser to the Foreign Office. Unfortunately for Berchtold, Wiesner was pedantic, cautious and unimaginative. He would not hazard any guesses without incontrovertible facts to back his argument. Indeed, he bent over the other way. After two days and nights sifting material he telegraphed to Vienna that, although the crime had been prepared in Belgrade and although the Serbian Government stimulated hostile propaganda in Bosnia, there was "nothing to prove, or even to cause suspicion of the Serbian Government's cognisance of the steps leading to the crime, or of its preparing it, or of its supplying the weapons. On the contrary there are indications that this is to be regarded as out of the question."[15]

Dr. Wiesner was to spend a life-time rueing the word "cognisance." Before sending his telegram he showed it to Governor Potiorek who condemned it as far "too conservative" and hastened to inform General Conrad von Hötzendorff, the Austrian Chief-of-Staff, of his dissent. "It is downright impossible," he wrote, "that some person or other in a democratic government in such a small country as Serbia should not have had knowledge of the preparations of the crime and the traitorous working methods of the whole propaganda . . . Furthermore in Serbia by the side of the official government, there is a rival military government, which takes its existence from the army. That Serbian officers in active service participated in the preparation of the assassination, and also participated in the whole propaganda, and are therefore among the instigators of the traitorous agitation stirred up in our country, is proven. The army, to be sure, is not part of the Government. But to try to maintain that the official Serbian Government does not know what the army is doing is by no means tenable."[16]

Potiorek was right. We know to-day that Pashitch was aware of the plot, and undoubtedly Pashitch informed the Regent, Prince Alexander. The Prime Minister may have learned the details from

Milan Ciganovitch, who was said to be his spy and whom he bundled out of Belgrade to evade trial after the crime. He certainly received a report from one of his border guards stating that armed youths had crossed the frontier, for he annotated it in his own hand. He ordered an investigation of Colonel Apis (who denied all knowledge of the affair) and informed several of his Cabinet colleagues that a plot was under way to murder the Archduke. One of these confederates, the Minister of Education, revealed this fact in 1923.

For years historians have argued as to whether or not Pashitch warned the Vienna Government. "On this issue there exists a vast literature of a most controversial character," writes Vladimir Dedijer, a Jugoslav historian who lives in Belgrade and has had an opportunity to study the archives.

"At least ten sources mentioned, either immediately after 28th June, 1914, or between the two world wars, that the Serbian Government had warned Vienna. Some of these sources claimed that Pashitch himself stated that the warning was sent to the Belgrade Government; but Pashitch denied this on two occasions. The Austrian Government on three different occasions denied that the warning was delivered.

"This writer believes that the Serbian Government did not officially inform Vienna of the results of its investigations before 28th June, as the archives of the Serbian Ministry of Foreign Affairs confirm. It is not clear whether the Serbian Minister in Vienna, Jovan Jovanovich-Pizon, on his own initiative, expressed his fears about the Archduke's visit to Sarajevo. There are several different versions of this issue, but it seems safe to say that Jovanovich-Pizon went to Count Bilinski and mentioned vaguely the dangers for the Archduke during his trip to Bosnia and Herzegovina."[17]

As Pashitch did not warn the Austrian Government, he was an accomplice to the crime, no matter how reluctant. Why did he remain silent? The answer lies with the formidable leader of *The Black Hand*.

In the spring of 1914 Colonel Dragutin Dimitrievich-Apis was the most feared and the most powerful man in Serbia. He lived in a world of conspiracy made all the more sinister by his modest demeanour and charming smile. "He met me in a polite way as he used to do with everyone," wrote a friend who called to see him some time during this period. "He expressed himself in an ambiguous way, never finishing his sentences, as if he remembered all of a sudden that it would be better not to say everything that he had on his mind. He had not yet recovered from his grave illness; there were still traces of poison in his body. He did not stand firmly on his legs which, wrapped in military bindings, looked giant-like. He was gaining weight because he did not move about enough. He had an unhealthy pale colour and his head was completely bald. Sitting at the table, with his huge body and bald head, he looked, as a foreign correspondent described him, like a giant Mongolian."[18]

The Colonel's indisposition was due to a rare disease known as Maltese fever which he had contracted in 1912 when he made a raid into Albania to win an important chieftain to the Serbian side. He was too ill to take part in the First Balkan War of 1912 but reached the apex of his career in June 1913 when he was appointed Chief of Intelligence for the Serbian General Staff.

This was the job he most wanted, as his thirst for power was not military but political. Although he already used *The Black Hand* to exert pressure on the Government, control of the state espionage apparatus opened exciting new vistas. It not only enabled him to enter the international field and to deal officially with Russia but to accelerate the activities of *The Black Hand* under cover of state affairs. By the end of 1913 *Black Hand* members were everywhere; they honey-combed the civil service and army, and had penetrated almost every secret society in the country. Even the Secretary General of the *Narodna Odbrana* swore allegiance to Apis, not to mention many of the organisation's workers in humbler capacities.

The Colonel was as aggressive and ruthless as any modern dictator; but as he had an almost childish love of "adventure, danger, secret meetings, mysterious activity" he preferred to play his hand behind the scenes. He exercised a great influence over the younger officers and had a knack of making "the worst deeds appear trifles, and the most dangerous schemes innocent and harmless." Although the Colonel's life was passionately dedicated to the realisation of a

Greater Serbia he was impossible to control for he was convinced that no one could achieve this but himself. "Anyone who disagreed with him," wrote a contemporary, "was in his eyes, neither honourable, nor clever, nor a patriot."[19] He was a born killer who preferred war and murder to any sort of temporisation. Consequently he despised Pashitch for his tendency to compromise. He had been at loggerheads with the Prime Minister ever since 1908 when he inveighed against his acceptance of the Austrian annexation as "treason." He claimed credit for the Serbo-Bulgarian Treaty of 1912 which led to the First Balkan War; and he prevented Pashitch from reaching agreement with Bulgaria over Macedonia which resulted in the Second Balkan War.

At the end of 1913 he was locked in a bitter quarrel with the Prime Minister over who should administer the vast new territories that Serbia had acquired in the wars—the civil or the military? The army, flushed with victory, arrogant and intolerant, was indignant that there should be any argument about it but Pashitch was determined to hold on to his authority. The clash became known as "the priority question" and had grown so fierce by May, 1913, that both the French and Austrian Ministers sent alarming dispatches to their Governments reporting that "the officers were in a ferment" and predicting "violent eruptions."[20]

The Colonel was a sinister opponent, for he not only had a following in the army but also controlled gangs of *Black Hand* terrorists who roamed about Macedonia. Just as Lenin's followers robbed banks to keep the Bolshevik Party in funds, these thugs killed and plundered to swell the coffers of *The Black Hand*, under pretext of "serbising" the population. "The worst crimes were committed by this secret organisation, known to all the world and under powerful protection," reported the Carnegie Commission on the Balkan Wars in 1914. ". . . Where complaints were made to the regular authorities they pretended to know nothing of the matter, or if the person complaining was obscure, they punished him . . ."

The truth was that the civil authorities were too frightened to oppose the terrorists. The Karageorgevich family quaked when Apis's newspaper *Piedmont* hinted darkly that there might be a repetition of the events of 1903. Early in June, when talk of a military *coup d'état* was on everyone's lips, the King accepted Pashitch's resignation. "The white-haired heads with long beards have now to be forgotten for ever," crowed *Piedmont*. "The Negroes have finished their jobs and they can go." But Apis was rejoicing too soon. The Russian Minister, Hartwig, intervened and persuaded King Peter to reinstate Pashitch. Peter agreed; but as such a reversal made his own position impossible, he abdicated and appointed his son Alexander as Regent. In the middle of this fierce clash Pashitch learned about the conspiracy to murder the Archduke. Although he made a few feeble attempts to scotch the plot it is assumed that he did not warn the Austrian Government because he was frightened of the vengeance of *The Black Hand*.

What was Colonel Apis's motive in encouraging the murder of the Archduke? This is the most controversial of all the questions dealing with Sarajevo. Apis was a man of the utmost secrecy, famous for keeping his own counsel. "Though very young I spent a whole year with him at his office during the World War," wrote his nephew in 1937. "I never heard him utter a word about the Sarajevo outrage. I have questioned some fifty people who were closest to him and they could none of them tell me anything definite that they had been told by him. Most of them had been told nothing while to others vague and evasive statements were made . . ."[21]

Historians, therefore, have been forced to speculate. In 1923 a Serbian professor, Stanojevich, was authorised by his government to produce an "official history," *The Murder of the Archduke Franz Ferdinand*. The object was to clear up the mystery and, of course, to absolve the Jugoslav Government. He claimed that Colonel Apis received a report through Russian military intelligence that Austria was planning to use the Bosnian manœuvres to make a surprise attack on Serbia; that the plan had been decided at Konopischt in the presence of the Kaiser William II of Germany and Franz Ferdinand. After much thought Apis decided to murder the Archduke in order to prevent the war. This naïve explanation was laughed out of court. First, the Konopischt meeting took place on 12th June, a fortnight after the assassins had crossed the frontier and proceeded to Sarajevo; second, as the Colonel's nephew pointed out, ". . . they forget that he was head of Military Intelligence of the General Staff and must have perfectly well known that Austria at that moment was not preparing for a war with Serbia"[21]; third, why should Austria be deterred from war by the murder of her Heir Apparent?

The interpretation put forward by Sidney Fay in his great classic, *Origins of the World War*, was more plausible and found acceptance among historians of every nationality. He portrayed Franz Ferdinand as the champion of "trialism" a reform which would give the Slavs the same autonomy as Germans and Magyars in the Dual Monarchy. Belgrade feared trialism for if Austria succeeded in satisfying her Slav population the dream of a Greater Serbia would end. The assassin Gavrilo Princip hinted this at his trial, ". . . as future Sovereign he would have prevented our union by carrying through certain reforms which would have clearly gone against our interests."

Yet even this explanation is not convincing. Although the Archduke favoured trialism in the early nineteen-hundreds he soon came to the conclusion that "three parliaments" would not work, and abandoned the idea in favour of Federalism which would give the Germans the upper hand. During the last five years of his life he frequently referred to trialism in disparaging terms. "If we want peace in Austria," he wrote to the Kaiser in 1909, "we must smash the *preponderance* of the Magyars. Otherwise we shall with absolute certainty become a Slav Empire, and trialism, which would be a misfortune, would be achieved."[22] As the Emperor Franz Joseph and his Government were also wholly opposed to trialism it is not credible to conclude that Colonel Apis murdered the Archduke for a hazy idea that had already been discarded.

Finally, we must keep in mind that almost everyone in Serbia believed that the murder of the Archduke meant war. The Vienna militarists had been straining at the leash for five years, warning the Government that if Serbia's policy of subversion and incitement remained unchecked, the Monarchy would crumble away before their eyes. Belgrade had become so arrogant that she was jibing at the "worm-eaten" Empire. "She keeps her parts joined with the help of old glue," shrilled *Piedmont* in January, 1914, "which might not survive a sharper crisis . . ." As soon as the assassination became known in the Serbian capital most people believed that a clash with Austria was inevitable. "About 5 p.m. an official from the Press Bureau rang me up on the telephone and told me what had happened at Sarajevo," wrote Ljuba Jovanovitch, the Minister of Education in the Pashitch Cabinet of 1914. "Although I knew what was being prepared there, yet, as I held the receiver, I felt as though someone had dealt me an unexpected blow; and a little later, when the first news was confirmed from other quarters I began to be overwhelmed with grave anxiety. I did not doubt for a moment that Austria-Hungary would make this the occasion for a war on Serbia."[23] If most responsible people in Belgrade believed that an outrage on the Archduke would lead to war, how was it that the Head of Serbian Intelligence should have been innocent enough to suppose that he could murder Franz Ferdinand and ignore the catastrophe that was bound to intervene?

This brings us to the most obvious motive of all: that Colonel Dimitrievich-Apis wished to provoke an attack by Austria which would result in a European war and pave the way for Greater Serbia. Ever since June 1913 Apis had been working in close cooperation with the Russian military attaché, Colonel Victor Artamonov, and from April onwards with Artamonov's assistant, the newly appointed Captain Verkhovsky. As Russia and Serbia regarded Austria as the common enemy the two Colonels pooled their resources, exchanged intelligence and even employed the same spies. "Of course I was in practically daily contact with Dimitrievich-Apis," Artamonov stated many years after the war. "I was military attaché, Dimitrievich was head of military intelligence of the Serbian General Staff. Serbia and Russia were on extremely friendly terms and had mutual co-operation in case of war. Moreover, I had to follow Austrian military preparations in Bosnia, because, as an enemy frontier, it was of concern to the Russian General Staff in case of war. My relations with Dimitrievich were entirely confined to intelligence on military matters."[24]

Not entirely, it seems. Artamonov approved of the belligerent tone of Colonel Apis's *Piedmont* which frequently referred to the "inevitability" of a war with Austria, for he contributed to the journal's funds. And in May, 1914, he listened intently when Apis confided the plan for the assassination of the Archduke, and asked him what he thought Russia would do if Austria attacked Serbia. Artamonov could not give a reply, he said, until he consulted his superiors. But a few days later he had the answer. "Just go ahead! If you are attacked you will not stand alone."

This incident was revealed after the war by Colonel Simich, a member of *The Black Hand*. It appeared in an interview with Victor Serge which was published in the Paris review *Clarté* in May, 1925. When the Italian historian, Luciano Magrini, consulted Simich in 1937 and asked him if he could vouch for the truth of the story, he confirmed that it was correct except for certain references to the Russian Minister, Hartwig. "His opinion was that Hartwig was kept in the dark about the plot but that Artamonov—who sympathised with *The Black Hand* to which he had contributed 8,000 francs, and above all with its chief Dimitrievich, with whom he was in daily co-operation—was fully informed of everything. Simich added that he had no idea whom Artamonov could have consulted in St. Petersburg before giving Dimitrievich his reply, but it must have been somebody of more authority than himself, possibly the Russian General Staff, possibly the War Minister Soukhomlinov, possibly some Grand Duke, certainly not Hartwig, because in that case there would not have been a delay of several days before he could give his answer."[24]

It was not surprising that the Russian General Staff gave a belligerent reply for, as the reader has seen, in the spring of 1914 the Russian Army, backed by the Panslavists, was in a dangerous mood. If the Russian military attaché, Colonel Artamonov, consulted the War Minister, M. Soukhomlinov, or the Grand Duke Nicholas or even the Chief of the General Staff, General Yanoushkevitch—as he was said to have done—the reply was bound to have been aggressive.

Nevertheless, historians have been reluctant to accept the theory of collusion, first because Colonel Artamonov repeatedly denied that Apis had confided his murder plan to him; secondly because Artamonov went on leave between 19th June and 28th July, which appeared to be a perfect alibi. Would the Russian military attaché have taken a holiday if he had known what was being planned? While most scholars shook their heads, the Italian historian, Luigi

Albertini, answered the question by inserting a negative. Would Artamonov have gone on leave if he had *not* known what was being prepared? In 1937 Artamonov described to Albertini's collaborator, Luciano Magrini, the duties of a Russian military attaché. "I had to follow Austrian military preparations in Bosnia, because, as an enemy frontier, it was of concern to the Russian General Staff in case of war." When Magrini remarked that "it was strange that he should absent himself from Belgrade at the very moment when the Austrian manœuvres were on the point of beginning on the Bosnian frontier and the Archduke was expected at Sarajevo, Artamonov, after some embarrassed hesitation, said that he had not been given any furlough for three years and permission had been given him in the first half of June . . ." This was three weeks before the start of manœuvres. "The present writer," Magrini continues, "must honestly say he remained unconvinced by the behaviour of this officer, who struck him as being of limited intelligence with little strength of character, or by his explanations for his absence from Belgrade even after the outrage. He showed the present writer his note-book of June-July 1914, a bald list of Swiss and Italian hotels, giving the room-numbers of the accommodation occupied by himself and his family in each hotel and the account of the day's expenses and nothing else. No mention of the Sarajevo outrage or Hartwig's death. Only at the top of the page bearing the date 24th July, 1914, under the name of his hotel at Lovrana are the words: *Austrian ultimatum to Serbia*, followed by the usual record of the day's expenditure beginning with: coffee—2 lire!"[25]

In June, 1917 Colonel Apis was executed by the Serbian Government on charges of conspiring with the enemy and plotting to kill the Regent, Alexander. As Serbia was overrun by Austrian and German troops the Government had taken refuge in Greece and the trial took place before a secret military tribunal in Salonika. Others were tried with Apis, among them the two Moslems, Mehmedbasitch and Golubic who had attended the Toulouse meeting.

The chief witness for the prosecution was Milan Ciganovitch the man who had provided Princip and Chabrinovitch with weapons for the Sarajevo murder. From start to finish the proceedings were a legal farce. Although not a shred of evidence was produced to show that Apis and his associates were guilty of treason, the Colonel and two companions, Malobabitch and Vucinovitch were executed, the rest being sentenced to prison. The Serbian captain who drove Apis and his two followers to the place of execution claims that the Colonel remarked to him: "Now it is clear to me and clear to you, too, that I am to be killed to-day by Serbian rifles solely because I organised the Sarajevo outrage."[26]

Was Pashitch fearful that Colonel Apis might reveal the fact that he, Pashitch, knew about the Sarajevo plot? As the Prime Minister had failed to warn Vienna his only alternative was to deny flatly any fore-knowledge. This he did throughout his life. "Had we known of the plot," he told a reporter from the *New York Herald* (Paris edition) on 20th July, 1914, "assuredly we would have informed the Austro-Hungarian Government." The importance Pashitch attached to guarding his guilty secret throughout the war-years sprang from the conviction that the future of Greater Serbia was bound up with the goodwill of the victors.

Other writers claim that Pashitch believed that the Central Powers were likely to win the war and contemplated opening negotiations with Austria-Hungary. He could not risk disclosures that the Chief of Serbian Military Intelligence had planned the Sarajevo outrage and gone unpunished, for this would not only incriminate the Serbian Army but do great damage to the Government. Undoubtedly this argument was impressed on Apis in private for in the first two lines of his will he wrote: "Although sentenced to death by two competent courts, and deprived of the mercy of the Crown, I die innocently, and in the conviction that my death is necessary to Serbia for higher reasons."[27]

The trial had the bizarre quality that we have come to associate with Russia. No one was allowed to refer to the Sarajevo murder, although behind the scenes confessions were extracted from those involved. Torture was applied to Malobabitch, who broke under it, and to Mehmedbasitch and Golubic, who withstood it. We do not know whether Apis was tortured, but there is evidence that he was promised his freedom if he would write letters pleasing to his captors. On 12th April he wrote two letters, one to King Peter pleading guilty to every charge brought against him, and another to Alexander shamelessly begging for mercy. On the previous day, 11th April, he had revealed his part in the Sarajevo murder in a written statement as patently false as the other two documents. This "confession" came to light when the Nazis overran Belgrade in the Second World War.

> As the Chief of the Intelligence Department of the General Staff I engaged Rade Malobabitch to organise the information service in Austria-Hungary. I took this step in agreement with the Russian military attaché, Artamonov, who had a meeting with Rade in my presence. Feeling that Austria was planning war with us, I thought that the disappearance of the Austrian Heir Apparent would weaken the power of the military clique he headed, and thus the danger of war would be removed or postponed for a while. I engaged Malobabitch to organise the assassination on the occasion of the announced arrival of Franz Ferdinand to Sarajevo. I made up my mind about this only when Artamonov assured me that Russia would not leave us without protection if we were attacked by Austria. On this occasion I did not mention my intention for the assassination, and my motive for asking his opinion about Russia's attitude was the possibility that Austria might become aware of our activities and use this as a pretext to attack us. Malobabitch executed my orders, organised and performed the assassination. His chief accomplices were in my service and had small payments from me. Some of their receipts are in the hands of the Russians, since I got money for this purpose from Mr. Artamonov, as the General Staff did not have funds available for this increased activity.[28]

Confessions were also extracted from Golubic and Mehmed-basitch but were never published as they did not support Apis's declaration. After the trial Ciganovitch was sent to America at the expense of the Serbian Government; when he returned in 1919 he was given agricultural land near Uskub as a reward for his services. Colonel Victor Artamonov was also received warmly. As a refugee from Russia he spent the remainder of his life in Belgrade living on a Serbian state pension.

Colonel Milan Bogitchevich, a Serbian diplomat who was stationed in Berlin from 1907-14, and who was Colonel Apis's closest friend (his *probratim* or blood brother) declared, long before the Colonel's "confession" came to light, that Apis had written all he knew of the Sarajevo crime, taking sole responsibility, but making it clear that Alexander, Pashitch, Artamonov and Hartwig (the Russian Minister) knew of the preparations. Bogitchevich returned to Serbia when war began and in 1915 spent some weeks with Apis at his headquarters. As he defected to Germany in 1916 his revelations are treated gingerly by historians. Nevertheless time has proved so many of his assertions true that one cannot ignore them, particularly when they provide the only logical explanation for mystifying happenings. Hartwig's dispatches to St. Petersburg during the crucial period from May to July 1917, are missing from the Soviet files. It is alleged, but not proven, that they were stolen from the Foreign Office archives in St. Petersburg during the revolution.[29]

After sentence was passed on Colonel Apis, Britain and France made representations to Prince Alexander for clemency. An even more urgent intervention was made by Russia's Kerensky Government. The Minister of War in this Cabinet was none other than the former assistant military attaché at Belgrade, Captain Verkhovsky.

The Captain's name came up again some years later. In 1926 a Russian-Polish archæologist Louis de Tyrdar-Burzynski, who moved to Italy after the war, published his memoirs. "The assassination," he wrote, "was perpetrated with the support of the Russian military attaché at Belgrade. Captain Verkhovsky, who was assistant to the military attaché [Artamonov] and was later War Minister in the Kerensky Government, a young man whom I had known very well for years and all his family, told me quite frankly the truth about the origins, preparations and execution of the plot."[30]

The final mystery of Sarajevo leads back to Switzerland in the weeks before the murder. Vladimir Gatchinovich was not as discreet as Colonel Apis. He liked to talk, and confided to Natanson-Bogrov and other Russian revolutionary friends—with whom he practised throwing bombs in the Alps—about the preparations being made at Sarajevo. After the Archduke's death he wrote to friends in Serbia that his Russian comrades had advised him to leave Switzerland without delay; if his name came up in the trial the Austrian Government might ask for his extradition and the Swiss authorities were certain to comply.

Although Gatchinovich escaped mention he was compelled to leave Switzerland a few weeks later for financial reasons, as his subsidies from the Government and *The Black Hand* came to an end with the outbreak of war. He went to Paris and for the next year lived a hand-to-mouth existence. He served for a brief while in the French Navy, but apparently did not care for the life, for soon he was back in Paris moving in Russian and French revolutionary circles. He worked as a newsboy selling *Humanité*; dug trenches, drove a truck; wrote articles at the request of Trotsky who paid a brief visit to the capital.

By the middle of 1915 Gatchinovich had picked up some sort of secret job for he returned once more to Switzerland. Here he met Karl Radek who, with Natanson-Bogrov, was to become a member of Lenin's Bolshevik Government. Radek must have been fascinated by Gatchinovich for he never ceased to take a deep interest in the Sarajevo controversy. In 1934 he wrote an article criticising the Soviet historian, Poletika, for accusing the Serbian Government of complicity; he did not, however, censure Poletika for claiming that the crime had been engineered by the Russian General Staff. Gatchinovich, meanwhile, remained on such close terms with Natanson that when the latter accompanied Lenin back to Russia, through Germany, in 1917, he invited the young Serb to accompany them. Gatchinovich was longing to go but refused because, according to his brother, he feared that the Germans might arrest him for his part in the Archduke's murder.

In August, 1917, two months after Colonel Apis's execution, Gatchinovich was found dead in his flat. All his letters and papers were missing. Who killed him? The Serbian Government? *The Black Hand*? Some writers believe that agents of Austria poisoned him, but in that case the stolen letters eventually would have come to light.

In 1937 when Karl Radek—by this time one of the "Old Guard"

—was brought to trial in a Stalin purge, he made a statement to the Court that deepened the mystery of Sarajevo.

". . . And we must also tell the world what Lenin—I tremble to mention his name from this dock—said in the letter, in the directions he gave to the delegation that was about to leave for The Hague, about the secret of war. A fragment of this secret was in the possession of the young Serbian nationalist, Gabriel Princip, who could die in a fortress without revealing it. He was a Serbian nationalist and felt the justice of his cause when fighting for the secret which was kept by the Serbian national movement. I cannot conceal this secret and carry it with me to the grave, because while in view of what I have confessed here, I have not the right to speak as a repentant Communist, nevertheless the 35 years I worked in the labour movement despite all the errors and crimes with which they ended, entitle me to ask you to believe one thing—that, after all, the masses of the people with whom I marched do mean something to me. And if I concealed this truth and departed this life with it, as Zinoviev did and as Mrach-kovsky did, then when I thought over these things, I would have heard in my hour of death the execrations of those people who will be slaughtered in the future war, and whom, by my testi-mony, I could have furnished with a weapon against the war that is being fomented . . ."[31]

Radek was cut off and not allowed to continue. What letter? What conference? What secret? Were there two plots to kill the Archduke, one inspired by the revolutionaries, the other by the mil-itarists? Had the two-tiered policy of Czarist Russia, which made use alike of Panslavists and revolutionaries to pursue its expansionist aims, collided at Sarajevo? Or did Colonel Dragutin Dimitrievich-Apis combine these dual rôles in his own person? Dr. Jevto Dedijer, a Serbian writer and a close friend of Apis, firmly believed that the Colonel was, in the jargon of modern Jugoslavia, a "progressive." In 1914 it required a stretch of imagination to think of a "National-Socialist" or "a Communist-Imperialist," but it is not so difficult to-day. Although Dedijer's son, a historian who lives in Belgrade, does not share his father's views, he feels that scholars would do well to study "Apis's relations with unofficial Russia, particularly with revolutionary circles."[32]

The feverish negotiations that were crammed into the four and a half weeks before the outbreak of the World War have no place in this book. The fundamental quarrel was between Russia, determined to extend her influence in the Balkans at the expense of Austria; and Austria, determined to defend herself by attacking Serbia whom she regarded as a Russian Trojan Horse. Germany was regarded by the Panslavs as a major enemy because she had a treaty of alliance with Austria, and Austria would not dare to defy Russia without the backing of German might. It was natural, wrote the British historian, Dr. G. P. Gooch, "that Austria should resolve to defend herself against the openly proclaimed ambition to rob her of the provinces which she had held for centuries. After the Bosnian crisis Serbia had promised to be a good neighbour; but she had not kept her word, and her intrigues with Russia were notorious. [For Austria] to sit with folded arms and wait till her enemies felt strong enough to carry out their programme of dismemberment was to proclaim her impotence and invite disaster; and the murder of the heir to the throne by Jugoslav assassins appeared to demand some striking vindication of the authority of the State.

". . . As Berchtold saw the hand of Russia in the tragedy of Sarajevo, so Sazonov felt the ultimatum as a blow struck at Nicholas II not less than at Prince Peter Karageorgevitch. Had she left her protégé to the tender mercies of Austria, she would have forfeited all claim to be the champion of the Slavonic races, and have handed over the Near East to the unchecked domination of the Central Powers. Though bound by no treaty obligation, Russia could no more be expected to remain neutral in face of an Austrian attack on Serbia than England in face of a German attack on Belgium. The same instinctive pride of a Great Power which prompted Vienna to throw down the glove compelled Petrograd to take it up. It is true that while Austria fought under the banner of self-preservation, Russia, whom nobody threatened to attack, marched out to battle in the name of prestige . . ."[33]

At the time, not everyone felt that Russian prestige merited a world war. On 26th July, the British Ambassador in Paris, Lord Bertie, wrote in his diary: ". . . Russia comes forward as the protectress of Serbia; by what title except on the exploded pretensions that she is, by right, the protectress of all the Slavs? What rubbish! And she will expect, if she adheres to her present attitude, France and Britain to support her in arms . . ."[34]

That same week the French President, Poincaré, visited the Russian capital and the French Ambassador in St. Petersburg, Maurice Paléologue, gives us a vivid picture of the enthusiasm of the Panslavs. "We returned to the village of Krasnoe Selo," he wrote on 22nd July, "where the Grand Duke Nicholas Nicholaevich, Commander of the Imperial Guard, G.O.C. the St. Petersburg military area and subsequently generalissimo of the Russian armies, gave a dinner to the President of the Republic and the sovereigns. Three long tables were set in half-open tents around a garden which was in full flower. The beds had just been watered and from them the fresh scent of flowers—a delicious change after a baking day—rose into the warm air. I was one of the first to arrive. The Grand Duchess Anastasia, the wife of the Grand Duke Nicholas, and her sister, the Grand Duchess Militzia, gave me a boisterous welcome. The two Montenegrins burst out talking at once:

" 'Do you realise that we're passing through historic days, fateful days! . . . At the review to-morrow the bands will play nothing but the *Marche Lorraine* and *Sambre et Meuse*. I've had a telegram from my father to-day. He tells me we shall have war before the end of the month . . . What a hero my father is! . . . He's worthy of the Iliad! Just look at this little box I always take around with me. It's got some Lorraine soil in it, real Lorraine soil I picked up over the frontier when I was in France with my husband two years ago. Look there, at the table of honour: it's covered with thistles. I didn't want to have any other flowers there . . . Militzia go on talking to the ambassador. Tell him all to-day means to us while I go and receive the Czar. . . .'

"At dinner I was on the left of the Grand Duchess Anastasia and the rhapsody continued, interspersed with prophecies: 'There's going to be a war . . . There'll be nothing left of Austria . . . You're going to get back Alsace and Lorraine . . . Our armies will meet in Berlin. Germany will be destroyed . . .' Then suddenly: 'I must restrain myself. The Emperor has his eye on me.' Under the Czar's stern gaze the Montenegrin sybil suddenly lapsed into silence."[35]

President Poincaré departed from Russian soil on the 23rd and that night Austria sent Serbia a formidable ultimatum demanding the dismemberment of all anti-Austrian societies, a cessation of hostile propaganda and the right of Austrian officials to take part in the search for members of the conspiracy which had provoked the assassination. From that moment onwards the Russian High Command began to prepare for war. General Yanoushkevitch, the Chief of Staff, received a visit from Sazonov who proposed a partial mobilisation directed against Austria—the same plan which War Minister Soukhomlinov tried to initiate during the Balkan Wars in 1913. Yanoushkevitch sent for General Dobrorolski, Chief of the Mobilisation Section, and asked: "Have you everything ready for the proclamation of the mobilisation of our army?" Dobrorolski replied in the affirmative and the Chief of Staff continued: "In an hour bring to me all the documents relative to preparing our troops for war, which provide, in case of necessity, for proclaiming partial mobilisation against Austria-Hungary alone. This mobilisation must give no occasion to Germany to find any grounds of hostility to herself."[36]

Dobrorolski was just as dumbfounded as Prime Minister Kokovtsov when he had heard the proposal in 1913. A partial mobilisation was technically impossible. Indeed, no such plan had ever been drawn up as it had always been assumed that, if Russia struck at Austria, Germany was bound to honour her alliance and enter the conflict. Furthermore, to strike at Austria effectively from the East and North, it was necessary for troops to advance through the Warsaw District. "Yet in order not to alarm Germany the Warsaw District was to remain untouched! And if no preparations were made in the Warsaw District, the part of it which bordered on Austria would remain uncovered and unprotected. Moreover, if a general mobilisation should follow the partial mobilisation, the utmost confusion would take place, because the reservists for the Warsaw District were drawn partly from the Moscow and Kazan

Districts, where partial mobilisation would already have taken place." As General Yanoushkevitch had been appointed Chief of Staff on grounds of amenability rather than efficiency perhaps it is not surprising that he should have been unaware of the total impracticability of partial mobilisation. Nevertheless he stood his ground, and refused to take no for an answer. He "ordered me anew," wrote Dobrorolski, "to make a detailed report to him after an hour in accordance with his decision . . ."[36]

Meanwhile the Czar and many members of St. Petersburg society were still at Krasnoe Selo watching the summer review of Russian troops. By this time the atmosphere was electric. On the night of the 24th a banquet and a theatrical performance was held at which the Grand Duke Nicholas made inflammatory speeches, provoking a great demonstration for war. The St. Petersburg military cadets were promoted to the positions of regular officers in the army, instead of later in the year as was customary. Many of them openly expressed their joy at "starting something against Austria." Even St. Petersburg had caught the fever, for the streets resounded to the clatter of horses' hooves as the Imperial Guard returned, a month early, to their barracks. "At seven o'clock," wrote Paléologue, "I go to the Warsaw Railway Station [in St. Petersburg] to say good-bye to Isvolsky who is returning to his post in haste. On the platform there is lively animation: the trains are crowded with officers and soldiers. This already looks like mobilisation. We exchange rapidly our impressions, and come to the same conclusion: *Cette fois, c'est la guerre.*"[37]

By this time the militarists had the bit between their teeth. The High Command agreed with Dobrorolski that partial mobilisation was out of the question and were determined to get the order changed to a general mobilisation—even though general mobilisation meant war. "The whole plan of mobilisation is worked out ahead to its end in all its details," wrote Dobrorolski. "When the moment has been chosen, one only has to press the button and the whole state begins to function automatically with the precision of a clock's mechanism . . . Once the moment has been fixed everything is settled; there is no going back; it determined mechanically the beginning of war."[38]

The High Command believed that war was inevitable; some welcomed it because of "the glittering prizes of the Balkans," others because strikes had broken out in all the large cities of Russia and they argued that war was the only way to purge the country of "unpatriotic elements." But on 25th July when the Czar held a Ministerial Council he refused to give the order for a general mobilisation. The most he would do was to allow the military to make secret preparations under a regulation known as *The Period Preparatory to War.* "The following days," wrote Dobrorolski, "are well-known to everybody through the 'coloured books' and documents published by the European Governments. The war was already a settled matter . . ."[39]

Thus, for the next three days, Russia presented the not unusual spectacle of the right hand doing one thing, the left hand another. While Sazonov continued negotiations the High Command was cancelling leave, moving troops, shoeing horses, rounding up spies, organising supplies and a hundred other things. On the 28th Vienna, dissatisfied with Belgrade's reply to the Austrian ultimatum, declared war on Serbia. As Austrian mobilisation required two weeks no troops crossed the frontier but on the 29th Belgrade was bombarded from Austrian territory. This infuriated Sazonov to such an extent that he broke off negotiations and informed the Russian High Command that he would urge the Czar to declare General Mobilisation. Meanwhile reports of Russian troop movements were pouring into Berlin. Late on the night of the 28th the Kaiser was so alarmed that he sent a telegram to the Czar. "It is with the gravest concern," wired William II, "that I hear of the impression which the action of Austria against Serbia is creating in your country. The unscrupulous agitation that has been going on in Serbia for years has resulted in the outrageous crime to which Archduke Franz Ferdinand fell a victim. The spirit that led Serbians to murder their own king and his wife still dominates the country. You will doubtless agree with me that we both, you and I, have a common interest, as well as all Sovereigns, to insist that all the persons morally responsible for the dastardly murder should receive their deserved punishment. In this politics play no part at all.

"On the other hand I fully understand how difficult it is for you and your Government to face the drift of your public opinion. Therefore, with regard to the hearty and tender friendship which binds us both from long ago with firm ties, I am exerting my utmost influence to induce the Austrians to deal straightly to arrive at a satisfactory understanding with you. I confidently hope you will help me in my efforts to smooth over difficulties that may still arise. Your very sincere and devoted friend and cousin. Willy."[40]

Strangely enough the Kaiser's telegram, dispatched around midnight, was crossed by an urgent appeal from the Czar—two cries for help passing each other in the darkness.

"The Czar to the Emperor, Peterhof Palace, July 29th, 1914
His Majesty the Emperor, New Palace
Am glad you are back. In this most serious moment I appeal to you to help me. An *ignoble* war has been declared on a *weak* country. The *indignation* in Russia, *shared fully by* me, is *enormous*. I foresee that very soon I shall be *overwhelmed* by the *pressure* brought upon me, and be forced to take extreme measures which *will lead to war*. To try and avoid such a calamity as a European war, I beg you in the name of our old friendship to do what you can to *stop* your allies from *going too far*. Nicky."[41]

The Czar's telegram was dispatched at two in the morning. The "pressure" to which he referred was the feverish insistence of the military that General Mobilisation must be declared without further delay. Nicholas II knew that he could not withstand the combined strength of his Foreign Secretary and War Minister. The dreaded request was put to him on the 29th, nine hours after his telegram to the Kaiser, and he reluctantly assented to it. But the mobilisation order required the signatures of three specified ministers, and one of them could not be found. The missing minister did not return to the capital until that evening.

When Dobrorolski finally secured the necessary signature he hurried to the Central Telegraph Office to dispatch the order through the Empire. But there was another drama in store for him. "The

Chief Director of the Post and Telegraph had been notified before-hand that a message of extraordinary importance was to be sent out," he wrote. "After I had entered the cabinet of the St. Petersburg Telegraph office, I handed him the telegram, and waited to be present personally at the transmission of the telegram to the four corners of the Russian Empire. In my presence they proceeded to click off the telegram on several typewriters in order to send it at the same moment by all the wires which connected St. Petersburg with the principal centres of the Empire, from which the dispatch would be transmitted to all the towns in the governments and territorial districts. There existed a special instruction for the sending of the mobilisation telegram. During its transmission no other telegrams of any sort could be sent.

"The imposing room of the St. Petersburg Central Telegraph Office with its telegraph keys, to the number of some dozen, was ready to receive the mobilisation telegram.

"But at this moment—about 9.30 p.m.—General Yanoush-kevitch called me on the telephone and ordered me to hold back the telegram until the arrival of a Captain in the General Staff, Tugan-Baranovski. He entered and told me that he had hurried after me through the city to bring me a special order from the Czar not to send out the telegram for general mobilisation. General mobilisation was to be suspended, and in its place, by order of the Czar, partial mobilisation was to be adopted in accordance with the plan previously arranged.

"I at once took back the telegram for general mobilisation which I had delivered to the telegraph office and all the copies of the telegram. I notified the head of the telegraph office of the with-drawal which had taken place, and rode away."[42]

While Dobrorolski was on his way to the Post Office, at 9.40 p.m. on the 29th the Czar received another telegram from the Kaiser. "It would be quite possible for Russia to remain a spectator of the Austro-Serbian conflict without involving Europe in the most horrible war she ever witnessed. I think a direct understanding between your Government and Vienna possible and desirable, and as I already telegraphed you, my Government is continuing its exertions to promote it. Of course, military measures on the part of Russia which would be looked upon by Austria as threatening would precipitate a calamity we both wish to avoid, and jeopardise my position as mediator which I readily accepted on your appeal to my friendship and my help."[43]

The Czar was ready to clutch at any straw. He called War Minister Soukhomlinov and Chief of Staff Yanoushkevitch on the telephone and held a three-cornered conversation in which the two military men tried to convince him that he was making a terrible mistake. They used every argument they could conjure up, including the untrue statement that Germany had begun to mobilise and that if Russia did not hurry she would face a severe disadvantage. For once the Czar remained firm and Yanoushkevitch was forced to instruct Dobrorolski to hold the order for general mobilisation and to issue instead the order for partial mobilisation which was bound to result in crippling confusion.

A few hours later, at one-thirty in the morning of 30th July, before the Kaiser had gone to bed, he received a letter from the Czar (written several days earlier) announcing partial mobilisation against Austria. "The military measures which have come into force," wrote Nicholas, "were decided five days ago for reasons of defence on account of Austria's preparations. I hope with all my heart that these measures won't in any way interfere with your part as mediator which I greatly value. We need your strong pressure on Austria to come to an understanding with us. Nicky."

William II did not know, of course, how close Russia had come to general mobilisation; how the Czar had intervened just as the order was about to be sent over the wires and stopped it. Instead of being grateful to Nicholas he flew into one of his rages. "And these measures are for *defence* against *Austria*, which is in *no way* attacking him!!! I cannot agree to any more mediation, since the Czar who requested it has at the same time secretly mobilised behind my back. It is only a manœuvre in order to hold us back and to increase the start they have already got. My work is at an end."[44]

Meanwhile the Russian generals were working themselves into a state of despair. General Yanoushkevitch telephoned to the Czar on the morning of the 30th and begged him to return to the general mobilisation order. But the Czar was adamant and threatened to break off the conversation; General Yanoushkevitch prevented this by saying "that M. Sazonov was beside him and had something to ask. Sazonov then requested an immediate audience but the Czar replied that he was 'too busy.' After a pause he added: 'Is it all the same to you if I receive you at the same time with Tatischev at 3 o'clock, because otherwise I have not a minute of free time to-day?' Sazonov thanked the Czar and said that he would arrive at the time suggested.

"The generals begged Sazonov to use every argument he could conjure up, both political and military. If he was successful, he was to telephone General Yanoushkevitch from the Palace, so that he immediately could convert the partial mobilisation into general mobilisation. 'After this,' added the Chief of Staff, 'I will retire from sight, smash the telephone, and generally take all measures so that I cannot be found to give any contrary orders for a new postponement of general mobilisation.'

"Sazonov found the Czar pale and nervous, fully conscious of the awful responsibility resting upon him, for it was understood by all military men that mobilisation meant war. Furthermore, it was bound to provoke similar measures in Germany and once the machine began to move nothing would be able to stop it. 'Think of the responsibility which you are advising me to take!' said the Czar. 'Think of the thousands and thousands of men who will be sent to their deaths.' Sazonov argued that he would have nothing with which to reproach his conscience as war clearly had become inevitable. Diplomacy had finished its work. It was time for His Majesty to think of the safety of his Empire. The refusal to order general mobilisation would only dislocate the whole Russian military organisation and disconcert Russia's allies. 'It only remains to do everything necessary to meet war fully armed and under the conditions most favourable to us. Therefore it is better without fear to call forth a war by our preparations for it, and to continue these preparations carefully, rather than out of fear to give an inducement for war and be taken unawares.'

"The Czar sat silently staring into space, and could not bring himself to speak the decisive word. After an hour General Tatischev said: 'Yes, it is hard to decide.' In a burst of irritability the Czar said: 'I will decide,' and immediately gave the order for general mobilisation. Sazonov hurried to the telephone, notified General Yanoushkevitch and said: 'Now you can smash the telephone. Give your orders, General, and then—disappear for the rest of the day'."[45]

The Russian diplomat, Baron Rosen, was in St. Petersburg at the time and was horrified at what was happening. He was in close touch with ministers and generals and all day rumours swept the capital of mobilisation orders, cancellations, new orders. He described general mobilisation as an "unmitigated folly and arrant imbecility." "If it was meant to be a deliberate provocation," he wrote in his memoirs, "it was an appalling crime, the responsibility for which these three men, Sazonov, Soukhomlinov and Yanoushkevitch, must share with the equally guilty advisers of the German Emperor, who caused the Russian mobilisation to be answered by an ultimatum and a declaration of war. I prefer to think that it was due to their recklessness, incompetence and groundless belief in the possibility of a prompt and glorious victory, rather than to any thought-out intention. But it was an act that sealed the doom of an Empire—their own Fatherland—and the crushing consciousness of having advised it must be to the two of them, who are still alive, a punishment more cruel than any which human justice could devise."[46]

Russian mobilisation was so far advanced when war broke out that the first army to invade the soil of another was not the German divisions that forced their way through neutral Luxembourg and Belgium but the Russian divisions swarming into East Prussia on 1st August. The Kaiser had not wanted war but his blunders over the past fifteen years had convinced Europe that he thirsted for conquest. The English had not wanted war but they feared German sea-power and had not grasped the true nature of the quarrel. The war was the result of Russian and Austrian rivalry in the Balkans; yet England and Germany blamed each other bitterly. "England," wrote Professor Harnack of Berlin University, one of Germany's leading academicians, "cut the dyke which has preserved Western Europe and its civilisation from the encroaching desert of Russian and Paslavism. We must hold out, for we defend the work of fifteen hundred years for all Europe and for Great Britain herself . . ."

The Professor was not right but he was not wholly wrong. The dyke, as things turned out, was cut twenty years later by Hitler. But "the encroaching desert," even more withering with the passage of time, remains the same.

XI
The Red Czars

"Europe," they say at Petersburg, ". . . is enervating herself by a vain liberalism, while we continue powerful precisely because we are not free; let us be patient under the yoke; others shall some day pay for our shame."

La Russie en 1839, Marquis de Custine.

THE RUSSIA envisaged a hundred years ago by Danilevsky, the author of the Panslav Bible, included in its European possessions Poland, Finland, the Baltic States; Romania, Bulgaria, Hungary, what is now Czechoslovakia and Jugoslavia, and Greece.

In 1917 when the Bolsheviks seized power many people believed that Russian Imperialism had come to an end. Marxism, on paper at least, appeared to be the very negation of conquest by force. For twenty-six years Russia remained quiescent. But when war broke out between Nazi Germany and the Western Powers Stalin seized the opportunity to reconstruct the dream of the Czars. In 1939 he attacked Poland, in 1940 he invaded Finland. He devoured the Baltic States in 1942. At Yalta in 1944 he managed to wring from Roosevelt and Churchill a pledge that Russia would have "a preponderance of power" in Romania, Bulgaria, Hungary, Czechoslovakia and Jugoslavia.

He promised, of course, that all these countries would have the right of free elections. But Soviet Russia had inherited from the Czars a formidable apparatus of revolutionary and subversive techniques. Nothing had to be invented. Nechaev had written the code, and it was all there in its vile array from the cell system to the *agent provocateur*, from forced demonstrations to rigged elections; from torture and blackmail to betrayal and death. And over the whole, just as in the days of the Panslav movement, was flung the cloak of the Crusader, posing as the symbol of a sacred cause to which everything had to be sacrificed, particularly hope and honour.

One by one the Balkan countries were given the hug of the bear, a Communist bear to be sure, but still very Russian in the strength of its embrace. Jugoslavia managed to free itself partially after the war; but the only country named by Danilevsky to escape wholly was Greece. This ancient state came within a hair's breadth of the Communist domination that would have condemned it to Russia but was saved by Winston Churchill who sent British troops to support the legal government against Soviet-backed terrorists.

"I am resolved," a French diplomat told his Russian colleague, "to put forth every effort to fight against your influence and to thrust you back into Asia from whence you came. You are not a European Power, you should not be one . . . Let the ties attaching you to Europe be loosened, and of your own accord you will flow toward the East and become once more an Asiatic Power . . ."[47] This was said in 1854. A century later, almost to the same year, science had placed terrible weapons in Russia's hands and her presence in Europe was assured.

The last two decades have watched her forward march, into the Mediterranean, into the Middle Eastern territories that once belonged to Turkey, and along the shores of North Africa. They have also seen the savagery with which she has smashed the resistance of famous nations—or fragments of nations—whom she insults by referring to as her allies: Poland, East Germany, Hungary, and finally the civilised people of Czechoslovakia who asked for nothing more than the barest of freedoms and the right to treat each other with humanity.

The great slave country is expiating its sins by forcing its neighbours to share its shame—just as the Marquis de Custine prophesied in 1839. Are there any other lessons to be learned from history? Should we keep in mind the lines written by the poet Tyutchev in 1844?

Seven inland seas and seven mighty rivers
From the Nile to the Neva
From the Elbe to China
From the Volga to the Euphrates
From the Ganges to the Danube
Such is our Empire to be.

BIBLIOGRAPHICAL REFERENCES
AND ACKNOWLEDGMENTS

Bibliographical References

The full title of book and name of author is repeated in each chapter where subsequent references occur. The name of publisher and date of publication are given only once, however, the first time a work is mentioned.

CHAPTER I PHILOSOPHERS AT COURT, *pp.* 13-40

1. *Complete Works*, Vol. I, p. 389: V. A. Zhukovsky. Moscow. 1902.
2. Ficquelmont to Metternich, 26th April and 3rd July, 1839. Vienna State Archives.
3. *Victoria R.I.* p. 166: Elizabeth Longford. Weidenfeld and Nicolson. London. 1964.
4. *Russia*, p. 3: Marquis de Custine. Longmans Brown, Green and Longmans. London. 1854.
5. *The Downfall of Three Dynasties*, p. 12: Count Egon Corti. Methuen & Co. Ltd. London. 1934.
6. *Tsar Nicholas I*, p. 147: Constantin de Grunewald. Douglas Saunders with MacGibbon & Kee. London. 1954.
7. *The Letters of Queen Victoria*, First Series, Vol. II, p. 14. John Murray. London. 1911.
8. *Pensées et Réflexions morales et politiques*, Count de Ficquelmont. Paris. 1859.
9. De Grunewald, Nicholas I, op. cit. p. 155.
10. Ibid. p. 136. Quoted from Archives Winter Palace, 26th May, 1841.
11. Marquis de Custine, Russia, op. cit. p. 167.
12. *La Russie en 1839*, Vol. IV, pp. 66/7: Marquis de Custine. Paris. 1843.
13. *The Emperor Alexander II*, p. 63: E. M. Almedingen. The Bodley Head. London. 1962.
14. *Count Kisselev and His Times*, Vol. III, p. 306 et seq.: Zablotzky-Dessiatovsky. St. Petersburg. 1882.
15. *Readings in Russian Civilisation*, p. 317 (from the diary of P. A. Karatygin): edited by Thomas Riha. University of Chicago Press. 1964.
16. De Grunewald, Nicholas I, op. cit. p. 169.
17. Ibid. p. 170.

18. *The Mind of Modern Russia*, p. 142: Hans Kohn. Harper & Row. New York.
19. *My Past and Thoughts*, Vol. II, pp. 274/5: Alexander Herzen. Translated by Constance Garnett. Chatto & Windus. London 1924-7.
20. *New Republic*. New York. 26th June, 1950. Translated by George Kennan.
21. *Three Russian Prophets*, p. 69: Nicholas Zernov. S.C.M. Press. London. 1944.
22. Herzen, Past and Thoughts, op. cit. Vol. II, pp. 257 and 254.
23. Zhukovsky, Works, op. cit. Vol. I, p. 335.
24. *The Emergence of Russian Panslavism, 1856-60.* pp. 24/6: Michael Petrovich. Columbia University Press. New York. 1956.
25. Corti, Downfall, op. cit. p. 14.
26. The Letters of Queen Victoria, First Series, Vol. II, p. 562. (14th Nov., 1853).
27. Corti, Downfall, op. cit. pp. 75/6.
28. Petrovich, Panslavism, op. cit. p. 29.
29. Corti, Downfall, op. cit. pp. 77/8.
30. De Grunewald, Nicholas I, op. cit. pp. 274/5 and 268.
31. *Ein deutscher Artz am Hofe Kaiser Nicholas I von Russland*, p. 37 et seq.: Martin Mandt. München & Leipzig. 1917.

CHAPTER II THE NEW REIGN, *pp.* 41-73

1. *The Emperor Alexander II*, p. 123: E. M. Almedingen. Quoted from a letter written by Vera Liarsky, August 1856.
2. *The Letters of Queen Victoria*, First Series, Vol. III, p. 259.
3. Ibid. p. 260.
4. *The Downfall of Three Dynasties*, p. 103: Count Egon Corti.
5. *Selected Works*, pp. 132/3. M. E. Saltykov. Moscow. 1946.
6. Almedingen, Alexander II, op. cit. p. 166. Quoted from I. D. Sytin's *Alexander II.*
7. *Macmillan's Magazine*. Vol. 37. H. Sutherland Edwards.
8. *The Romanoffs*, p. 247: H. Sutherland Edwards. W. H. Allen. London. 1890.
9. *L'Instruction Publique en Russie*, p. 325/6: C. Hippeau. Didier. Paris. 1878.
10. *The Emperor Alexander II*, Vol. I, p. 401: S. S. Tatichev. St. Petersburg. 1903.
11. *Turgenev's Literary Reminiscences*, Vol. I, p. 107. Faber & Faber. London. Translated by David Margaschack.
12. Corti, Downfall, op. cit. p. 138.
13. Ibid. p. 370.
14. *Dearest Child*, pp. 132 and 133: Roger Fulford. Evans Brothers, Ltd. London. 1964.
15. Ibid. pp. 323 and 339.
16. *Modern Russian History*, Vol. II, pp. 112/13: Alexander Kornilov. Skeffington & Son, Ltd. London. 1916.
17. *Complete Works*, Tendentious Ballad: Count Alexis Tolstoy. Berlin. 1923.
18. *The Fortress*, pp. 173/5: Robert Payne. W. H. Allen. London. 1967.

19. *The Emergence of Russian Panslavism*, p. 118: Michael Petrovich.
20. Ibid. p. 212. Quoted from the Archives, Ministry of Foreign Affairs, Prague.
21. Ibid. pp. 237/8.
22. Corti, Downfall, op. cit. pp. 207/8.
23. *The Tragic Romance of Alexander II*, pp. 38/9: Maurice Paléologue. Hutchinson & Co. London. 1926.
24. Théophile Gautier quoted by Paléologue, p. 47.
25. Almedingen, Alexander II, op. cit. p. 258.
26. *Diplomatic Reminiscences*, Vol. II, p. 210: Lord Augustus Loftus. Cassell & Co., Ltd. London. 1894.
27. Ibid. p. 47.
28. Corti, Downfall, op. cit. p. 213.
29. *Victoria, R.I.*, p. 394: Elizabeth Longford.
30. *Letters of Queen Victoria*, Second Series, Vol. II, pp. 228/9.
31. Corti, Downfall, op. cit. p. 216.
32. Letters of Queen Victoria, op. cit. p. 337.
33. *The Russian Revolution*, p. 43: Alan Moorehead. Collins with Hamish Hamilton. London. 1958.

CHAPTER III FISHING IN TROUBLED WATERS, *pp.* 74-100

1. *The Vanished Pomps of Yesterday*, p. 88: Lord Frederick Hamilton. Hodder & Stoughton. London. 1920.
2. *Recollections of a Diplomatist*, Vol. II, p. 254: Sir Horace Rumbold. Edward Arnold. London. 1902.
3. *The Diary of a Writer*, p. 628: Feodor Dostoevsky. Charles Scribner's Sons. New York. 1949.
4. *The Emergence of Russian Panslavism*, pp. 268 and 257: Michael Petrovich.
5. Ibid. p. 257.
6. Ibid. p. 274.
7. Monson to Foreign Office. F.O. 7/882.
8. Monson to Foreign Office. 22nd August. F.O. 7/883.
9. Monson to Foreign Office. F.O. 7/882.
10. Letters of Queen Victoria, Second Series, Vol. II, pp. 485/6.
11. *The Downfall of Three Dynasties*, p. 222: Count Egon Corti.
12. Letters of Queen Victoria, op. cit. p. 466.
13. Ibid. p. 491.
14. *Slavonic Review*, Vol. X. *Memories of Count Ignatiev*, p. 387.
15. *Life of Robert, Marquis of Salisbury*, Vol. II, p. 110: Lady Gwendolyn Cecil. Hodder & Stoughton. London. 1921.
16. *Slavonic Review*, Vol. 10, op. cit. p. 391.
17. Ibid. p. 391.
18. *Pages from the Autobiography of a Bulgarian Insurgent*, p. 58: Zachary Stoyanoff. Edward Arnold. London. 1913.

19. *Russia and the Balkans, 1870-80*, p. 188: B. H. Sumner. Anchor Books. London. 1962.
20. *The Emperor Alexander II*, pp. 280/1: E. M. Almedingen.
21. Dostoevsky, Diary, op. cit. pp. 364 and 366.
22. *Anna Karenina*, (translated by Constance Garnett) pp. 884/5: Leo Tolstoy. Heinemann. London. 1901.
23. Report No. 243: F.O. 7/851.
24. *Two Months with Tchernayeff in Serbia*, pp. 230/4: Philip Salusbury. Chapman & Hall. London. 1877.
25. Sumner, Russia and Balkans, op. cit. p. 227.
26. *Russky Arkhiv* 1897, Vol. II, pp. 257/61.
27. *Diplomatic Reminiscences*, Second Series, Vol. II, p. 190: Lord Augustus Loftus.
28. Almedingen, Alexander II, op. cit. p. 283.
29. Account & Papers, Parliamentary Proceedings, 1877 XC 1640 No. 930.
30. *The Life of Benjamin Disraeli*, p. 62: Monypenny & Buckle. John Murray. London. 1920.
31. *Letters of Queen Victoria*, Second Series, Vol. II, p. 480.
32. Ibid. p. 488.
33. Monypenny & Buckle, Disraeli, op. cit. pp. 72/3.
34. Ibid. p. 112.
35. Ibid. p. 128.
36. *Disraeli*, p. 619: Robert Blake. Eyre & Spottiswoode. London. 1966.
37. Monypenny & Buckle, Disraeli, op. cit. Vol. VI. p. 130.

CHAPTER IV BITTER VICTORY, *pp.* 101-123

1. *The Life of Benjamin Disraeli*, Vol. VI. p. 132: Monypenny & Buckle.
2. Ibid. p. 133.
3. *The Siege of Plevna*, p. 70: Rupert Furneaux. Anthony Blond. London. 1958.
4. Ibid. p. 60.
5. *With Russia in Peace and War*, p. 195: Col. the Hon. F. A. Wellesley. J. E. Nash. London. 1905.
6. Furneaux, Plevna, op. cit. p. 80.
7. *The Tragic Romance of Alexander II*, p. 102: Maurice Paléologue.
8. *The Downfall of Three Dynasties*, pp. 231/2: Count Egon Corti.
9. Furneaux, Plevna, op. cit. pp. 138/9.
10. Wellesley, With Russia, op. cit. pp. 216/18.
11. Corti, Downfall, op. cit. p. 235.
12. Wellesley, With Russia, op. cit. pp. 277/8.
13. Furneaux, Plevna, op. cit. p. 216.
14. *Disraeli*, p. 637: Robert Blake.
15. *Kronberg Letters* 4th Jan., 1878.
16. *Slavonic Review*, Vol. XI. pp. 110 and 119. Memoirs of Count Ignatiev: Alexander Onou.

17. Corti, Downfall, op. cit. p. 241.
18. Ibid. pp. 242/4.
19. Monypenny & Buckle, Disraeli, op. cit. Vol. VI, pp. 317/18.
20. Ibid. p. 325.
21. *Modern Russian History*, Vol. II, p. 234: Alexander Kornilov.
22. *The Emperor Alexander II*, p. 308: E. M. Almedingen.

CHAPTER V THE KILLERS, *pp.* 124-149

1. *Tolstoy*, p. 385: Henri Troyat. Doubleday & Co. Inc. New York. 1967.
2. *The Court of Russia in the 19th Century*, p. 259: E. A. Brayley Hodgetts. Methuen & Co. London. 1908.
3. *Once a Grand Duke*, pp. 48/9: Grand Duke Alexander Mikhailovich. Cassell & Co. London. 1932.
4. *The Downfall of Three Dynasties*, p. 255: Count Egon Corti.
5. *Underground Russia*, p. 4: Stepniak. Smith Elder & Co. London. 1883.
6. *Vanished Pomps of Yesterday*, pp. 107/8: Lord Frederick Hamilton.
7. Almedingen, Alexander II, op. cit. p. 327.
8. *The Tragic Romance of Alexander II*, pp. 144/5: Maurice Paléologue.
9. Corti, Downfall, op. cit. p. 268.
10. Ibid. p. 272.
11. Grand Duke Alexander Mikhailovich, Once a Grand Duke, op. cit. pp. 61/2.
12. Ibid. p. 63.
13. Corti, Downfall, op. cit. pp. 271/2.
14. Almedingen, Alexander II, op. cit. p. 338.
15. Grand Duke Alexander Mikhailovich, Once a Grand Duke, op. cit. p. 70.
16. Stepniak, Underground, op. cit. pp. 229/30.
17. Grand Duke Alexander Mikhailovich, Once a Grand Duke, op. cit. p. 72.
18. Stepniak, Underground, op. cit. p. 232.
19. Paléologue, Tragic Romance, op. cit. p. 213.
20. Ibid. pp. 28/9.
21. Stepniak, Underground, op. cit. p. 234.
22. Ibid. pp. 237/8.
23. Troyat, Tolstoy, op. cit. p. 403.
24. Ibid. p. 406.

CHAPTER VI A COUSIN'S VENDETTA, *pp.* 150-188

1. *The Downfall of Three Dynasties*, p. 251: Count Egon Corti.
2. *Letters of Queen Victoria*, Second Series, Vol. III. Jan. 1879.
3. Corti, Downfall, op. cit. p. 259.
4. *Bulgaria Since the War*, p. 40; James G. Minchin. Kegan, Paul & Co. London. 1880.
5. Corti, Downfall, op. cit. p. 258.

6. Ibid. p. 259.
7. *Tsarist Russia and Balkan Nationalism*, p. 60: Charles Jelavich. University of California Press. 1958.
8. Ibid. p. 58.
9. *Alexander III*, pp. 253/4: Charles Lowe. William Heinemann. London. 1895.
10. *The Last Grand Duchess*, pp. 27/8: Ian Vorres. Hutchinson. London. 1964.
11. Jelavich, Russia and Nationalism, op. cit. pp. 84/5.
12. Corti, Downfall, op. cit. p. 284.
13. Wyndham to Granville, F.O. 78/3393.
14. Jelavich, Russia and Nationalism, op. cit. p. 118.
15. Ibid. p. 121.
16. Corti, Downfall, op. cit. p. 288.
17. *Alexander von Battenberg*, pp. 90/1: Count Egon Corti. Cassell & Co., Ltd. London. 1954.
18. Corti, Downfall, op. cit. p. 291.
19. *Stambuloff*, pp. 51/2: A. Hulme Beaman. Bliss, Sands & Foster. London. 1895.
20. *The Court of Russia in the 19th Century*, Vol. II, p. 252: E. H. Brayley Hodgetts.
21. *Vanished Pomps of Yesterday*, p. 107: Lord Frederick Hamilton.
22. Jelavich, Russia and Nationalism, op. cit. p. 137.
23. Corti, Battenberg, op. cit. pp. 119/21.
24. Ibid. p. 123.
25. Corti, Downfall, op. cit. p. 301.
26. Morier to Salisbury, F.O. 65/1219 No. 384 C, 11th Nov., 1885.
27. *Letters of Queen Victoria*, Second Series, Vol. III. op. cit. p. 699.
28. Corti, Battenberg, op. cit. pp. 176/7.
29. Corti, Downfall, op. cit. p. 312.
30. Ibid. p. 381.
31. Beaman, Stambuloff, op. cit. p. 79.
32. Jelavich, Russia and Nationalism, op. cit. p. 249/50.
33. Corti, Battenberg, op. cit. p. 226.
34. Ibid. p. 228.
35. *Letters of Queen Victoria*, Third Series, Vol. I, p. 187.
36. Corti, Battenberg, op. cit. p. 231.
37. *Letters of Queen Victoria*, op. cit. pp. 187/8.
38. Corti, Battenberg, op. cit. pp. 239/40.
39. *Grosse Politik*, Vol. V, p. 68.
40. Corti, Downfall, op. cit. p. 378.

CHAPTER VII POACHER TURNED GAMEKEEPER, *pp.* 189-216

1. *The Linings of Life*, Vol II, p. 432: Lady Paget. Hurst & Blackett. London. 1928.
2. *Queen Victoria's Relations*, p. 140: Meriel Buchanan. Cassell & Co., Ltd. London. 1954.
3. *The Letters of Queen Victoria*, Third Series, Vol. I, pp. 229, 337, 345.

4. *Recollections of a Bulgarian Diplomat's Wife*, p. 28: Anna Stancioff. Hutchinson & Co. London. 1933.
5. *Old Diplomacy*, pp. 37/9: Lord Hardinge of Penshurst. John Murray. London. 1947.
6. Stancioff, A Diplomat's Wife, op. cit. p. 36.
7. *Stambuloff*, pp. 164/5: A. Hulme Beaman.
8. *Heyday in a Vanished World*, pp. 180/1: Stephan Bonsal. Allen & Unwin, Ltd. London. 1938.
9. *Ferdinand of Bulgaria*, p. 55: Hans Roger Madol. Translated by Kenneth Kirkness. Hurst & Blackett. London. 1931.
10. *Forty Years of Diplomacy*, p. 108: Baron Rosen. Allen & Unwin, Ltd. London. 1938.
11. *The Empress Frederick Writes to Sophie*, p. 161: Edited by Arthur Gould Lee. Faber & Faber. London. 1955.
12. *A Royal Tragedy*, p. 64: Chedomille Mijatovich. Eveleigh Nash. London. 1906.
13. Bonsal, Heyday, op. cit. pp. 186/7.
14. Buchanan, Victoria's Relations, op. cit. p. 148.
15. Hardinge, Old Diplomacy, op. cit. p. 36.
16. Madol, Ferdinand, op. cit. p. 108.
17. *Letters of Queen Victoria*, Third Series, Vol. II. p. 124.
18. Beaman, Stambuloff, op. cit. p. 185.
19. Lee, Empress Writes to Sophie, op. cit. p. 163.
20. Beaman, Stambuloff, op. cit. pp. 203/4.
21. *The Times*, London, 28th August, 1894.
22. Beaman, Stambuloff, op. cit. pp. 210/11.
23. Ibid. p. 239.
24. *Letters of Queen Victoria*, Third Series, Vol. II. op. cit. pp. 538/41.
25. *Lord Carnock*, pp. 106/7: Harold Nicolson. Constable & Co., Ltd. London. 1930.
26. Madol, Ferdinand, op. cit. p. 94.

CHAPTER VIII UNEASY LIES THE HEAD, *pp.* 217-249

1. *The Last Grand Duchess*, p. 67: Ian Vorres.
2. *King Edward VII*, p. 248: Sir Philip Magnus. John Murray. London. 1964.
3. *Krasnyi Archiv*, Vol. II, p. 31.
4. *The Origins of the First World War*, p. 365: Sidney Fay: The Macmillan Company. New York. 1959.
5. *A Royal Tragedy*, p. 56: Chedomille Mijatovich.
6. Green to Paunceforte, F.O. 103/22. 19th April, 1883.
7. *Memoirs of a Balkan Diplomatist*, p. 130: Chedomille Mijatovich. Cassell & Co., Ltd. London. 1917.
8. *A King's Romance*, p. 145: Frances Gerard. Hutchinson & Co. London. 1903.
9. *Alexander von Battenberg*, pp. 206, 208/9. Count Egon Corti.
10. Gerard, King's Romance, op. cit. p. 147.

11. Ibid. pp. 177/8.
12. Mijatovich, Royal Tragedy, op. cit. p. 52.
13. Ibid. p. 96.
14. *Forty Years of Diplomacy*, pp. 107/10: Baron Rosen.
15. Mijatovich, Royal Tragedy, op. cit. p. 107.
16. *Das Ende der Obrenovitch*, p. 215: Dr. Vladau Georgevitch. Leipzig. 1905.
17. *Serbia Between East and West*, pp. 8/9: Wayne Vucinich. Stanford University Press. California. 1954.
18. Mijatovich, Royal Tragedy, op. cit. pp. 136/40.
19. Vucinich, Serbia, op. cit. p. 8.
20. Ibid. p. 51.
21. Mijatovich, Royal Tragedy, op. cit. p. 179.
22. Ibid. pp. 181/2.
23. Ibid. p. 201.
24. *Glimpses of High Politics*, p. 235: N. V. Tcharykov. Allen & Unwin, Ltd. London. 1931.
25. Mijatovich, Royal Tragedy, op. cit. p. 204.
26. Ibid. pp. 204/5.
27. Tcharykov, High Politics, op. cit. p. 236.

CHAPTER IX PROTECTRESS OF ALL THE SLAVS, *pp.* 250-280

1. *The Eclipse of Russia*, p. 133: Dr. E. J. Dillon. J. M. Dent & Sons, Ltd. London. 1918.
2. *Aseff, The Russian Judas*, pp. 90/1: Boris Nicolaievsky. Hurst & Blackett, Ltd. London. 1934.
3. *The Letters and Friendships of Sir Cecil Spring Rice*, p. 425: Constable & Co. London. 1929.
4. Nicolaievsky, Aseff, op. cit. p. 140.
5. Dillon, Eclipse, op. cit. p. 133.
6. *Lord Carnock*, p. 216: Harold Nicolson.
7. *The Origins of the First World War*, Vol. I, pp. 371/2: Sidney Fay.
8. *Grosse Politik XXII* 83 f.
9. *King Edward VII*, p. 417: Sir Philip Magnus.
10. Ibid. p. 420.
11. *The Letters of Czar Nicholas and Empress Marie*, p. 236: Edited by Edward Bing. Ivor, Nicholson & Watson. London. 1937.
12. Ibid. p. 240.
13. Nicolson, Carnock, op. cit. pp. 303 and 312.
14. Fay, Origins of War, Vol. I, op. cit. p. 401.
15. Ibid. p. 402.
16. *The Road to Sarajevo*, p. 180: Vladimir Dedijer. MacGibbon & Kee. London. 1967.
17. Ibid. pp. 178 and 208.

18. *Sarajevski Atentat*, p. 70: B. Jevtitch. Sarajevo. 1924.
19. *Sarajevo*, p. 52: Joachim Remak. Weidenfeld & Nicolson. London. 1959.
20. Dedijer, Sarajevo, op. cit. p. 373.
21. *The Origins of the War of 1914*, p. 27: Luigi Albertini. Translated by Isabella Massey. Oxford University Press. London. 1952-7.
22. *At the Court of the Last Czar*, p. 10: A. A. Mossolov. Edited by A. A. Pilinco. Translated by E. W. Dickes. Methuen & Co. London. 1935.
23. Nicolson, Carnock, op. cit. p. 225.
24. *Out of My Past*, p. 283: Count Kokovtsov. Edited by H. H. Fisher. Translated by Laura Matevev. Stanford University Press. California. 1935.
25. Dedijer, Sarajevo, op. cit. p. 425.
26. *Affaires Balkaniques*, Vol. I, p. 38, 111 ff: Ministère des Affaires Étrangères, 1912-14. Paris. 1922.
27. *Deutschland Schuldig*, p. 99: Deutches Weissbuch über die Verantwortlichkeit der Urheber des Krieges. Berlin. 1919.
28. Fay, Origins of War, op. cit. p. 452.
29. Nicolson, Carnock, op. cit. p. 390.

CHAPTER X WHO PLANNED SARAJEVO? *pp.* 281-320

1. *Russia's Ruin*, p. 42: E. H. Wilcox. Chapman & Hall, Ltd. London. 1919.
2. Out of My Past, op. cit. pp. 345/8.
3. Wilcox, Russia's Ruin, op. cit. p. 71.
4. The Minutes of this Conference are published in English in *Isvolsky and the World War*, pp. 219/29: Stieve.
5. Kokovtsov, Out of My Past, op. cit. pp. 349 and 439.
6. *Twenty-Five Years*, Vol. I, p. 308: Viscount Grey of Fallodon. Hodder & Stoughton. London. 1925.
7. *The Road to Sarajevo*, p. 181: Vladimir Dedijer.
8. *Sarajevski Atentat*, p. 23: B. Jevtitch. Sarajevo. 1923.
9. Dedijer, Sarajevo, op. cit. p. 181.
10. Ibid. p. 279.
11. *Three Who Made a Revolution*, pp. 607/8: B. D. Wolfe. Beacon Press. Boston. 1925.
12. *Le Procès de Salonique*, pp. 160/3: M. Bogitchevitch. Paris. 1927.
13. *The Origins of the War of* 1914, pp. 78/9: Luigi Albertini.
14. Ibid. p. 68.
15. *Origins of the World War*, Vol. II, p. 237: Sidney Fay.
16. *Aus Meiner Dienstzeit*, Vol. II, pp. 82/85: Feldmarschall Conrad von Hötzendorff. Vienna. 1921-5.
17. Dedijer, Sarajevo, op. cit. p. 395.
18. Ibid. p. 385.
19. *Die Ermordung des Erzherzogs Franz Ferdinand*, pp. 50/1: S. Stanojevich. Frankfurt. 1923.

20. Albertini, Origins First War, op. cit. p. 34.
21. Ibid. p. 81.
22. Dedijer, Sarajevo, op. cit. p. 137.
23. *Journal of Royal Institute of International Affairs.* March. 1925. London.
24. Albertini, Origins First War, op. cit. p. 84.
25. Ibid. p. 85.
26. Ibid. p. 81.
27. Bogitchevitch, Le Procès de Salonique, op. cit. p. 68:
28. Letter in the Belgrade Archives quoted by Vladimir Dedijer in *The Road to Sarajevo*, p. 398.
29. Dedijer, Sarajevo, op. cit. p. 513, note 17. Quotes from Osterreich Zwischen Russland und Serbien, pp. 297/8.
30. *Le Crépuscule d'une Autocratie*, Louis de Tyrdar-Burzynski. Paris. 1926.
31. Dedijer, Sarajevo, op. cit. p. 436.
32. Ibid. p. 431.
33. *Recent Revelations of European Diplomacy*, pp. 207/8: G. P. Gooch. British Institute of International Affairs. London. 1923.
34. *The Diary of Lord Bertie of Thame*, Vol. I, p. 1. Hodder & Stoughton. London. 1924.
35. *An Ambassador's Memoirs*, Vol. I, pp. 22/3: Maurice Paléologue. Translated by F. A. Holt. Hutchinson. London. 1923-5.
36. *Die Mobilmachung der russischen Armee 1914*, pp. 17/19. S. Dobrorolski. Berlin. 1921.
37. Paléologue, Memoirs, Vol I, op. cit. p. 27.
38. Dobrorolski, Die Mobilmachung, op. cit. p. 9 f.
39. Ibid. p. 21. f.
40. German Documents collected by Karl Kautsky No. 335. Edited by Max Montgelas. Carnegie Endowment for International Peace. Oxford University Press. New York. 1924.
41. Ibid. No. 332.
42. Dobrorolski, Die Mobilmachung, op. cit. p. 25 f.
43. How The War Began in 1914: Being the Diary of the Russian Foreign Office, p. 55. Introduction by Baron Schilling. Translated by Major W. E. Bridge. London. 1925.
44. Kautsky Documents. No. 390.
45. Schilling's Diary, op. cit. p. 65 f.
46. *Forty Years of Diplomacy*, p. 172: Baron Rosen.
47. A conversation between Count de Reisat, former First Secretary of the Russian Embassy in St. Petersburg and M. de Poggenpohl, incorporated in the Nesselrode Papers. From Constantin de Grunewald's *Tsar Nicholas I*, p. 268.

Acknowledgments

I would like to thank the following publishers for permission to quote from books published by them: The Stanford University Press of California for *Serbia Between East and West* by Wayne Vucinich, and *Out of My Past* by Count Kokovtsov; the Columbia University Press of New York for *The Emergence of Russian Panslavism* by Michael Petrovich; the Macmillan Company of New York for *The Origins of the First World War* by Sidney Fay; the Bodley Head, London, for *Emperor Alexander II* by E. M. Almedingen; Cassell & Co., Ltd., London, for *Alexander von Battenberg* by Count Egon Corti and *Once a Grand Duke* by Alexander Mikhailovich; Doubleday & Company, Inc., for *Tolstoy* by Henri Troyat, translated by Nancy Amphoux; Ivor Nicholson & Watson Ltd., London, for *The Letters of the Czar Nicholas II and Empress Marie,* edited by Edward J. Bing; George Allen & Unwin Ltd., London, for *Forty Years of Diplomacy* by Baron Rosen; Granada Publishing Ltd., London, for *Tsar Nicholas I* by Constantin de Grunewald; John Murray, London, for *The Letters of Queen Victoria;* The Clarendon Press, Oxford, for *The Origins of the War of 1914* by Luigi Albertini; Anthony Blond, London, for *The Siege of Plevna* by Rupert Furneaux; Simon & Schuster, Inc., for *The Fortress* by Robert Payne and *The Road to Sarajevó* by Vladimir Dedijer.

I am also grateful to Count Egon Corti for the extracts from *The Downfall of Three Dynasties;* to Mr. Nigel Nicolson for quotations from *Lord Carnock* by Sir Harold Nicolson; and to Collins-Knowlton-Wing for the material from *The Last Grand Duchess* by Ian Vorres.

INDEX

Index